APPLIED STOCHASTIC MODELS
AND CONTROL IN MANAGEMENT

Advanced Series in Management   Volume 12

Series Editors: **A. BENSOUSSAN**   and   **P. A. NAERT**

University of Paris-Dauphine   *INSEAD*
and INRIA   *Fontainebleau, France*
Paris, France

NORTH-HOLLAND
AMSTERDAM · NEW YORK · OXFORD · TOKYO

APPLIED STOCHASTIC MODELS AND CONTROL IN MANAGEMENT

Charles S. TAPIERO
Lewis-Progressive Professor of Management
Case Western Reserve University
and
The Hebrew University of Jerusalem

1988

NORTH-HOLLAND
AMSTERDAM · NEW YORK · OXFORD · TOKYO

ISBN: 0 444 70362 4

Publishers:

ELSEVIER SCIENCE PUBLISHERS B.V.
P.O. Box 1991
1000 BZ Amsterdam
The Netherlands

Sole distributors for the U.S.A. and Canada:

ELSEVIER SCIENCE PUBLISHING COMPANY, INC.
52 Vanderbilt Avenue
New York, N.Y. 10017
U.S.A.

LIBRARY OF CONGRESS
Library of Congress Cataloging-in-Publication Data

Tapiero, Charles S.
    Applied stochastic models and control in management / Charles S.
Tapiero.
        p.   cm. -- (Advanced series in management ; v. 12)
    Includes bibliographies and index.
    ISBN 0-444-70362-4 (Elsevier)
    1. Management--Mathematical models. 2. Stochastic analysis.
3. Mathematical optimization. 4. Management science. I. Title.
II. Series.
HD30.25.T36 1988
658.4'033--dc19   87-32462
                                                      CIP

PRINTED IN THE NETHERLANDS

For Josepha

Daniel

Dafna and

Oren

My guiding lights

PREFACE

Time, change and uncertainty are essential forms of complexity that, increasingly beset managers' ability to function. Further, the instability and increasingly dynamic character of our technological, economic and business environment, has rendered management, unavoidably, a far more difficult and speculative function. Today more than ever, management has become at the same time more of an art and more of a discipline which requires the latest tools technology can afford. Thus, office automation, sophisticated communication and information systems etc., awhile ago unknown, have become a necessity. For management, tomorrow is now, which means that the intricacies of the past, the present and the future and how they relate to one another has to be deciphered. As a result, management has begun to reason explicity in terms of processes, alternative scenarios and plan in a perspective of time and uncertainty.

Simultaneously, quantitative tools dealing with such problems have penetrated the science of management and with the common use of computers, threy are assuming a greater part in the practice of management. With the massive use and availability of micro-computers and the ensuing demystification of operations research methodologies, further gains and inroads in the factory, in management offices etc. are likely to take place. Domains such as nonlinear programming, optimal control theory and stochastic control will no longer be esoteric domains involving a few initiated managers, but instruments essential to management and methodologically imbedded in the software available on any machine.

In this vein, the purpose of this book is twofold. First, to present at an introductory level, the modeling and management optimization (over time) of selected problems in management science. Second, to explain and outline, the kind of tools that are necessary for the solution of such problems. In this latter case, we use the dynamic programming framework developed by Bellman and recently extended to a large class of problems also called stochastic control. At the same time, the book will seek to bridge a gap between theory and applications by emphasizing the latter and simplifying the former. Thus, the required quantitative background for reading this book is kept as low as possible, with special quantitative sections, such as proofs or complicated applications, starred or put in appendices. In this way, it is possible to maintain a conceptual understanding of the material at hand without being "bogged down" by proofs and justifications for each result.

This book follows several books and a long list of papers that have been published in the management science literature. Foremost among these are books by Bensoussan, Hurst and Naslund [1] published in 1974, my own two volumes book [5] published in 1977 as well as the more recent Sethi and Thompson [4] book. In addition, Bensoussan, Kleindorfer and Tapiero [2,3] have edited a collection of papers on Applied Optimal Control and Applied Stochastic Control in Econometrics and Management Science. These are in addition to an extremely large literature that has appeared in engineering, biology, economics, computer science, etc., each field emphasizing his relevant domain of applications. Throughout these literatures, the stochastic effects of processes and their conceptual- methodological implications have not been emphasized as it is done here.

We begin by a first conceptual notion on Dynamic Models and Uncertainty, outlining applications in firms and by pointing out several sources of uncertainty which requires management. The second chapter provides an introduction to the modelling of stochastic processes, including essentially the random walk approach and its limiting cases in the Wiener and Poisson processes. This forms the basis for defining stochastic differential equations with Wiener noises and jump processes. Other models dealt with, include Markov discrete state processes and reflected (constrained) processes. In the third chapter, applications in Operations Management (such as production and inventory management, dispatching, maintenance, etc.) are outlined with solutions given in the next chapter.

In Chapter 4, the dynamic programming approach and the dynamic programming equations for special processes and special criteria are established. These are also applied by obtaining a series of analytical results for the operations management problems defined earlier.

For numerical and computer results, we refer to Chapter 8 where a program written by Jean Pierre Quadrat is used for generating special computer programs for the solution of stochastic dynamic programming problems. As a result, for the practitioner, it is sufficient to define the problem and let the computer write the relevant optimization routines.

In Chapter 5, conceptual and strategic notions of marketing under uncertainty and the advertising problem (both from qualitative and quantitative points of view) is treated in some detail. In addition, selected applications in consumer behavior, pricing and new product sales are considered.

Chapter 4 is a broad outline and applications in insurance, finance and cash management. These domains have particularly evolved in the use of the techniques of the book and, therefore, the reader is referred to the many papers indicated in the text. Nonetheless, in this chapter portfolio theory, options and insurance problems are treated in general and made relevant to other (non-finance) problems of firms. In addition, problems of cash management, the growth of firms, and insurance firms' dynamic models are outlined.

The seventh chapter is a Pot-Pourri of selected applications and treatment of topics such as filtering, dual control, natural resources, etc. providing further motivation for the approach used. Finally, as was pointed out earlier, the last chapter provides numerical applications Here computer programs are provided for solving specific problems. In addition, a brief introduction to simulation of dynamic systems is outlined, with references given for simulation programs and applications.

The book as outlined above, provides an applied and comprehensive view of dynamic and stochastic models in management science, and can be used in both business and industrial engineering schools for second year Master's students. The book may also be used as a complementary source for finance and economic students increasingly involved in dynamic economics and finance. For such students, Chapters 2, 4 and 6 are particularly useful.

Charles S. Tapiero
May 1, 1987

Bibliography

[1] Bensoussan, A., Hurst, G., Naslund, B. *Management Applications of Modern Control Theory*, North-Holland Pub. Co., Amsterdam, 1974.

[2] Bensoussan, A., Kleindorfer, P., Tapiero, C.S. (Eds.) *Applied Optimal Control* TIMS Studies, North Holland, Amsterdam, 1978.

[3] Bensoussan, A., Kleindorfer, P., Tapiero, C.S. (Eds.) *Stochastic Control in Econometrics and Management Science* Contributions to Economic Analysis Series, North-Holland Pub. Co., Amsterdam, 1980.

[4] Sethi, S.P., and Thompson, G.L. *Optimal Control Theory Applications to Management* M. Nijhoff & Co., Boston, 1981.

[5] Tapiero, C.S. *Managerial Planning: An Optimum and Stochastic Control Approach*, Gordon Breach Science Publishers, New York, 1977.

ACKNOWLEDGEMENTS

This book was written with the support of the following institutions, in which I had the privilege to be a Visiting Professor; Department of Mathematics, Ecole Polytechnique Federale de Lausanne, Switzerland; Department of Operations Research, Case Western Reserve University, Cleveland, Ohio; The Institut Nationale de Recherche sur l' Informatique et l'Automatisme (France); Department of Decision Sciences, Wharton School, University of Pennsylvania, Philadelphia; and the Graduate School of Business, the Hebrew University, Jerusalem with which I am affiliated.

In the course of these visits, and while writing this book, I have benefited from discussions and comments by numerous colleagues. Foremost, I wish to thank, Alain Bensoussan, Paul Kleindorfer, Dominique de Werra, Jean Pierre Quadrat, Robert Pyndick, Suresh Sethi, Arnold Reisman, Hamilton Emmons and Ranganathan Ramaswamy.

TABLE OF CONTENTS

Chapter 1

DYNAMICAL MODELS, UNCERTAINTY AND MANAGEMENT SCIENCE

1.1   *Introduction*

The increased complexity and dynamic character of our social, economic
and business environment are currently raising some of the greatest challenges yet faced by managers. Old answers may no longer be appropriate.
Instead, managers are required to understand, to cope and to adapt to
change. To do so, knowhow, experience and better decision-making procedures must find their link to increase the ability of managers to manage
in a perspective of time and uncertainty. These require an understanding
of dynamic processes under uncertainty and an ability to manipulate such
processes. The fields of stochastic dynamic programming and stochastic
control provide an avenue we may embark on to augment our ability to
ensure that what is intended will likely occur.

For example, planning in a perspecitive of time and uncertainty is meant
to "organize" events in time (control) and manage the uncertainty unfolding
over time (risk management). The combined functions of planning events,
and risk management, are expressed naturally in a stochastic dynamic programming (SDP) framework. In this view, planning attempts to replace a
set of possible and uncontrolled events by a set of possible and more desirable events. Thus, through such plans, we seek to influence and program
not only the future events but also their probable occurrences. Such functions require, of course, that we "infer" and "imagine" the possible futures
and the mechanisms (i.e., the dynamic model) leading to these futures. It is
also required that learning mechanisms be devised to assess and reduce the
uncertainty as information unfolds over time. Only then, by manipulating
and optimizing the dynamical model of the given process, can we obtain
credible time paths and strategies for learning and deciding what to do as
the veils of the future are raised to reveal the present. For example, when a
manufacturer investigates the potential demand for something he plans to
produce, he is essentially "imagining" (perhaps intelligently) a future. By
gathering information, he achieves more relevant and credible knowledge
of his environment and thus increases the manageability of his firm. This
"environment" may be, in this case, the existence of similar and competing
products, the intensity of competition, and the needs and demands of consumers. Given an assessment of potential future needs, the manufacturer
can face the future with greater confidence and justified expectations. In
this process, the manufacturer has not specified the future, but he has iden-
tified it in terms of a probable succession of events which he is willing to
accept (or protect himself from) by designing a course of action now.

Time and uncertainty are the prevalent forms of complexity that this book will deal with in order to lead to better and adaptive management practices. Further, a wide variety of decision science problems of current interest, such as problems of production management, marketing, insurance, transport and others will be used as applications. These will demonstrate how answers to decision problems are to be obtained when time and uncertainty are essential dimensions of the science of decisions.

1.2 *On Dynamical Models*

The purpose of dynamical models is to represent the process of change. To do so, it is necessary to "construct" the mechanisms through which change actually occurs, or could be influenced. This may seem at first, simple, but it is in fact, extremely complicated requiring a deep understanding of the underlying process at hand, and how it can be patterned as a set of time dependent activities. The process of change may be affected by a large number of variables, acting at different times and in an uncertain manner. As a result, such models generally involve a great deal of uncertainty, a function of the premises (or hypotheses) regarding the process of change.

For example, consider the process of change in inventory and seek all the causes for such a change. A partial list is given in Table 1.1 including production, demands, deterioration, etc. Further, can we be sure about the effects of each of these on inventory? Can demands be forecasted with certainty? Is the process through which stored products become obsolete, breakdown, or deteriorate be completely known? The answers to such questions are negative. They also necessitate that both the causes and the uncertainty effects on change be clearly defined and combined to obtain a relevant dynamical model of the process under investigation.

Other variables such as prices, sales, wealth, a machine state, are considered in Table 1.1. Evidently, there are many other such variables that may be considered.

To construct dynamical models, we substitute dynamical modes of analysis for static ones. Instead of considering a function evaluated at one instant of time, we use derivatives, integrals and differential and integral equations to express the tendency of the process as it evolves over time. Therefore, past behavior and its effect on the current state of a variable is "memorized" by certain equations which can be used to retrace past states. In this sense, a model is "dynamic" when there is a mechanism such that the past (or an expectation of the future) can functionally be traced to a present.

Throughout the book, we shall use differential and difference equations (albeit amended to include uncertainty effects) to represent processes of

Table 1.1: Change and its Causes

Change In	*Causes*
Inventory	Production, demands, stolen goods, deterioration, . . .
Sales	Competition, market change, marketing mix activity such as advertising, sales effort, distribution, . . .
Wealth	Speculative profits or losses, salary income, consumption, investments, returns, . . .
Prices	Competition, new cost-reducing technologies, product differentiation, . . .
Machine State	Usage, maintenance, aging, . . .

change. For this reason, it is useful to consider the underlying mechanisms of such equations. Define any of the variables expressed in Table 1.1 at a given time t (such as inventory, price, machine state). We begin by defining "change" as the incremental difference between the states (or values) the variable takes on in successive instants of time. Let the time interval between two successive instants of time equal Δt, then

$$\begin{array}{ccc} \text{Change in the specified} & = & \text{The variable state} \quad - \quad \text{The variable state} \\ \text{time interval } \Delta t & & \text{at time } t + \Delta t \qquad \text{at time } t \end{array}$$

If x_0 denotes the variable under study, we write instead

$$\Delta x_0(t) = x_0(t + \Delta t) - x_0(t)$$

A dynamical model can then be defined as a relationship between a number of variables $x_0, x_1, ...x_n$ (including x_0) and the process of change represented schematically in Figure 1.1.

If such a relationship can be maintained (or recorded) in time, then we construct a mathematical model of this relationship and call it a dynamical model. To construct such a model, we can proceed in several ways, each assuming information and knowledge we may not readily have.

Postulate that a function $F(.)$ over the variables $(x_0, x_1...x_n)$ defines inclusively the potential changes in x_0 over the time interval $(t, t + \Delta t)$ or

$$\Delta x_0 \in F(x_0, x_1...x_n, t, t + \Delta t) \tag{1.1}$$

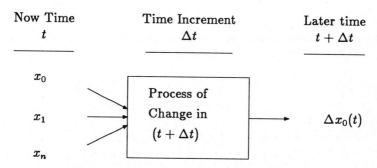

Figure 1.1: Effects on the Process of Change

In this case, we define an inclusive dynamical model which is difficult to handle (see [2] for such model equations). By assuming and seeking more information regarding the process of change, we may postulate an inequality relationship.

$$\Delta x_0 \geq F(x_0, ... x_n, t, t + \Delta t) \tag{1.2}$$

and preferably to simplify the quantitative problem, an equality relationship. In this case,

$$\Delta x_0 = F(x_0, ... x_n, t, t + \Delta t) \tag{1.3}$$

To construct such equalities, we can parametrize the inclusion relationship (1.1) such that it may be transformed into an equality. For example, if

$$\Delta x_0(t) \leftarrow \{x_0, x_1, ... x_n, t + \Delta t \leftarrow t\}$$
$$\Delta x_0 \in \begin{cases} x_1 & \text{linearly in time and state} \\ x_2 & \text{linearly in time and state} \end{cases}$$

then we can define two parameters a and b such that

$$\Delta x_0 = [ax_1 + bx_2]\Delta t \tag{1.4}$$

or for $\Delta t \neq 0$

$$\Delta x_0/\Delta t = ax_1 + bx_2$$

when $\Delta t = 1$ this defines a difference equation. When Δt becomes very small, $\Delta t \rightarrow 0$ then by definition of the derivative

$$\frac{dx}{dy} = \lim_{\Delta t \to 0} \frac{x(t + \Delta t) - x(t)}{\Delta t}$$

we obtain the differential equation

$$\frac{dx_0}{dt} = ax_1 + bx_2; \ x_0(0) = x_0, \text{ a given initial condition} \qquad (1.5)$$

whose solution below clearly expresses the current value as a function of past effects

$$x_0(t) = x_0(0) + \int_0^t [ax_1(t) + bx_2(t)]dt \qquad (1.6)$$

In such modeling situations, the parameters, a, b, are not known exactly, and must be estimated (often from less than perfect data). As a result, such parameters induce uncertainties which lead such differential equations to being stochastic (i.e., uncertain) as we shall see in the next chapter.

Alternatively, an identity-equation model as in (3) can be constructed by describing the process of change as an "accounting" identity (or a truism). In this case, by definition of change, we have

$$\Delta x_0 = F(x_0, x_1..., x_n, t)\Delta t \qquad (1.7)$$

and at the limit

$$\frac{dx_0}{dt} = F(x_0, x_1..., x_n, t); \ x_0(0) = x_0 \qquad (1.8)$$

Since some of the effects on Δx_0 may have uncertain sources, the evolution of x_0 may be uncertain. For example, define from Table 1.1 the following variables; $x_0(t) = $ Inventory at a given time t, $x_1(t) = $ Production rate in $(t, t + \Delta t), x_2(t) = $ Demand rate in $(t, t + \Delta t)$.

The change in inventory $\Delta x_0 = x_0(t + \Delta t) - x_0(t)$ can be, for our purposes, modeled as follows

Change in		Production		Demand
Inventory	=	Rate $*\Delta t$	-	Rate $*\Delta t$
in Δt				

or

$$\Delta x_0(t) = x_1(t)\Delta t - x_2(t)\Delta t$$

which is an "accounting" identity. For $\Delta t \to 0$, we obtain

$$\frac{dx_0(t)}{dt} = x_1(t) - x_2(t); \ x_0(0) = \text{initial inventory}$$

Note that if the demand is deterministic, the equation for inventory is deterministic and can be forecasted perfectly, provided $x_1(t)$ is specified. If the demand is uncertain, however, the inventory and the differential equations above will be stochastic, but the structure of the equation expressing the functional (accounting) identity will remain the same. Finally, in Table 1.2, we add a number of examples that provide an appreciation of a few of the relationships that can be considered. As a result of the foregoing, the ways in which we construct dynamical models to represent change depend crucially on humanly defined problems, the conceptions and the views of the world held by the ultimate users of such models - the decision makers. Thus, models (whether they are dynamic or not) originate in human intentionality and are a function of one's personal knowledge, experience and insights. For these reasons, the variety of dynamical models that can be constructed is truly great, bounded only by our imagination of potential realities and the instruments available for the purpose of such modeling.

To appreciate further the problems of dynamic modeling and the interplay of time and change, uncertainty and decision makers, we refer to Figure 1.2, expressing the simultaneity of those three components in most dynamic decision problems. More specifically, we define three classes of issues addressed to in management;

(i) The time structure of preferences, the capacity to take decisions over time, flexibility and the reversibility (i.e., regrets) of decision making.

(ii) The relationship between risk and decision makers' attitudes, and risk management.

(iii) The time structure of transformation processes (i.e., the process of change), uncertainty, information seeking and processing, adaptation and learning.

We shall discuss some of these issues.

(i) Preference and Decision Flexibility

The time structure of preferences and decision flexibility (see Koopmans [12, 13], Beckmann [4], and also [1], [11], [21]) involve the determination of mechanisms scaling the desirability of outcomes as they occur over time. The difficulties in obtaining a measurement of temporal preference originates in two essential factors,

(a) Incomparability of current versus future outcomes; and

(b) Assessment of managers' decision-making flexibility and defining quantitatively the "value" of flexibility (meaning the number of alternative courses of action that can be taken by management which will lead to

Table 1.2: Change and Decision Making

Change ΔX	Function of	Decision Making on	Potential Uncertainty
Inventory	Production Demand	Production	Demand
Capital	Investment, Losses of capital	Investment	Losses of capital
Wealth	New Income - Consumption	Consumption	New Income
Mineral Reserves	New Discovery - Extraction Rate of Reserves	Extraction, Research	New Discoveries of Reserves
Fish Population	Reproduction Rate - Fishing Rate - Death Rate	Fishing Rate	Death Rate, Reproduction Rate
Waiting Persons in a Line	New arrivals, Servicing of Waiting Customers (if any)	Servicing	New Arrivals, Servicing
Machine State	Maintenance Deterioration	Maintenance	Deterioration and Maintenance Effects
Goodwill	Losses due to Forgetting, Advertising	Advertising	Advertising Effectiveness, Forgetting
Sale of New Product	Potential and Probabilities of Adoption, Marketing Mix	Marketing Effort (Pricing and Advertising)	Potential and Probabilities of Adaption
Transport	New Arrivals, Dispatched Persons	Dispatching	New Arrivals

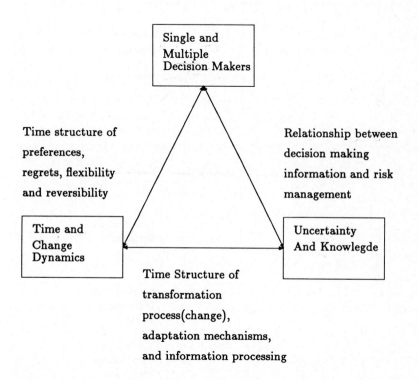

Figure 1.2: Time, Uncertainty and Decision Makers

different results).

The first difficulty is a function of the evolution of "tastes" over time, as well as an attitude towards postponement of choice, costs and rewards. Operationally we deal with changing tastes by the use of adaptive mechanisms for selecting objectives and priorities (as change is observed).

The attitude toward postponement of choice, costs and rewards is, on the other hand, resolved by introducing discounting procedures. The choice of procedures and of the discount rate is not a simple task. Discounting expresses the relative present value of resources expressed in dollars. Typically, the value of future income is in relative terms, smaller than the same income realized now or, in the words of the well known adage, "A bird in the hand is worth two in the bush". Discounting, however, is not without pitfalls. It may, for example, defer beyond any reason the cost of current consumption. "Buy now, pay later" is a marketing philosophy and psychological attitude for the selling of products and services, where the structure of temporal preferences is used to induce current consumption.

To appreciate more fully the problems of discounting, consider the desirability of obtaining a certain sum of money now versus later (say in a month), as shown below, and fill in the question marks. Can we obtain a smooth curve describing the changing value of money as payment is defered, that diverse individuals can agree on?

payment Now	versus	payment in a Month	payment in a Year
$ 1		?	?
$ 10		?	?
$ 100		?	?
$ 1000		?	?
$ 10,000		?	?

Of course, such substitution is difficult, a function of other alternatives, attitudes, hopes, etc., so that it may not be defined easily. Therefore, discounting, although analytically attractive, is not a mechanism which may be applied without careful consideration of the short-term and long-term perspectives of the problem. Further research dealing with such problems is greatly needed.

The second difficulty originates in the desirability of maintaining and expressing quantitatively the value of temporal flexibility. Actually, the degree of flexibility is a consequence of solving a dynamical problem under uncertainty. Over time, management values the freedom of action and the development of opportunities. If future outcomes can be forecasted with certainty, then there is indeed little reason to plan for flexibility. However, in practice, management is faced with an uncertain future and has to plan for possible contingencies. If programs are designed as an extrapolation of current reality, then these programs may not be able to withstand changing tastes, new political climates, expanding technological possibilities, or disasters. In other words, our inability to forecast structural and functional changes within a process prescribes a need to plan for unlikely and harmful disturbances. In Chapter 6, we shall see that the use of options can be useful for such purposes.

To assess states of knowledge, we distinguish between two extremes, *Certainty* and *Complete Ignorance*. All intermediate states can be characterized by special types of information (or a lack of it). For example, say that the state of an environment (e.g., the demand for the product of a firm, the probable effect of an advertising plan on a firm's sales, etc.) is characterized in probability terms. This means that if x is a variable describing possible values of the state, then we associate to each one of these values a probability $F(x/\phi)$, a function of a set of parameters. The fact that x may take on different values with probabilities $F(x/\phi)$ is in itself a statement of knowledge. Further, knowledge may then be expressed in terms of our ability to specify F and ϕ. Or, a state of knowledge is a function of the information we have about a process, while information is that quality and quantity which will reduce our uncertainty. Over time, such information is required for obtaining a better assessment of the process at hand, forecasting (or predicting), decision making and/or to relieve managers' intolerance of ambiguities. For example, if planning is defined as "an activity augmenting the chances that what is intended will occur", then, of course, uncertainty is an element that is to be "avoided", "reduced", "protected from" or "absorbed". When this is not possible, it is essential that a decision making flexibility allowing regrets and reversibility of some course of action be maintained. The decision making process involving several agents is a further source of uncertainty. Multiple agents, each with an identical (or not) goal and information creates conflict and a lack of mutual knowledge about agents behavior. The theory of games (e.g., Luce and Raiffa [16]) as well as the theory of large systems, centralization, decentralization and systems' organization, has dealt with aspects of this problem, establishing organizational models (such as cooperative, competitive, mutual information exchange, etc. between agents) that can provide a "solution" to the added complexity of having agents involved in decision making. The desires to *augment control*, (as a means to avoid uncertainty) have, therefore, led to management strategies of "buying" competition, vertical integration, and to develop organizational forms that recognize that information is to be distributed in a firm in a certain way. Design problems involve then the combination of information, decision making and control coordination. Although these problems are extremely important, they will not receive here great attention (see Kleindorfer [11] for further study of these issues and problems). Subsequently, in section 1.3, we shall return to the problem of uncertainty and its implication to risk and information systems.

(ii) Time Structure of Transformation Processes

Here, we mean the functional identity or technology transforming a set of inputs into a set of outputs at a specific instant of time (as we discussed it in dynamical modeling). To obtain an appropriate model of transformation processes relating the "past to the future", it is necessary to construct a model of change over time. If the future has no relation to the past, we use static models to describe the effects of one or a set of acts at a given time. If the future is a function of the past, the relationship between specific instants is *a model of change*. Basically, it is a hypothesis about the underlying process and must be continually assessed and tested. For example, in advertising models with carry-over effects, we may hypothesize that there are two dynamic processes at hand: forgetting and recall. The modeling of such processes, being a hypothesis about consumer behavior, includes a great deal of uncertainty, not only on the processes themselves, but on how these are maintained over time. The prime task of the model builder is, therefore, to construct from an intimate knowledge of the management problem, the structure of the transformation process and use statistical techniques to study the correspondence of the model to the record of reality.

Once a dynamic model has been constructed, however, the problems to be faced consist of investigating the properties of the model (stability, sensitivity, reliability, fit, etc.), and devising techniques for assessing and optimizing the courses of action to be followed.

1.3 *Applications*

Below we discuss several essential functions dealt with by managers when decision making involves time and uncertainty in a crucial manner. These functions include planning, risk management and information systems.

In the next section, we shall discuss several specific applications including production and inventory management, maintenance, marketing, etc.

1.3.1 Planning

Planning, in a broad sense, deals with temporal aspects of management and is particularly important for managerial problems involving future uncertainties and a changing environment. In planning, as in management, we seek to increase our ability to manage change and ensure (or encourage) that desirable future states may occur. In a perspective of time and uncertainty, planning includes two essential activities; future modeling and risk management. Future modeling is a basic activity which consists in transforming a set of possible and future oriented events into a coherent whole. This is complicated, because it requires a very clear understanding of the causes of change. That is, we seek to establish not only casual links between events, but how these links are maintained over time. In planning, we face an unmanageable number (indeed an unlimited number) of possible futures. Therefore, if we are to make a reproduction of the future in the present, we must determine a substitute for it. This substitute is not what will necessarily occur; it is our guess about what may occur. When managers' intentionality are combined with such guesses of the future, then we engage in learning, adaptation and, more generally, in uncertainty reduction, i.e., replace a string of unknown events by another (or the same) string of events with an altered likelihood of occurrence. In this manner, managers seek to influence and possibly control the risks of the environments within which they function. This will be called risk management, and will be detailed in the next section. Whenever a model of the future and a reduction of uncertainty has been achieved, alternative courses of action can be tested for their future impact. By manipulating the model on the basis of credible assumptions, we obtain credible time paths of the variables with which we are most directly concerned. Planning may then be defined as an activity in time designed to attain a set of desired states using a series of actions and strategies. It would be concerned with the following (Figure 1.3):

1) The elaboration of goals (expressed as desired states with appropriate probabilities of occurrences) and their realization in time.

2) The elaboration of available means over time.

3) The allocation in time of the available means necessary to achieve the desired goals.

Planning in this sense is at the core of a great many managerial activities. To render relevant choices more manageable and to gain more information concerning the impact of an action upon the future, we require information as will be discussed in 3.3.

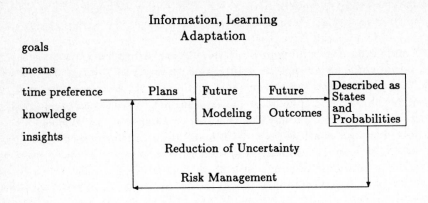

Figure 1.3: Planning

1.3.2   Risk Management

Risk management consists in altering in a desirable manner the states a system may reach and their probabilities. This can be reached by various instruments risk managers may have at their disposal. These include (see Figure 1.4):

Insurance
Loss Prevention
Technological Change

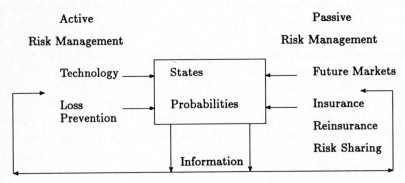

Figure 1.4: Risk Management - A Simplified View

Insurance is a medium, or a market for risk, substituting payments now for potential damages later. The size of such payments and the potentiality of damages being intertwined in a consumer, a firm or government objectives leads to widely distributed market preferences and to the possibility of exchange. Insurance firms have recognized the opportunities of such differences and have, therefore, provided mechanisms for pooling and redistributing the "willingness to pay to avoid losses" of say consumers. It is because of such rationality, combined with goals of personal gains, social welfare and economic efficiency, that markets for fire and theft insurance, as well as sickness, unemployment, accident insurance, etc., have come to be as important as they are today. It is because of persons or institutions' desires to avoid too great a loss (even with small probabilities) which would have to be borne alone, that markets for reinsurance (i.e., sub-selling portions of insurance contracts) and mutual protection insurance (based on the pooling of risks) have also come into being. However, while insurance is, in fact, a *passive form of risk management*, based on exchange mechanisms only, loss prevention and technological innovations are *active forms for managing risks*. Loss prevention is a managerial mean to alter the probabilities and the states of undesirable, damaging states. For example, an inventory policy, as well as a machine's maintenance policy, are a form of loss prevention seeking to alter the chances that a firm will be caught short when a product demand materializes or to alter the effects of costly machines' breakdowns. Similarly, driving carefully, locking one's own home effectively, installing fire alarms, etc. are all forms of loss prevention. Of course, insurance and loss prevention are, in fact, two means to the similar end of risk protection. Car insurance rates tend, for example, to be linked to a person's past driving record. Certain clients (or areas) might be classified as "high risk clients", required to pay higher insurance fees. Inequities in insurance rates will occur, however, because of an imperfect knowledge of the probabilities of damages and because of the imperfect distribution of information between insured and insurers. Thus, situations may occur where persons might be "over-insured" and have no motivation to engage in loss prevention. Such outcomes, known as "moral hazard", are in fact just counter to the basic purposes of insurance. It is a phenomenon that can recur in a society in widely different forms. Over-insuring unemployment may stimulate persons not to work, while under-insuring may create uncalledfor social inequities. Low car insurance rates (for some) can lead to reckless driving, leading to unnecessary damages inflicted on others, on public properties, etc. Risk management would, therefore, seek to ensure that risk protection does not become necessarily a reason for not working. Technological innovation means that the structural process through which a given set of inputs is transformed into output states with various probabilities of occurrences is altered. For example, the replacement of a machine by another newer, more reliable machine is essentially a change of the "production function" of the machine. Building a new six lane highway can be viewed as a way for the public to change the "production-efficiency function" of transport servicing. Environment protection regulation and legal procedures have, in fact, had an impact on some firms production technologies by requiring them to *change* the way in which they have converted inputs into products, by considering as well the treatment of refuse.

Finally, it should be pointed out that learning and information are parts and essential ingredients and of risk management. Asymetries in information between insured and insurers, between buyers and sellers, etc., are creating a wide range of opportunities and problems that provide great challenges to risk managers. Several of these issues will be dealt with later in the context of special problems.

1.3.3   Information Systems

The *raison d'être* of information systems can be attributed to two essential functions: reducing uncertainty and organizing complexity. The first function, *uncertainty reduction*, presupposes that events occur randomly, and that managers can make better decisions by reducing this randomness. For example, a production manager facing an uncertain demand for a product can develop more efficient production schedules if he can devise mechanisms which can reliably predict the demand. The quality of the predictions are then measured in terms of how well they replicate the actual demands. The better the predicitions, the better the information system. Here, the "proof of the pudding is in the eating". In other words, the information system is evaluated *aposteriori* in terms of the predictions and actual outcomes. To reduce uncertainty, managers search, collect, accumulate, absorb, manipulate and transform data. The combination of these activites defines the information system. When the transformed data is used by managers, they assume that it is a "deterministic equivalent representation" of the uncertain environment. In other words, the information system absorbs the uncertainty inherent in the environment and replaces it by measures which are essentially deterministic and on the basis of which actions or descriptive statements of the system processes can be reached (see Figure 1.5).

There may be uncertainty with respect to one or all of a system's components - input, transformation process and output. When an input is uncertain, the information systems seeks to define forecasts of future inputs by using data, models and other mechanisms. When a transformation process in unknown, the information system attempts alternative *parameters and functional representations* of the transformation processes and uses a given set of criteria to choose a particular representation. Finally, when the output is uncertain, the information system measures the output and

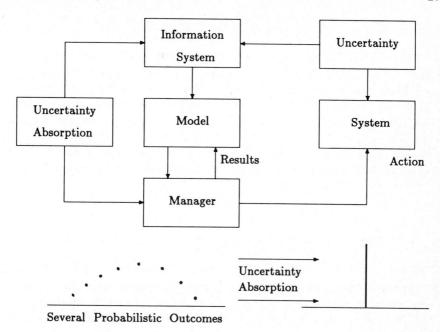

Figure 1.5: The Absorption of Uncertainty by Managers

replaces it by an estimate which is essentially a deterministic equivalent to the actual but uncertain recorded output. This measure results in a reduction of uncertainty and is achieved by an appropriate use of statistical techniques.

For example, consider social indicators as an instance of a public information system. Such indicators (it is hoped) provide the social information for determining underlying social processes, social changes, needs and goals for public policy.

> These are, therefore, an *information base* which may be used to: "assess where we stand and where we are going with respect to our values and goals, and to evaluate specific programs and determine their impact" (Bauer [3]), p. 1).

Basically, such indicators would:

(1) Provide a consistent and continuous body of data which may be used to determine adaptively the structure of social transformation processes.

(2) Provide a set of indicators for establishing an empirical measure of social conditions and quality of life and their rates of change.

(3) Provide criteria for measuring the cost/effectiveness of social programs.

The information imbedded in social indicators is therefore important and is usually recognized as such by city administrators. They provide a useful collection of tools for monitoring state variables - a prerequisite for effective decision making. Social indicators are not by themselves useful variables; but, combined with political and administrative action, they become a means for learning about and improving our social environment. Examples for specific problems of public interest are given in Table 1.3.

Table 1.3: Social Policy and Processes

Social Transformation Process	Social Indicators/ Information	Social Policy	Example Measure of Effectiveness
Relationship between Crime Rate and Society, Police, Freedom etc.,	Crime Rate	Increased Police, Limit Freedom	Increases and Decreases in Crime Democracy
Atmospherics	Pollution Count	Emission Control	Alternative Costs in Reducing Pollution Counts
Roads, Locations, Speed	Ambulance, Response Time	Location of Ambulances, Quality, Cost Equipment, Number of Vehicles, etc.	Costs of Obtaining Particular Configuration of Ambulances and Benefits Derived
Health Care	Quality of Health Care Proportion of Sick which is Properly Cared for	Hospital Beds No. of Doctors Configuration of Hospital System	Cost/Benefits

1.4   *Application in the Firm*

All firms face at one time or another decision making uncertainty. Their attitude and behavior toward such uncertainty, of course, varies because their function and purposes differ. They all need, however, information, seek to operate efficiently, and implicitly (or explicitly) attempt to manage risk. Here, we shall discuss several aplications from a decision making point of view. The managerial, economic, and financial issues relating to a firm's strategy and their facing competition has been dealt with in Porter [20], for example, who provides a very broad understanding of firms' and industries' decision making strategies imbedded in the kind of uncertainties firms seek to reduce or are motivated by. Since the kind of problems we may consider is very diverse, we shall draw attention to a few cases only.

Consider a firm functioning in a given industry. Evidently, competition by other firms, as well as explicit (or implicit) goverment interventions through regulation, tax rebates for special environment protection investments, grants or subsidized capital budgets in distress areas, etc., are instances where firms are required to be sensitive to these external forces. Since these forces are not in the control of a firm's management, and may (as in the case of competition) be detrimental to the firm's purposes, they also provide a great deal of uncertainty. Managers, of course, will seek to reduce and manage the risk implied by such uncertainty. Thus, firms may look for ways to augment their control of market forces (such as through vertical integration, acquisition of competition, etc.), or they may diversify risks by seeking activities in unrelated markets.

In Table 1.4, we construct as examples, a list of uncertainties faced by both industries and firms and how these may be met. The list provided in Table 1.4 is by no means exhaustive and provides only an indication of the kind of problems that we can address.

More specifically, consider a firm in terms of its operations and marketing. Operations have to do with the actual on-going processes which transform a set of inputs into a set of outputs. Problems such as purchasing and production, capacity expansion, manufacturing, research and development, quality control and inspection, maintenance and replacement, etc., are operational problems involving many sources of uncertainty. Some of these are given in Table 1.5.

Marketing has to do with a firm's interface with markets, including the use of a marketing mix to expand market shares, product design, marketing channels development, sales force management, etc. Problems that might be considered are pricing practices, sales effort and sales force management, advertising, design of quality, products warranties, product line design, assessing response functions, consumer behaviors, and competition behaviors. All involve time and uncertainty in several way as will be shown in Section 1.5.

The firm logisitic system can be viewed as an interface between the operation and marketing functions. Here, the firm is concerned with problems

Table 1.4: Sources of uncertainty

Uncertainty	Actions Taken
Long range changes in market growth	Research and development on new products, diversification to other markets
Inflation	Indexation of assets, and accounts receivables
Technological developments	Adaptation by "absorbing" new technologies, price reduction, barriers to technolocial change
Consumer behavior and choice	Marketing effort activity, advertising, education
Production quality	Quality control, sampling, warranties, servicing
Demand for product	Marketing intelligence, forecasting, contracting supplies
Price uncertainty of input materials	Building up inventory, buying options and hedging techniques
Competition	Acquisition, cartels, price-fixing, advertising and marketing effort, diversification

of location/allocation, problems of transportation and dispatching, the distribution system of physical goods, but possibly also the distribution system of information and its flow between geographically remote parts of the firm. Specific "distribution" problems such as dispatching will be considered below. Next, we consider particular operational problems.

Table 1.5: Selected Operations Problems and Uncertainty

Funtion	Uncertainty
Purchasing	Product quality, required quantities, time delays, cost and price changes
Manufacturing/ Production	Quantities demanded, machines breakdown, inventory loss to deterioration, production rejects
Research and Development and Technology	New products, new processes, uncertain payoffs of research
Capacity Expansion	Development cost, long term demands, availability of raw materials, plants obsolescence and maintenance
Quality Control	Production (risk) of defects, risks of marketing defective products, sampling - inspection errors in production

1.4.1 Production and Inventory

Production and inventory are two intertwined decisions designed to meet probable demands and smooth the production process in an economic and efficient manner. The importance of inventory arises from its ability to serve as a buffer between uncertain demands and the firm's production process. Inventory is thus a hedge against unforseen and probablistic demands for a product. Production managers may also build up inventories to facilitate the organization of work. Costs incurred, such as the maintaining of warehouses, investment in finished goods inventories, etc., may be outweighed by more efficient production schedules, consumers loyalty (since their demands will be satified with greater likelihood) and so on.

Evidently, the "structure" of inventory and production models, being of a general nature has been adapted to a large class of problems. Outstanding examples are cash reserves management, manpower hiring-firing, dam and reservoir problems, etc. We shall return to these problems in Chapter 3, section 3, in far greater detail.

1.4.2   Dispatching and Transportation Policies

A vehicle dispatching policy consists in determining the capacity and instants in time at which vehicles are dispatched along a route (see Figure 1.6). This problem is widely encountered in mass transit vehicle dispatching, freight transportation and aircraft shuttle scheduling. In dispatching, the following processes are involved:

(1) Traffic demand forecasting and modeling. This includes the definition of the probabilistic processes of passengers arrivals, the parameters of these probability distributions, the relationships between arrivals and advertising, promotions, fares, service levels and competing companies and transportation modes. (2) Definition and computation of routes structures, fares stuctures, levels of service (times and capacity of dispatches), priorities. (3) Monitoring of vehicles' positions, availability, reliability, safety, maintenance, operations costs, waiting times, market share, etc.

The applicability of dispatching processes is varied. For example, in automated mass transit, dispatching by computer decisions on a real- time basis can be implemented by designing information sensitive (feedback) decision rules. The same feedback principle could also apply to an airline's shuttle service. On the basis of passenger patterns of arrival, the decision to send a plane along a particular route can be taken. In section 3.6, a dispatching problem is considered in detail.

1.4.3   Maintenance, Replacement and Inspection

The problem of maintenance and replacement is to maximize the value of machines and other equipment used. (For a review of such a problem see Pierskalla and Voelker [9]). Planning acquisition of a new machine involves complex analyses and considerable uncertainty about the future. This uncertainty concerns the effective life of the machine (that is, the period during which it is used), new technological developments which renders the machine obsolete, possible breakdowns and failures, and the probabilistic effects of

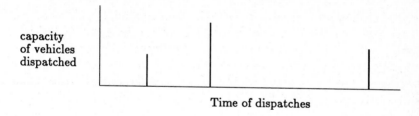

Time of dispatches

A Dispatching Policy

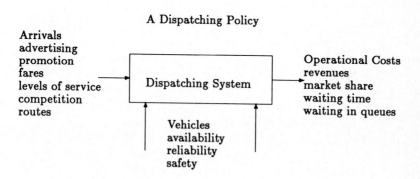

Figure 1.6: Dispatching System

maintenance programs and deterioration. These important considerations impel managers to consider both the economic and the risk implications of a machine's value in reaching decisions to acquire, maintain or replace machines. When a machine is deteriorating maintenance expenditures are incurred to compensate for and prevent such deterioration. The effects of deterioration (including the effects of a machine's usage, aging, production and technical obsolescense), and maintenance may also be considered uncertain, thereby defining maintenance and replacement as decision problems under uncertainty.

1.4.4 Queueing

Queueing is an inquiry into the organization, the nature and environment of waiting lines and how specific service configurations influence a system's performance. Examples of queues are numerous, e.g. in communication traffic (telephony), transportation traffic on highways, people queueing for service (in supermarkets, airline terminals, banks, etc.), air traffic control, etc. can all be interpreted as instances of queueing models.

Queueing models are characterized by three elements: (1) Patterns of arrivals; (2) Service patterns (or mechanisms); and (3) Queue discipline. The relationship between these elements is of great importance in defining the structure of a queueing model. A very simple input/output queueing model is described in Figure 1.7.

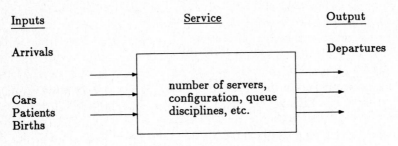

Figure 1.7: A Queueing System

A survey of such models can be found in [14]. Considerable research has been conducted in such models using long run equilibrium assumptions which may not always be realistic. More recently, however, queueing models are used in decison problems under uncertainty where states of nature are the arrival rates of "customers" and alternatives are the various priority classes (or service configurations) which may be specified. The queueing problem is then to specify the cost to be associated with a given set of arrival rates and a set of priority classes. In Section 3.4, we present several queuing models which are, subsequently, investigated in a decision making under uncertainty framework.

1.5   *Other Applications*

1.5.1   Marketing and Uncertainty

Under uncertainty, marketing management consists in altering in a desirable manner the market states and probability distributions the marketing system may reach at a given time and in a given market. To do so, marketing managers engage in

(1) Markets research

(2) Response and Consumer Behavior Modeling and Analysis
(3) Marketing Mix Management
(4) Marketing Risk Management

Through market research, the market and competitive structure, industry demands, the marketing environment, the available marketing channels, technology, tastes, culture, etc. are defined. Typically, such market research is based on field studies, surveys, economic studies, etc., and provides a probabilistic assessment of opportunities and potential problems for a prospective marketing activity. Such information once accumulated provides the information for understanding consumers' behavior and more generally, for assessing the market and consumers response to marketing. Of particular interest is the assessment of responses to marketing resources as summarized in Figure 1.8. Examples to this effect abound. Lipstein [15], Howard & Seth [8], Massy et al. [17] have pointed out a large number of models for describing the "probabilistic" response of consumers' behaviors when faced with the choice of selecting a product (e.g., see also [18], [28]). Similarly, the uncertainty implicit in models of sales response to advertising, pricing and other marketing resources have been the subjects of intense studies (Horowitz [9], Tapiero [23], as well as [24], [25]).

Given such models, their integration with marketing resources has led to what we have called marketing mix management, earlier in (iii). This is an attempt to alter the market states in a desirable manner, by seeking a proper mix of the marketing resources such as advertising, selling effort, distribution channels design, pricing, etc. This mix, called the marketing mix is also used to manage both the expected returns that might be derived from the market activity as well as the risks in such returns (see Figure 1.10).

For example, when it is used for the purpose of differentiating one product from the other, pricing is essentially an instrument of "uncertainty resolution" (in a consumer's mind, conveying the message that since products have "very" different prices, they are also very different in fact). Of course, the choice of a price will be intended to lead to an expectation of greater profitability. Alternatively, pricing can be used to provide an incentive for consumers to try a new product and thereby allow the firm to penetrate a given market. Warranties are used to alter consumer's confidence in product quality, advertising is used to convey information, convince and build up goodwill, etc. Thus, almost every activity of marketing can be thought of as a direct (or indirect) effort to alter the distribution of some market variable which is critical to the firm's or business' profitability.

In a temporal perspective, the effects of the marketing mix are not only

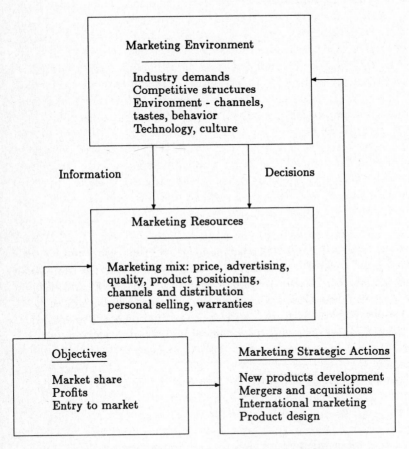

Figure 1.8: A Global View of Marketing

to affect the distribution of such variables, but also their time phasing. This occurs because there are time delays, carry over effects in time, etc. that alter the response time that such variables (and hence profitability as expressed in Figure 1.9) have to a marketing mix activity. As a result, over time, marketing under uncertainty requires that an assessment and a substitution in the time-risk-return space be defined, on the basis of which a desirable marketing mix might be selected.

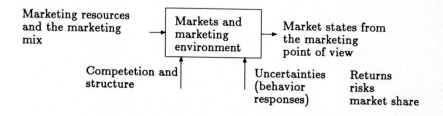

Figure 1.9: Risk Management Examples

Marketing resources have predictably varying effects on market variables. As in section 1.3, on risk management, we may define these effects as "active" and "passive". By active, we shall mean that either the market is altered in some direct way or it involves a direct outlay of marketing resources. Passive forms of risk management will essentially be indirect ways to alter these variables. Although, a clear cut distinction between active and passive forms of marketing risk management is difficult, such an attempt is made in Table 1.6 for a number of marketing decisions.

Some of these problems (in particular, advertising) will be dealt with in Chapter 5, and solutions obtained by stochastic dynamic optimization.

1.5.2 Insurance

Insurance is an instrument used to substitute certain for uncertain payments at different times. To elaborate on this statement, we shall consider a simple insurance decision framework and describe key elements of the insurance dynamic decision problem.

Say that an insurance firm has assets A_t and liabilities L_t at time t. These assets consist of cash, cash equivalents, bonds, morgages, stocks, real estate, and other investments. Liabilities consist, for example, of benefit payments (resulting from claims), withdrawals, expenses, dividends and the negative of future premiums. Of course, liabilities for a period consist of

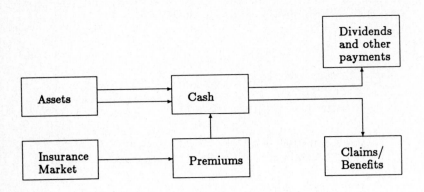

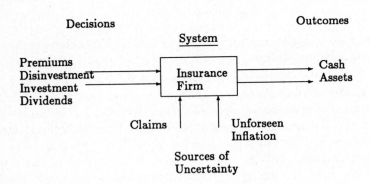

Figure 1.10: An Insurance Firm Model

Table 1.6: Managing Marketing Risk

Active	Passive
Product design (quality)	Market research (survey, field studies, etc.)
Pricing, advertising information dessimination	Warranties
Cartels, price fixing and markets collusion	Product liabilities and insurance
Patents, innovations, R & D	Agents contracting and channels-agreement
Sales force management and motivation	

certain and uncertain components that vary in time. The difference between assets and liabilities defines a surplus. A "rough" model of the insurance firm we might contemplate is given in Figure 1.10.

The model relating the outcomes over time together with the instruments used by the insurance firms (the decisions) provide a dynamic model of the insurance firm. In essence, these outcomes are states that can be thought of as *summarizing* the past history of the insurance firm's economic performance. This history is defined as a function of the actions taken by the firm, the unforeseen disturbances and uncertainties the firm has been subjected to, and, of course, the mechanism for combining these into economic indicators of the firm's health, valuation and assets accounting.

Once such a model, representing realistically the mechanisms of the insurance firm's function, has been constructed it becomes an *instrument* of management, providing information regarding the firm's economic state (such as economic viability, financial position, worth, etc.), an instrument for testing alternative policies and finally, an instrument for *designing* actual and financial procedures. To do so, however, it is required that a valuation approach (or that an objective for the design of insurance policies) be defined. Given such objectives (such as earning capacity, solvency, dividend distribution to shareholders, etc.), the choice of decisions by the insurance firms could include:

- the choice of investment assests

- a learning mechanism in terms of the various implicit costs of uncertainty sustained by the firm

- risk absorption approaches used by the firm, insofar as portfolio, diversification strategies, etc. are followed

- risk sharing approaches such as indexed and linked premium formulae, co-insurance, re-insurance approaches, etc.

In summary, the dynamic decision problems faced by insurance firms can be stated as follows:

Optimize the (Dynamic)
Temporal Objective
<u>Subject to</u>
A State-Space Representation
of the Insurance Firm
+
Solvency Regulation
Constraint
+
Other Constraints
<u>To Obtain</u>
Management Strategies for Investment
and Liquidity Maintenance
+
Premium Rates Policies Sensitive or
Insensitive to Temporal Change
+
Constitute Reserves for
Unforeseen Contingencies
+
Learning Mechanism for
Adaptation to Change

Within such strategies many questions such as the following might be answered:

- What is the optimal surplus required to protect the insurance firm against insolvency, and assets depreciation? Generally what should be the surplus management and investment policy?

- What is the surplus policy required for protection against pricing inadequacy resulting from uncertainty (or partial information)?

- What should the premium policy be?

- What is the economic value of learning more precisely consumers risk classifications? And so on. To reach such solutions, however, the problems defined earlier will necessitate a specification of the insurance firm's structure and process and the definition of the changes it is subjected to. It will also lead to quantitative problems that will be dealt with in great detail in Chapter 6.

Next, we shall consider the mathematical modeling of processes which involve time and uncertainty. Applications to the techniques used in Chapter 2 are given in Chapter 3 such that the next two chapters may be "read" at the same time.

Further Reading

The interested reader may find it useful to complement this chapter with reading of Fraisse [7], Psychology of Time, Tofler [27], Future Shock; Shackle [22], Time in Economics; as well as my own Time and Management paper [26]. For an introduction to deterministic models and decisions over time using techniques such as the calculus of variations and optimal control theory, the reader may consult the books referred to in the Preface as well as Connors and Teichroew [5], and Kamien and Schwartz [10].

Bibliography

[1] Arrow, K.J., 1971, *Essays in the Theory of Risk Bearing*, Markham Publishing Co, Chicago, Ill.

[2] Aubin, J.P., 1980, *Mathematical Methods of Games and Economic Theory*, Ceremade, University of Paris IX.

[3] Bauer, R.A. (ed.) 1966, *Social Indicators*, The MIT Press, Cambridge, Mass.

[4] Beckmann, M.J., 1972, Decisions Over Time, in C.B. McGuire and R. Radner, (eds.), *Decisions and Organizations*, North-Holland/Elsevier, New York, pp. 141-161.

[5] Connors, M.M. and D. Teichroew, 1967, *Optimal Control of Dynamic Operations Research Models*, International Textbook, Scranton, PA.

[6] Crabill, T.B., D. Gross and M.J. Magazine, 1973, *A Survey of Research on Optimal Design and Control of Queues*, Working Paper, September 19, 1973, Rand Institute, New York.

[7] Fraisse, P., 1957, *Psychologie du Temps*, P.U.F., Paris.

[8] Howard, J.A. and J.N. Seth, 1969, *The Theory of Buyer Behavior*, Wiley, New York.

[9] Horowitz, I., 1970, A Note on Advertising and Uncertainty, *Journal of Industrial Economics*, 18, 151-161.

[10] Kamien, M.I. and N.L. Schwartz, 1981, *Dynamic Optimization: The Calculus of Variations and Optimal Control in Economics & Management*, North Holland, Amsterdam.

[11] Kleindorfer, P.R., 1981, Group Decision Making Methods for Evaluating Social and Technological Risks, W-P. 81-09-01, U. of Pennsylvania, *Decision Sciences*.

[12] Koopmans, T.C., 1964, On Flexibility of Future Preference, in M.W. Shelly II and G.L. Bryan (Eds.) *Human Judgment and Optimality*, Wiley, New York.

[13] Koopmans, T.C., 1972, Representation of Preference Orderings Over Time in C.B. McGuire and R. Radner (Eds.) *Decisions and Organizations*, North Holland, Elsevier, New York, pp. 79-101.

[14] Levhari D. and E. Sheshinsky, 1974, The Economics of Queues: A Brief Survey, in M.S. Balch, D.L. Fadden, S.Y. Wu (Eds.) *Essays in Economic Behavior Under Uncertainty*, North Holland, Amsterdam, pp. 195-212.

[15] Lipstein, B., 1965, A Mathematical Model of Consumer Behavior, *Journal of Marketing Research 2*.

[16] Luce, R.D. and H. Raiffa, 1957, *Games and Decisions*, Wiley, New York.

[17] Massy, W.F., D.B. Montgomery and D.G. Morrison, 1970, *Stochastic Models of Buying Behavior*, MIT Press, Cambridge, Mass.

[18] Naert, P. and Leafland, 1978, *Building Implementable Marketing Models*, Martinus Nijhoff, Leiden.

[19] Pierskalla, W.P. and J.A. Voelker, 1976, A Survey of Maintenance Models: The Control and Surveillance of Deteriorating Systems, *Naval Res. Log. Quart.*, 23, 353-388.

[20] Porter, M.E., 1980, *Competitive Strategy: Techniques for Analyzing Industries and Competitors*, The Free Press, New York.

[21] Radner, R., 1981, Utility Over Time: The Homothetic Case, *Journal of Economic Theory*, 25, 219-236.

[22] Shackle, G.L.S., 1958, *Time in Economics*, North Holland, Amsterdam.

[23] Tapiero, C.S., 1975, Random Walk Models of Advertising, Their Diffusion Approximation and Hypothesis Testing, *Annals of Economics and Social Measurement*, 4, 293-309.

[24] Tapiero, C.S., 1975, On Line and Adaptive Optimum Advertising Control by a Diffusion Approximation, *Operations Research*, 22, 890-907.

[25] Tapiero, C.S., 1977, Optimum Advertising and Goodwill Under Uncertainty, *Operations Research*, 26, 450-963.

[26] Tapiero, C.S., 1978, Time, Dynamics and the Process of Management Modeling, in A. Bensoussan, P. Kleindorfer and C.S. Tapiero, (Eds.), *Applied Optimal Control*, TIMS Studies, North Holland, Amsterdam.

[27] Tofler, A., 1971, *Future Shock*, Bantam Books, New York.

[28] Wind, Y., 1982, *Product Policy: Concept Methods and Strategy*, Addison Wesley, Reading, Mass.

Chapter 2

INTRODUCTION TO MODELING

2.1   *Introduction*

Under uncertainty, the construction of models requires that we distinguish known from unknown realities and find some mechanisms (such as constraints, theories, common sense and more often intuition) to reconcile our knowledge with our lack of it. For this reason, modeling is not merely a collection of techniques but an art in blending the relevant aspects of a managerial problem and its unforeseen consequences with a descriptive, yet tractable, mathematical methodology.

To model under uncertainty, we typically use probability distributions (explicitly or implicitly in constructing mathematical models of processes) to describe quantitatively the set of possible events that may unfold over time. Specification of the structure of the probability distributions (for example, whether these are binomial, Poisson, Normal etc.) are important and based on an understanding of the process. Moments of such processes (particularly the mean and the variance) tend to reflect the trend and the degrees to which we are more or less certain about the events as they occur.

Throughout this chapter we shall deal with the construction of stochastic processes. In particular, random walks, Wiener and Poisson processes as well as stochastic differential equations and jump processes are introduced. This chapter should be read simultaneously with Chapter 3 where numerous applications in operations management are given. A simplified treatment is given in the text while a more formal treatment of some specific processes considered here are outlined in the appendix. In our quest for simplicity, the mathematical rigour of the presentation is sacrificed. For a broad and formal study of stochastic processes, references such as Arnold [1], Cinlar [8], Cox and Miller [9], Gihman and Skorohod [12, 13], Prabhu [22], Bartlett [3], Ross [23, 24] Saaty [25], Snyder [27] and others as will be indicated throughout the chapter should be consulted.

2.2   *Random Walk Models*

Consider a line representing the prices a product may take (or the possible sales levels of a firm, a stock price etc.). We denote by Δx the increment in price changes so that the distance between any two points on the line equals Δx. A position on the line at a given time stands therefore for the price, and movements on the line stand for increases or decreases in prices in a given time interval Δt. We shall hypothesize that at a given time, prices may increase with a probability p and if not, decrease with a probability $1 - p$. Denote by $\Delta \xi(t)$ the random event of jumps denoting the price change. Thus,

$$\Delta \xi(t) = \begin{cases} +\Delta x \text{ w.p. } p \\ -\Delta x \text{ w.p. } 1-p \end{cases} \tag{2.1}$$

If $x(t)$ is the price at the discrete time t, and if it is *only* a function of the last price $x(t - \Delta t)$ with time increments Δt and the random price changes $\Delta \xi(t)$ during $(t - \Delta t, t)$, then an evolution of the price is given by:

$$x(t) = x(t - \Delta t) + \Delta \xi(t) \tag{2.2}$$

The values $x(t)$ at the various instants of time $x(0), x(\Delta t), x(2\Delta t), ... x(t - \Delta t), x(t), x(t + \Delta t), ...$ denote a random function or a stochastic process of $x(t)$. We shall provide a probability distribution for the possible values of x at time t, or $P(x, t)$. Say that we start at a given price x_0 at time $t_0 = 0$. At time $t_1 = t_0 + \Delta t$, we obtain a price $x_1 = x(t_1)$;

$$x(t_1) = x(t_1 - \Delta t) + \xi_1, \text{ or}$$

$$x(t_1) = x(t_0) + \Delta \xi_1$$

which can take two values at time t_1

$$x(t_1) = \begin{cases} x_0 + \Delta x \text{ w.p. } p \\ x_0 - \Delta x \text{ w.p. } 1-p \end{cases}$$

Now consider an instant of time later $t_2 = t_1 + \Delta t = t_0 + 2\Delta t$. Here again,

$$x(t_2) = x(t_2 - \Delta t) + \Delta \xi_2 \text{ or}$$

$$x(t_2) = x(t_1) + \Delta \xi_2 \text{ or}$$

$$x(t_2) = x(t_0) + \Delta \xi_1 + \Delta \xi_2 \text{ or}$$

x at t_2 is thus

$$x(t_2) = \begin{cases} x_1 + \Delta x \text{ w.p. } p \\ x_1 - \Delta x \text{ w.p. } 1-p \end{cases}$$

or

$$x(t_2) = \begin{cases} x_0 + 2\Delta x & \text{w.p.} \quad p^2 \\ x_0 & \text{w.p.} \quad 2p(1-p) \\ x_0 - 2\Delta x & \text{w.p.} \quad (1-p)^2 \end{cases}$$

We generalize to n jumps (increases or decreases in prices, sales etc.) and seek the probability distribution $P(x_n, t_n)$. We have

$$x(t_n) = x(t_{n-1}) + \Delta\xi_n \quad or$$

$$x(t_n) = x(t_0) + \sum_{i=0}^{n} \Delta\xi_i \qquad (2.3)$$

or, the probability distribution of $x(t_n) - x(t_0)$ is equal to that of the sum of $\Delta\xi_i (i = 1...n)$ where each $\Delta\xi_i$ is as defined in (1). This distribution can be computed in several manners. If the price jumps $\Delta\xi_i$ are independent, we can compute the moment generating function G of each jump[1]. The moment generating function of the sum is then equal to the n product, $G \times G \times ...G = G^n$. It is easy to verify that this leads to a binomial distribution. Since in our case,

$$G = p exp(m\Delta x) + q exp(-m\Delta x)$$

where $q = 1 - p$ and $m = 1$. Thus,

$$G^n = [p exp(\Delta x) + q exp(-\Delta x)]^n$$

which is the moment generating function of the binomial distribution. Alternatively, let y be the number of positive jumps (i.e. cases where $\Delta\xi = \Delta x$, or "successes") in n trials. Since each jump is essentially a Bernoulli experiment with probability of success, p, the probability of y successes in n independent trials is binomial and given by

$$P_y^n = \binom{n}{y} p^y (1-p)^{n-y}, y = 0, 1, 2, 3, ...$$

If y is the number of positive jumps, then $n - y$ is the number of negative jumps (i.e. cases where $\Delta\xi = -\Delta x$). The distance d covered in n jumps is therefore equal to

---

[1]From probability theory, this moment generating function is given by $G = E exp(m\Delta\xi_i)$, where E is the expectation operator. Further, a sum of independent random variables has a moment generating function equalling the product of the individual generating functions.

$$d = [y - (n - y)]\Delta x$$

The mean distance and its variance are given by $E(d)$ and $var(d)$, with $q = 1 - p$. Or,

$$E(d) = n(p - q)\Delta x; \quad var(d) = 4npq(\Delta x)^2$$

This is easily proved by noting that, since $E(y) = np$ and $var(y) = npq$. Then,

$$
\begin{aligned}
E(d) &= E[y - (n - y)]\Delta x = E[2y - n] \\
&= (2np - n)\Delta x \\
&= n(p - q)\Delta x
\end{aligned}
$$

Also

$$
\begin{aligned}
Var(d) &= (\Delta x)^2 Var[y - (n - y)] \\
&= (\Delta x)^2 var[2y - n] \\
&= 4npq(\Delta x)^2
\end{aligned}
$$

as written above.

The stochastic process above is unrestricted, meaning that it can take values on the whole line ($-\infty$ to $+\infty$). Inserting restrictions on the number of positions and on the probabilities of jumps will lead to different random walks. Restrictions include reflecting barriers, absorbing barriers etc. as will be defined at the end of this chapter.

The results above are expressed in terms of small increments of distance jumped in small increments of time. Letting these increments get smaller and smaller, we obtain in the limit a continuous time form for the equation of motion. In a time interval $[0, t]$, the number of jumps n is given by $n = [t/\Delta t]$, since at each Δt a jumps occurs. When Δt is a small time increment, then (with $t/\Delta t$ integer):

$$E(d) = \frac{t(p - q)\Delta x}{\Delta t}$$

$$var(d) = \frac{4tpq(\Delta x)^2}{\Delta t}$$

For the problem to make sense, the limits of $(\Delta x/\Delta t)$ and $((\Delta x)^2/\Delta t)$ as $\Delta x \to 0$ must exist. If we let these limits be:

$$\lim_{\Delta x \to 0} \frac{(\Delta x)^2}{\Delta t} = 2D, \quad \lim_{\Delta t \to 0} \frac{\Delta x}{\Delta t} = 2C,$$

and also let $p = 1/2 + (C/2D)\Delta x$, then the expected displacement $m(t)$ and $\sigma^2(t)$ its variance become

$$m(t) = 2Ct; \; \sigma^2(t) = 2Dt \tag{2.4}$$

This can be shown by elementary manipulations. From the above

$$
\begin{aligned}
E(d) &= t(p-q)\frac{\Delta x}{\Delta t} = t[(\frac{1}{2} + \frac{C}{2D}\Delta x) - (\frac{1}{2} - \frac{C}{2D}\Delta x)]\frac{\Delta x}{\Delta t} \\
&= t\frac{C}{D}\frac{(\Delta x)^2}{\Delta t} = t\frac{C}{D}.2D = 2Ct = m(t)
\end{aligned} \tag{2.5}
$$

and finally

$$
\begin{aligned}
Var(d) &= 4t[(\frac{1}{2} + \frac{C}{2D}\Delta x)(\frac{1}{2} - \frac{C}{2D}\Delta x)]\frac{(\Delta x)^2}{\Delta t} \\
&= 4t(\frac{1}{4} - \frac{C^2}{4D^2}\Delta x^2)\frac{\Delta x^2}{\Delta t} \\
&= t(1 - \frac{C^2}{D^2}\Delta x^2).2D = 2Dt = \sigma^2(t)
\end{aligned}
$$

where $(\Delta x)^2 \approx 0$, since $D\Delta t \to 0$ as Δt becomes very small.

Q.E.D.

When $\Delta x \to 0$ and $\Delta t \to 0$, the number of jumps is extremely large and from *probability arguments*, the binomial distribution of displacement can be approximated by a normal distribution with mean and variance $m(t)$ and $\sigma^2(t)$ respectively, or

$$f(x,t) = [\frac{1}{\sqrt{2\pi}\sigma(t)}]exp\{-\frac{1}{2}\frac{[x - m(t)]^2}{\sigma^2(t)}\} \tag{2.6}$$

An alternative procedure to deriving the normal distribution above can be obtained from *mathematical arguments*. This consists in describing the physical characteristics of movement, representing them quantitatively and by approximations obtain a partial differential equation representing the movement of the particle over time.

Let $f(x,t)$ be the probability of having reached a position x (in time t). Say that in the time interval $(t, t + \Delta t)$, we can reach the distance x either if we were at $(x - \Delta x)$ at t and increased the distance covered by Δx (with probability p), or if we were at $(x + \Delta x)$ at t and decreased the distance by Δx (with probability q). This is written as follows:

$$f(x, t + \Delta t) = pf(x - \Delta x, t) + qf(x + \Delta x, t)$$

Two and three terms Taylor series approximation of the arguments above around $f(x, t)$ yield;

$$f(x, t + \Delta t) \quad = f(x, t) + (\Delta t)\frac{\partial f(x, t)}{\partial t} + o(\Delta t)^2$$

$$f(x - \Delta x, t) \quad = f(x, t) - (\Delta x)\frac{\partial f}{\partial x} + (\frac{1}{2})(\Delta x)^2\frac{\partial^2 f(x, t)}{\partial x^2} + o(\Delta x)^3$$

$$f(x + \Delta x, t) \quad = f(x, t) + (\Delta x)\frac{\partial f}{\partial x} + \frac{1}{2}(\Delta x)^2\frac{\partial^2 f(x, t)}{\partial x^2} + o(\Delta x)^3$$

Inserting these approximations into the equation of motion $f(x, t)$, we obtain (using the definitions for p above in terms of C and D)

$$\frac{\partial f}{\partial t} = -(\frac{C}{D})[\frac{(\Delta x)^2}{\Delta t}]\frac{\partial f}{\partial x} + \frac{1}{2}[\frac{\Delta x^2}{\Delta t}]\frac{\partial^2 f}{\partial x^2} + o(.)$$

When $\Delta x \to 0$ and $\Delta t \to 0$, we obtain a partial differential equation named the Fokker-Planck equation,

$$\frac{\partial f}{\partial t} = -2C(\frac{\partial f}{\partial x}) + D(\frac{\partial^2 f}{\partial x^2})$$

where $(f(x, t) \to 0$ as $x \to \pm\infty)$. A solution to this equation is the normal distribution $f(x, t)$ found earlier.

Finally, the stochastic process considered so far can be represented from a different point of view. We return to equation (2.2) and assume that $\eta(t)$ is now an instantaneous (to be clarified later on) random disturbance, so in the time interval $[t - \Delta t, t]$, the disturbance is given by $\Delta x(t) = \eta(t)\Delta t$. We rewrite $x(t - \Delta t)$ by

$$x(t - \Delta t) = x(t) - (\Delta t)\frac{dx(t)}{dt}$$

Inserting into (2.2) we obtain for $\Delta t \to 0$,

$$\frac{dx(t)}{dt} = \eta(t) \tag{2.7}$$

which is a linear differential equation with an "instantaneous" disturbance given by $\eta(t)$, or better called a stochastic differential equation with a representation due to Langevin. When $x(t)$ has a mean of $2Ct$ and variance $2Dt$. We can rewrite (2.7) as:

$$\frac{dx}{dt} = 2C + \sqrt{2D}\eta(t)'$$

where $\eta(t)'$ is now defined by the diffusion;

$$dw = \eta(t)'dt, \text{ or}$$

$$dx = 2Cdt + \sqrt{2D}dw$$

Equations with such representations are known as Ito-stochastic differential equations, and will be discussed in greater detail below. A summary of these equivalent approaches, in determining in a quantitative manner the stochastic movement of a particle on a line are given in Table 2.1. Generalizations to far more complex movements will be presented in the sequel. Nonetheless, the approaches presented outline clearly that there is more than one way to conceive and formalize stochastic models.

Throughout the cases treated, the evolution of movements were entirely independent of their past history. A position at an instant of time depends only on the position at the previous instant of time. Such assumptions, compared to real economic and social processes we usually face, are extremely simplistic. They are, however, required if we are to gain a measure of analytical tractability. Decision scientists must therefore be aware of the limitations of quantitative model building of time related activities when the past, the present, and the future are characterized in probabilistic terms. As a larger measure of realism is introduced into models, their analytical tractability tends to be correspondingly lessened. The stringency of the assumptions required to construct probabilistic models over time (stochastic processes) thus indicates that these can be useful to study systems which exhibit small variations in time. Models with large and unpredictable variations must be based therefore on an intuitive understanding of the problem at hand and the choice of appropriate courses of action based on the wisdom of managers. Finally, the dynamic models, especially in their continuous forms, exhibit behaviors which may not be physically realizable. This is

Table 2.1: The Random Walk

Representation	Comment
$x(t) = x(t - \Delta t) + \xi(t)$	Random Walk with disturbance $\Delta\xi(t)$
$P_{ij}^n = \binom{n}{a}p^a q^b; a = (n + j - i)/2,$ $b = (n - j + i)/2$	Discrete jump process. At the limit, we obtain the normal $f(x,t)$ with mean 2Ct and variance 2Dt
$f(x, t + \Delta t) =$ $pf(x - \Delta x, t) + qf(x + \Delta x, t)$	Jump process. At the limit $\Delta x \to 0, \Delta t \to 0$ given by the partial differential equation below
$\partial f/\partial t = -2C\partial f/\partial x + D\partial^2 f/\partial x^2$	Fokker Planck diffusion equation whose solution is a normal distribution with mean $2Ct$ and variance $2Dt$
$dx/dt = 2C + \sqrt{2D}\eta$	Langevin's representation of a stochastic differential equation
$dx = 2Cdt + \sqrt{2D}\ dw$	Ito representation of a stochastic differential equation

seen when we seek to comprehend the meaning of a stochastic differential equation. Although this will be the concern of Sections 2.3(i) and 2.4, it is evident that such a differential equation must exist and must be integrable. Due to the random character of the equation, a special treatment and/or clear understanding of what we mean by such an equation is required.

2.3   *Special Processes*

The random walk models discussed earlier belong to a large and important class of processes called Markov processes. These processes have the property that at any time t, the state of the process depends on the immediately preceding state. As a result, all the past is reflected in the last value the process has attained. Below we consider several special processes including the Wiener, the Poisson and discrete state Markov processes.

(i) The Wiener Process

A Wiener process is a Markov stochastic process $x_t = \{x, t; t \geq 0 \}$ for which the increments Δx_t and Δx_s, where

$$\Delta x_i = x_{i+\Delta t} - x_i; \; i = t, s \qquad (2.8)$$

are *stationary*, *independently* and *normally distributed* with mean zero and variance $\sigma^2 \Delta t$, that is $E\{\Delta x_t\} = 0$, $var\{\Delta x_t \Delta x_s\} = 0$ for $s \neq t$. Equivalently, if we let $N(\mu, \sigma^2)$ stand for the normal distribution with mean μ and variance σ^2, we have for the above process that $\Delta x_t \sim N(0, \sigma^2 \Delta t)$. Thus, if we let

$$\Delta x_t = \sigma \Delta w \qquad (2.9)$$

where $\Delta w \approx N(0, \Delta t)$. Then two instants of time t, s, we have $(x_t - x_s) \approx N(0, \sigma^2 |t - s|)$, or by letting $x_s = 0$, $s = 0$, we have

$$f(x, t) = \frac{1}{\sqrt{2\pi\sigma^2 t}} exp(\frac{-x^2}{2\sigma^2 t}) \qquad (2.10)$$

Einstein was the first to show that this is a unique solution to a Fokker Planck Equation (FPE) of the form

$$\frac{\partial f}{\partial t} = \frac{1}{2}\sigma^2 \frac{\partial^2 f}{\partial x^2}; \qquad (2.11)$$

$$f(x, 0) = 0, x \neq 0 \text{ and } ; \frac{\partial f}{\partial x}(x, t) \to 0 \text{ as } x \to \pm\infty$$

thus bridging a gap between the random walk (probability) approach and the mathematical (functional) approach.

An alternative approach to obtaining the Wiener process consists in considering directly the FPE and solving it. In this case it is convenient to use the characertistic function ϕ of $f(x, t)$, (or $\phi(\theta, t) = exp(i\theta f(x, t))$, $i = \sqrt{-1}$)

$$\phi(\theta, t) = \int_{-\infty}^{+\infty} exp(i\theta x) f(x, t) dx; i = \sqrt{-1} \qquad (2.12)$$

which transforms the FPE into

$$\frac{\partial \phi}{\partial t} = -\frac{\sigma^2}{2}\theta^2 \phi; \quad (\phi(0, t) = 1) \qquad (2.13)$$

A solution by integration is straightforward and yields

$$\phi(\theta,t) = exp(-\sigma^2 t\theta^2/2) \qquad (2.14)$$

which is the characteristic function of a normal random variable with mean zero and variance $\sigma^2 t$.

We now let Δt, the time increment, become very small and tend to zero, and interpret the continuous random variable $\xi(t)$. That is, let

$$\frac{\Delta x_t}{\Delta t} = \frac{\sigma \Delta w}{\Delta t} \qquad (2.15)$$

Formally we may use derivatives to denote the ratio $\Delta x_t/\Delta t$ and $\Delta w/\Delta t$ as Δt tends to zero. But what is the meaning of taking derivatives of a random function? What physical sense can we have? Say that (with $\xi_t \equiv \xi(t)$, for notational convenience),

$$\xi_t \approx \lim_{\Delta t \to 0} \frac{\Delta w}{\Delta t} = \frac{dw}{dt} \qquad (2.16)$$

where ξ_t is called a $White-Noise$ Gausian process. This is a zero-mean, normal and uncorrelated random function, with

$$E\{\xi_t\} = 0; E\{\xi_t \xi_s\} = \delta_D(t-s) \qquad (2.17)$$

where $\delta_D(t-s)$ called a Dirac delta function, is an impulse function defined by the integrals

$$\int_{-\infty}^{+\infty} \delta_D(t-s)dt = 1$$
$$\lim_{\varepsilon \to 0} \int_{s-\varepsilon}^{s+\varepsilon} \delta_D(t-s)dt = 1 \qquad (2.18)$$

Thus, $\delta_D(t-s)$ is an ε neighborhood of s, equalling 1 at $t = s$ and because of the first integral, it equals zero elsewhere. Informally we may understand it to be:

$$\delta_D(t-s) = \begin{cases} 1 \text{ for t} = \text{s} \\ 0 \text{ elsewhere} \end{cases} \qquad (2.19)$$

Now if $dx_t/dt = \lim_{\Delta t \to 0} \Delta x/\Delta t$, then

$$\frac{dx_t}{dt} = \frac{\sigma dw}{dt} = \sigma \xi_t \qquad (2.20)$$

which is a Langevin's stochastic differential equation. As we pointed out earlier this is only a formal representation because there is no physical sense to the white noise ξ_t consisting of impulses. There is a physical sense to its integral, however. That is, if we write

$$dx_t = \sigma \xi_t dt = \sigma dw \tag{2.21}$$

Table 2.2: Alternative Representations of
the Wiener-Levy-Einstein Process

$\Delta x_t = \sigma \Delta w$ $\Delta w \sim N(0, \Delta t)$	Probability Model in Δt
$\dfrac{\partial f}{\partial t} = \dfrac{1}{2}\sigma^2 \dfrac{\partial^2 f}{\partial x^2}$ $F(x,0) = 0$ for $x \neq 0$ $\dfrac{\partial f}{\partial x} \to 0$ as $x \to \pm\infty$	Fokker Planck Equation formulation
$\dfrac{dx_t}{dt} = \sigma \xi_t$ ξ_t white noise	Langevin's s.d.e
$dx_t = \sigma dw$	Ito s.d.e
$x_t = x_s + \displaystyle\int_s^t \sigma dw$	Stochastic integral

and formally let

$$x_t = x_s + \int_s^t \sigma \xi_t dt = x_s + \int_s^t \sigma dw \tag{2.22}$$

Then;

$$x_t = x_s + \sigma(w_t - w_s) \tag{2.23}$$

where the term $(w_t - w_s)$ is meaningful (it is a zero mean random variable with variance $|t - s|$ as pointed out earlier). We return to these considerations in far greater detail in 2.4, but it is now clear that a Wiener process summarized in Table 2.2 is a fundamental process, defined in its integral sense as above. The integral is called a *stochastic integral*, and it is to be distinguished from the usual integral of calculus.

(ii) The Poisson Process

The Poisson process, as the Wiener process, consists of *stationary independent increments* which are *identically distributed as a Poisson probability distribution*. That is, for an increment Δx_t, we have $E(\Delta x_t) = \lambda \Delta t$ where λ is the mean rate of a Poisson distribution, or

$$p(\Delta x_t = n) = exp(-\lambda \Delta t)(\lambda \Delta t)^n/n!, \ n = 0, 1, 2... \quad (2.24)$$

To define this process we let the transition probabilites be defined as follows:

$$\begin{aligned}
Prob(\Delta x_t = 1) &= \lambda \Delta t \\
Prob(\Delta x_t = 0) &= 1 - \lambda \Delta t \\
Prob(\Delta x_t \geq 2) &= o(\Delta t)
\end{aligned} \quad (2.25)$$

Let $P(x_t)$ be the probability of x_t (integer) at time t. Then;

$$P(x_{t+\Delta t}) = P(x_t - 1)\lambda \Delta t + P(x_t)(1 - \lambda \Delta t) \quad (2.26)$$

with initial condition

$$P(x_{t+\Delta t}) = P(x_t)(1 - \lambda \Delta t) \text{ at } x = 0 \quad (2.27)$$

Graphically, the possible transitions are given in Figure 2.1.

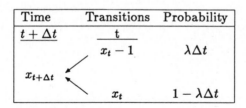

Time	Transitions	Probability
$t + \Delta t$	t	
	$x_t - 1$	$\lambda \Delta t$
$x_{t+\Delta t}$		
	x_t	$1 - \lambda \Delta t$

Figure 2.1: The Poisson Process

at the limit $\Delta t \to 0$ (where the index t is dropped) we obtain the Kolomogorov equations;

$$\frac{dP(x)}{dt} = \lambda P(x - 1) - \lambda P(x); \ x = 1, 2, 3, ... \quad (2.28)$$

$$\frac{dP(0)}{dt} = -\lambda P(0)$$

We can verify easily that the Poisson distribution satisfies the differential-difference equations above. Alternatively, we can solve these equations by defining the probability generating function $F(z,t) = E\{z^z\}$, or

$$F(z,t) = \sum_{x=0}^{\infty} z^x P(x,t) \qquad (2.29)$$

We can show that the Kolmogorov equation is reduced to a simple differential equation

$$\frac{\partial F(z,t)}{\partial t} = \lambda(z-1)F(z,t) \qquad (2.30)$$

whose solution is

$$F(z,t) = exp[(z-1)\lambda t] \qquad (2.31)$$

which is the probability generating function of the Poisson distribution with parameter λt. We shall use this technique for solving Kolmogorov equations repeatedly.

An alternative representation of the Poisson process in an equation form can be reached by considering the Poisson process as a jump process. Such processes are introduced in the next section. Say that

$$\Delta x_t = \lambda \Delta t + \sigma \tilde{\mu}(\Delta t) \qquad (2.32)$$

For the Poisson process, we have the special case $\lambda = \sigma^2$ and $\tilde{\mu}(\Delta t)$ is a Poisson noise standardized in the following manner. We let

$$\tilde{\mu}(\Delta t) = \mu(\Delta t) - \Delta t \qquad (2.33)$$

where $\mu(\Delta t)$ is a random variable with parameter Δt, thus:

$$\begin{aligned} Prob[\mu(\Delta t) = 0] &= 1 - \Delta t + o(\Delta t) \\ Prob[\mu(\Delta t) = 1] &= \Delta t + o(\Delta t) \\ Prob[\mu(\Delta t) \geq 2] &= o(\Delta t) \end{aligned} \qquad (2.34)$$

or $E\{\tilde{\mu}(\Delta t)\} = 0$ and $var\{\tilde{\mu}(\Delta t)\} = \Delta t$. When Δt becomes very small, we define formally a stochastic differential equation for the Poisson process;

$$dx_t = \lambda dt + \sigma \tilde{\mu}(dt); \ \sigma^2 = \lambda \tag{2.35}$$

Evidently, $\tilde{\mu}(dt)$ represents now a discrete state process, taking on values of zero and one only. A generalization of this approach will lead to a class of stochastic models we shall call in the next section, jump processes. It is also evident that if we approximate the Poisson process by the Wiener process, we shall have equations of the form:

$$dx_t = \lambda dt + \sigma dw \tag{2.36}$$

where dw is a Wiener process. The representation of a discrete random process (such as Poisson), by a continuous one (diffusion approximation) is made however, for convenience.

(iii) Finite State Markov Process.

Assume that a discrete time stochastic process $\{x, t_i \geq 0; \ i = 1, 2, ...\}$ can take on only a finite set of values $S_1, S_2, ..., S_n$, or

$$x \in \{S_1, S_2, ...S_n\} \tag{2.37}$$

Further we let $t_1, t_2, ...t_m, ...$ the instants of times or stages in a process be denoted by the index m, $m = 1, 2, ...$. Between any two successive instants of time t_{m-1} and t_m (or stages $m - 1$ and m) and given that we are in a state i, $(S_i, \ i = 1, ...n)$, we may transit to a state j (S_j) with a known probability $Prob\{S_i|S_j\} = P_{ij}$. This probability is called the transition probability and for all states i, j, it defines a matrix $P = [P_{ij}]$ called the Markov Chain. Since the m states define exhaustively the sample space of the process $\{x, t \geq 0\}$, then of course:

$$\sum_{j=1}^{n} P_{ij} = 1 \tag{2.38}$$

Further, if the probability of being in state i at time t_{m-1} is denoted by P_i^{m-1} and if the probability P_j^m depends on the previous state at t_{m-1} and the transition (probability) possibilities, then clearly (see also Figure 2.2)

$$P_j^m = \sum_{k=1}^{n} P_k^{m-1} P_{kj}$$

Now assume that we begin at t_0, with P_j^0. Then at t_1,

$$P_j^1 = \sum_{k=1}^{n} P_k^0 P_{kj}$$

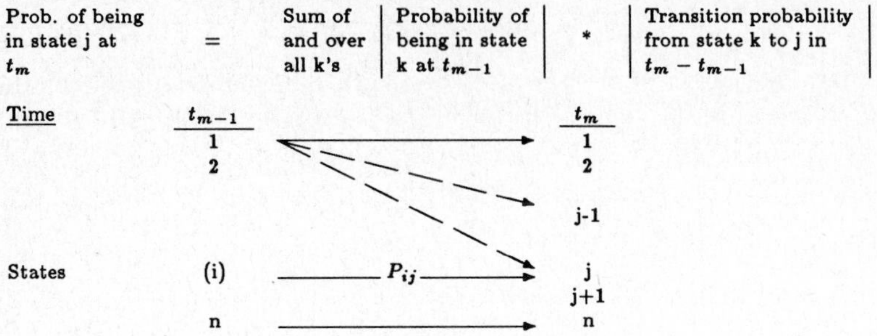

| Prob. of being in state j at t_m | = | Sum of and over all k's | Probability of being in state k at t_{m-1} | * | Transition probability from state k to j in $t_m - t_{m-1}$ |

| Time | | t_{m-1} | | | t_m |
| States | (i) | $\xrightarrow{\quad\quad P_{ij} \quad\quad}$ | | | j |

Figure 2.2: Transition Probabilities

also at t_2

$$P_j^2 = \sum_{i=1}^{n} P_i^1 P_{ij}$$

Inserting P_i^1

$$P_j^2 = \sum_{i=1}^{n} \sum_{k=1}^{n} P_k^0 P_{ki} P_{ij} = \sum_{i=1}^{n} \sum_{k=1}^{n} [P_{ki} P_{ij}] P_k^0$$

which we rewrite as follows:

$$P_j^2 = \sum_{k=1}^{n} P_{kj}^2 P_k^0$$

$$P_{kj}^2 = \sum_{i=1}^{n} P_{ki} P_{ij}$$

where P_{kj}^2 is interpreted as the probability of transition from state k to state j in two stages, or in the time interval $t_2 - t_0$. By recursion, it is clear that for two successive instants of time t_{m-1} and t_m we have,

$$P_{ij}^m = P_{i1}^{m-1} P_{1j} + P_{i2}^{m-1} P_{2j}^j + ... + P_{in}^{m-1} P_{nj}$$

or

$$P_{ij}^m = \sum_{k=1}^{n} P_{ik}^{m-1} P_{kj} \tag{2.39}$$

This latter recursive equation is called the *Chapman Kolmogorov Equation* in discrete and finite state Markov processes. If we use a matrix notation, we note that P_{kj}^2 is the (kj^{th}) entry of the product matrix $P * P$ of transition probabilities, as a result,

$$[P_{ij}^m] = [P_{ij}^{m-1}] * [P_{ij}]$$

And by recursion

$$P^m = P * P * \ldots * P, \quad m \text{ times}$$

Thus, the transition probability from one state to another in m stages (or time $t_m - t_1$) is given by raising the transition matrix P to the mth power. The resultant probabilities thus defined describe completely how we might characterize the evolution of a discrete time, stationary (time invariant) Markov process.

Now assume that the time interval between stages $1, 2, \ldots$ is very small (see also Appendix A.2 for a formal treatment of continuous time Markov processes) and is denoted by Δt.

Specifically let the transition probality in a small time interval Δt, be $P_{ij}^{\Delta t}$, or

$$\{P_{ij}^{\Delta t} = Q_{ij}^{\Delta t} + o(\Delta t), o(\Delta t) \to 0 \text{ as } \Delta t \to 0\}$$

The Chapman-Kolmogorov equations indicate that:

$$P_{ij}^{m\Delta t} = \sum_{k=1}^{n} P_{ik}^{(m-1)\Delta t} P_{kj}^{\Delta t}$$

Or, if we denote $(m-1)\Delta t = t$ and $m\Delta t = t + \Delta t$, and if we write for convenience $P_{ij}^t = P_{ij}(t)$, then

$$P_{ij}(t + \Delta t) = \sum_{k=1}^{n} P_{ik}(t) P_{kj}(\Delta t)$$

Replace P_{kj} by $Q_{kj}\Delta t + o(\Delta t)$, then (dropping the kj terms in $o(.)$), we have

$$P_{ij}(t + \Delta t) = \sum_{k=1}^{n} P_{ik}(t) Q_{kj}\Delta t$$

Since "$Q_{kj}\Delta t$" is a distribution summing to one, we obviously have

$$Q_{jj}\Delta t = 1 - \sum_{j\neq i}^{n} Q_{ij}\Delta t$$

and

$$P_{ij}(t + \Delta t) = \sum_{k\neq j}^{n} P_{ik}(t)Q_{kj}\Delta t + P_{ij}(t)Q_{jj}\Delta t$$

and

$$P_{ij}(t + \Delta t) = \sum_{k\neq j}^{n} P_{ik}(t)Q_{kj}\Delta t + P_{ij}(t)[1 - \sum_{j\neq i}^{n} Q_{ij}\Delta t]$$

Rearranging the terms in the above equation and dividing by Δt yields

$$(1/\Delta t)\{[P_{ij}(t + \Delta t) - P_{ij}(t)]\} = \sum_{k\neq j}^{n} P_{ik}(t)Q_{kj} - P_{ij}(t)\sum_{j\neq i}^{n} Q_{ij}$$

Finally, when $\Delta t \rightarrow 0$, the left hand side of the above equation becomes an ordinary differential equation which we write as follows;

$$\frac{dP_{ij}(t)}{dt} = [-Q_i P_{ij}(t) + \sum_{k\neq i}^{n} P_{ik}(t)Q_{kj}]$$

$$Q_i = \sum_{j\neq i}^{n} Q_{ij}; \quad P_{ij}(0) = P_{ij}^0; i = i,...n; j = 1,...n \qquad (2.40)$$

These latter equations are called the *forward Kolmogorov differential* equations and characterize the continuous time probability distribution of transiting from state i to a state j in a continuous time. It is an $(n \times n)$ set of ordinary linear differential equations that can in some cases be integrated analytically. Evidently, numerical integration of these equations is clearly possible.

In stationary state, when the transition probabilities are time invariant,

$$\frac{dP_{ij}(t)}{dt} = 0 \text{ and } P_{ij}(t) = \bar{P}_{ij}, \text{ or}$$

$$\sum_{i\neq j}^{n} Q_{ij}\bar{P}_{ij} = \sum_{k\neq i}^{n} Q_{kj}\bar{P}_{ik}$$

(2.41)

which is a system of simultaneous $(n \times n)$ linear equations which may be resolved by the usual methods.

When the probabilities Q_{ij} are time variant, then the Kolmogorov differential equation must be dealt with directly, leading to the evolution in time of transition probabilities. These probabilities, do not exhibit a random behavior, but they provide a deterministic characterization of the process' uncertain evolution.

Applications of discrete state markov processes are numerous, and have been used extensively in describing certain queueing processes, brand switching processes in marketing etc. In subsequent chapters we shall deal with applications as well as approximations by continuous state processes.

2.4   *Stochastic Differential Equations*

A straightforward generalization of the Wiener process considered in the previous section leads to stochastic difference and differential equations. For simplicity, let us assume that

$$x(t + \Delta t) = x(t) + \sigma \Delta w$$

where $\Delta w = w(t + \Delta t) - w(t)$, with $w(t)$ a Weiner process: a zero mean normal random variable with variance t. Then clearly, $\Delta x(t)$ is a zero mean normal random variable with variance $\sigma^2 \Delta t$ where σ is a constant. If instead $\sigma = \sigma(x)$, then evidently,

$$\Delta x = \sigma(x) \Delta w$$

which need not lead, necessarily, to a normal process in x. For example, say that $\sigma(x) = \sigma_0 x$ and $\Delta t \to dt$ such that $(dx/x) = d(lnx) = \sigma_0 dw$ and $lnx \approx N(0, \sigma^2 \Delta t)$. As a result, x has a lognormal distribution rather than a normal one. The increments $\{\Delta x, t \geq 0\}$ are normal however. Generally, we can define a certain type of stochastic process whose increments are driven by a Wiener process as shown in Figure 2.3. Such a process will be called a stochastic differential equation and can be written formally as follows:

$$x(t + \Delta t) = x(t) + f(x,t)\Delta t + \sigma(x,t)\Delta w$$

Examples for such equations are considered in the next chapter. If $\Delta t = 1$, we obtain a stochastic difference equation

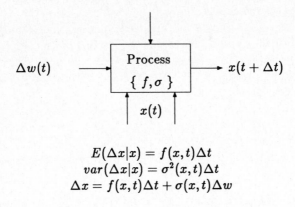

$$E(\Delta x | x) = f(x,t)\Delta t$$
$$var(\Delta x | x) = \sigma^2(x,t)\Delta t$$
$$\Delta x = f(x,t)\Delta t + \sigma(x,t)\Delta w$$

Figure 2.3: A Stochastic Differential Equation Process

$$X_{t+1} = X_t + f_t(X) + \sigma_t(X)\varepsilon_t; \ \varepsilon_t \sim N(0,1), \ \ t = 0,1,2,... \qquad (2.42)$$

with ε_t a zero mean, unit variance and normally distributed random variable.

If we let $\Delta t \to 0$, in continuous time, then we can formally write:

$$dx(t) = f(x,t)dt + \sigma(x,t)dw; \ x(0) = x^0 \text{ given} \qquad (2.43)$$

The stochastic variable x is defined, however, if the above equation is meaningful or if in the equation below

$$x(t) = x(t_0) + \int_{t_0}^{t} f(x,t)dt + \int \sigma(x,t)dw \qquad (2.44)$$

the integrals are meaningful and computable. The first integral is well defined in calculus. The second integral involves however, a random variable with an unbounded variation due to the Wiener process, $w(t+dt) - w(t)$. This unbounded variation introduces some difficulty requiring that we specify precisely what we mean by random (or stochastic) integrals.

Specifying a computational method for the integral will provide a definition of the stochastic differential equation. Namely, we shall distinguish in Appendix A.2 between Ito and Stratonovich stochastic differential equations. To define the integral we partition the time interval $[t, t_0]$ into N steps of length $t^\ell_{j+1} - t^\ell_j, j = 0, 1, ...N - 1$ where

$$\ell = max(t_{j+1} - t_j)$$

and let $t = t_N$. Then we proceed by letting ℓ the maximum time difference $(t_{j+1} - t_j)$ tend to zero (See Appendix A.2 for a formal treatment and definition of stochastic integrals), and obtain

$$\int \sigma(x,t)dw = \lim_{\ell \to 0} \sum_{j=1}^{N-1} \sigma(x(t_j), x, t_j)[w(t_{j+1}) - w(t_j)]$$

as Ito's integral

$$\int \sigma(x,t)dw = \lim_{l \to 0} \sum_{j=1}^{N-1} \sigma(\frac{x(t_j) + x(t_{j+1})}{2}, t_j)[w(t_{j+1}) - w(t_j)]$$

(2.45)

as Stratonovich's integral.

Although the Ito and Stratonovich definition of integrals are not the same they are related to one another by a relationship which holds with probability one (Sethi and Lehoczky[26]). For

$$dx(t) = f(x(t), t)dt + \sigma(x(t), t)dw(t); x(0) = x^0 \qquad (2.46)$$

it will be understood that a solution exists if the stochastic integrals above exist. That is, the limit in the mean of the area of step functions with infinitesimally small step lengths exists. A solution to Ito's stochastic differential equation by "stochastic integration" provides a solution in terms of random functions. A different but complementary solution to Ito's equation consists in determining the evolution in time of the probability distributions p(x,t) of the stochastic process $\{x(t); t > 0\}$. Remembering that Ito's stochastic differential equation is a Markov process, and assuming existence and continuity of the partial derivatives

$$\frac{\partial p}{\partial t}, \frac{\partial p}{\partial x}, \frac{\partial^2 p}{\partial x^2}$$

it can be shown that $p(x, t)$ is given by the solution of a Fokker-Plank equation; (see also appendix A.2)

$$\frac{\partial p(x,t)}{\partial t} = -\frac{\partial}{\partial x}[f(x,t)p(x,t)] + \frac{1}{2}\frac{\partial^2}{\partial x^2}[\sigma^2(x,t)p(x,t)] \qquad (2.47)$$

with initial conditions $p(x, t_0)$ given. This is called the backward equation, since its solution is taken as a function of $x(t_0)$, the initial state. An equivalent equation can be shown to be given by (see Cox and Miller [9])

$$-\frac{\partial p(x,t)}{\partial t} = f(x_0)\frac{\partial p}{\partial x_0} + \frac{1}{2}\sigma^2(x_0)\frac{\partial^2 p}{\partial x_0^2} \qquad (2.48)$$

which is the foreward (or Kolmogorov) equation.

In general, a solution of the Fokker Planck equation is difficult. Special cases with specific assumptions regarding f, and σ may be resolved however. When $f = 0, \sigma = 1$ we showed earlier that

$$p(x,t) = (2\pi t)^{-\frac{1}{2}} exp\{-x^2/2t\} \qquad (2.49)$$

which is the normal distribution with mean zero and variance t. It can also be verified that for $f = \mu, \sigma^2(x) = \sigma^2$, that with intial conditions $t_0, x(t_0)$,

$$p(x,t|x_0,t_0) = \frac{1}{\sqrt{2\pi\sigma^2(t-t_0)}} exp[-\frac{(x-x_0-\mu t)^2}{2\sigma^2(t-t_0)}] \qquad (2.50)$$

When the state space is restricted, either because of absorption or rejection at some boundary, then boundary restrictions on $p(x,t)$ are required. This will be shown in the next section.

Finally, when we use such random processes, it is necessary to manipulate them carefully. These require a special set of rules (for say multiplication, division etc. of the random variables) which are called Ito's calculus, when we use stochastic differential equations defined in the sense of Ito. The basic rules are summarized below, but the reader is encouraged to read some of the following references, Ito [15], McKean [21], Ito and McKean [16], Jaswinsky [17], Bensoussan [4], Sethi and Lehoczky [26].

<u>Ito's Calculus Rules</u>

a. <u>Addition</u>

Let x_1 and x_2 be two processes satisfying the following stochastic differential equations

$$dx_i = f_i(x,t)dt + \sigma_i(x,t)dw_i; i = 1,2 \qquad (2.51)$$

where dw_1 and dw_2 are independent standard Wiener processes, f_i and σ_i, $i = 1,2$ are assumed independent of future Wiener processes (i.e. these are called adapted processes). Define the sum process

$$y = x_1 + x_2$$

then

$$dy = dx_1 + dx_2$$

b. Multiplication of Functions

Consider two twice continuously differentiable real scalar functions $F = F(x_1, t)$ and $G = G(x_2, t)$ and consider the product of these two functions

$$H(x_1, x_2, t) = F(x_1, t)G(x_2, t)$$

then, the stochastic differential equation of the product is

$$dH = FdG + GdF + \frac{\partial F}{\partial x_1}\frac{\partial G}{\partial x_2}(dx_1)(dx_2)$$

with dG and dF given by the differential rule below. In particular when $x_1 = x_2$ (i.e. these are the same process), then

$$dH = FdG + GdF + \sigma^2\frac{\partial F}{\partial x}\frac{\partial G}{\partial x}dt \tag{2.52}$$

c. Division of Functions

Let $G(x_2, t) > 0$ and consider again the twice continuous differentiable function $F(x_1, t)$ and $G(x_2, t)$. Define the quotient.

$$H(x_1, x_2, t) = \frac{F(x_1, t)}{G(x_2, t)}$$

and let x_1 and x_2 be the same process. Then,

$$d(F/G) = (1/G)dF - (F/G^2)dG - [\sigma^2\frac{\partial F}{\partial x}\frac{\partial G}{\partial x}/G^2]dt + [F\sigma^2\frac{\partial F}{\partial x}\frac{\partial G}{\partial x}/G^3]dt \tag{2.53}$$

d. The Differential Rule

Let $F(x, t)$ be a continuous (twice differentiable) function in x and t, with continuous derivatives $\partial F/\partial t, \partial F/\partial x, \partial^2 F/\partial x^2$, then

$$y = F(x, t) \tag{2.54}$$

has a stochastic differential equation

$$dF = \frac{\partial F}{\partial t}dt + \frac{\partial F}{\partial x}dx + \frac{1}{2}\frac{\partial^2 F}{\partial x^2}(dx)^2$$

and

$$dF = \frac{\partial F}{\partial t}dt + \frac{\partial F}{\partial x}dx + \frac{1}{2}\sigma^2\frac{\partial^2 F}{\partial x^2}(dw)^2$$

or

$$dF = \{\frac{\partial F}{\partial t} + \frac{\partial F}{\partial x}f(x,t) + \frac{1}{2}\sigma^2\frac{\partial^2 F}{\partial x^2}\}dt + \frac{\partial F}{\partial x}\sigma(dw) \qquad (2.55)$$

For a two variable process, we have

$$y = F(x_1, x_2, t) \text{ and}$$
$$dy = \frac{\partial F}{\partial t}dt + \frac{\partial F}{\partial x_1}dx_1 + \frac{\partial F}{\partial x_2}dx_2 +$$

$$\frac{1}{2}\frac{\partial^2 F}{\partial x_1^2}(dw_1)^2 + \frac{1}{2}\frac{\partial^2 F}{\partial x_2^2}(dw_2)^2 + \frac{\partial^2 F}{\partial x_1 \partial x_2}(dw_1)(dw_2) \qquad (2.56)$$

or

$$dy = \{\frac{\partial F}{\partial t} + \frac{\partial F}{\partial x_1}f_1(x_1,t) + \frac{\partial F}{\partial x_2}f_2(x_2,t) +$$

$$\frac{1}{2}\sigma_1^2\frac{\partial^2 F}{\partial x_1^2} + \frac{1}{2}\sigma_2^2\frac{\partial^2 F}{\partial x_2^2} + \sigma_1\sigma_2\frac{\partial^2 F}{\partial x_1 \partial x_2}E(dw_1.dw_2)\}dt + \qquad (2.57)$$

$$\sigma_1\frac{\partial F}{\partial x_1}dw_1 + \sigma_2\frac{\partial F}{\partial x_2}dw_2$$

When x is a vector stochastic process with x *an* n vector, f *an* m vector, σ *an* $n.m.$ matrix and dw is an m vector Wiener process with $E(dw'dw) = Q(t)dt$, then

$$F = F(x_1, ...x_n, t) \qquad (2.58)$$

has a stochastic differential equation

$$dF = \frac{\partial F}{\partial t}dt + \frac{\partial F'}{\partial x}dx + \frac{1}{2} \; trace \; \sigma Q\sigma'\frac{\partial^2 F}{\partial x^2}dt \qquad (2.59)$$

where

$$\frac{\partial F}{\partial t} = \frac{\partial F}{\partial t}$$

$$\frac{\partial F'}{\partial x} = [\frac{\partial F}{\partial x_1}, ..., \frac{\partial F}{\partial x_n}]$$

$$\frac{\partial^2 F}{\partial x^2} = \begin{bmatrix} \dfrac{\partial^2 F}{\partial x_1^2} \cdots \dfrac{\partial^2 F}{\partial x_1 \partial x_n} \\ \\ \dfrac{\partial^2 F}{\partial x_1 \partial x_n} \cdots \dfrac{\partial^2 F}{\partial x_n^2} \end{bmatrix}$$

e. The Derivative Rule

Let $F(x)$ be a twice continuously differentiable function of the real variable x and let

$$G(x) = \frac{\partial F}{\partial x} \tag{2.60}$$

(consider the Wiener process $\{w, t \geq 0\}$ with variance σ^2(or $dx = \sigma dw$). Then for $t_0 < T$,

$$\int_{t_0}^{T} G(w) dw = F(w(T)) - F(w(0)) - \int_{t_0}^{T} \frac{\partial^2 F}{\partial x^2}(w) \sigma^2 dt \tag{2.61}$$

These rules will be used repeatedly in applications. But, we note that they are similar to "deterministic calculus", except for our considerations of the second order terms involving $(dx)^2$. These terms are included since $(dw)^2$ is of order dt rather than $(dt)^2$ and cannot therefore be neglected.

2.5 *Processes with Jumps*

We simplify the presentation of jump processes and refer the reader to Bensoussan and Lions [5], Snyder [27], Feller [11], Bensoussan and Tapiero [6] for a formal treatment. Assume at first that a process $y(t)$ is described by a differential equation, given by:

$$dy = f(y, t)dt; y(s) = x \tag{2.62}$$

At random times $\tau_i, s < \tau_1, < \tau_2 < ... < \tau_i < ...$ the process above jumps by a known (or random) quantity z_i. This means that at time τ_i, the value of the variable $y(\tau_i)$ instantly increases to $y(\tau_i^+) = y(\tau_i^-) + z_i$, as is shown in Figure 2.5. That is, instead of (2.62) we can write

$$y(t+dt) = \left\{ \begin{array}{l} y(t) + f(y,t)dt \text{ at } t \in (\tau_i, \tau_{i+1}) \\ y(t) + z_i \text{ at } t = \tau_i, i = 0, 1, 2, ... \\ y(s) = x \end{array} \right\} \qquad (2.63)$$

where it is convenient to write $\tau_0 = s$. In such a process, the equation behaves between jumps as if it were an ordinary differential equation, while at the jump times it creates a discontinuous change in the process variable $y(t)$ which may be deterministic or stochastic. For example, if the jumping process is Poisson as discussed earlier, then the probability of a jump occuring in dt is λdt where λ is a known parameter and the inter-jump times are exponential. That is, if $n(dt)$ denotes the number of jumps occurring in dt, then

$$\begin{array}{l} P(n(dt) = 1) = \lambda dt + o(dt) \\ P(n(dt) = 0) = 1 - \lambda dt + o(dt) \\ P(n(dt) \geq 2) = o(dt). \end{array} \qquad (2.64)$$

Process

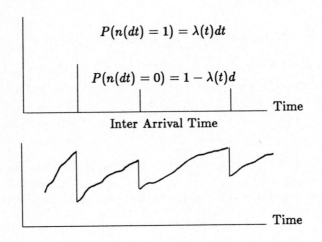

Figure 2.4: Jump process

and the size of the jump equals one. Equation (2.63) would then be written as follows:

$$y(t + dt) = \begin{cases} y(t) + f(y,t)dt \\ y(t) + 1 \text{ at } t = \tau_i = 1, 2... \\ y(s) = x \end{cases} \tag{2.65}$$

where τ_i is defined by a Poisson probability distribution with parameter λ.

Next, let the size of the jump z be arbitrary, possibly defined by a probability distribution $F(z)$. For simplification purposes, we assume that the jump times (τ_i) and the jump magnitudes (z) are statistically independent leading therefore to a compound Poisson (jump) process. We then write for notational convenience.

$$dy = f(y,t)dt + \mu(z, n(dt))$$

$$\mu(z, n(dt)) = \begin{cases} 0 \text{ if } n(dt) = 0 \\ z \text{ if } n(dt) = 1 \end{cases} \tag{2.66}$$

Since $n(dt)$ is a Poisson process, we have

$$P(dy) = \Sigma P[dy|n(dt)]P[n(dt)] \tag{2.67}$$

where $n(dt) = 1, 0$. Thus

$$P(dy) = P[f(y,t)dt][1 - \lambda dt] + P(z)\lambda dt \tag{2.68}$$

where $P(.)$ denotes the probability distribution of its argument.

Generally, it is convenient to write formally a stochastic differential equation with jumps as follows:

$$dy = f(y,t)dt + \sum z_i \delta(t - \tau_i); \quad y(s) = x \tag{2.69}$$

where $\delta(.)$ is the Dirac Delta function, z_i is the ith jump at time τ_i, both possibly random. Further, if the underlying process (without jumps) is also stochastic, or given by a Wiener process, we can proceed as before and write more generally:

$$dy = f(y,t)dt + \sigma(y,t)dw + \sum z_i \delta(t - \tau_i); \quad y(s) = x; \tag{2.70}$$

Applications of such processes are numerous as we shall see subsequently. These include insurance problems where claims arrive following a Poisson process and claims size have a known distribution, transportation, scheduling, quality control, etc.

2.6   *Processes with Barriers : Reflection and Absorption*

Barriers are constraints on stochastic processes. We distinguish between two sets of barriers, reflecting and absorbing. The proper use of such barriers in representing certain processes can be useful. For example, an absorbing barrier can be thought of as the stopping time for a search process, or the first instant of time where a firm's financial health indicator (assumed to be a stochastic process) reaches a given (bankruptcy) level, etc. To represent the kind of problems encountered when introducing such barriers we shall consider some simple examples.

Consider the simple random walk of section 2.2, taking on the values i = 1,2,3 . . . where at zero we assume a reflecting barrier. Further, let the transition probabilities be given as follows,

$$P_{i,i+1} = p \text{ probability of a positive move (increase)}$$

$$P_{i,i-1} = q \text{ probability of a negative move (decrease)}$$

Since we have a reflection at zero, it is impossible, once at zero to go b elow to -1. To account for such an impossibility say that at the zero boundary;

$$P_{0,0} = q \text{ the probability of remaining on the lower boundary}$$

Of course, at this point we return back into the domain of definition with the probability p, or

$$P_{0,1} = p$$

If the process is restricted to values i=0, . . . N, then reflection at i=0 and i=N means that in addition at N

$$P_{NN} = p, \ P_{N,N-1} = q$$

In absorption, at say i=0, however, we require that the absorbing state have a unit mass probability, (since once having reached this state, we can no longer switch to another state). This means that

$$P_{0,0} = 1$$

A solution of the above probability process with appropriately specified values at the boundaries (of absorption or reflection) provides a probability distribution of the constrained process.

Generally, in continuous time and in continuous state Markov processes, we can write the general kinematic equation (see equation (A.115) in the appendix) as follows;

$$\frac{\partial P(x,t)}{\partial t} + \frac{\partial G(x,t)}{\partial x} = 0$$

$$G(x,t) = \sum_{k=1}^{\infty} -(\frac{1}{k!}\frac{\partial}{\partial x})^k (u_k P)$$

(2.71)

where u_k is the kth moment of the process. Note that in the special case, when summing over the first two moments only, we obtain the Fokker Planck equation used earlier, or

$$G = u_1 P - \frac{1}{2}\frac{\partial}{\partial x}(u_2 P)$$

(2.72)

and

$$\frac{\partial P}{\partial t} = -\frac{\partial}{\partial x}(u_1 P) + \frac{1}{2}\frac{\partial^2}{\partial x^2}(u_2 P)$$

(2.73)

To obtain the probability distribution $P(x,t)$, it is necessary to integrate the above partial differential equation, with appropriately specified boundaries. In other words, there are two specific problems to answer; what is the domain of definition of the state space and time dimensions and second, how does the process act on the boundary (i.e., if it is absorbed or reflected and how). To see the effects of boundaries, consider the case $u_1 = 0$ and $u_2 = 1$, then the Fokker Planck equation takes the form

$$\frac{\partial P}{\partial t} = \frac{1}{2}\frac{\partial^2 P}{\partial x^2}$$

(2.74)

Assume that at $t = 0$, the probability distribution is concentrated on a point, or

$$P(x,0) = \delta(x)$$

where $\delta(.)$ is the Dirac-Delta function. Further if x is unconstrained ($x \rightarrow \pm\infty$), then (as we have shown earlier)

$$P(x,t) = (2\pi t)^{1/2} exp[-x^2/2t]$$

(2.75)

Now let $P(x,0) = f_0(x)$ and let the state space be constrained to (a,b), or

$$a \leq x \leq b$$

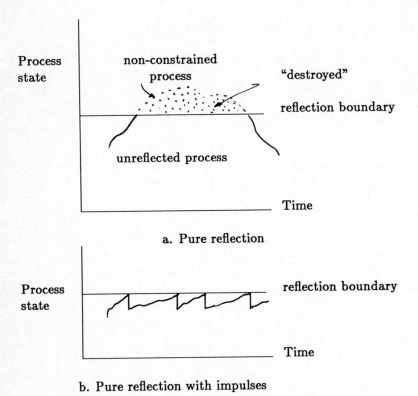

a. Pure reflection

b. Pure reflection with impulses

Figure 2.5: Process with Reflection

Application of Green's function in integrating the Fokker-Planck equation shows that (see Keilson [18] for an extensive treatment of this method in probability theory),

$$P(x,t) = \int_a^b f_0(y)g(x-y,t)dy - \int_0^t I_a(z)g(x-a,t-z)dz$$

$$- \int_0^t I_b(z)g(x-b,t-z)dz \tag{2.76}$$

where $I_a(z)$ and $I_b(z)$ are unknown functions, to be determined by the restrictions on the boundary. In particular, if we have absorption at $x = a, b$, then

$$P(a,t) = 0; P(b,t) = 0$$

These two conditions provide conditions for $I_a(.)$ and $I_b(.)$.

When we impose reflection boundaries, at $x = a$ and $x = b$, then the boundaries on the Fokker Planck equation become, (since P is necessarily a probability distribution);

$$\int_a^b P(x,t)dx = 1; G(x=a,t) = 0, G(x=b,t) = 0 \tag{2.77}$$

Specifically, for the Wiener process,

$$- u_1 P + \frac{\partial}{\partial x}(u_2 P) = 0 \text{ at } x = a, b \tag{2.78}$$

This can be proved by noting that $\int_a^b (\partial P/\partial t)dx = 0$ and replacing it by $- \partial G/\partial x$. Then integrating by parts we obtain

$$G(b,t) - G(a,t) = 0 \tag{2.79}$$

and by convention $G(a,t) = 0, G(b,t) = 0$ as pointed out above.

When we construct a reflective process, it is particularly important to understand the underlying mechanism and the behavior of the stochastic process on the reflection boundary. Further, there may be more than one way to handle such boundaries. As is shown in Figure 2.5a where a pure reflection is considered. Here the reflected and the unreflected process are separated and note that the shaded area above the reflection boundary is "destroyed". This means that a stochastic process with reflection is described by the unreflected process as long as we are below the boundary, but as soon as we move above the boundary, it is necessary to compensate the "shaded area" such that the process remains in the domain of definition. Alternatively, if the process is a Weiner process, such as

$$dx = adt + \sqrt{b}dw; x(0) > 0 \qquad (2.80)$$

we can exert an impulse of say ε, each time we reach the reflection boundary, as shown in Figure 2.5b. Specifically, let $\theta_i, i = 1, 2, \ldots$ be the times at which the reflection boundary and the unreflected process intersect, then the resulting process is (see section 2.5),

$$dx = adt + \sqrt{b}dw - \sum_i \varepsilon\delta(t - \theta_i); x(0) \qquad (2.81)$$

The basic idea is to set the process off the boundary whenever it reaches the reflection boundary and "seeks" to escape into the forbidden domain of the state space definition. Let the impulses ε be very small ($\varepsilon \to 0$) and let the i's be extremely large (since there will be an infinity of intersections if the process remains for some time on the boundary). In this case, we should be looking for a description of the process $\sum \varepsilon\delta(t-\theta_i)$ on the boundary as $\varepsilon \to 0$ and the intersections become continuous; this is done (see [5] and Chapter 5) by representing the limit process on the boundary by the product of a right continuous process $d\xi \geq 0$ (of the impulses θ_i) and a function $\gamma(x,t)$ such that off the boundary, $\gamma(x,t) = 0$ and the process behaves as if it is reflected and on the boundary, $\gamma(x,t) \neq 0$, equalizing the size of the "escape" above the boundary. For this reason, we shall write formally a reflected process as follows,

$$dx = adt + \sqrt{b}dw - \gamma(x,t)d\xi; x(0) = x_0 \qquad (2.82)$$

Bensoussan and Lions [5] have shown that such a process is indeed the limit of the impulse-jump process we have described above. Evidently, when the size of jumps are controlled (such as borrowing money at a cost each time we are on the reflection boundary, or investing excess funds above a given boundary), then the reflected process is a controlled pure reflection process.

For reflective processes, the application of Ito's differential rule is ammended. Namely for all twice continuous and differentiable function $h \in C^2$, we have in expectation (e.g. see [5] for a proof and a development)

$$E\{h(x)\} = h(x_0) + E\int_0^t (\frac{b}{2}\frac{\partial^2 h}{\partial x^2} + a\frac{\partial h}{\partial x})dt - E\int_0^t \gamma\frac{\partial h}{\partial x}d\xi(s) \qquad (2.83)$$

In differential equation form we have

$$dh = (\frac{\partial h}{\partial x} + \frac{b}{2}\frac{\partial^2 h}{\partial x^2})dt + \sqrt{b}\frac{\partial h}{\partial x}dw - \frac{\partial h}{\partial x}\gamma d\xi; h(x_0) \text{ given} \qquad (2.84)$$

These equations will be found useful in chapter 5.

Finally, an approach to reflection, and discussed very briefly for random walks, is based on probability arguments. This was also used explicitly while constructing the Poisson process (whose domain of definition is the set of positive integers) in section 2.3 (ii). Then at the zero reflection boundary, the process can either remain on the boundary with a given probability (equalling $1 - \lambda dt$) or it can move by a unit with probability λdt. All other possibilities, including a movement below the zero boundary are ruled out and as a result, the process can never venture outside the domain of definition of the process. The outcome of such an approach is to create a mixture probability distribution of the unrestricted process, (by the process of reflection and as specified by a behavioral equation at the boundary).

Further Reading

The literature on stochastic processes and their uses in management science is extremely large and expanding rapidly. Useful references for the management scientist include the two books of Ross [23, 24], Saaty's book on queueing [25], as well as Prabhu's book on Queue's, Dams and Storage [22]. In addition, Cox and Miller [9], Bartlett [3], Doob [19], Tintner and Sengupta [30], Buhlmann [7], Bartholomew [2], Feller [11], Cinlar [8] and more recently Heyman and Sobel [14] provide an up to date introduction to the uses of stochastic processes. For a more formal treatment of continuous stochastic processes, books by Arnold [1], Gihman and Skorohod [12, 13], Ito and McKean [16], Bensoussan [4], Bensoussan and Lions [5], Kushner [5], Kushner [19, 20] and Jazwinsky [17] can be usefully consulted, as we pointed out throughout the chapter.

APPENDICES

A.1 *The Markov Process*

The random walk discussed earlier belongs to a large and important class of processes called Markov processes. These processes have the property that at any time t, the state of the process depends on the immediately proceding states. Specifically, a stochastic process $\{x(t), t > 0\}$, is a Markov process if for a finite set of time $t_1, t_2, ..., t_n, t_{n+1} (t_{i+1} > t_i)$, the conditional probability distribution of $x(t_{n+1})$ depends on the state of the previous instant, that is;

$$Prob\{x(t_{n+1})|x(t_1), ...x(t_n)\} = Prob\{x(t_{n+1})|x(t_n)\} \qquad \text{(A.85)}$$

The value of the previous state determines the probability of the next state. For exposition purposes we let $t_n = n\Delta t$, or $t_{n+1} = t_n + \Delta t$ and by dropping the n subscript, any two successive time instants are given by $(t, t + \Delta t)$. Equation (A.85) defines then a transition probability

$$p[x(t_{n+1}), x(t_n)] = Prob\{x(t_{n+1})|x(t_n)\} \qquad (A.86)$$

or in terms of time intervals Δt, we write

$$p(x_{t+\Delta t}, x_t) = P[x_{t+\Delta t}|x_t] \qquad (A.87)$$

where P replaces the probability notation $Prob\{.\}$. Since $p(x_{t+1}, x_t)$ is a probability distribution, we have for continuous states x,

$$\int p(x_{t+\Delta t}, x_t) dx_{t+\Delta t} = 1 \qquad (A.88)$$

When the values a state may take on are finite, it is necessary to replace the integral in (A.88) by a sum. For two successive instants, the joint probability distribution is given by

$$P[x_{t+\Delta t}, x_t] = P[x_{t+\Delta t}|x_t]P[x_t] \qquad (A.89)$$

or

$$P[x_{t+\Delta t}, x_t] = P(x_{t+\Delta t}, x_t)P[x] \qquad (A.90)$$

By recurrence, a joint probability distribution of n successive instants of time is given by (dropping the t subscript)

$$P[x_{n\Delta t}, x_{(n-1)\Delta t}, ...x] = \Pi_{j=1}^{n} p(x_{j\Delta t}, x_{(j-1)\Delta t})P[x] \qquad (A.91)$$

Of course, by integration of the joint distribution over any of the states $x_{t+j\Delta t}$, we reduce the dimensionality of the joint distribution. By considering two successive instants of time t, $t + \Delta t$, for simplicity we have

$$\int P(x_{\Delta t}, x) dx = P(x_{\Delta t}) \qquad (A.92)$$

In terms of the transition probabilities we also obtain by substitution in (A.89)

$$P(x_{\Delta t}) = \int P(x_{\Delta t}, x)P(x) dx \qquad (A.93)$$

For two successive instants of time $[t, t + \Delta t), [t + \Delta t, t + 2\Delta t)$, we obtain by inserting in (A.93):

$$P(x_{2\Delta t}) = \int p(x_{2\Delta t}, x_{\Delta t}) P(x_{\Delta t}) dx\Delta t = \int p(x_{2\Delta t}, x_{\Delta t}) p(x_{\Delta t}, x) P(x) dx_{\Delta t}$$

$$(A.94)$$

If we define:

$$p(x_{2\Delta t}, x) = p(x_{2\Delta t}, x_{\Delta t}) p(x_{\Delta t}, x) \tag{A.95}$$

then

$$p(x_{2\Delta t}, x) = \int p(x_{2\Delta t}, x_{\Delta t}) p(x_{\Delta t}, x) dx_{\Delta t} \tag{A.96}$$

An equation of the form (A.96), is called a *Chapman-Kolmogorov equation.* Generally we have

$$p(x_{n\Delta t}, x) = \int .. \int .. \int \prod_{j=1}^{n-1} p(x_{j\Delta t}, x_{(j-1)\Delta t}) dx_{j\Delta t} \tag{A.97}$$

with the Chapman-Kolmogorov equation we obtain by repeated integration, the direct states transitions probability from and to arbitrary instants of time.

We consider next the probability distribution of movement and seek to represent the evolution in time of the states x. We follow Stratonovich's [28,29] approach and define the characteristic function of the movement Δx in a time interval Δt. That is,

$$\Delta x = x_{\Delta t} - x \tag{A.98}$$

The characteristic function is defined by $\theta(s; x)$;

$$\theta(s; x) = E\{e^{is\Delta x}\} = \int exp(-is\Delta x) p(x_{\Delta t}, x) dx_{\Delta t} \tag{A.99}$$

where E is the expectation operator and $i = \sqrt{-1}$ is the imaginary number. By inverse integration, of the characteristic function we have:

$$p(x_{\Delta t}, x) = \frac{1}{2\pi} \int exp(-is\Delta x) \theta(s; x) ds \tag{A.100}$$

Inserting (15) into (9), we have;

$$P(x_{\Delta t}) = \frac{1}{2\pi} \int \int exp(-is\Delta x) \theta(s; x) ds P(x) dx \tag{A.101}$$

Writing the characteristic function in terms of the moments of movements Δx,

$$m_k(x) = E\{(\Delta x)^k\} = E\{(x_{\Delta t} - x)^k\} \tag{A.102}$$

we note:

$$\theta(s,x) = 1 + \sum_{k=1}^{\infty} \frac{(is)^k}{k!} m_k(x) \qquad (A.103)$$

Inserting (A.103) into (A.101), we obtain:

$$P(x_{\Delta t}) = \sum_{k=0}^{\infty} \frac{1}{k!} \frac{1}{2\pi} \int \int exp(-is\Delta x)(is)^k ds\, m_k(x) P(x) dx \qquad (A.104)$$

Since

$$\frac{1}{2\pi} \int exp(-is\Delta x)(is)^k ds = (-\frac{\partial}{\partial x_{\Delta t}})^k \frac{1}{2\pi} \int exp(-is\Delta x) ds \qquad (A.105)$$

and since the right hand side integral of (A.105) is the characteristic unit function $\delta(\Delta x) = \delta(x_{\Delta t} - x)$.

$$\delta(\Delta x) = \begin{cases} 1 \text{ if } x_{\Delta t} = x \\ 0 \text{ otherwise} \end{cases} \qquad (A.106)$$

we obtain combining (A.106) and (A.105) together with (A.104);

$$P(x_{\Delta t}) - P(x) = \sum_{k=1}^{\infty} \frac{1}{k!} (-1\frac{\partial}{\partial x})^k [m_k(x)P(x)] \qquad (A.107)$$

Dividing both sides of (A.107) by Δt and letting Δt tend to zero we obtain a partial differential equation

$$\frac{\partial P}{\partial t} = \sum_{k=1}^{\infty} \frac{1}{k!} (-\frac{\partial}{\partial x})^k (u_k P) \qquad (A.108)$$

where the limit

$$u_k(x) = \lim_{\Delta t \to 0} m_k(x)/\Delta t \qquad (A.109)$$

exists, and expresses the instantaneous probability moments of the process of movement of Δx. Equation (A.108) is called the *Stochastic or the Kinetic Equations for Markov Processes*. A special case (often called the diffusion) consists in considering the first two moments u_1 and u_2 of the instantaneous movement Δx. In this case, (A.108) is reduced to

$$\frac{\partial P}{\partial t} = -\frac{\partial}{\partial x}(u_1 P) + \frac{1}{2}\frac{\partial^2}{\partial x^2}(u_2 P) \qquad (A.110)$$

which is the Fokker-Plank partial differenital equation with mean u_1 and variance u_2. That is, we define

$$dx = \lim_{\Delta t \to 0} \Delta x \qquad (A.111)$$

we have

$$E\{dx\} = u_1 dt \text{ and } var\{dx\} = u_2 dt \qquad (A.112)$$

and as we have shown, the probability process described by (A.110) corresponds to a stochastic differential equation with instantaneous mean and variance given by (A.112), or

$$dx = u_1 dt + \sqrt{u_2} dw \qquad (A.113)$$

where dw is a normal random variable with mean zero and variance dt. It is also called a Brownian Motion. The differential ratio,

$$\xi = dw/dt$$

is called a White noise. We return to the Fokker-Planck Equation (FPE), and write

$$G = u_1 P \frac{1}{2} - \frac{\partial}{\partial x}(u_2 P). \qquad (A.114)$$

Inserting into (26) we have instead

$$\frac{\partial P}{\partial t} + \frac{\partial G}{\partial x} = 0 \qquad (A.115)$$

This representation of the FPE is often used and is called the *Equation of Conservation of Probability*. It is similar in form to heat equations describing the flow of heat or of a mass of molecules in a gas. Because of these similarities, some FPE are also called Heat Equations. To solve FPE it is necessary however to specify boundary conditions. Examples to that effect were considered in the main text.

A.2   *Stochastic Differential Equations*

Below, we shall provide a definition and an existence theorem for stochastic differential equations (see Arnold [1], Jazwinsky [17], Bensoussan [4]).

Let $\rho = \max_j (t_{j+1} - t_j)$ on a partition of T.

$$T : t_0 < t_1 ... < t_{j+1} ... < t_N = T$$

Let $g(x,t)$, a random function, be mean-square continuous on T and be statistically independent of $[w(t_{j+1}) - w(t_j)]$, where $w(t)$ is a Wiener-Levy process with variance $\sigma^2(x,t)$. Finally, let $E(g(x,t)^2)$ be finite for all $t \in T$. Then the Ito stochastic integral equals the mean-square limit.

$$\lim_{\rho \to 0} \sum_{j=0}^{N-1} g(x,t_j)[w(t_{j+1}) - w(t_j)] = \int_T g(x,t)dw(t)$$

<u>Theorem:</u> Existence of Solution of Stochastic Differential Equations. Supose that a stochastic differential is given by:

$$dx = f(x,t)dt + g(x,t)dw \ \ on \ t_0 \leq t \leq T$$

where the real functions f and g and the initial condition $x(t_0)$ satisfy the hypotheses given below:

(1) f and g satisfy uniform Lipschitz conditons in x. That is, there is a $K > 0$ such that for x_2 and x_1,
$$|f(x_2,t) - f(x_1,t)| \leq K|x_2 - x_1|$$
$$|g(x_2,t) - g(x_1,t)| \leq K|x_2 - x_1|$$

(2) f and g are continuous in t on $[t_0, T]$

(3) $x(t_0)$ is any random variable with $E|x(t_0)|^2 < \infty$, independent of the increment stochastic process $\{dw(t), t \in [t_0, T]\}$

Then,

(1) The stochastic differential equation has, in the mean square sense, a solution on $t \in [t_0, T]$, given by

$$x(t) - x(t_0) = \int_{t_0}^{t} f(x,\tau)d\tau + \int_{t_0}^{t} g(x,\tau)dw(\tau)$$

(2) x(t) is mean square continuous on $[t_0, T]$

(3) $E[|x(t)|^2] \leq M$ for all t on $[t_0, T]$ and arbitrary M

(4) $\int_{t_0}^{T} E[|x(t)|^2]dt < \infty$

(5) $x(t) - x(t_0)$ is independent of the stochastic process $\{dw,(\tau); \tau > t\}$ for every t on $[t_0, T]$

(6) The stochastic process $[x(t), t \in [t_0, T]]$ is a Markov process and, in a mean square sense, is uniquely determined by the initial condition $x(t_0)$.

Bibliography

[1] Arnold, L., 1974,*Stochastic Differential Equations*, Wiley, New York.

[2] Bartholomew, D.J., 1973,*Stochastic Models for Social Processes*, Wiley, New York.

[3] Bartlett, M.S., 1982, *An Introduction to Stochastic Control by Functional Analysis Methods*, North-Holland, Amsterdam.

[4] Bensoussan, A., 1982, *Stochastic Control by Functional Analysis Methods*, North-Holland, Amsterdam.

[5] Bensoussan, A. and J.L. Lions, 1978, *Applications des Inequations Variationelles et Controle Stochastique*, Dunod, Paris

[6] Bensoussan, A. and C.S. Tapiero, 1982, Impulsive Control in Management: Prospects and Applications, *Journal of Optimization Theory and Applications*, 37, 419-442.

[7] Buhlman, H., 1970, *Mathematical Methods in Risk Theory*, Berlin, Springer-Verlag, Berlin.

[8] Cinlar, E., 1975, *Introduction to Stochastic Processes*, Prentice Hall, Englewood Cliffs, N.J.

[9] Cox, D.R. and H.D. Miller, 1965, *The Theory of Stochastic Processes*, John Wiley & Sons, New York.

[10] Doob, J.L., 1953, *Stochastic Processes*, Wiley, New York.

[11] Feller, W., 1957, 1966 *An Introduction to Probability Theory and its Applications*, Vol. I and II, Wiley, New York.

[12] Gihman, I.I. and A.V. Skorohod, 1970 *Stochastic Differential Equations*, Springer Verlag Press, New York.

[13] Gihman, I. & A.V. Skorohod, 1975, 1979, *The Theory of Stochastic Processes*, Vol. I and II, Springer Verlag, New York.

[14] Heyman, D.P. and M. Sobel, 1984, *Stochastic Models in Operations Research*, Wiley(volumes 1 and 2), New York.

[15] Ito, K., 1961, *Lectures on Stochastic Processes*, Lecture Notes, Iata Inst. on Fundamental Research, Bombay, India.

[16] Ito, K., and H.P. McKean, 1967, *Diffusion Processes and their Sample Paths*, Academic Press, New York.

[17] Jazwinski, A.H., 1970, *Stochastic Processes and Filtering Theory*, Academic Press, New York.

[18] Keilson, J., 1965 *Green's Function Methods in Probability Theory*, Charles Griffing and Co., Ltd, London.

[19] Kushner, H.J., 1966, *Stochastic Stability and Control*, Academic Press, New York.

[20] Kushner, H.J., 1977, *Probability Methods in Stochastic Control and for Elliptic Equations*, Academic Press, New York.

[21] McKean, H.P.,1969 *Stochastic Integrals*, Academic Press, New York.

[22] Prabhu, N.U., 1980, *Stochastic Storage Processes*, Springer-Verlag, Berlin.

[23] Ross, S.M., 1970, *Applied Probability Models with Optimization Applications*, Holden-Day, San Francisco.

[24] Ross, S.M., 1982, *Stochastic Processes*, Wiley, New York.

[25] Saaty, T.L., 1961, *Elements of Queueing Theory*, McGraw Hill Book Co., New York.

[26] Sethi, S.P. and J.P. Lehoczky, 1983, A Comparison of the Ito and Stratonovich Formulations of Problems in Finance, *J. of Econ. Dyn. and Control*.

[27] Snyder, D.L., 1975, *Random Point Processes*, Wiley, New York.

[28] Stratonovich, R.L., 1966, A New representation for Stochastic Integrals and Equations, *SIAM J. on Control*, 4, 362-371.

[29] Stratonovich, R.L., 1968, *Conditional Markov Processes and their Application to the Theory of Optimal Control*, American Elsevier, New York.

[30] Tintner, G. and S.K. Sengupta, 1972, *Stochastic Economic: Stochastic Processes, Control and Programming*, Academic Press, New York.

Chapter 3

APPLIED MODELING: OPERATIONAL PROBLEMS

3.1   *Introduction*

The concepts outlined in Chapter 1 and modeling techniques of Chapter 2 are applied next in the formulation of specific problems in management science. Further, this chapter formulates decision problems that will be resolved in Chapter 4. We begin by a cursory introduction to decision criteria which are used in applications to production and inventory management, queueing, machines maintenance and replacement, dispatching, and so on.

3.2   *Decision Making*

Say that a planner takes decision u, a state x occurs, and he obtains a random reward of $R(x, u)$. Aware of the uncertainty inherent in both the state and reward, the planner will expand both time and resources to study (1) the functional and probabilistic relationships between x and u, i.e., establish the conditional probabilistic correspondence $P(x|u)$, (2) the functional and probabilistic correspondence between R, x and u, i.e., establish the conditional probability correspondence $P(R|x, u)$. Once these probabilities are found, the manager chooses a decision u which reflects his preference towards the uncertain returns R, and the information he has accumulated to make this decision. If managers use an expected reward criterion, the decision problem would be to maximize;

$$\text{Maximize } J(u) = E\{R(x, u)\}$$
$$u \in U$$

$$(3.1)$$

$$E\{R(x, u)\} = \int_{x \in \Omega} R(x, u) P(x|u) dx$$

where Ω is the sample space of the random variable x, and U a constraint set. Now assume that the manager faces a decision problem over time and let t be the current time. Denote by $R_t(x_t, u_t)$ the rewards obtained at time t when state x_t occurs at t and decision u_t is taken. Further, assume (as we have shown in Chapter 2) that there is a Markov process relating the states at successive instants of time,

$$(x_{t-1}, u_t) \rightarrow x_t$$

Explicitly, there is a probability relationship for such a model which we write by

$$P(x_t|x_{t-1}, u_t)$$

Let Y^t and U^t be the records (or past measurements) of the states x_t and decisions u_t where;

$$Y^t = \{y_0, y_1, ... y_t\}$$

$$U^t = \{u_0, u_1, ... u_t\}$$

If states are perfectly measured (as it will be assumed throughout this book), then $y_t = x_t$ and Y^t denotes the actual realizations of the states x_t as they occur in time. If decisions must be based on available information, then clearly, $u_t = u_t(Y^t)$ and more generally, $U^t = U^t(Y^t)$. Thus, at two successive instants of time t, $t+1$, we note that

$$x_{t+1} \leftarrow \text{ is determined } \begin{cases} \text{past state } x_t \leftarrow \text{ past acts} \\ \text{by past measurement } Y^t \\ \text{current act } u_{t+1}(Y^t) \end{cases}$$

which yields a probability relationship

$$P(x_{t+1}|x_t, Y^t, U^t, u_{t+1})$$

When an act u_t is taken, and state x_{t+1} occurs, a reward is obtained, given by $R_{t+1}(x_{t+1}, u_{t+1})$. As in (3.1), the objective of the decision maker is to select some act u such that an expectation of the reward can be maximized, or at $t+1$,

$$\text{Max } J(u_{t+1}) = E\{R_{t+1}(x_{t+1}, u_{t+1})\}$$
$$u_{t+1} \in U$$
$$E\{R_{t+1}(x_{t+1}, u_{t+1})\} = \tag{3.2}$$
$$\int_{x_{t+1} \in \Omega} R_{t+1}(x_{t+1}, u_{t+1}) P(x_{t+1}|x_t, Y^t, U^t(Y^t), u_{t+1}(Y^t)) dx_{t+1}$$

where Ω is the sample space of the state variable at time $t+1$. In this expression we clearly note both the importance and the place of the information pattern Y^t, the conditionality of states x_{t+1}, x_t and, of course, the effects of decisions on the reward R_{t+1}. When $y_t = x_t$, then the probability distribution P in (3.2) can be written as $P(x_{t+1}|x_t, u_t)$ only. That is, at times $i = 1, 2, 3, ...$, we obtain the following conditional distributions:

$$i = 1; \quad P(x_1|x_0, u_1)$$
$$i = 2; \quad P(x_2|x_1, u_2) \rightarrow P(x_2|x_0, u_1, u_2)$$
$$i = 3; \quad P(x_3|x_3, u_3) \rightarrow P(x_3|x_0, u_2, u_3)$$

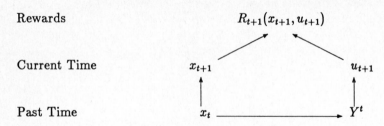

Figure 3.1: The Computation of Rewards

At time $t + 1$, we have

$$P(x_{t+1}|x_t, u_{t+1}) \to P(x_{t+1}|x_0, u_1, u_2, ...u_{t+1})$$

where " $\to$ " points out ·to a functional dependence. In other words, to resolve the apparently single period optimization problem (3.2), we must find the best decisions $u_1, u_2, ...u_{t+1}$, requiring the solutions of a multi-period problem. This dependence, shown in Figure 3.1, renders our decision problem a dynamic one. A dynamic decision problem may, therefore, be stated as follows: (1) Given a probability model relating the evolution of states x and the controls u (or a probability $P(x_{t+1}|x_t, u_{t+1})$), (2) given constraints on the $x's$ and the $u's$, and (3) given an objective defined in terms of the states and the act.

Optimize: The Expected Objective Subject to: (a) The stochastic model for the process of change (b) The constraints on the states (c) The constraints on the controls

In this sense, (3.2) is a dynamic decision problem. Other decision problems can be constructed by specifying the nature of the objective function, the stochastic process of change and the constraints. These lead to difficult problems some of which will be resolved in Chapter 4. A summary of several objective functions is given in Table 3.1. These are (i) the expected terminal rewards (as in (2)), with T, a final time, replacing $(t + 1)$, (ii) the expected sum of rewards in $t = 0, 1, ...T$, (iii) the expected function of the sum of rewards, (iv) the average reward and, finally, (v) the probability criterion. These objectives will be discussed in specific applications throughout the remaining parts of the book. By replacing the "summation" signs, we will obtain, of course, objectives for continuous time stochastic models. For example, say that $R(x_t, u_t)$ is an instantaneous reward at time t expressed in terms of the process variables x_t and control u_t. Further, let x_t be given by a stochastic process such as outlined in the previous chapter. If this process is defined by an Ito stochastic differential equation we then write,

$$dx_t = a(x_t, u_t)dt + b(x_t, u_t)dw; \quad x(0) = x_0, \text{ given} \qquad (3.3)$$

If r denotes a discount rate and $G(x_T)$ is a terminal reward at time T, the final time, a typical optimization problem could be written as follows:

$$\text{Max } J(T) = E \int_0^T e^{-rt} R(x_t, u_t) dt + e^{-rT} G(x_T) \qquad (3.4)$$

$$u_t \in U$$

Subject to equation (3.3)

Other problems, involving infinite horizons $(T \to \infty)$, average cost criteria, etc., can be formulated as we shall next see.

Table 3.1: Selected Objectives

OBJECTIVE	DISCRETE TIME	CONTINUOUS TIME
Expected rewards at the final time	$Max\ E\{R_T(x_T, u_T)\}$ $u_1...u_T$	$Max\ E\{R(x(T), u(T))\}$ $u(t)$
Sum of expected rewards	$Max\ E\{\sum_{t=1}^T R_t(x_t, u_t)\}$ $u_1...u_T$	$Max\ E\{\int_0^T R(x, u, t) dt\}$ $u(t)$
Expected function of sum of rewards	$Max\ E\{f(\sum_{t=1}^T R_t(x_t, u_t))\}$ $u_1...u_T$	$Max\ E\{f(\int_0^T R(x, u, t) dt)\}$ $u(t)$
Expected average reward	$Max\ (1/T)E\{\sum_{t=1}^T R_t(x_t, u_t)\}$ $u_1...u_T$	$Max\ (1/T)E\{\int_0^T R(x, u, t) dt\}$ $u(t)$
Probability criterion for rewards	$Max\ Prob[R_T(x_T, u_T) \geq \mu]$ $u_1...u_T$	$Max\ Prob[R(x, u, T) \geq \xi]$ $u(t)$

3.3 *Production and Inventory Problems*

The classical production-inventory equation is used to relate inventories at two successive instants of time t, $t + \Delta t$ where Δt is a time interval. That is, if x_t is the inventory on hand at time t, u_t and s_t are the production and demand rates during the interval of time Δt, we then have;

$$x_{t+\Delta t} = x_t + u_t \Delta t - s_t \Delta t; \ x_0 \text{ given}$$

If Δt is small and tends to zero, the equation above is reduced to a differential equation;

$$\frac{dx_t}{dt} = u_t - s_t; \; x_0 \text{ given}$$

Now assume that demand is uncertain, and described by a stochastic process,

$$s_t \Delta t = a_t \Delta t - b_t \Delta w$$

where a_t is the mean demand rate, b_t is the standard deviation and Δw is a Wiener process. The inventory equation is therefore;

$$x_{t+\Delta t} = x_t + u_t \Delta t - a_t \Delta t + b_t \Delta w$$

If $\Delta t = 1$, we have

$$x_{t+1} = x_t + u_t - a_t + b_t \varepsilon_t \tag{3.5}$$

where ε_t is a zero-mean, unit variance normal random variable.

A continuous time formulation is similarly defined by,

$$\Delta x_t = x_{t+\Delta t} - x_t = (u_t - a_t)\Delta t + b_t \Delta w \tag{3.6}$$

$$\xi_t = \lim_{\Delta t \to 0} \frac{\Delta w}{\Delta t} \text{ or } \xi_t dt = dw \tag{3.7}$$

we obtain

$$dx_t / dt = u_t - a_t = b_t \xi_t$$

or in Ito's form;

$$dx_t = (u_t - a_t)dt + b_t dw \tag{3.8}$$

We shall return to such equations later on. Evidently, if demand for a product is discrete and "Poisson" distributed, we can proceed in a similar manner and obtain a stochastic differential equation with Poisson noise, that is,

$$dx_t = (u_t - a_t)dt + b_t \tilde{\mu}(dt) \tag{3.9}$$

where $\tilde{\mu}(dt)$ is a standard Poisson random variable (i.e. with zero mean and variance dt). A generalization to a Wiener jump process can similarly be defined.

The inventory equation would then be: (in differential equation form)

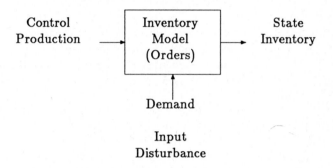

Figure 3.2: Inventory Type Models

$$dx_t = (u_t - a_t)dt + b_t dw - \sum_i \xi_i \delta(t - \tau_i), \quad x_0 \text{ given} \qquad (3.10)$$

where ξ_i are the demands (random variables) occurring at the random instants of time τ_i. Now assume that inventories are replenished by quantitites q_i at the decision times θ^i i.e., the inventory control policy is defined by a series of impulses.

$$q_1, q_2, ..., q_i ...$$

$$s \le \theta^1 < \theta^2 < ....\theta^i,$$

(instead of the continuous time production schedule u_t). Such policies are particularly important when fixed or transaction costs are an essential part of a problem's definition. The selection of such a policy

$$(q_i, \theta^i, i = 1, 2, ...)$$

by minimization of an appropriate objective function, defines an impulsive control problem which we shall define later in far greater detail. In its integral form, the inventory equation is then written as follows:

$$x_t = x_s - \int_s^t a_\lambda d\lambda - \int_s^t b_\lambda dw - \int_s^t \int_R z\mu(d\lambda, z) + \sum_{\{i|\theta^i \le t\}} q_i \qquad (3.11)$$

These equations are models we can use in defining dynamic decision making problems in production and inventory management. There are many problems that can be formulated by inventory type models, however (see Table 3.2). Some of these problems will be dealt with subsequently. Outstanding examples include dams and reservoirs, cash management, maintenance, etc., summarized in Table 3.2, organized according to the controls, the states, and the disturbances (input) defined by each problem. Of course, for each problem there may be a variety of objectives, disturbances and constraints. Next, we turn our attention to three special problems.

Table 3.2: Control Examples

Problems	Uncertainty Disturbance	Control u	Objective & State,x	Constraints
production-Inventory	Demand	Production of orders	inventory	Minimize production inventory costs subject to inventory capacity constraints
Queueing Control	Arrivals of Persons	Servicing	Waiting Lines	Minimize servicing costs subject to queue's constraints and waiting lines
Maintenance	Deteriortaiton of machine	Maintenance and selling date (replacement) of machines	Machine's productivity or salvage	Max, net worth of machines operation subject to maintenance possibilities
Cash Management	Income and Expenditures	Investments of excess cash borrowings	Cash on hand	Minimize cash holding costs subject to specified minimum requirements
Portfolio of Stocks	Rates of Return	Investment strategy in	Wealth	Maximize the utility of returns stocks and wealth subject to the wealth availability
Consumption and investment	Return on investment period (or investment)	Consumption during the	Current Wealth	Maximize expected consumption and/or terminal (bequest) wealth

(i) *A Discrete Stochastic Production Smoothing with Convex Costs*

We are concerned with a production smoothing problem with convex costs (Kleindorfer and Glover [22]) with successive demands represented as independent random variables. We denote by x_t, z_t and D_t the ending inventory, the production and the demand in period t respectively. The demands $D_t, t = 1, ...T$ are non-negative random variables, with compact range Ω_t. We let u_t be the *change in production* from period t to $t+1$. We define a cost function $f_t(u_t, x_t, z_t)$, a function of $u_t, x_t,$ and z_t. A simple unconstrained production smoothing problem is then defined as follows,

$$\text{Min } E\{\textstyle\sum_{t=0}^{T-1} f(u_t, x_t, z_t) + f_T(x_T, z_T)\}$$
subject to:

$$x_{t+1} = x_t + z_t + u_t - D_{t-1}; \quad x_0 \text{ given} \qquad (3.12)$$

$$z_{t+1} = z_t + u_t; \quad z_0 \text{ given}$$
$$t = 0, 1, 2, ..., T - 1$$

Because of the stochastic nature of D_t, problem (3.12) defines a stochastic control problem with u_t the control variable and x_t, z_t state variables. We may also add constraints and other specifications to this problem to render it more realistic for applications.

(ii) *A Continuous Stochastic Production Problem*

We use now a continuous stochastic differential equation model to define a simple production problem with a convex cost function. Generalizing the objective function used by Modigliani and Hohn [24], where C is production cost and H an inventory cost, we have (with $\partial C/\partial u > 0, \partial^2 C/\partial u^2 \geq 0, \partial H/\partial x > 0, \partial^2 H/\partial x^2 > 0$);

$$\text{Min } E\{\textstyle\int_0^T [C(u_t) + H(x_t)]e^{-rT}dt + e^{-rt}pX_T\}$$
$$u_t \geq 0 \qquad (3.13)$$
subject to:

$$dx_t = u_t dt - d\phi_t; \quad x_0 \text{ given}$$
$$d\phi_t = a_t dt + b_t dw$$

where ϕ_t is the demand probability distribution given in this case by a Wiener process. Constraints such as [14]

$$E \int_0^T [u_t dt - d\phi_t] + x_0 \geq 0$$

i.e., the expected value of net inventory at time T should be non-negative, or probability constraints such as

$$\text{Prob}\{x_t \geq 0\} \geq \alpha$$

might be added also. Note that if $\alpha = 1$, then this is equivalent to requiring that the inventory process has a reflection boundary at $x = 0$.

(iii) *An Inventory Impulsive Control Problem*

Consider the following costs: an ordering (fixed) cost, an inventory holding and a shortage cost. The cost of an order quantity q is given by

$$C(q,t) = \begin{cases} 0 \text{ if } q = 0 \\ k(t) + cq \text{ where } q \in Q \\ \infty \text{ if } q \in Q \end{cases}$$

where $k(t)$ is the fixed order cost (which may be a variable function of time t), c is the per unit (or price) ordering cost while Q denotes the constraint set imposed on the ordering quantity q (such as given by budget constraints, physical constraints, etc.). The inventory carrying and shortage cost is given by $f(y,t)$ where,

$$f(y,t) = \begin{cases} \text{holding cost if } y \geq 0 \\ \text{shortage cost if } y < 0 \end{cases}$$

Over a planning time (t,T), the expected inventory cost is therefore given by:

$$J = E\{\int_t^T f(y,s)ds + \sum_i C(\theta_i, q_i)\} \tag{3.14}$$

where θ_i is the (decision variable) order time and $E(.)$ is the expectation operator. A minimization of J subject to the appropriate dynamical inventory process, defines an impulsive control problem. Such problems have wide applicability and include among others barrier policies (such as the well known (s,S) policies [10, 42, 6]).

3.4   *Queueing*

"Queueing managers" can influence a queueing system through one or a combination of: (i) the input arrival rate (ii) the service mechanism (iii) queues discipline and parameters (such as the queue's capacity). For the most part, queueing problems have been considered as stationary discrete state stochastic processes whose limiting distributions provide the queueing system's operational and economic performance parameters. Although some non-stationary (time variant) problems have been dealth with, these require complex analytical techniques and mostly use approximations (a useful survey can be found in Crabill and Magazine [12]). Below, we shall follow the approach of section 2.3 in chapter 2 in formulating queueing birth-death processes and in providing continuous approximations (as well as generalizations) which can lead to simpler and approximate results for dynamic queueing design problems.

(i) *Birth Death Processes*

Birth-death processes are important stochastic models used to describe specific queueing models. Their applications are varied, spanning the field of operations management, biology, economics, etc. Such models are discrete state Markov processes as we shall see next. Consider a "system" and denote by $n = 0, 1, 2, \ldots$ the states of the system (such as the number of persons in the queue). For two consecutive instants t and $t + \Delta t$, where Δt is small, hypothesize that;

Probability of one arrival in Δt when there are n units $= \lambda_n \Delta t$

Probability of one departure in Δt when there are n units $= \mu_n \Delta t$

Since the probability of having more than one arrival is very small, the probability of no arrival in Δt is $(1 - \mu_n \Delta t)$, and of no departure is $(1 - \lambda_n \Delta t)$. To construct the equations for the birth-death process, we use these properties and determine the set of possibilities and their probabilities for transiting from t to $t + \Delta t$ when there are n persons in the system. This is represented in Figure 3.3 where we note that transitions to n occur from $n - 1$, n and $n + 1$ only (since only one person may arrive or leave in Δt). Further, because of the statistical independence of the probabilities, these can be summed in constructing the simple "identity",

$$P_n(t + \Delta t) = \lambda_{n-1} \Delta t P_{n-1}(t) + [(1 - \lambda_n \Delta t)(1 - \mu_n \Delta t)] P_n(t) + \mu_{n+1} \Delta t P_{n+1}(t)$$

After some elementary mathematical manipulations (noting that $(\Delta t)^2$ is of zero order), we obtain, when Δt tends to zero, a "differential-difference equation", which is, in this special case, also called the birth-death process. (below we drop the time subscript t for convenience)

$$dP_n/dt = -(\lambda_n + \mu_n)P_n + \lambda_{n-1}P_{n-1} + \mu_{n+1}P_{n+1} \qquad (3.15)$$

Since no departure may occur when $n = 0$, we have at the reflection boundary $n = 0$;

$$dP_0/dt = -\lambda_0 P_0 + \mu_1 P_1 \qquad (3.16)$$

Other boundaries may be obtained, depending upon the special character-isitics of the queueing problem we analyze. The solution of the birth-death equation in the time domain is expectedly difficult. Further, since we may often be interested in the long-run performance of a queueing system and not its dynamic (time dependent) properties, we can consider the steady state solution of the birth-death process. Then the probabilities $P_n(t)$ do not change in time and $dP_n/dt = 0$ yields,

$$0 = \lambda_{n-1}P_{n-1} - (\lambda_n + \mu_n)P_n + \mu_{n+1}P_{n+1}$$

$$0 = -\lambda_0 P_0 + \mu_1 P_1$$

(3.17)

A solution of this equation (for P_n) by iteration, yields:

$$P_n = [\Pi_{i=0}^{n-1}\lambda_i / \Pi_{i=1}^{n}\mu_i]P_0; \quad \sum_{n=0}^{\infty} P_n = 1 \qquad (3.18)$$

A solution, for specific assumptions concerning the dependence of λ_n and μ_n will provide the probability distribution P_n. Using this distribution, the operational characteristics of the queueing system can be calculated (see standard Operations Research texts [42]). An alternative formulation to the kind of processes defined above, consists in considering the state

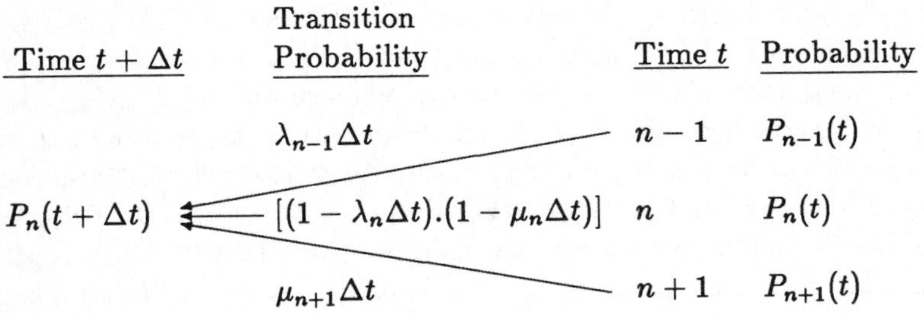

Time $t + \Delta t$	Transition Probability		Time t	Probability
	$\lambda_{n-1}\Delta t$	$n-1$		$P_{n-1}(t)$
$P_n(t + \Delta t)$	$[(1 - \lambda_n\Delta t).(1 - \mu_n\Delta t)]$	n		$P_n(t)$
	$\mu_{n+1}\Delta t$	$n+1$		$P_{n+1}(t)$

$P_n(t)$ = Probability of n units in the system at time t

$\lambda_n\Delta t$ = Probability of one arrival in Δt when there are n units in the system

$\mu_n\Delta t$ = Probability of one departure in Δt when there are n units in the system

Figure 3.3: Transition Probabilities and the Birth-Death Process

space equations directly. Thus, we express the model dynamics directly in terms of probability statements regarding the process of transition among states in a given small time interval. To demonstrate this approach, assume that $\{x, t \geq 0\}$ is a discrete state stochastic process taking on real values on the whole line at time t. The dynamics of the process is characterized by jumps $\Delta x(t) = x(t + \Delta t) - x(t)$ in a given time interval $(t + \Delta t, t)$. Jumps may originate from various sources but are assumed to be of given sizes in a given time interval. Let (v, w) be controls influencing the jumps $\Delta x(t)$. Specifically, we shall state that there is some probability $q(x, v, t)\Delta t$ which increases $\Delta x(t)$ by $+\varepsilon$ in Δt and a probability $h(x, w, t)\Delta t$ which decreases $\Delta x(t)$ by $-\varepsilon$ in Δt. In other words, the effects of controls (v, w) are exerted on the transition probabilities of the process and are given by

$$\Delta x(t) = \begin{cases} +\varepsilon & \text{w.p. } q\Delta t \\ -\varepsilon & \text{w.p. } h\Delta t \\ 0 & \text{w.p. } (1 - q\Delta t)(1 - h\Delta t) \\ x = 0, 1, 2... \end{cases} \tag{3.19}$$

Here, effects of order $0(\Delta t)^2$ are assumed to be very small and are, therefore, dropped (as is stated in deriving Kolomogrov equations for discrete state stochastic processes).

Say that $\varepsilon = 1$, then $x(t)$ may denote the number of persons in a queueing system, $q(x, v)$ is the arrival rate which may be a function of birth x and an intensity control v and $h(x, w)$ is a "death" rate also a function of x and the control w. The linear birth-death process is given by $q(x, v) = q_0 x$ and $h(x, w) = h_0 x$. In the long run $(t \to \infty)$, the stationary Kolmogrov equations corresponding to the linear birth-death process and letting $x \geq 0, x = 0, 1, 2, ...$ lead to a Poisson distribution of x. This result is well known in the queueing literature (See also Chapter 2, section 2.2). Given a stochastic model as above, we define an objective function of the state x and controls (u, w). Over a planning horizon $[0, T]$, the expected discounted objective cost is defined by

$$J(x, s) = E\left\{ \int_0^T e^{-r(t-s)} L(x, v, w)dt + e^{-rT} G(x, T) \right\} \tag{3.20}$$

which is optimized with respect to the controls v and w, constraints on the control and for small time intervals $\Delta t \to dt$, to;

$$dx(t) = \begin{cases} +\varepsilon & \text{w.p. } q(x, v)dt \\ -\varepsilon & \text{w.p. } h(x, w)dt \\ 0 & \text{w.p. } 1 - [q(x, v) + h(x, w))]dt \end{cases} \tag{3.21}$$
$$x(s) = x, \text{ Prob } [x \geq 0] = 1$$

Here, r is the rate of discount, $G(x, T)$ is the terminal cost, s is the initial time and x is the initial state condition at time s. For busy queueing systems, (denoting emptiness) $x \leq 0$ may not be reached so that approximations may assume away the non-negativity constraint. This, of course, will result in a simplified problem. Further, instead of the discounted criterion above, average cost criteria could be considered. In this case, it is required to select optimal policies v and w such that the objective below is minimized

$$J(x) = lim_{T \to \infty} \frac{1}{T} \int_0^T EL(x, v, w) dt \qquad (3.22)$$

(ii) *Continuous Approximations*

Continuous approximations in queueing are numerous, seeking to simplify the mathematical treatment of the problems at hand. Foremost among the techniques used are diffusion approximations which seek to represent a queue's line (or some other property) by a diffusion process. In the simplest case, we want to imposes conditions on the parameters a and b of a diffusion process

$$dx = adt + \sqrt{b}dw \qquad (3.23)$$

such that it will be "closest" to the queue's true (non-approximated) behavior. A FPE representation of this process in its backward and forward setting, as pointed out in Chapter 2, is respectively, (with appropriate boundary constraints)

$$-\frac{\partial P}{\partial t}(x, t : x_0) = a\frac{\partial P}{\partial x_0}(x, t : x_0) - \frac{1}{2}b\frac{\partial^2 P}{\partial x_0^2}(x, t : x_0) \qquad (3.24)$$

$$\frac{\partial P}{\partial t}(x, t) = a\frac{\partial P}{\partial x}(x, t) + \frac{1}{2}b\frac{\partial^2 P}{\partial x^2}(x, t) \qquad (3.25)$$

where x_0 is the initial condition of the process at time $t = 0$. A first approximation impose a reflection constraint at $x = 0$, meaning that there cannot be a negative number of (say) persons waiting on the line. In this case, (see Chapter 2, section 2.10) we can solve the backward equation by imposing at $x = 0$, that

$$-aP(x, t) + \frac{1}{2}b\frac{\partial P}{\partial x}(x, t) = 0 \text{ at } x = 0 \qquad (3.26)$$

Kobayashi [23] has shown in particular that a solution of such an equation is given by

$$P(x, t : x_0) = p(x) + \exp[\alpha(x - x_0 - at/2)] \sum_{n=1}^{\infty} \phi_n(x)\phi_n(x_0)\exp[(a/2)\lambda_n t] \qquad (3.27)$$

where $p(x)$ is defined by

$$p(x) = lim_{t \to 0} P(x, t : x_0) = 2\alpha \exp(2\alpha x)/[\exp(2\alpha N) - 1]$$

$$0 \le x \le N \text{ where } \alpha = a/b \tag{3.28}$$

and

$$\lambda_n = n\pi/N$$

$$\phi_n(x) = \frac{2\lambda_n^2}{N(\lambda_n^2 + \alpha^2)} \cos[\lambda_n x + \frac{a}{\lambda_n} \sin \lambda_n x]$$

In busy periods, i.e. when the queue does not often become empty, the unreflected difffusion approximation is a good one (since the reflection boundary is almost never active) and the queue's length would have a normal distribution with mean at and variance bt. In a similar manner, approximations to queues with multiple servers, etc. can be constructed (as we shall see later on). Evidently, the increased use of time shared computers with complex (queueing) organizational rules, as well as computer communication networks, has rendered imperative the study of approximate queueing problems. This is today a burgeoning field (see Chapter 2 on diffusion approximations).

An alternative approach consists in modeling directly the queueing problem as a continuous one. This is particularly useful in queueing design and decision problems. In this case, assume that units representing jobs to be processed on machines, persons incoming for service, etc. arrive at a rate given by a stochastic differential equation. Thus, if x is the number of units in the system at time $s, f(y, t)$ is a deterministic arrival rate, dw is a standard Wiener process while $\sigma^2(t)$ is the variance component of the diffusion process and if jump "arrivals" occur at times τ_i, in quantitites $\xi_i, i = 1, ...$ we can then write $y(t)$ as a differential equation (see also [15], [16])

$$dy = f(y, t)dt + \sigma(y, t)dw + \Sigma_i \xi_i \delta(t - \tau_i); \; y(s) = x \tag{3.29}$$

where (τ_i, ξ_i) are appropriately defined stochastic processes and $\delta(.)$ is the usual Dirac Delta function. At present, we model the service process as a deterministic (or stochastic) process and derive the ensuing waiting line (queue) process. If there are significant probabilities of a queue being empty, we might then impose reflection boundaries on the resultant process. Typical boundaries are the queue's waiting space capacities and, of course, the non-negative constraint on the number of waiting units (or the reflection boundary at zero). To make these matters clear, we consider several special service design problems. We begin by a clearing service process (e.g. see Stidham [23], Robin and Tapiero [30]) and subsequently introduce deterministic and stochastic service rates.

Assume a queueing problem with a fixed service capacity Q, expressing the number of service agents obtained by an investment of say $G(Q)$. In this case, assume that service is a clearing-instantaneous process, and takes place at some times $\theta_j, j = 1, 2, \ldots$ when there are $y(\theta_j)$ units waiting on line. Then, the number of waiting units is given by,

$$dy = f(y,t)dt + \sigma(y,t)dw + \sum_i \xi_i \delta(t - \tau_i) - \sum_j min(y(\theta_j), Q)\delta(t - \theta_j) \tag{3.30}$$

$$y(0) = x$$

The min (.) term above is justified by the impossibility of servicing more than Q units at the same time, the service capacity constraint. More simply, we can let θ_j be a series of impulses triggered by Q, then

$$\theta_j = \{t > \theta_{j-1}; \ y = Q, j = 1, 2, \ldots\} \tag{3.31}$$

with $\theta_0 = 0$ as a convention.

Design problems may then involve objectives with one or all of the following costs,
   (i) impulse (fixed) cost for providing service
   (ii) processing costs
   (iii) waiting and customers costs
Let the first two costs be given by

$$H(z) = k + h(z, Q)$$

where

$$h(z, Q) = (c - p)min(z, Q)$$

where p is the price extracted from a unit being serviced and c is the corresponding variable cost. Also, $\phi(z)$ is the waiting cost such that over an infinite horizon and with a constant rate of discount, the economic (design) objective of our queueing problem is

$$\text{Min} \ J(x) = E \int_0^\infty e^{-rt}(\phi(y) + rG(Q))dt + \sum_j exp[-r\theta_j](k + h(y, Q))$$

$$\{\theta_1, \theta_2 \ldots\} \tag{3.32}$$

where the processing cost of servicing is assumed null compared to $G(Q)$ which is introduced directly in the integral. The decision problem is to select θ and Q when the remaining parameters of the model are known. Other problems can be considered in a similar fashion. If we control the arrival rate as well, then f and σ, for example, could be constructed to reflect the effects of our controls and their implications on the performance objective of the queueing system. If service time takes a deterministic amount of time, say udt per server, then for a reflected process

$$dy = -[min(y, K)u]dt + f(y,t)dt + \sigma(y,t)dw + \sum_i \xi_i \delta(t - \tau_i)$$
$$y(0) = x \tag{3.33}$$

with reflection at $y = 0$ and at $y = R$ where R is the number of waiting positions available for the queue. A design problem would use an objective which is compatible with management's decision criteria and the model parameters. When service takes a stochastic amount of time then the variance component in (3.33) above will be amended appropriately, as we shall show in Chapters 4 and 7.

3.5   *Machines Maintenance and Replacement*

A classic model for determining the optimum maintenance policy and replacement date of a machine, is given by Thompson [39] in a deterministic setting, as follows

Maximize $V(T)$ with respect to $T, m(.)$

$$V(T) = S(T)e^{-rT} + \int_0^T Q(t)e^{-rt}dt$$

Subject to: (3.34)

$$0 \leq m(t) \leq M$$
$$Q(t) = p(t)S(t) - m(t)$$
$$dS(t)/dt = -a(t) + f(t)m(t); \quad S(0) = K$$

where
V(t)	=	present value of the machine at time t
S(t)	=	salvage value of the machine at time t
Q(t)	=	net operating receipts at time t
m(t)	=	maintenance policy - hours of maintenance at time t, expressed in $/unit time
f(t)	=	"obsolescence" function at time t, subtracted from $S(t)$
p(t)	=	production rate at time t; output value at $t/S(t)$
r	=	constant rate of discount
T	=	sale date of the machine
K	=	purchase cost of the machine

$V(t)$ and $S(t)$ are state variables, while $m(t)$ is the control variable under management discretion.

A generalization to this problem and its solution in the deterministic domain has been dealt with in many papers (e.g., see [28]). Here, we shall consider several stochastic dynamic extensions. Let the salvage value process $S(t)$ be described by a discrete state stochastic process. Thus, the salvage value of a machine at time t, is a random variable x_t with $P(x_t = x) = P(x, t)$ describing the time variant distribution of the salvage value. The range X_t is $(0, 1, 2, ...)$, and at time $t + \Delta t$, the probability that the salvage value is $X_{t+\Delta t}$ is given by transitions probabilities such as:

$[a(t) + b(t)]\Delta t =$ the probability that the machine deteriorates by one unit in the time interval $(t, t + \Delta t)$.

This probability is a function of $a(t)$, the obsolescence rate and $b(t)$, the depreciation rate which is proportional to the salvage value of the machine at time t:

$f(t)m(t)\Delta t =$ the probability that the machine appreciates in value by one unit through maintenance.

Movements increasing the salvage value of the machine are controlled by maintenance expenditures, while movements decreasing it are due to deterioration and obsolescence. Without difficulty, we can show that this problem is similar to the kind of problems dealt with earlier in queueing models. The uncertainties in the maintenance-replacement problem are varied, however. New technologies, changing production processes, the "real effects of maintenance", etc. are factors we cannot always measure or predict accurately. Further, the variety of operational maintenance and replacement problems is such that there is no global and unique formulation to this important problem. For this reason, we shall consider below alternative formulations to emphasize the workings of time and uncertainty in maintenance and replacement of productive machines.

(i) *Intermittent Breakdowns and Repair*

Say that we consider a model with intermittent breakdowns and repairs (Alam and Sarma [1]), and assume that the machine's breakdown and repair times are taken as random variables with exponential distributions with parameters λ and μ respectively. We say that the machine is in state 0 if it is working and in state 1 if it is being repaired. The differential equations for the probabilities $P_i(t), i = 0$ or 1, of finding the machine in state i at time t, are given by

$$dP_0(t)/dt = -\lambda P_0(t) + \mu P_1(t); \quad P_0(0) = 1$$

$$dP_1(t)/dt = \lambda P_0 - \mu P(t)_1; \quad P_1(0) = 0$$

(3.35)

These probabilities determine the operating time of machines (and, hence, computation of their values) and the time spent in repair. Now, combine these states with the deterministic Thompson model. To do so, let k_1 be the cost of the machine being in the down time state "1", and take expectation of the objective function (3.34) to yield for $E(Q(t)) = \{pS(t)P_0(t) - m(t) - k_1 P_1(t)\}$, where $S(t)$ is as defined in (3.34). The problem we obtain in this manner is a deterministic problem where the probabilities of being in the operating ("0") mode or the repair mode ("1") are given explicitly by (3.35). Extensions to more than one machine and a limited number of servers has been considered by Alam and Sarma [1] and provide an ingenious approach to transforming stochastic problems to deterministic ones.

(ii) Maintenance and Overhaul of Continuous Production Processes

If instead of continuous time we consider the machine production process to be continuous in the number of units produced, we obtain a different formulation of the maintenance problem (see Vickson [40] for an interesting formulation). For example, such a production process would model a car's mileage, an automated machine performing a given function (such as cutting, boring, etc.) continuously. Maintenance resources would then be applied as a function of the machine state and its production history. Such a procedure is followed in may cases where there is little meaning to time (as compared to production history) as a dimension along which the machine's state can be assessed.

To construct such models, assume that a machine has produced over its lifetime n units. This results in a degradation state we denote by $x(n)$. This degradation expresses a deviation from an operational standard the machine is in when it is in perfect condition. Over large quantities produced the machine deteriorates and the quality of products declines too. To compensate usure of the machine, maintenance, overhaul and the replacement of certain components (or the machine itself) might be required.

Given a machine deterioration state x, we focus our attention on some state $y = Q(x)$, $Q \in C_2$ which defines the quality of products, and provide maintenance policies in terms of such qualities. In particular, we let $y \in [0, 1]$, such that it can be interpreted as propensities for product failure. In this case, maintenance is introduced to manage production quality directly rather than implicitly through the machine's operational states. Let the production sequences n be continuous and let $n, n \geq 0$ be the degradation state of the machine which we approximate by a diffusion process;

$$dx(n) = \alpha(x, n)dn + \beta(x, n)dw; \quad x(0) = x_0 \geq 0 \qquad (3.36)$$

where $w(.)$ is a standard Wiener process, $\alpha(x, n)dn$ is the mean growth (of deterioration) rate and $\beta^2(x, n)dn$ is its finite and continuous variance, per additional unit produced on the machine. For example, we could state $\alpha(x, n) = \alpha$, a constant mean rate of deterioration and $\beta^2(x, n) = \beta^2 n$ to specify that this rate has a variance which increases with the quantity produced.

Say that after a production sequence of n, that a maintenance program $u(n)$ is implemented, reducing the rate of degradation. Dropping the production index n, we shall let;

$$dx = (\alpha - u)dn + \beta dw; \quad x(0) = x \geq 0 \qquad (3.37)$$

The quality production "dynamics" is, $y = Q(x)$, thus, applying Ito's differential rule we have

$$dy = [\frac{\partial y}{\partial x}(\alpha - u) + \frac{\partial^2 y}{\partial x^2}\frac{\beta^2}{2}]dn + \frac{\partial y}{\partial x}\beta dw; \quad y(0) = Q(x_0) = y_0 \qquad (3.38)$$

If we replace in (3.38), x by $Q(y)$, an equation in y and n is obtained, or

$$dy = f(y, n, u)dn + g(y, n)dn; \quad y(0) = y_0 \qquad (3.39)$$

which is an (Ito) stochastic differential equation of the quality production process with f and g appropriately defined functions. In particular, if we assume that

$$y = Q(x) = e^{-kx} \qquad (3.40)$$

where k is an index estimated from past production performance. Then $\partial y/\partial x = -ky, \partial^2 y/\partial x^2 = k^2 y$ and

$$dy = [-k(\alpha - u) + k^2\beta^2/2]ydn - ky\beta dw$$

$$(3.41)$$

$$y(0) = y_0 \leq 1, \text{ and reflection at } y = 1$$

If we assume further that $\alpha(x, n) = \alpha(n)$ and $\beta(x, n) = \beta(n)$, then (3.41) is an equation with two reflecting boundaries at $y = 1$ (corresponding to $x = 0$) and at $y = 0$, when the machine is of infinitely poor quality. Thus, better quality will be associated to higher values of y. Alternatively, we can assume that the degradation process is a lognormal process with $\alpha(x, n) = \alpha x$ and $\beta(x, n) = \beta x$, then since $y = exp(-kx), x = (-1/k) \log y$ which leads to:

$$\frac{dy}{y} = [\alpha \log y + \frac{\beta^2}{2}(\log y)^2 + ku]dn + \beta \log y dw$$

$$(3.42)$$

$$y(0) = exp(-kx_0) \leq 1 \text{ and } 0 \leq y \leq 1$$

Note that in this process, there are no reflecting barriers, it is however nonlinear in y and bilinear in the control as in (3.41). We may, therefore, rewrite (3.42) as follows:

$$dy/y = (f(y) + ku)dn + g(y)dw$$

$$(3.43)$$

$$y(0) = y_0 \leq 1, 0 \leq y \leq 1 \text{ (naturally)}$$

and consider (3.43) as a slight generalization of (3.41) where f and g are constants (in addition to reflection at $y = 0, 1$). Of course, by changing the assumption regarding the degradation process and the quality production function, we shall obtain other processes.

For a given quality y, assume that the net return per unit produced is $p(y)$ and let $m(u)$ be the maintenance cost. The profit rate is thus $[p(y) - m(u)]dn$. Over a production sequence of N units, at which level we stop production and incur a cost $K(y(N), N)$ (such as for overhaul, replacement of the machine, etc.), the objective is the minimization of the expected costs;

$$\text{Minimize } J(y_0) = E\{\int_0^N [m(u) - p(y)]dn + K(y(N), N)\}$$

$$(3.44)$$

Subject to the quality-production process (3.41) (or (3.43))

Maintenance is constrained physically by the potential improvement it can make on the machine's quality production process. The constraint set is given by U, and for our purpose we let $U = \{\alpha, 0\}$ or maintenance can only slow down or stop deterioration processes. The quantity N, at which we stop production can be a planned production level at which the machine is overhauled. Such procedures are commonly observed in industry where machine's maintenance and overhaul programs are established on the basis of the expected machine's performance. Alternatively, N can be random, induced by some major breakdown in the machine (whose probability characteristics we are able to define) or by a cumulative deterioration of the machine to production of qualities that are below acceptable standards. Further, the machine quality production may be observed only when quality control samples are collected. In this case, the machine's quality performance is imperfectly observable and requires a measurement (sampling) model. This will necessitate a filter for y to select the optimum maintenance policy. Finally, the objective defined in (3.44) includes a wide variety of cases depending upon the functional characteristics of $m(.), p(.)$ and $K(.)$, depending upon N and the objective J we might deem relevant.

3.6 *A Dispatching Problem*

Consider a specific dispatching stochastic problem with Poisson noise. In Chapter 4, a solution to this problem will be given. Say that $x(t)$ denotes the number of "persons" waiting on a line and to be dispatched on a route. If arrivals occurs following a non- stationary poisson process (i.e., a time variant parameter stochastic process) then $\Delta x(t)$ the number of new arrivals in the line in the time interval $(t, t + \Delta t)$ is given by,

$$\Delta x(t) = x(t, t + \Delta t) = n(t)\Delta t + q(t)\tilde{\mu}(\Delta t)$$

with

$$
\begin{array}{ll}
\Delta t & = \text{ time increment and} \\
n(t) & = \text{ mean arrival rate} \\
q^2(t) & = \text{ arrival's rate variance} \\
\tilde{\mu}(\Delta t) & = \text{ a standardized Poisson noise .}
\end{array}
$$

Now assume that at some times $\tau^i, i = 1, 2, \ldots$ the dispatching times, *all passengers* board the vehicle (i.e., we assume in effect that vehicles have an infinite capacity). Denote by x_{τ_i} the number of persons at time τ^i, the evolution of the state (the number of persons waiting at time t) can then be shown at the limit $(\Delta t \to 0)$, to be

$$dx(t) = n(t)dt + q(t)\tilde{\mu}(dt) - \sum \delta(t - \tau^i)x_{\tau_i} \tag{3.45}$$

where Δt is replaced by dt and $\delta(t - \tau^i)$ is a set of impulses given by

$$\delta(t - \tau^i) = \begin{cases} 1 & \text{if } t = \tau^i \\ 0 & \text{otherwise} \end{cases}$$

and x_{τ_i} is the number of persons waiting on the line, at time τ_i, the ith vehicle dispatching time. The sum $\sum \delta(t - \tau^i)x_{\tau_i}$ represents the total number of persons dispatched up to and including time t. The waiting persons stochastic model has the decision variable, τ^i, the dispatching time which is a set of impulses. To determine an optimal dispatching policy, it is necessary to determine first a cost function. This is done next.

Say that $u(t, x)$ is the optimal future cost in a time interval (t, T) when there are x persons waiting to be transported at time t. This cost is obtained by optimizing a cost function consisting of (i) waiting time cost and (ii) a transport cost. It is evident that other costs such as crowding, revenues, availability of vehicles, reliability, etc., may be defined. These may require a more extensive definition of the dispatching system considered here. Say that $f(t, x)$ is the per unit waiting time cost when there are x persons waiting and let $c(t, x)$ be the transport cost of x persons, with

$$c(t, x) \geq k \geq 0$$

Here, k is used to denote a fixed cost for dispatching a vehicle on the route. If V denotes the dispatching policy; $V = \{\tau^i, i \geq 1\}$, with τ^i monotonically increasing, then $u(t, x)$ the expected optimum future (cumulative in (t, T)) cost at time t is given by

$$u(t, x) = \underset{v = (\tau^i \geq 1);\ \tau^i < T}{Inf}\ E\{\textstyle\int_t^T f(s, x(s))ds + \sum c(\tau^i, x_{\tau^i})\} \tag{3.46}$$

Minimization of $u(t, x)$ subject to the passengers waiting process provides a formulation of the dispatching (impulsive) stochastic control problem. If the planning horizon T is infinite and we use a discounted cost; then the objective cost can be stated as follows:

$$u(x) = \underset{v = (\tau^i, i \geq 1)}{Inf}\ E\{\textstyle\int_0^\infty \exp[-\alpha s]f(x(s))ds + \sum \exp[-\alpha \tau^i]c(x_{\tau_i})\} \tag{3.47}$$

where $\alpha > 0$ is the discount rate, f and c are independent of time. Minimization of $u(x)$ subject to the passengers waiting process is another stochastic control problem with infinite horizon.

Next, we consider a continuous state approximation of the dispatching problem. Say that "arrivals" follow a diffusion process with mean rate α and variance β^2;

$$dx = \alpha dt + \beta dw;\ x(0) = x_0 > 0$$

Note that due to the unbounded variation of the normal process, x might take on negative values, rendering the persons (cumulative) arrival process unrealistic. To compensate for such a flaw, and render the process physically realizable, we impose a reflection (or constraint) at $y = 0$ or

$$\text{Prob}[x \geq 0] = 1, \forall t \geq 0$$

In other words, we define the arrival process by $\{x, t \geq 0 | x \geq 0\}$. To construct such a process, we proceed as in Chapter 2, Section 2.6 and write

$$dx = \alpha dt + \beta dw + \gamma(x) d\xi \tag{3.48}$$

where $d\xi$ is a right continuous adapted process $(d\xi \geq 0)$ and $\gamma(x)$ is a function defined to be normal to the reflection boundary. Further, $\gamma = 0$ off the boundary, since the reflection constraint is not effective, while on the reflection constraint, $\gamma \neq 0$, equalling the size of the jump below the reflection constraint.

Assume that a dispatching schedule is defined again by a sequence of stopping times $\theta_j, j = 1, 2, \ldots$ in which $x(\theta_j)$ waiting persons board the vehicles, and the waiting persons process is reduced to zero, i.e.

$$dx = \alpha dt + \beta dw - \sum \delta(t - \varepsilon_j) x(\theta_j) + \gamma(x) d\xi; \quad x(0) = y_0 \geq 0 \tag{3.49}$$

This equation provides a dynamical system with dispatching decision times, $\theta_j, j = 1, 2, \ldots$ where all waiting persons board the vehicle, and the waiting persons process is a diffusion process with reflection at $x = 0$. Given such a process, we can consider the above objective (3.46) in selecting a dispatching policy.

3.7 *Capacity Expansion*

Capacity expansion deals with increasing a productive capacity in response to anticipated demand growth. Given a demand forecast, characterized by a stochastic model, the problem consists in selecting

a. Expansion Sizes
b. Expansion Times
c. Expansion Types (or locations)

The decision to expand capacity involves much uncertainty about the future and large outlays in the present. For this reason, these are basically risky decisions (for a survey of capacity expansion problems, see H. Luss [26]). For example, there may be significant probabilities that an expansion project incurred in the anticipation of a given demand growth will turn out to be obsolete if the demand does not materialize. Inversely, an insufficient capacity involves large opportunity losses of profits. Although, the capacity expansion decision is basically a strategic corporate decision, we shall outline below an example emphasizing the problems of expansion sizes and times. The expansion sizes will be denoted by $K_1, K_2, ...$ while the expansion times by $\theta_1, \theta_2, ...$ For simplicity, assume a firm facing at time s a probabilistic demand whose evolution is modeled by a diffusion process;

$$dy = \alpha dt + \sigma dw; \quad y(s) = y_s \text{ given} \tag{3.50}$$

where α is the mean demand growth and σ^2 its variance while dw is a standard Wiener process. At some random times $\tau_i, \tau_1 < \tau_2...\tau_i < ...$ demands are assumed to jump by say ξ_i. For example, τ_i may be the random time event of a government policy which could necessarily expand demand for our product. In this case the firm must consider in its expansion programs the possiblities of such a demand ξ_i to materialize. Since it cannot be sure if the governmnt will actually adopt a "favorable" policy to expansion plans, it can use a probability characterization of this event to quantify its own belief. In this way, the demand process can be written specificially as follows:

$$dy = \alpha dt + \sigma dw; \quad t \in [\tau_i, \tau_{i+1}]$$
$$y(\tau_{i+1}) = y(\tau_{i+1} - 0) + \xi_{i+1}; \quad y(s) = y_0 \tag{3.51}$$

The decision to expand capacity at time θ_i depends on the information (regarding future demand) at time t, while K_i depends on the information available at the random (decision) time θ_i. The couples $\{K_i, \theta_i\}, i = 1, 2, ...$ defines an implusive capacity expansion program as is shown in Figure 3.5. In the time interval (θ_i, θ_{i+1}), the capacity excess (shortage) evolves according to

$$x(\theta_i) - y(t)$$

where $x(\theta_i)$ is the capacity level in (θ_i, θ_{i+1}) while at time θ_{i+1}, we have a capacity growth;

$$x(\theta_{i+1}) = x(\theta_{i+1} - 0) + K_{i+1}$$

If $v(t) = x(t) - y(t)$, then we can rewrite

$$dv(t) = -\alpha dt - \sigma dw - \sum \xi_i \delta(t - \tau_i) + \sum K_i \delta(t - \theta_i); \quad v(s) = v_s \tag{3.52}$$

where τ_i is a Poisson random variable with mean $q(t)$, ξ_i has a probability distribution $f(\xi)$ and δ are Dirac-delta functions.

To select an optimal expansion plan, we define an objective function consisting of $C(K_i, \theta_i - s)$, the expansion cost at time θ_i and an excess (and/or shortage) capacity cost $g(.)$ which expresses the utility of being above or below capacity. These costs, discounted over an infinite horizon, at the given discount rate r yield an expected objective given by:

$$J = E\{\int_s^\infty e^{-r(t-s)} g(v) dt + \sum_i exp[-r(\theta_i - s)] C(K_i, \theta_i - s)\} \qquad (3.53)$$

Minimization of this cost subject ot (3.52) will provide a capacity expansion program $(K_i, \theta_i), i = 1, 2, ...$ This is evidently an impulsive control problem.

3.8 *Quality Control*

There is an increased awareness that producing units of higher quality and quality control have become of strategic importance for cost cutting in manufacturing and for increasing sales and profitability (see [11], [38] for a cursory review of the importance of quality control). Further, the increased inter-dependence of production, marketing, servicing and other vital functions of the firm will be increasingly dominant in management (a particularly useful survey of such relationships can be found in Juran [20]). In this section, we shall provide a dynamic framework for quality control which will be extended to include several problems in management science [35, 36, 37].

(i) *Quality Control as a Stochastic Process*
Define by $\{X(t), t \geq 0\}$ a discrete state stochastic process (such as Poisson), taking real values on the line at time t. This state may reflect the number of units previously sold and that have failed, a firm product "reputation" etc. Consider two subsequent instants of time $(t, t + \Delta t)$ and define by $\Delta X(t) \equiv X(t + \Delta t) - X(t)$, the incremental change in $X(t)$ the relevant time interval. For simplicity, let $\Delta X(t)$ be the number of returned items due to failure at time t and let units bought be "instantly consumed" such that product returns in $(t, t + \Delta t)$ are from the production output (and sales) in the same period. Now define by Φ, a quality control procedure consisting of a sample inspection f drawn from the production output and on the basis of which the sold output is accepted (i.e. sold as is) or rejected (i.e., the output is completely inspected and then shipped). Of course, the quality control procedure which may be acceptance sampling, bar chart, double or sequential sampling, etc. will affect the quantity of units inspected, the quality of the output, etc. Let $y(\Phi)$ be the probability of accepting the product lot when a quality control procedure Φ is used, then the number

of units returned in $(t, t + \Delta t)$ is $Z_1(t|\Phi)\Delta t$ or $Z_2(t|\Phi)\Delta t$ depending on Φ and whether the sampled output was accepted or rejected. Particularly, let Z_1 and Z_2 be approximated by Poisson distributions with parameters $\lambda_1(\Phi)$ and $\lambda_2(\Phi)$ respectively. Thus,

$$\Delta X(t) = \begin{cases} Z_1\Delta t & \text{with} \quad y(\Phi) \\ \\ Z_2\Delta t & \text{with} \quad 1 - y(\Phi) \end{cases} \tag{3.54}$$

If units returned are also Poisson, then the return rate is given by $\lambda(\Phi)$ where

$$\lambda(\Phi) = \lambda_1(\Phi)y(\Phi) + \lambda_2(\Phi)[1 - y(\Phi)] \tag{3.55}$$

and

$$\Delta X(t) = \begin{cases} +1 \text{ with } \lambda(\Phi)\Delta t \\ \\ 0 \text{ with } 1 - \lambda(\Phi)\Delta t \end{cases} \tag{3.56}$$

In other words, a unit sold in $(t, t + \Delta t)$ is returned due to "failure" with a probability of $\lambda(\Phi)\Delta t$, where $\lambda(\Phi)$ can be computed in terms of the sold output production quality and quality control.

The costs incurred by the manufacturer are then given by the inspection costs $C_i(\Phi)$ (a function of the number of units inspected), the returned unit costs $C_f(X, \Phi)$ and finally the direct production costs, $C_0 N$ where N is a production rate at time t. Over a planning time $[0, T]$, this defines an objective given by:

$$\text{Minimize } J = E\{\int_0^T [C_0 N + C_i(\Phi)]dt + C_f(X(T); \Phi)\} \atop \Phi \in \theta \tag{3.57}$$

Subject to (3.55) - (3.56)

where θ is the feasible quality control procedure. Prior to extending this problem, consider a simple acceptance sampling quality control procedure where n is the inspection sample, q the acceptance number, and let $(1 - \theta)$ be the probability of producing a unit which is not acceptable (i.e. faulty, or below standard), then the probability of accepting the sample $y(\Phi)$ given by $P(u \leq q)$ is

$$y(\Phi) = \sum_{u=0}^{q} \binom{n}{u}(1 - \theta)^u \theta^{n-u} \tag{3.58}$$

If a sample is accepted and the failed units of that sample are repaired and shipped, then the probability distribution of units being returned is

$$P(z_i(t) = z) = \binom{N-n}{z}(1-\theta)^z \theta^{N-n}; \quad z = 0, 1, \ldots N - n \qquad (3.59)$$

If the sample is rejected and the whole production lot is inspected and repaired then $Z_2 = 0$. As a result, using the Poisson approximation we have instead of $\lambda(\Phi)$ in (3.55);

$$\lambda(\Phi) = (N - n)(1 - \theta) \sum_{u=0}^{q} \binom{n}{u}(1 - \theta)^u \theta^{n-u} \qquad (3.60)$$

Further, $I(t)$ the inspection sample size at t is given by

$$I(t) = \begin{cases} n & \text{if sample is accepted }; y(\Phi) \\ \\ N & \text{if sample is rejected }; 1 - y(\Phi) \end{cases} \qquad (3.61)$$

If we ignore the repair costs, the expected inspection costs $C_i(\Phi)$ are then;

$$E(C_i(\Phi)) = C_i(n)y(\Phi) + C_i(N)[1 - y(\Phi)] \qquad (3.62)$$

Inserting these into our problem, we obtain an optimization problem with n, the inspection sample size, a control variable, which can be resolved without great difficulties.

The quality control problem can now be extended in several directions. For example, if X denotes a number of units to be serviced and there are S "repairmen" each repairing one unit in Δt with probability, $\mu \Delta t$, then (see also section 3.6)

$$\Delta X = \begin{cases} +1 & \text{with } \lambda(\Phi)\Delta t \\ -1 & \text{with } \mu \text{ Min } (x, Q)\delta t \\ 0 & \text{with } 1 - \lambda(\Phi)\Delta t - \mu \text{ Min } (X, Q)\Delta t \end{cases} \qquad (3.63)$$

$$X = 0, 1, 2, \ldots$$

A decision problem involving both Φ, the quality control procedure and the servicing parameters (μ, Q) can be constructed and resolved simultaneously in terms of the costs and the benefits each induce.

(ii) *Quality Control and Post-Sales Failure* [38]

The next problem we consider provides a discrete formulation of the dynamic quality control problem. For generality we shall establish a link between a "product reputation" and quality control within a specific optimization problem. Let t be the time index and N_t be the sales at that time, which are assumed to be a function of the sales price p_t and a (stochastic) variable X_t called the "product reputation", i.e.

$$N_t = N(p_t, X_t) \tag{3.64}$$

The product reputation is defined explicitly as a moving average of the faulty units sold. Thus if $Z_t(\Phi)$ is the number of defective units sold at t when the quality control procedure is Φ, then

$$X_{t+1} = \alpha X_t + (1 - \alpha) Z_t(\Phi)/N_t$$

$$X_0, \text{ given}, \alpha \in [0, 1] \text{ and } X_t \in [0, 1] \tag{3.65}$$

where α is a smoothing constant. Unlike the previous case we shall distinguish between two types of failures; a failure probability due to manufacturing only which is given by $1 - \theta$ and a designed failure probability which is denoted by $1 - r$, that is, a unit sold has reliability (or a failure probability given by its complement) which is

$$R = \begin{cases} r & \text{with } \theta \\ 0 & \text{with } 1 - \theta \end{cases} \tag{3.66}$$

In other words, if we sell an inspected output N_i the number of returned units can be interpreted as a random variable whose distribution is a binomial mixture $B(N_i, 1 - R)$ where R is given by (3.66).

For demonstration purposes, assume that a sample of n units is inspected at time t for manufacturing defects only. If at least one unit is found to be defective, then the whole output is inspected. Proceeding as before, the number of units inspected I_t is:

$$I_t = \begin{cases} n & \text{with } y(\Phi) = \theta^n \\ \\ N & \text{with } 1 - y(\Phi) = 1 - \theta^n \end{cases} \tag{3.67}$$

and the number of post sales failures is;

$$Z_t \sim \begin{cases} B(N - n; 1 - R) \text{ with } \theta^n \\ \\ B(N, 1 - r) \text{ with } 1 - \theta^n \end{cases} \tag{3.68}$$

If $c(r, \theta)$ is a unit's production cost and π_t denotes the period profit,

$$\pi_t = [p_t - c(r, \theta)]N(p_t, X_t) - C_i(I_t) - C_f(Z_t) \tag{3.69}$$

Then, over a planning time T, the manufacturer's quality control problem consists in optimizing the discounted profit;

$$\text{Max } V(X_0) = E\{\sum_{t=1}^{T}(1+\gamma)^{-t}\pi_t + (1+\gamma)^{-T}Q(X_T)\}$$

$$\theta \in \Gamma$$

(3.70)

Subject to (3.65) - (3.69)

where γ is the discount rate used for profit maximization.

This problem can be extended in several manners as shown in [38] and continuous time approximation used to obtain a problem formulation which may be simpler to resolve.

Further Reading

The topics we have covered in this chapter are the tip of an iceberg of past and current research in dynamic operational models and management. In the production-inventory area important work was realized by Bather [5], Bensoussan, Crouhi and Proth [9], Bensoussan and Lions [9] and many others [41], [34]. Similarly for queueing related problems and their diffusion approximations. For example, Iglehart [18], Gaver [13], Heyman [17] are initial and starting references for a reader interested in diffusion approximations. Levhari and Sheshinsky [25], Lefevre [24] together with the references given in the text (in particular Crabill et al. [12]) provide first steps for queueing systems optimization. In maintenance and replacement, Barlow, Proschan and Hunter[4], Jorgenson, McCall and Radner [19] are important books in this area while Kamien and Schwarts [21] can be used as another example of the economic approach to maintenance and replacement decisions (see also [28]). Storage and dam process are covered in Puterman [29] for example. Finally, in the quality control and monitoring areas, considerable and varied results have been achieved. These include Anderson and Friedman [2], Bather [7], Balmer [3], Shiryaev [31] and Willsky [19] (for a survey of such problems from an engineering point of view). More recently, however, Tapiero [35] and Tapiero et al [36, 37, 38] have devised an approach based on reputation, sales and learning in assessing the net benefits of quality control.

Bibliography

[1] Alam M. and V.V.S. Sarma, 1974, "Optimum Maintenance Policy for an Equipment Subject to Deterioration and Random Failure," *IEEE Trans. Syst. Man. Cybern.* SMC - 4, 172-175.

[2] Anderson, R. and A. Friedman, 1977, "A Quality Control Problem and Quasi Variational Inequalities," *J. Rat. Mech. Quality* 63, 205- 252.

[3] Balmor, D.W., 1976, "On a Quickest Detection Problem with Variable Monitoring," *Journal of Applied Prob.* 13, 760-767.

[4] Barlow, R.E., F. Proschan and L.C. Hunter, 1965, *Mathematical Theory of Reliability*, New York, Wiley.

[5] Bather, J.A., 1966, "A Continous Time Inventory Model," *Journal of Applied Prob.* 3, 539-549.

[6] Bather, J.A., 1967, "On a Quickest Detection Problem," *Ann Math Stat* 38, 711-724.

[7] Bather, J.A., 1971, "Free Boundary Problems in the Design of Control Charts Trans of the 6th Prague Conf," *Information Theory, Statistical Decision Function and Random Process*, 89-106.

[8] Bensoussan, A., M. Crouhi and J.M. Proth, 1983, *Mathematical Theory of Production Planning*, North-Holland, Amsterdam.

[9] Bensoussan, A. and J.L. Lions, 1974, "Nouvelles Methodes de Controle Impulsionnel," *Applied Mathematics and Optimization*, 289-312.

[10] Bensoussan, A. and C.S. Tapiero, 1982, "Impulsive Control: Prospects and Applications," *Journal of Optimization Theory and Applications*.

[11] Business Week, 1982, Quality; The US Drives to Catch Up, Special Report, Nov., 9, 66-80.

[12] Crabill, T.B., D. Gross and M.J. Magazine, 1970, "A Survey of Research of Optimal Design and Control of Queues, *Rand Institute*, New York.

[13] Gaver, D.P., 1968, "Diffusion Approximations and Models for Certain Congestion Problems, *Journal of App. Prob* 5, 607-623.

[14] Gonedes, N.J. and Z. Lieber, 1974, "Production Planning for a Stochastic Demand Process," *Operations Research* 22, 771-787.

[15] Halachmi, B. and W.R. Franta, 1978, "A Diffusion Approximation to the Multi-Server Queue, *Management Science* 24, 522-529.

[16] Harrison, J.M. and A.J. Taylor, 1978, "Optimal Control of a Brownian Storage System," *Stoch. Processes and Applications*, 6, 179-194.

[17] Heyman, D.P., 1975, "A Diffusion Model Approximation for the GI/G/1 Queue in Heavy Traffic," *Bell System Tech. Journal* 54, 1637-646.

[18] Iglehart, D.L., 1965, "Limiting Diffusion Approximations for the Multi Server Queue and the Repairman Problem, *J. Appl Prob* 2, 429-441.

[19] Jorgensen, D.W., J.J. McCall and R. Radner, 1967, *Optimal Replacement Policy*, North-Holland, Amsterdam.

[20] Juran, J.M. and F.M. Gryna Jr., 1970, *Quality Planning and Analysis*, McGraw Hill Book Co., New York.

[21] Kamien M. and N.L. Schwartz, 1971, "Optimal maintenance and Sale Age for a Machine Subject to Failure," *Management Science*, 17, 495-504.

[22] Kleindorfer, P.R. and K. Glover, 1973, "Linear convex Stochastic Optimal Control with Applications in Production Planning," *IEEE Trans in Automatic Control*, AC-18, 56-59.

[23] Kobayashi, H., 1974, "Applications of the Diffusion Approximation to Queueing Networks," I, *JACM*, 21, 316-328.

[24] Lefevre, C., 1981, "Optimal Control of a Birth and Death Epidemic Process," *Operations Research* 29, 971-982.

[25] Levhary, D. and E. Sheshinsky, 1974, "The Economics of Queues: A Brief Survey," in M.S. Balch, D.F. McFadden and S.Y Wu (eds.), *Essays in Economic Behavior Under Uncertainty*, North-Holland, Amsterdam, 195-212.

[26] Luss, H., "Operations Research and Capacity Expansion Problems: A Survey," *Operations Research*, 30, 907-947.

[27] Modigliani, F. and F. Hohn, 1955, "Production Planning over time and the Nature of the Expectations and Planning Horizon," *Econometrica*, 23, 46-66.

[28] Pierskalla, W.P. and J.A. Voelker, 1976, "A Survey of Maintenance Models, the Control and Surveillance of Deteriorating Systems," *Naval Research Logistics Quarterly*, 23, 353-388.

[29] Puterman, M., 1975, "A Diffusion Process Model for a Storage System," in M. Geisler (ed.), *Logistics, TIMS Studies in Management Science*, 1, North Holland, Amsterdam, 143-159.

[30] Robin, M. and C.S. Tapieros, 1982, "A Simple Vehicle Dispatching Policy with Non-Stationary Stochastic Arrival Rates," *Transp. Res*, 6, 449-457.

[31] Shiryaev, A.N., 1963, "On Optimum Methods in Quickest Detection Problems," *Theor. Prob. Appl*, 8. 22-46.

[32] Stidham, S., 1974, "Stochastic Clearing Systems," *Stoch. Processes and Appl.*, 2, 85-113.

[33] Stidham, S., 1977, "Cost Models for Stochastic Clearing Systems, *Operations Research*, 25, 100-127.

[34] Tapiero, C.S., 1977, *Managerial Planning: An Optimum and Stochastic Control Approcah*, Gordon Breach Science Publ., New York.

[35] Tapiero, C.S., 1986, "Quality Control by the Control of Discrete State Stochastic Process," *International Journal of Production Research*, 24, 927-937.

[36] Tapiero, C.S., 1987, "Production Learning and Quality Control" *AIIE Transactions*.

[37] Tapiero, C.S. and H. Lee, 1987, "Quality control and Servicing," *Europ. J. of Operations Research*.

[38] Tapiero, C.S., A Reisman and P. Ritchken, 1987, "Product Failures, Manufacturing Reliability and Quality Control: A Dynamic Framework," *Infor.*.

[39] Thompson, G.L, 1968, "Optimal Maintenance Policy and Sale Date of a Machine," *Management Science*, 14, 543-550.

[40] Vickson, R.G., 1982, "Optimal Control of Production Sequences: A Continuous Parameters Analysis," *Operations Research*, 30, 659-679.

[41] Vickson, R.G., 1982, "Schedule Control for Randomly Drifting Productions Sequences," *Infor.*, 19, 330-346.

[42] Wagner, H., 1969, *Principles of Operations Research*, Prentice Hall, Englewood Cliffs, N.J.

[43] Willsky, A.S., 1976, "A Survey of Design Methods for Failure Detection of Dynamic Systems," *Automatica*, 12, 601-611.

Chapter 4

DYNAMIC OPTIMIZATION

4.1   *Introduction*

In this chapter we turn to the solution of dynamic decision models under uncertainty. Specifically, we shall use the stochastic dynamic programming approach. This is based on an approach developed by Bellman [6,7], stating essentially that:

> "An optimal policy has the property that whatever the initial conditions are, the remaining decision must constitute an optitmal policy with regard to the state resulting from the first decision."

This basic and rational premise enables us to relate the optimum solution of a problem of two periods to a similar problem in three periods. More generally, it provides an approach for stating a recurrence relationship between the solution of an nth period problem and that of an $(n+1)^{st}$ period. It is noteworthy that there are conceptually no differences between a problem's formulation when uncertainty is, or is not, considered. The special considerations in formulating and solving a stochastic dynamic programming problem (SDP) will be the concern of sections 4.2 - 4.4, while in 4.5, numerous examples and applications of Chapter 3 are dealt with.

To comprehend the dynamic programming approach, we consider first the problem of decision-making over time and under certainty. Suppose that at an initial time, $t = 0$, we have an initial state, x_0, and assume that some decision u_0, is taken. This decision can be reached as a function of current information (or forecasts), which means that $u_0 = u_0(x_0)$, where x_0 parametrize all the information which is available initially. Given $[x_0, u_0(x_0)]$ a next state is reached which we denote by x_1. A repetition of such a process finally leads to an evolution of states, or a dynamic process. For simplicity, we can write the between periods transition in functional form, F, or

$$x_{i+1} = F(x_i, u_i) \tag{4.1}$$
$$i = 0, 1, \ldots, N - 1$$

The fundamental question that remains, however, is how to select a decision u_i at $i = 0, 1, \ldots$ To do so, four sets of assumptions are required. These consist in specifying:

1) The objective function

2) The process structure, or evolution in time, i.e., F

3) The usable information available at any given time for reaching a decision.

4) The relevant constraints on both states and decisions to be considered in seeking a decision, at a given time.

Given such assumptions, we can proceed and solve the dynamic decision problem. Supose that at each period of time i, the state x_i and the decision u_i induce a loss $L_i(x_i, u_i)$ over N periods starting from the initial time $i = 0$. The total loss would be:

$$J_0(x_0) = \sum_{i=0}^{N-1} L_i(x_i, u_i) \tag{4.2}$$

where x_0 is the only information available at $i = 0$. Evidently, as time goes by, the cost J is altered. For example, at time 1:

$$J_1(x_1) = \sum_{i=1}^{N-1} L_i(x_i, u_i) \tag{4.3}$$

The relationship between these two quantities, however, is obviously:

$$J_0(x_0) = L_0(x_0, u_0) + J_1(x_1) \tag{4.4}$$

Now we use our knowledge of the process structure and note that $x_1 = F_1(x_0, u_0)$, thus

$$J_0(x_0) = L_0(x_0, u_0) + J_1[F_1(x_0, u_0)] \tag{4.5}$$

which is one function in u_0 only whose solution can be obtained if we knew the functional form J_1. Further, specification of constraint X_1 on x_1 - the next state, and the constraints U_0 on u_0, lead to an optimization problem of the following form:

$$J_0^0(x_0) = \min\{L_0(x_0, u_0) + J_1(F_1(x_0, u_0))\} \tag{4.6}$$

$$x_1 = F_1(x_0, u_0) \in X_1; u_0 \in U_0$$

which is a constrained optimization problem in *one variable*, even though our original problem involves N decisions. This has been achieved by foregoing the knowledge of the functional form J_1, and rendering (4.6) indeterminate. To circumvate this difficulty, the dynamic approach, as stated in Bellman's principle, uses an inductive logic which is implicit in our recurrence relationship (4.4). Specifically, by repeating the above procedure and defining $J_i(X_i)$ = the cost-to-go at time i until the end in period N, we have

$$J_i^0(x_i) = \min\{L_i(x_i, u_i) + J_{i+1}(x_{i+1})\},$$
$$x_{i+1} = F_i(x_i, u_i), x_{i+1} \in X_{i+1}, u_i \in U_i \tag{4.7}$$
$$i = 0, 1, \ldots, N-1$$

This is called the backward recurrence equation of dynamic programming whose final value, (treated as a first value in solving the equation) is given by

$$J_N^0(x_N) = \min\{L_N(x_N, u_N)\} \qquad (4.8)$$
$$x_N \in X_N, u_N \in U_N$$

Define a solution to (4.8) by $u_N^0(x_N)$, and as a result

$$J_N^0(x_N) = L_N[x_N, u_N^0(x_N)] \qquad (4.9)$$

Next, given J_N^0 we find J_{N-1}^0 by substitution into (4.7),

$$J_{N-1}^0(x_{N-1}) = \min\{L_{N-1}(x_{N-1}) + J_N^0(F_{N-1}(x_{N-1}, u_{N-1}))\} \qquad (4.10)$$

A substitution of (4.9) into (4.10) finally leads to an equation where all functional forms are given and with u_{N-1}, the unknown decision variable, we optimize

$$J_{N-1}^0(x_{N-1}) = \min\{L_{N-1}(x_{N-1}, u_{N-1}) + \qquad (4.11)$$
$$+L_N(F_{N-1}(x_{N-1}, u_{N-1}), u_N^0(F_{N-1}(x_{N-1}, u_{N-1})))\}$$
$$\text{subject to:} \quad x_{N-1} \in X_{N-1}, u_{N-1} \in U_{N-1}$$

whose solution is

$$u_{N-1}^0 = u_{N-1}^0(x_{N-1}) \qquad (4.12)$$

Substituting again into (4.11), we obtain J_{N-1}^0 which is used for substitution into (4.7) and so on until the initial stage.

Evidently, for problems of special forms, it is possible to obtain analytical expressions for $J_i(x_i)$, while in other cases, it is necessary to use numerical techniques. In this chapter, we concentrate on an analytical approach, while in Chapter 8, we shall use numerical techniques in solving the SDP problems to be formulated.

The discrete time procedure followed so far can be extended without difficulty to continuous time problems. To do so, we consider a special problem in Table 4.1 and treat it in parallel in discrete and continuous time.

For optimum decisions, we minimize at each stage of the decision process with respect to u. The procedure in discrete time follows the method outlined earlier. In continuous time, however, it is possible to make several simplifications by assuming that the objective J is a differentiable function of time t and state x. Then, if we take a two terms Taylor series approximation of $J(x + dx, t + dt)$, we have:

$$J(x + dx, t + dt) = J(x,t) + \frac{\partial J}{\partial x}dx + \frac{\partial J}{\partial t}dt \qquad (4.13)$$

Table 4.1: The Principle of Optimality

Discrete Time	Continuous Time
$x_{t+\Delta t} = x_t + f_t(x_t, u_t)\Delta t$ x_0 given $J_0 = Q_t(x_t) + \sum_{t=0}^{T} L_t(x_t, u_t)\Delta t$	$dx = f(x, u, t)dt$ x_0 given $J(T) = Q(x,t) + \int_0^T L(x, u, t)dt$
$J_t(x_t) =$ Cost to go at t where $x = x_t$	$J(x,t) =$ Cost to go at t where $x = x(t)$
The Principle of Optimality $J^0 = \text{Min } \{J\}$ $u_t \in U$	
$J_t(x_t) = L_t(x_t, u_t)\Delta t + J_{t+\Delta t}(x_{t+\Delta t})$ $J_T(x_T = Q_T(x_T)$	$J(x,t) = L(x, u, t)dt + J(x + dx, t + dt)$ $J(x,T) = Q(x,T)$

which leads at the optimum to

$$-\frac{\partial J(x,t)}{\partial t} = \min_{u \in U}\{L(x,u,t) + \frac{\partial J(x,t)}{\partial x}\frac{dx}{dt}\} \qquad (4.14)$$

where u_0 is a solution (if it exists) given in terms of x and t in the minimization problem above. Or, for an optimal $J(x,t)$,

$$u^0 = u(x, \partial J/\partial x, t) \qquad (4.15)$$

Substituting u^0 in Bellman's equation, we obtain the Hamilton-Jacobi partial differential equation;

$$-\frac{\partial J}{\partial t} = L(x,u^0,t) + \frac{\partial J}{\partial x}(\frac{dx}{dt}) = H^0(x, \frac{\partial J}{\partial x}, u^0, t) \qquad (4.16)$$

where H^0 is called the Hamiltonian evaluated along an optimum trajectory, and is given by:

$$H^0(x, \frac{\partial J}{\partial x}, u^0, t) = \text{Min } H(x, \frac{\partial J}{\partial x}, u, t) \qquad (4.17)$$

$$H^0(x, \frac{\partial J}{\partial x}, u^0, t) = L(x, u^0, t) + z(dx/dt)$$

where $z(t)$ is a Lagrange multiplier, with its usual interpretation

$$z(t) = \partial J/\partial x \qquad (4.18)$$

Thus, the Hamilton-Jacobi-Bellman equation is given by:

$$-\frac{\partial J}{\partial t} = H^0(x, \frac{\partial J^0}{\partial x}, u^0, t) \qquad (4.19)$$

$$H^0(x, \frac{\partial J^0}{\partial x}, u^0, t) = \underset{u \in U}{\text{Min }} H(x, \frac{\partial J}{\partial x}, u, t)$$

and is a first order partial differential equation. If u is unconstrained, and H, L are differentiable functions in u, then when a solution exists,

$$\frac{\partial H}{\partial u} = 0$$

$$\qquad (4.20)$$

$$\frac{\partial L}{\partial u} + \frac{\partial J}{\partial x}\frac{\partial f}{\partial u} = 0$$

and $\partial^2 H/\partial u^2 \geq 0$. This latter inequality is known as the Legendre condition.

Of course, by changing our assumption regarding the dynamics of the process studied, the equations above will also be altered. This will become evident when deriving the dynamic programming equations under uncertainty.

4.2   The Dynamic Programming Approach : Under Uncertainty

Next we develop the Bellman equation for stochastic decision problems. In the next section, specific equations for special processes will be developed. Especially we shall consider processes driven by Wiener, Poisson-Jump processes, with finite, infinite and random planning horizons. In addition, we shall introduce impulsive control problems. Consider first the discrete time optimization problem defined by:

$$\text{Minimize } J(0) = E\sum_{t=0}^{T} L_t(y_t, v_t) + G(y_{T+1}) \tag{4.21}$$

where

T = the final, planning time
$J(z)$ = the cost at time z, $z = 0, 1, \ldots, T$
L_t = the period's t loss
v_t = a managerial discretion variable (a control variable)
y_t = state (random) variable at t

Evidently, there is in addition a stochastic process relating the states at subsequent stages. We can write

$$y_{t+1} = F(y_t, v_t, w_t) \tag{4.22}$$

where w_t is a random disturbance with known (or unknown) probability characteristics. Define by $\lambda_T(y_T)$ the optimum cost-to-go at the decision time T and starting with the state variable y_T. Evidently, $\lambda_0(y_0) = \text{Min } J(T)$ so that, $\lambda_T(y_T)$ is the cost incurred at the final time or,

$$\lambda_T(y_T) = \min_{v_T \in U} \{EL_T(y_T, v_T) + G(y_{T+1})\} \tag{4.23}$$

Insert y_{T+1}, and obtain:

$$\lambda_T(y_T) = \min_{v_T \in U} EL_T(y_T, v_T) + G(F(y_T, v_T, w_T)) \tag{4.24}$$

which is an equation in y_T alone (since y_T is given and w_T is a random process). Our problem is to represent a recurrence equation for λ_t so that $\lambda_0(y_0)$ can be found. Consider a previous instant $T - 1$, then of course

$$\lambda_{T-1}(y_{T-1}) = \min_{v_{T-1} \in U} EL_{T-1}(y_{T-1}, v_{T-1}) + \lambda_T(y_T) \tag{4.25}$$

replacing y_T, we obtain

$$\lambda_{T-1}(y_{T-1}) = \operatorname*{Min}_{v_{T-1} \in U} EL_{T-1}(y_{T-1}, v_{T-1}) + \lambda_T(F(y_{T-1}, v_{T-1}, w_{T-1}))$$

(4.26)

And, by recurrence

$$\lambda_{T-k}(y_{T-k}) = \operatorname*{Min}_{v_{T-k} \in U} EL_{T-k}(y_{T-k}, v_{T-k}) + \lambda_{T-k}(F(y_{T-k}, v_{T-k}, y_{T-k}))$$

(4.27)

which is the backward recurrence equation, expressing the principle of optimality. Evidently, such equations are quite difficult to resolve, although many cases have been dealt with and numerical methods developed (see Chapter 8).

We persue this problem by considering its continuous time formulation. For future convenience, we formulate a discounted cost problem. The procedure we follow, although simplified, can be found in many recent texts of stochastic dynamic programming and stochastic control (for example, Krylov [38], Fleming and Rishel [30], Bensoussan [11], Ross [57], Bertsekas and Shreve [19]).

Define a minimizing criterion as follows:

$$J(T) = E \int_0^T e^{-rt} L(y, v, t) dt + G(y(T)) e^{-rt}$$

(4.28)

where r is a discount rate and T is a known planning horizon. The functions L and G are the continuous and instantaneous loss and terminal objectives respectively and y and v are the state and control variables. Say that at some initial time s, the value of the state $y(s)$ equals a known value x, or $y(s) = x$. At time s, the objective J, a function of x and s, will be written as follows:

$$J(x, s) = E \int_s^T e^{-r(t-s)} L(y, v, t) dt + G(y(T)) e^{-r(T-s)}$$

(4.29)

and expresses the "future" expected cost at time s when $y(s) = x$, and when a control $v(.)$ is applied. The optimum (minimum) objective is then defined by some function $\phi(.)$;

$$\phi(x, s) = \inf_{v \in U} J(x, s)$$

(4.30)

In maximization terms, we can write instead

$$-\phi(x, s) = \sup_{v \in U} -J(x, s)$$

(4.31)

where "$-J$" is interpreted as an expected profit (or benefits) at time s when $y(s) = x$. In this sense, and assuming that we function optimally, $-\phi(x, s)$

is a "value", function of s and x. As a result, its derivative with respect to say x is the marginal change in expected future income due to a change in the state x. In this sense, it can be thought of as a "shadow price" $p(x, s)$ associated to the resource x, where

$$p(x, s) = -\frac{\partial \phi(x, s)}{\partial x} \tag{4.32}$$

For example, if x stands for inventory on hand at time s, or a stock of capital, then the imputed price of this stock or capital is given by $p(x, s)$. The Dynamic programming approach under uncertainty, technically, provides a means to expressing $J(x, s)$ (and hence $\phi(x, s)$) as a partial differential equation whose solution we might be able to solve analytically, or numerically. Our concern in the next section is to obtain such equations for alternative formulations of stochastic dynamic programming problems.

To obtain the fundamental equation of dynamic programming consider a small time interval $(s, s+\Delta t)$ where Δ is small. Using the Bellman principle:

$$\phi(x, s) = \inf_{v \in U} E \int_s^{s+\Delta t} e^{-r(t-s)} L dt + e^{-r\Delta} \phi(y(s + \Delta t), s + \Delta t) \tag{4.33}$$

The first term (within the integral) is the cost incurred during the interval $(s, s + \Delta t)$ while the second term is the discounted future cost, which is by definition the optimum value at $s + \Delta t$. This cost however is different than $\phi(x, s)$ since at $(s+\Delta t)$, the state $y(s)$ was altered (probabilistically or not) to a new state $y(s + \Delta t)$ For small $\Delta t, \Delta t \to dt$ we have

$$\lim_{\Delta t \to dt} E \int_s^{s+\Delta t} e^{-r(t-s)} L dt = e^{-rdt} E(L) dt \tag{4.34}$$

As a result, the recurrence equation (4.34) can be written (for $\Delta t \to dt$) as follows:

$$\phi(x, s) = e^{-rdt} E(L) dt + E\phi(y(s + dt), s + dt) \tag{4.35}$$

Since $r\, dt$ is expectedly very small, $\exp(-rdt) \approx (1 - rdt)$ and replacing x by $y(s)$, we can write more completely,

$$\phi(y(s), s) = \inf_{v \in U} E(1 - rdt)[Ldt + \phi(y(s + dt), s + dt)] \tag{4.36}$$

The right hand terms of the equation above can be developed by Taylor series approximations, or expressed explicitly as a function of the "driving" stochastic process $y(t)$. Nonetheless, the equation above provides a departure point for obtaining alternative characterizations of the ϕ-function.

4.3 *The Dynamic Programming Equations*

Below we shall derive the dynamic programming equations for several
dynamic processes and problem formulations.

4.3.1 Wiener Process

As in Chapter 2, consider a stochastic (Wiener Process) differential equation
given by

$$dy = F(y, u)dt + \sigma(y, u)dw; \quad y(s) = x \qquad (4.37)$$

where $u(.)$ is a control variable and $dw = w(t + dt) - w(t)$ is a standard
Wiener process, with $E(dw) = 0$, $\text{var}(dw) = dt$. Evidently,

$$y(s + dt) = y(s) + [F(y, u)dt + \sigma(y, u)dw] \qquad (4.38)$$

Such that $\phi(y(s + dt), s + dt)$ can be written as $\phi(y(s) + dy, s + dt)$ with
dy defined above. Now suppose that we approximate ϕ by a Taylor series
approximation and retain only the terms of order less or equal to dt (terms
in $(dt)^k, k \geq 2$ are assumed negligible). Then,

$$E\{\phi(y(s+dt), s+dt)\} = E\{\phi(y(s), s) + \frac{\partial \phi}{\partial y}dy + \frac{1}{2}\frac{\partial^2 \phi}{\partial y^2}(dy)^2 + \frac{\partial \phi}{\partial s}dt\} \quad (4.39)$$

Taking expectations and letting the y process be independent of future
disturbances (which is called an adapted process), we also note that:

$$E\{dy\frac{\partial \phi}{\partial y}\} = f(y, u)(\frac{\partial \phi}{\partial y})dt \qquad (4.40)$$

and

$$E\{\frac{1}{2}(dy)^2\frac{\partial^2 \phi}{\partial y^2}\} = \frac{1}{2}\sigma^2(y, u)(\frac{\partial^2 \phi}{\partial y^2})dt \qquad (4.41)$$

Inserting these equations above in $\phi(y(s + dt), s + dt)$ and back into our
fundamental dynamic programming equation in the previous section, we
obtain the following parabolic partial differential equation

$$\frac{\partial \phi}{\partial s} + F(y, u)\frac{\partial \phi}{\partial y} + \frac{1}{2}\sigma^2(y, u)\frac{\partial^2 \phi}{\partial y^2} + L(y, u) - r\phi = 0 \qquad (4.42)$$

with the boundary condition at $s = T$

$$\phi(y(T), T) = G(y(T)) \qquad (4.43)$$

The optimum control, found by minimizing the above, is given by solving for u in:

$$\inf_{u \in U} \{F(y,u)\frac{\partial \phi}{\partial y} + \frac{1}{2}\sigma^2(y,u)\frac{\partial^2 \phi}{\partial y^2} + L(y,u)\} \qquad (4.44)$$

and inserting back into the parabolic equation. This equation can be solved analytically only seldom. Numerical results can be obtained as we shall point out in Chapter 8.

4.3.2 Random Walks

Say that a stochastic (random walk) process is described as follows

$$dy = \begin{cases} +\varepsilon & \text{w.p. } \alpha(y,u)dt \\ 0 & \text{w.p. } 1 - \alpha(y,u)dt - \beta(y,v)dt \\ -\varepsilon & \text{w.p. } \beta(y,v)dt \end{cases} \qquad (4.45)$$

Then

$$\phi(y(s+dt),s+dt) = \begin{cases} \phi(y(s)-\varepsilon,s) & \text{w.p. } \alpha(y-\varepsilon,u)dt \\ \phi(y(s),s) & \text{w.p. } 1 - \alpha(y,u)dt - \beta(y,v)dt \\ \phi(y(s)+\varepsilon,s) & \text{w.p. } \beta(y+\varepsilon,v)dt \end{cases} \qquad (4.46)$$

Or in expectation

$$\begin{aligned} \phi(y(s+dt),s+dt) = \ & \alpha(y-\varepsilon,u)\phi(y(s)-\varepsilon,s)dt + \\ & \beta(y+\varepsilon,v)\phi(y(s)+\varepsilon,s)dt + \\ & \phi(y(s),s) - [\alpha(y,u)+\beta(y,v)]\phi(y(s),s)dt \end{aligned} \qquad (4.47)$$

Inserting into the basic dynamic programming equation (4.36) in 4.2 we obtain at the limit:

$$\begin{aligned} & \frac{\partial \phi}{\partial s} - [\alpha(y,u)\phi(y,s) - \alpha(y-\varepsilon,u)]\phi(y-\varepsilon,s) + \\ & +[\beta(y+\varepsilon,v)\phi(y+\varepsilon,s) - \beta(y,v)\phi(y,s)] + L(y,u,v) \\ & -r\phi(y,s) = 0 \end{aligned} \qquad (4.48)$$

where L is now a cost function expressing both the costs of u and v. At the boundary, $s = T$ we have as before

$$\phi(y(T),T) = G(y(T)) \qquad (4.49)$$

If we define the operators

$$\Delta_e H = H(y + \varepsilon, s) - H(y, s) \left.\right\}$$
$$\Delta_{-e} H = H(y, s) - H(y - \epsilon, s) \left.\right\}$$

(4.50)

Then, a compact way to write ϕ will be

$$\frac{\partial \phi}{\partial s} - \Delta_e \alpha \phi + \Delta_{-e} \beta \phi + L - r\phi = 0;$$

(4.51)

$$\phi(y(T), T) = G(y(T))$$

Evidently, if these operators are approximated by Taylor series, we can obtain instead continuous state equations rather than discrete ones. For example, a first term approximation,

$$\Delta_{\pm e} = \frac{\partial(.)}{\partial y}$$

(4.52)

leads to

$$\frac{\partial \phi}{\partial s} - (\alpha - \beta)\frac{\partial \phi}{\partial y} + L - r\phi = 0$$

(4.53)

which is the dynamic programming equation of a deterministic system with objective L and with dynamics given by:

$$\frac{dy}{dt} = \alpha - \beta$$

(4.54)

4.3.3 A Jump Process

Now consider the stochastic process whose evolution is described by a jump process. Let $s \leq \tau_1 \leq \tau_2, \ldots \leq \tau_i \leq \ldots$, be the jump times. Then we have (see Chapter 2)

$$dy = f(y, v, t), t \in [\tau_i, \tau_{i+1})$$

(4.55)

$$y(\tau_{i+1}) = y(\tau_{i+1}^-) + \xi_{i+1}$$

(4.56)

where ξ_i denotes the jump at time τ_i. The objective cost to minimize is J of (4.44). As before, let the functional $\phi(x, s)$ be defined by:

$$\phi(x, s) = E\{\int_s^T L(y, v, t)dt\}$$

(4.57)

or written explicitly as follows:

$$\phi(x, s) = E\{\int_s^{s+\delta} L(y, v, t)dt\} + E\{\int_{s+\delta}^T L(y, v, t)dt\}$$

(4.58)

The first integral is computed by

$$E\{\int_s^{s+\delta} L(y,v,t)dt\} = \delta L(x,v,s) + \delta\phi(\delta) \tag{4.59}$$

The second integral is computed by separating the two possibilities, (i) a jump occurs in $(s, s+\delta)$ and (ii) a jump does not occur in $(s, s+\delta)$, and by taking their expectation. Specifically, write

$$\alpha_i = E\{\int_{s+\delta}^T L(y,v,t)dt\}$$
$$i = 1, \text{ if a jump occurs in } (s, s+\delta) \tag{4.60}$$
$$i = 2, \text{ if no jump occurs in } (s, s+\delta)$$

Then, evidently, unconditional on a jump occurring, the second integral in (4.58) is defined by

$$E\{\int_{s+\delta}^T L(y,v,t)dt\} = \text{Prob}[i=1]\alpha_1 + \text{Prob}[i=2]\alpha_2 \tag{4.61}$$

We shall consider each of these cases separately. Say first that a jump of size ξ occurs in $(s, s+\delta)$, this results in a change of $\phi(x,s)$ to $\phi(x+\xi,s)$ or

$$\alpha_1 = \phi(x+\xi,s) + o(\delta) \tag{4.62}$$

If the size of the jump is random with a known probability distribution $P(z,s)$, then

$$\alpha_1 = \int \phi(x+z,s)P(z,s)dz \tag{4.63}$$

The probability of a jump occuring however is $q(s)\delta(s)$ at time s, thus, unconditional on the jump occuring, the expectation $E\{\alpha_1\}$ is:

$$E\alpha_1 = q(s)\delta s \int \phi(x+z,s)P(z,s)dz \tag{4.64}$$

When no jump occurs in $(s, s+\delta)$ (with probability $1 - q(s)\delta s$), the process is deterministic and evolves by:

$$\alpha_2 = [1 - q(s)\delta s]\{\phi(x,s) + \frac{\partial\phi}{\partial s} + \delta s\frac{\partial\phi}{\partial x}f(x,v)\} \tag{4.65}$$

Gathering these terms, we note that ϕ satisfies the following equation

$$O = r\phi + \frac{\partial\phi}{\partial s} + f(x,v)\frac{\partial\phi}{\partial x} + L(x,v) + q(s)\int[\phi(x+z,s) - \phi(x,s)]P(z,s)dz \tag{4.66}$$

to which we add the terminal condition

$$\phi(x, T) = O \tag{4.67}$$

These last two equations provide a characterization of the dynamic programming equation for processes defined with a Poisson rate $q(s)\delta s$ of jump occurrences.

A generalization to diffusion processes with jumps is straightforward. Thus, if our stochastic process was defined by

$$dy = f(y, v, t)dt + \sigma(y, v, t)dw; \quad t \in [\tau_j, \tau_{j+1}] \tag{4.68}$$

$$y(\tau_{j+1}) = y(\tau_{j+1}^-) + \xi_{i+1}; \quad y(s) = x$$

where $w(t)$ is a standard Wiener process. Proceeding as before, we simply note that in computing $E\alpha_2$, we have instead

$$E\,\alpha_2 = \phi(x, s) + \delta\frac{\partial\phi}{\partial x}f + \delta\frac{\sigma^2}{2}\frac{\partial^2\phi}{\partial x^2} + \delta\frac{\partial\phi}{\partial s} + \delta(.) \tag{4.69}$$

This relationship follows from the fact that given that there is no jump in interval $(s, s + \delta)$, then $y(s + \delta)$ is given by a Wiener process. Specifically

$$y(s + \delta) = x + \delta F + \sigma w(\delta) + o(\delta) \tag{4.70}$$

where $w(\delta)$ is a normally distributed random variable with mean zero and variance δ. Then,

$$E\alpha_1 = [1 - \delta q(x, s)]\{\phi(x, s) + \delta\frac{\partial\phi}{\partial x}F + \delta\frac{\partial\phi}{\partial s} + \delta\frac{\sigma^2}{2}\frac{\partial^2\phi}{\partial x^2} + \delta o(\delta)\} \tag{4.71}$$

When we gather these results together with $E(\alpha_1)$ we obtain (with (4.65))

$$-\frac{\partial\phi}{\partial t} = -r\phi + F(x, v)\frac{\partial\phi}{\partial x} + \frac{1}{2}\sigma^2\frac{\partial^2\phi}{\partial x^2} + \tag{4.72}$$

$$L(x, v) + q(s)\int[\phi(x + z, s) - \phi(x, s)]P(z, s)dz$$

which generalizes the previous results.

4.3.4 Random Planning Time

"Random" Planning times occur when the horizon over which optimization is conducted is not known at the start. Such a horizon may be defined conditionally by the state attaining a certain absorption boundary, terminating the process. Examples to such boundaries are numerous, including bankruptcy states, machines breaking-apart, "death" etc. Specifically, let $x(t) = \{x, t \geq 0\}$ be a stochastic process and define an open set Ω as follows:

$$\text{If } x \in \Omega, \text{ process is continued}$$

$$\text{If } x \in \overline{\Omega}, \text{ process is stopped (absorbed)} \tag{4.73}$$

The boundary to the open set, within which the process is defined is $\Gamma = \Omega \cap \overline{\Omega}$ expressing the intersecton of Ω and $\overline{\Omega}$. For example, if $\Omega = \{x; x \geq 0\}$ then $\overline{\Omega} = \{x; x \leq 0\}$ and $\Gamma = \{x; x = 0\}$. Define by τ the first instant of time (since the initial time $t = 0$) that the process reaches the boundary Γ thus,

$$\tau = \inf\{t \geq 0; \; x(t) \in \Gamma\} \tag{4.74}$$

and a random planning time stochastic control problem can be defined as follows (at the starting time s);

$$\underset{u \in U}{\text{Min }} J(x) = E\{\textstyle\int_s^\tau e^{-(t-s)r} L(x,u)dt + e^{-r(\tau-s)} G(x(\tau))\} \tag{4.75}$$

subject to (4.74) and

$$dx = f(x,u)dt + \sigma(x,u)dw; \; x(t) = y \tag{4.76}$$

The objective function $J(x)$ in x is only a function of x. Assume that F is a Wiener process operator for this discounted problem, is defined by;

$$F = f(x,u)\frac{\partial}{\partial y} + \frac{1}{2}\sigma^2(x,u)\frac{\partial^2}{\partial y^2} - r \tag{4.77}$$

As long as $t < \tau$, then the expected cost J is given by a solution of

$$L + FJ = 0 \tag{4.78}$$

But at τ, on the boundary Γ, we have by definition

$$J_{|x \in \Gamma} = G \tag{4.79}$$

Equations (4.78) and (4.79) are thus the dynamic programming equations for equation (4.75). More generally, when the state process is given by a Wiener plus a jump process, the dynamic programming equation is (see Section 4.3):

$$FJ + BJ + L = 0 \tag{4.80}$$

where the operator B of the jump process is

$$BJ = q \int [J(x+z) - J(x)]p(z)dz \tag{4.81}$$

and, on the boundary Γ, condition (4.79) remains valid. Finally to obtain the optimum control policy we proceed as before by letting

$$J^0 = \underset{u \in U}{\text{Min}} \quad J(u) \tag{4.82}$$

and

$$\underset{u \in U}{\text{Min}} \ FJ^0 + BJ^0 + L = 0 \tag{4.83}$$

A solution of (4.82), (4.83) together with (4.79) provides the solution of the stochastic control problem with random planning time.

When the planning time is either a known constant T, or the random time τ - whichever comes first, then the objective is written as follows:

$$J(x) = E\{\int_0^{\tau \wedge T} e^{-rt} L(x, u) dt +$$

$$+ e^{-r\tau} G(x(\tau)) I_{\tau < T} + e^{-rT} H(x(T)) I_{t=T}\} \tag{4.84}$$

where $\tau < T$ and

$$I_{\tau < T} = \begin{cases} 1 \text{ if } \tau < T \\ 0 \text{ otherwise} \end{cases}$$

$$\tag{4.85}$$

$$I_{\tau = T} = \begin{cases} 1 \text{ is } \tau = T \\ 0 \text{ otherwise} \end{cases}$$

In other words, if the objective cost is stopped at T, then the boundary condition is (see also Section 4.3.1), $J(x, T) = H(x(T))$, or if it is stopped before at time $\tau < T$, it is $J(x, \tau) = G(x(\tau))$. As a result, as long as the process is not stopped, (and in case of a Wiener process only):

$$\frac{\partial J}{\partial t} + FJ + L = 0; \ t < \tau, t < T \tag{4.86}$$

Now as long as $\tau < T$ and the process *is not stopped* then clearly

$$J(x, s) \le G(x(s)) \tag{4.87}$$

If $J(x, s) > G$, it will be optimal to incur the cost G and stop. But at $s = \tau$, $J(x, \tau) = G(x(\tau))$ and the inequality in (4.87) becomes an equality. As a result, the dynamic programming equations are

$$\text{(i)} \quad \frac{\partial J}{\partial t} + FJ + L \leq 0$$

$$\text{(ii)} \quad J(x,s) - G(x) \leq 0$$

$$\text{(iii)} \quad (i) \ * \ (ii) = 0 \tag{4.88}$$

$$\text{(iv)} \quad J(x,T) = H(x(T))$$

4.3.5 Infinite Time

Consider next an optimization problem with an objective defined over an infinite horizon. Specifically, we define:

$$J(x,s) = E\{\int_s^\infty e^{-r(t-s)} L(y,v) dt\} \tag{4.89}$$

where $y(s) = x$, and

$$\phi(x,s) = \inf_{v \in U} J(x,s) \tag{4.90}$$

Say that all parameters of the stochastic dynamic process are stationary, so that at any time s, the value of J depends on x only, the initial condition. This means that $\partial\phi/\partial s = 0$ and provided $\phi(x)$ is a bounded function for all x, we have (in case of equation (4.80) above):

$$\begin{cases} F\phi + B\phi - r\phi + L = 0 \\ \phi \text{ bounded} \end{cases} \tag{4.91}$$

where F and B are operators as defined earlier (with $r = 0$).

The introduction of an infinite horizon introduces however some difficulties. Technically, this occurs since we have to solve a differential equation with boundary conditions given implicitly by the convergence (and existence) requirement that ϕ is finite for all x , in particular for $x \to \pm\infty$. Alternatively, we can "think of" the infinite time problem as a random (absorption) planning time problem where the absorption states are in fact not accessible (see section (4) earlier). Then let ϕ^x and ϕ^{-x} be the value of the objective at absorbing states $\pm x$. Evidently, the objective ϕ would be given by (4.91) above together with the requirement that

$$\lim_{x \to \pm\infty} = J^{\pm\infty} \tag{4.92}$$

which provides two additional equations for computing the constants implicit in equation (4.91).

4.3.6   Optimum Stopping Times

Optimum stopping time problems are classical applications of stochastic control and have been used profusely in statistics and management science. They have been used by Wald [68] in sequential analysis and in a large class of problems having to do with job search, and the economics of information acquisition (e.g., see Wilde [70], McCall [46]).

Wald's sequential analysis problem consists in reaching a decision about two courses of action, when the preference for one or the other involves uncertainty. Given a sample of n observations relating to these courses of action, the decision problem is stated as a "hypothesis testing" problem, where the sample size is the "stopping time" necessary to reach a decision.

Let X (a set of observations on R^n) be the observation (given by means of feedback in a decision making problem), and let a_1 and a_2 be the two actions we might follow, when the uncertainty in these actions is characterized by the probability distributions

$$f_1(x; a_1) \text{ and } f_2(x; a_2)$$

The "test" is the rule we adopt for selecting (based on X) one or the other distributions f_1 or f_2. The simplest such rule is

(i) if $x \in C$ choose f_1

(ii) if $x \in S - C$ choose f_2

where C is some set and S is the entire space. In this formulation a decision must be taken and the space of all possibilities is divided exactly into two parts, $(C, S - C)$. Note that x is a sample of information, or alternatively, it can represent the actual realization of a stochastic process. Say that C and $S - C$ are divided over time by a line as shown in Figure 4.1. Then, for x's above the line, we can choose a_1 (since $x \in C$) and for x's below the line we choose a_2 (since $x \in S - C$). If f_1 and f_2 are the costs to be incurred under both courses of actions, then if $EL_i(f_i), i = 1, 2$ is the expected loss under both actions, we have clearly

$$
\begin{array}{cccc}
\text{Choose action} & \text{if } E(L_1(f_1)) & < & E(L_2(f_2)) \\
a_1 & x & & x
\end{array}
$$

$$
\begin{array}{cccc}
\text{Choose action} & \text{if } E(L_1(f_1)) & \geq & E(L_2(f_2)) \\
a_2 & x & & x
\end{array}
$$

Or the best action is a solution of

$$\underset{a = (a_1, a_2)}{\text{Min}} \quad E\{L_1(f_1(x; a_1)), L_2(f_2(x; a_2))\}$$

In this case, we characterize the division of space by C and $S - C$. By the same token, if a decision has to be taken about stopping a process or not, we can define;

$f_1(x; a_1)$: cost of process if state x occurs and action a_1, a non stopping action, is taken

$f_2(x; a_2)$: cost of process if state x occurs and a stopping action a_2 is taken,

then the optimum solution a^* will clearly be

if $f_1(x; a_1) < f_2(x; a_2) \rightarrow a^* = a_1$

if $f_1(x; a_2) \geq f_2(x; a_2) \rightarrow a^* = a_2$

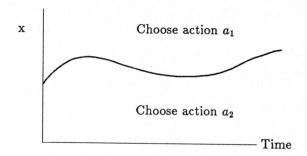

Figure 4.1: The Action Space

More generally, we can divide the space S into three regions C_1, C_2 and $S - C_1 - C_2$ and state

if $x \in C_1$, choose f_1
if $x \in C_2$, choose f_2
if $x \in S - C_1 - C_2$, continue sampling

The stopping time problem is then when to stop the process and reach a course of action. In Wald's terms, this is equivalent to stating how many (optimal) samples should be collected to reach a decision about a given set of competing hypotheses, while in our case, it amounts to asking "how long" should a process be left to persue its course of action until it is stopped. Of course, the procedure we shall follow in constructing the spaces $S - C$ and C for reaching a decision are quite different than Wald's since we shall use

Bellman's equation as an estimate of future costs (at a given time) compared
to the stopping cost of a process (at that same instant of time).

The job search problem on the other hand is a series of random (job)
wage offers $x_1, \ldots, x_n$, the job prospector obtains. For each job, the search
cost is c such that after n searches, the best offer is accepted and a cost of
nc is paid, or

$$Y_n = \max\{x_1, \ldots, x_n\} - nc$$

The problem is when to stop searching and select the best offer? In other
words, to select the stopping rule N such that

$$\max_N \{Y_N\}$$

This problem is solved as follows: let ε be the optimal gain (i.e., if we use
an optimal search); and let x be a recorded gain, then obviously,

if $x \geq \varepsilon$: accept the outcomes

if $x < \varepsilon$: reject the outcome and continue the search

As a result, the optimal gain is

$$E \, \max \, (x, \varepsilon) - c$$

Since ε is optimal

$$E \, \max \, (x, \varepsilon) - c = \varepsilon$$

and

$$c = E \, \max \, (x, \varepsilon) - \varepsilon$$

In other words, the optimum ε is a solution of the above equation which,
for a random density function $dF(x), x \in (-\infty, \infty)$ of job offers, is a solution
of

$$c = \int_\varepsilon^\infty (x - \varepsilon) dF(x) = H(\varepsilon), \text{ and } \varepsilon = H^{-1}(c)$$

The number ε is also called the reservation wage and the policy is called
the reservation wage policy and is another answer to our earlier problem of
dividing the decision space into $S - C$ and C. These simple ideas can be
used in dynamic programming formalism, as will be shown next.

Consider a dynamic process with a planning time T. The process can
be terminated beforehand however, at say, θ. For example, T might be
the natural time at which a machine is retired, while θ is the decision time
to retire the machine beforehand as its function and profitability becomes
apparent in practice. Thus, we define by $\text{Min}(T, \theta) \equiv T \wedge \theta$, the first instant
at which the machine is retired. In such a context we define the following
optimization problem:

$$\text{Min } J = E\{\int_0^{T \wedge \theta} \rho(y,s)ds + \Psi(y(\theta),\theta)\chi_{\theta<T} + G(T)\chi_{\theta<T}\}$$
$$\theta < T \tag{4.93}$$

Subject to:
$$dy = f(y,t) + \sigma(y,t)dw; \ y(0) = x;$$

Here ρ is the cost incurred during the operating time of the machine, Ψ is its cost if we change the machine prior to its final time T (at time θ) and G is the cost at the final time T. Finally f and σ are parameters in the machine's dynamics. Say that the machine is kept until time t, then we are in the special situation of sections (i), and

$$-\frac{\partial J}{\partial t} + FJ + \rho(x,s) = 0$$

where F is the Weiner process operator

$$F = f\frac{\partial}{\partial x} + \frac{1}{2}\sigma^2\frac{\partial^2}{\partial x^2}$$

At the final time

$$J(x,T) = G(x(T))$$

Assume that the process may be stopped and let $J(x,t)$ be the cost at time t (when there are $T - t$ periods to go) and the machine state is x. As in the "job search" example, we can at any time, stop the process and incur a cost Ψ or let the process continue its function. In the latter case, costs J evolve by the Bellman equation above, but this will occur if the cost-to-go at t will be smaller than the stopping cost $\Psi(x,t)$. This means that

$$-\frac{\partial J}{\partial t} + FJ + \rho(x,t) = 0; \ J < \Psi(x,t) \tag{4.94}$$

if the process is not stopped. At stopping time, however

$$J(x,\theta) = \Psi(x,\theta);$$
$$-\frac{\partial J}{\partial t} + FJ + \rho(x,t) \leq 0 \tag{4.95}$$

Thus, (4.94) and (4.95) together yield the desired Bellman equations.

4.3.7 Average Cost Criteria

Define by $\{x(t), t \geq 0\}$ the stochastic process (such as diffusion or jump processes) and let $u(t)$ be the controls. If $L(x,u)$ is the instantaneous cost then an average cost problem can be defined as follows:

$$J(u) = \min_{u\in U} \lim_{T\to\infty} \frac{1}{T}E\int_0^T L(x,u)dt \tag{4.96}$$

Such problems have been profusely used in the context of discrete time processes to resolve inventory control problems, queueing optimization, dispatching, etc., (see Bellman [7], Lanery [42] and Ross [55], [56] for example). Below we consider the continuous time average cost problem. Subsequently, we provide the dynamic programming equations for the discrete time problem.

The continuous time problem is intimately related to the long run discounted cost problem presented in section 4.3.5. This problem is defined as follows:

$$J^r(y) = \min_{u \in U} \int_0^\infty e^{-rt} L(x, u) dt; x(0) = y \tag{4.97}$$

where x is a stochastic process with operator F. For example, if x is a diffusion process defined by the following stochastic differential equation:

$$dx = f(x, u)dt + \sigma(x, u)dw; x(0) = y \tag{4.98}$$

then

$$F = f(x, u)\frac{d}{dx} + \frac{1}{2}\sigma^2(x, u)\frac{d^2}{dx^2} \tag{4.99}$$

and the dynamic programming equation corresponding to (4.97) is

$$rJ^r(y) = \min_{u \in U}\{FJ^r + L(x, u)\} \tag{4.100}$$

Of course, if x is a jump process, the operator F will be defined accordingly. Now assume that $rJ^r(y)$ as $r \to 0$ exists and equals a constant λ (see Robin [53] for a survey and tutorial).

$$\lambda = \lim_{r \to 0} rJ^r(y) \tag{4.101}$$

Next define a new variable $W^r(y)$ as follows:

$$W^r(y) = J^r(y) - J^r(0); W^r = 0 \tag{4.102}$$

and again assume that $W^r(y)$ exists and is continuous. Further consider

$$W(y) = \lim_{r \to 0} W^r(y) \tag{4.103}$$

Then by inserting (4.100) and (4.102) into (4.103) we can obtain an equation for $W(y)$ which is given in this case by:

$$\lambda = \min_{u \in U}\{FW(y) + L(y, u))\};$$

$$\tag{4.104}$$

$$W(0) = 0$$

Our next purpose is to prove that λ is the optimal average cost (4.96). To do so, consider $W(y)$ and apply to it Ito's differential rule. That is (in expectation)

$$E(dW) = EFW\,dt \qquad (4.105)$$

Integrate $E(dW)$ between $t = 0$ and $t = T$ then

$$E(W(T, x(T)) - W(y)) = E\int_0^T FW\,dt \qquad (4.106)$$

For optimal controls we add the Min sign to the above integral. From equation (4.104) we have however an expression for FW in terms of L and λ. Inserting (4.104) into (4.106) we obtain obviously

$$E(W(T, x(T)) - W(y)) = \lambda T - \min_{u \in U} \int_0^T L(x, u)\,dt$$

which is rearranged to yield:

$$\lambda = \frac{1}{T}\int_0^T L(x, u)\,dt + \frac{EW(T, x(T))}{T} - \frac{W(y)}{T} \qquad (4.107)$$

When $T \to \infty$, we are left in (4.107) with an average cost λ. Thus, following the intuitive treatment of the average cost problem we note that a solution is obtained by finding a pair (λ, W) where λ is a constant and W is a smooth function such that equation (4.104) is satisfied. If the W function is regular such that the Ito differential rule can be applied, then by (4.107) we see that λ is an average cost. Moreover, if we assume that a solution exists, we can solve first a discounted infinite time problem to obtain J^r then compute $rJ^r \to \lambda$. Thereafter, the solution for $W(x)$ can be obtained as specified by equation (4.104).

The results we have obtained here can be generalized easily to random time problems (i.e. T is replaced by $T\Lambda\tau$, where τ is a stopping absorption time). This will be done in 4.5.3 while solving a dispatching problem (a more complete treatment can be found in Robin and Tapiero [54]).

In discrete time, similar results can be obtained. For example, if the average cost is defined by:

$$\varphi(u) = \lim_{N \to \infty} \frac{1}{N}E\sum_{n=0}^N l(x_n, u_n) \qquad (4.108)$$

where x is given by a discrete time markov process, and

$$\lambda = \min_{u \in U} \varphi(u) \qquad (4.109)$$

If V^r is the discounted cost problem and if

$$V^r = \min_{u_n \in U} E \sum_{n=0}^{\infty} l(x_n, u_n)(1+n)^{-r} \qquad (4.110)$$

$$x(0) = y \; with$$
$$W(y) = \lim_{r \to 0}[V^r(y) - V^r(0)] \qquad (4.111)$$

Then the dynamic programming equation for the average cost problem is given by

$$\lambda + W(y) = \min_{u \in U}\{l(x, u) + rE_z W(z)\} \qquad (4.112)$$

where expectation is taken over the random states the process reaches from the state y. A formal treatment of the discrete time case can be found in Ross [57], p. 95.

4.3.8   Optimization with Reflection

The dynamic programming equations we obtain in this section will be derived by an application of the differential rule for reflected processes. This is given by equation (2.84) in chapter 2, section 2.6 (see also Mandl [45], Bensoussan and Lions [51]). Again, we proceed in an intuitive manner. Consider for example, the following objective

$$J(y) = \min_{u \in U} E \int_0^T L(x, u)dt + G(x(T)) \qquad (4.113)$$
$$x(0) = y, x \in R \text{ with } R \text{ a reflection boundary}$$

where x is a diffusion process for example. Further, assume that J is regular and at least twice differentiable in x and differentiable in time t. Then by equation (2.84) in 2.6, we have

$$\min_{u \in U}\{E(dJ) - E(FJdt) + E(\frac{\partial J}{\partial x}\gamma d\xi) = 0\} \qquad (4.114)$$

where $F = f\partial/\partial x + (\frac{1}{2})\sigma^2\partial^2/\partial x^2$. When x is off the boundary then as discussed in 2.6, $d\xi = 0$ and the dynamic programming equation is given by the "regular" (unreflected) equation $FJ - L = 0, J(x, T) = G(x, T)$. On the reflection boundary R, however, $d\xi \geq 0$ and therefore for (4.114) to hold, it is necessary that $\partial J/\partial x = 0$ which yields (if reflection is costless).

$$\frac{\partial J}{\partial x} = 0, x \in R \qquad (4.115)$$

when relection is costly, then as long as we are on the boundary the cost increases at a rate equalling the reflection cost, say α, or

$$\frac{\partial J}{\partial x} = \alpha, x \in R \qquad (4.116)$$

The boundary condition (4.115) (or (4.116)) provides an additional condition which is used for the dynamic programming equation when attempting to solve it.

4.4 *Impulsive Control*

Impulsive control problems provide solutions to management problems defined in continuous time, and on which only discrete time actions are exercised. For example, although a firm's production capacity process is continuous in time, the decision to expand capacity can be realized only at discrete instants of time. Of course, this particular decision structure arises not only from practical necessity but also since expansion costs are non-convex, and involve large fixed costs in expansion. In the past, such problems have been resolved by discretizing the continuous time process and by solving mixed (0,1) programming problems, where "1" might denote the decision to expand a facility. Such a procedure is, of course, an approximation of the real dynamic process and may involve a large number of variables if many discrete time states are used.

Alternatively, impulsive control may be used to control several processes with, say, a single controller. Then, costs of switching from one process to the other involve fixed costs, leading again to an impulsive control structure. As a case in point, we might consider a "machine robot", which has the capactiy to perform n tasks, which it can perform only one at a time. The decision problem is then, how to manage the machine such that it performs, over time, the required tasks, by minimizing some objective function, including the fixed switching costs. These problems can be handled by dynamic programming. Below we consider the case of optimum impulses. For further study refer to [14, 15, 17, 51].

In impulsive control, the objective function ϕ we computed previously by dynamic programming is no longer a solution of some differential equation but satisfy a set of inequalities and complementary slackness conditions. To understand these conditions we proceed as follows. At any one time, there may be two situations, either we apply an impulse policy, or we do not. Say that $\phi(x, s)$ is the optimal objective at time s with state $y(s) = x$. If at time $t = s$, it is optimal to apply an instantaneous control of say ξ, then at this time the state would also jump by ξ, and the objective ϕ would take on the value $\phi(x + \xi, s)$. To exert such an impulse, a cost is incurred. Let

$$c(\xi, s) \geq k > 0 \qquad (4.117)$$

be this impulse cost, where k is a fixed decision cost. Then at the impulse time, the optimum cost is given by

$$c(\xi, s) + \phi(x + \xi, s) \qquad (4.118)$$

Hence for an optimum impulse, we can state that

$$\phi(x,s) \leq \inf_{\xi}\{c(\xi,s) + \phi(x+\xi,s)\} = M\phi \qquad (4.119)$$

with the equality holding when the impulsive control is applied. Say that we do not apply an impulse control. In this case, ϕ will evolve as any one of the equations we have defined in the previous section, depending upon the kind of stochastic process used. Let these result (without impulsive control) in objective costs ϕ_1, then, clearly

$$\phi(x,s) \leq \phi_1(x,s)$$

$$\phi(x,s) \leq M\phi(x,s) \qquad (4.120)$$

where at least one of the above inequalities must hold with equality. This fact can be summarized by the following relation

$$[\phi - M\phi][\phi - \phi_1] \qquad (4.121)$$

Finally, we add the boundary condition:

$$\phi(x,T) = 0 \qquad (4.122)$$

It turns out that the set of relations (4.119) - (4.121) define the function ϕ in a unique way ([11]).

To obtain a solution we may proceed as follows. We set

$$C = \{x,s | \phi(x,s) < \phi_1(x,s)\} \qquad (4.123)$$

which is called the continuation set. Then define: $\theta_1 =$ first time after s when $y(\theta_1), \theta_1 \notin C$, $\xi_1 = \xi(y(\theta_1), \theta_1)$ where $\xi(x,s)$ is a function such that

$$\inf_{\xi}[c(\xi,s) + \phi(x+\xi,s)] = c(\xi(x,s),s) + \phi(x+\xi(x,s),s) \qquad (4.124)$$

This equation is the optimal objective function after the jump ξ. We may prove (Section [4.3.6]) that θ_1 is the first optimal impulse time and ξ_1, is the corresponding impulse. Repeating this procedure we may construct step by step the optimal impulse control W.

Similar arguments as those applied for the impulsive control policies can be applied to barrier or threshold policies. This will be shown by means of applications. We may therefore state that barrier policies are also impulsive policies. In both impulsive and barriers policies, the control is in effect an optimum stopping time as shown in Section 4.3 (vi) where the stopping time is either a decision (as in case of an impulsive control) or triggered by some conditions on the state of our system. Evidently, the trigger state can be optimal as well, reflecting the value of realizable competing trigger values from the objective point of view.

4.5   *Selected and Solved Problems*

The applications we shall consider here are based on some of the models in Chapter 3. In particular, we shall emphasize the analytical approach, and obtain solutions to specific problems.

4.5.1   Production Control

We consider a production control problem in discrete and continuous time, which we formulate in Table 4.2. The variables are defined by

t = time

x = inventory on hand at time $t(i)$

u = production at time $t(i)$

ξ_i = demand at time i, a random variable (discrete model)

D = mean demand rate

σ = standard deviation of demand in $dt(\xi dt = Ddt + \sigma dw)$

dw = standard Wiener process

T = planning horizon

$c(u)$ = production convex cost

$h(x)$ = inventory convex cost

U = production control constraint

X = constraint on inventory.

As a case in point, say that the objective is discounted and quadratic. Specifically, there is some desired production and inventory levels, deviations from which, we incur quadratic costs with (in continuous time)

$$\min_{u \geq 0} J \;=\; E \int_0^T [c(u - u_1)^2 + h(x - x_1)^2] e^{-rt} dt + gx(T) e^{-rT} \quad (4.125)$$

The dynamic programming equation and optimum controls are then given by:

$$0 \;=\; \max_{u \geq 0}\{-c(u - u_1)^2 - h(x - x_1)^2 + \frac{\partial J}{\partial t} + (u - D)\frac{\partial J}{\partial x} + \frac{1}{2}\sigma^2 \frac{\partial^2 J}{\partial x^2} - rJ\}$$

$$(4.126)$$

$$J(x, T) = gx(T); \quad u = \frac{1}{2c}\partial J/\partial x$$

Take $c = 1, h = 1, u_1 = 0, x_1 = 0$ for example and substitute the optimum control u into the Bellman equation which leads to (Sethi and Thompson [58]),

$$O = (\frac{\partial J}{\partial x})^2 \frac{1}{4} - x^2 + \frac{\partial J}{\partial t} - \frac{D\partial J}{\partial x} + \sigma^2 \frac{1}{2}\frac{\partial^2 J}{\partial x^2} - rJ \quad (4.127)$$

Table 4.2: A Production Problem

	Discrete Time	Continuous Time
Objective	Minimize $J_T = E\{\sum_{i=1}^{T-1}[c_i(u_i) + h_i(x_i)] + g(x_T)\}$	Minimize $J = E\{\int_0^T [c(u) + h(x)]dt + g(x(T))\}$
System	$x_{i+1} = x_i + u_i - \xi_i;$ $x_0 =$ given; $i = 1,...T-1$	$dx = (u - D)dt + \sigma dw$ $x(0) = x_0$
Constraints	$u_i \in U,\ x_i \in X, i = 1,...T$	$u \in U, x \in X$
Backward Dynamic Programming Equation	$J_n(x) = h_n(x) + Inf\{c_n(u_n) + J_{n+1}(x + u - \xi_{n+1})\}$ $u \in U, x \in X$	$J(x,t) = h(x) + Inf\{c(u) + J(x + dx, t + dt)\}$ $u \in U, x \in X$
Final Condition	$J_T(x) = g(x_T)$	$J(x,T) = g(x(T))$
Bellman's Equation		$(u - D)\frac{\partial J}{\partial x} + \frac{\sigma^2}{2}\frac{\partial^2 J}{\partial x^2} + c(u) + h(x) = -\frac{\partial J}{\partial t}$ $J(x,t) = g(x(T))$
Optimum Control	Min $\{c_n + J_{n+1}(x + u - \xi_{n+1})\}$ $u \in U$	Min $[u\frac{\partial J}{\partial x} + c(u)]$ $u \in U,\ x \in X$

Although this seems a complicated partial differential equation, it can be solved analytically (and numerically as it will be shown in Chapter 8). For $r = 0$, we can show that a solution is given by the quadratic form:

$$\phi(x,t) = Q(t)x^2 + R(t)x + M(t) \tag{4.128}$$

with $\partial\phi/\partial t = x^2 dQ/dt + x dR/dt = dM/dt$ and $\partial\phi/\partial x = 2Qx + R$, $\partial^2\phi/\partial x^2 = 2Q$. By inserting these into the partial differential equation, an ordering of terms leads to:

$$x^2[\dot{Q} + Q^2 - 1] + x[\dot{R} + RQ - 2DQ] + \dot{M} + R^2/4 - RD + \sigma^2 Q = 0 \tag{4.129}$$

which holds for all x's. Thus, for a solution we require that Q, R and M satisfy;

$$\begin{aligned} \dot{Q} &= 1 - Q^2; \ Q(T) = 0 \\ \dot{R} &= 2DQ - RQ; \ R(T) = B \\ \dot{M} &= RD - R^2/4 - \sigma^2 Q; \ M(T) = 0 \end{aligned} \tag{4.130}$$

A solution of these ordinary differential equations is straightforward and leads to

$$Q = (y - 1)/(y + 1), \ \text{where } y = e^{2(t-T)} \tag{4.131}$$

For $D =$ a constant,

$$R = 2D + [2(g - 2D)\sqrt{y}]/(y + 1) \tag{4.132}$$

and

$$M(t) = -\int_t^T [RD - R^2/4 - \sigma^2 Q]\,dt \tag{4.133}$$

since

$$u^* = \frac{1}{2}\frac{\partial\phi}{\partial x} = Qx + \frac{R}{2} = D + \frac{(y+1)x + (q - 2D)\sqrt{y}}{y + 1} \tag{4.134}$$

which means that the optimum production rate equals the mean demand, plus a correction term, depending upon the level of inventory on hand. If $r \geq 0$, and the planning horizon is infinite $T \to \infty$ then the Bellman equation is reduced to a simple ordinary differential equation

$$\frac{1}{4}\left(\frac{d\phi}{dx}\right)^2 - x^2 - D\frac{d\phi}{dx} + \frac{1}{2}\sigma^2\left(\frac{d^2\phi}{dx^2}\right) - r\phi = 0 \tag{4.135}$$

This is a Riccatti differential equation whose solution can be verified to be quadratic with (for $D =$ constant),

$$\begin{aligned} Q &= (r - \sqrt{r^2 + 4})/2 = m_1 \\ R &= 2D(rm_1 + 1) \\ M &= [m_1^2 D^2(m_1^2 - 2) + \sigma^2 m_1]/r \end{aligned} \tag{4.136}$$

The optimal production rate is also

$$u^* = m_1^2 D + m_1 x \qquad (4.137)$$

which is a weighted function of the current demand and inventory on hand. Now consider the discrete time problem and interpret it as a discretization of the continuous time problem. Specifically, consider the following problem:

$$\min J = E\{\sum_{i=1}^{N} c(u_i - u^*)^2 + h(x_i - x^*)^2 + B(x_{N+1})\} \qquad (4.138)$$

subject to

$$x_{i+1} = [x_i + u_i - D_i] + \sigma_i \xi_i; \quad x_s > 0$$

$$(4.139)$$

$$x_i \in X; u_i \in U, \quad i = 1, 2, ..., N$$

where ξ_i is a zero mean, unit variance random variable, X and U are constraint sets on the inventory and production levels respectively. The recursive equation of dynamic programming is clearly with $r = 0$; (see Table 4.2);

$$J_n(x) = h(x - x^*)^2 + \inf_{u \in U, x \in X}\{c(u - u^*)^2 + J_{n+1}(x_{n+1})\}; \qquad (4.140)$$

$$J_{N+1} = B(x_{N+1})$$

where x_{n+1} is the inventory at the next stage, which is given by the production inventory dynamics, or

$$J_n(x) = h(x - x^*)^2 + \inf_{u \in U, x \in X}\{c(u - u^*)^2 + J_{n+1}(x + u - D + \sigma\xi)\} \qquad (4.141)$$

with all variables calculated at the appropriate state n. Assuming that the inventory constraint set is not effective, the optimum production level is given by solving at each stage, the single variate optimization problem:

$$\min_{u \in U} c(u - u^*)^2 + J_{n+1}(x + u - D + \sigma\xi) \qquad (4.142)$$

whose solution can be found analytically only in a very limited number of cases. To obtain numerical results, we proceed recursilvely by starting (in case of backward dynamic programming) at the last stage. Or, at

At N+1   (4.143)
$$J_{N+1} = EB(x_{N+1}) = EB(x_N + u_N - D_N + \sigma_N \xi)$$
with solution $u_N^0(x_N)$

In other words, the above equation is one equation in one unknown u_N which can be solved for a given value of x_N. Quantitatively, if x_N can take on 10 values, then there will be 10 "production solutions" corresponding to each one of the values. In this case, the optimum (production) decision is conditioned by the (inventory) information on hand at the decision stage, which is what we have called in Chapters 1 and 5, "feedback".

At x=N

$$J_N = E\{h(x_{N-1} - x^*)^2 + \inf_{u \in U}[c(u_{N-1} - u^*)^2 + J_{N+1}(x_N)]\}$$

$$(4.144)$$

or, inserting J_{N+1}, calculated earlier,

$$
\begin{aligned}
J_N &= E\{h(x_{N-1} - x^*)^2 + \inf[c(u_{N-1} - u^*)^2 \\
&\quad + B(x_N + u_N^0(x_N) - D_N + \sigma_N \xi)]\}
\end{aligned}
\qquad (4.145)
$$

or

$$
\begin{aligned}
J_N &= E\{h(x_{N-1} - x^*)^2 + \inf[c(u_{N-1} - u^*)^2 \\
&\quad + B(x_{N-1} + u_{N-1} - D_{N-1} + \sigma_{N-1}\xi) \\
&\quad + u_N^0(x_{N-1} + u_{N-1} - D_{N-1} + \sigma_{N-1}\xi) - D_N + \sigma_N \xi)]\}
\end{aligned}
\qquad (4.146)
$$

which is again an equation to optimize for the production level u_{N-1}, which leads to

$$u_{N-1} = u_{N-1}^0(x_{N-1}; u_N^0)$$

By repeating this procedure, we obtain again and again one equation in one unknown, the production decision. If it can be found analytically, then of course, the solution is readily specified at each stage of the decision process. If not, some numerical technique has to be applied.

Finally, repeating this procedure, we obtain a solution for the optimum production levels which can be summarized by a table such as the one below, where all states have been reduced by transformation to be in the [0,1] state space definition

The operational meaning of such a solution is simply:

"If you observe an information inventory level $x \in [0,1]$, the optimum (production) decision at the nth stage (or $N - n$ stages before the end of optimization), is given by $u_n^0(x)$."

In this sense, Table 4.2, is a Production Decision Table which prescribes clearly what to produce and when. Over time, inventory levels attained and

Table 4.3: The Optimal Control

		1	2	......	N
Stage					
	0	$u_1^0(0)$	$u_2^0(0)$	......	$u_N^0(0)$
State	.1	$u_1^0(.1)$	$u_2^0(.1)$	......	$u_N^0(.1)$
	⋮	⋮	⋮	⋮	⋮
	1	$u_1^0(1)$	$u_2^0(1)$	......	$u_N^0(1)$

costs incurred will be random and given by a solution (in case of inventory) of the stochastic difference equation:

$$x_{i+1} = x_i + u_i^0(x_i) - D_i + \sigma_i \xi; \quad x_0 = \text{ given} \qquad (4.147)$$

which is subject to the uncontrollable events implicit in the random variable ξ. Thus, to obtain uncertain realizations of costs and inventories, we turn to simulation. In Chapter 8, we shall return to the numerical aspects of such problems. It should be clear however that a decision table together with simulation provide the possibility of assessing optimum plans.

(ii) The (s, S) Inventory Problem

We shall resolve below the well known (s,S) inventory problem (e.g., see [17], [62]) by an application of impulsive control arguments. Quantitatively, the problem is defined by:

$$\min J(x, s) = E\{\int_0^\infty e^{-rt} f(x)dt + \sum (k + cu_i)e^{-r\tau_i}\} \qquad (4.148)$$
$$\{u_i, \tau_i, i = 1, 2, ...\}$$

subject to

$$dx = -Ddt + \sigma dw + \sum_i u_i \delta(t - \tau_i)$$

where $Ddt + \sigma dw$ is the randon (normal) demand in dt, x is the inventory, $u_i, \tau_i; i = 1, 2, ...,$ is the impulse policy with u_i denoting the quantity ordered and τ_i the order time. The cost $f(x)$ includes both the holding and shortage inventory costs such that:

$$f(x) = \begin{cases} -px & \text{if } x < 0 \\ qx & \text{if } x \geq 0 \end{cases} \qquad (4.149)$$

Finally, k is the fixed ordering cost, c is the variable ordering cost and r is the discount rate. Application of section 4.4, leads to

$$A\phi \le f(x); \phi \le M\phi \qquad (4.150)$$

where

$$A\phi = -\frac{1}{2}\sigma^2\frac{d^2\phi}{dx^2} + D\frac{d\sigma}{dx} + r\phi$$

$$M\phi = k + \inf_{u\ge 0}\{cu + \phi(x+u)\} \qquad (4.151)$$

where one of the two (at least) inequalities above holds with equality. In addition, because of the infinite horizon, we require the convergence of ϕ.

If we impose an (s, S) inventory policy as in Figure 4.2, then the impulsive policy is in fact triggered by the (s, S) barriers.

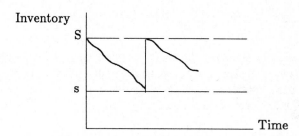

Figure 4.2: The (s, S) Policy

Specifically, when $x = s$, we order $S - s$ (the impulse size) bringing us back to the S inventory level. This means that at $x = s$,

$$\phi(s) = k + c(S - s) + \phi(S) \qquad (4.152)$$

and for optimum S:

$$\frac{d\phi}{dx} = -c \text{ at } x = S \qquad (4.153)$$

when $x \le S$, we solve the differential equation $A\phi = f(x)$ which is given by

$$\phi(x) = \frac{1}{\lambda_1 - \lambda_2}\{\frac{2}{\sigma^2}\int_s^x f(\tau)\exp[-\lambda_1(x-\tau)] - \exp[-\lambda_2(x-\tau)]\}d\tau$$

$$\qquad (4.154)$$

$$+[c - \lambda_2\phi(s)]\exp[-\lambda_1(x-s)] - [c - \lambda_1\phi(s)]\exp[-\lambda_2(x-s)]\}$$

where λ_1 and λ_2 are roots given by

$$\lambda_i = -D/\sigma^2 \pm \sqrt{D^2/\sigma^4 + 2r/\sigma^2}$$

$$i = 1, 2$$

(4.155)

A further condition (due to the infinity of the horizon) is a sublinear growth as $x \to \infty$ or (see Section 4.3),

$$\lim_{x \to \infty} \frac{\phi(x)}{f(x)} < \infty$$

(4.156)

which ensures convergence of ϕ. When $x \geq 0$, integration yields:

$$
\begin{aligned}
\phi(z) &= e^{-\lambda_2(x-s)} \frac{\lambda_1}{\lambda_2} [p(1 - \lambda_2 s) - (p + q)e^{-\lambda_2 s}] + \lambda_1 \phi(s) - c \\
&\quad + e^{\lambda_1(x-s)} \frac{p\lambda_2}{r}(\frac{1}{\lambda_1} - s) - \lambda_2 \phi(s) + c \\
&\quad - \frac{\lambda_2}{\lambda_1 r}(p + q)e^{-\lambda_1} - q\frac{(\lambda_1 - \lambda_2)}{r}(\frac{D}{r} - x)
\end{aligned}
$$

(4.157)

But as indicated earlier , as $x \to \infty$, ϕ must converge so that the term multiplying $exp[-\lambda_2(x - s)]$ should equal zero (otherwise ϕ diverges), or

$$\phi(s) = \frac{c}{\lambda_1} - \frac{1}{\lambda_2}[p(1 - \lambda_2 s) - (p + q)e^{\lambda_2 s}]$$

(4.158)

Replacing (4.158)into (4.157) we obtain (4.159);

$$
\begin{aligned}
\phi(s) &= \frac{q}{r}(x - \frac{D}{r}) + \frac{1}{\lambda_1}(c - \frac{p}{r})e^{-\lambda_1(x-s)} \\
&\quad + \frac{(p + q)}{r(\lambda_1 - \lambda_2)} e^{-\lambda_1 x}(e^{(\lambda_1 - \lambda_2)s} - \frac{\lambda_2}{\lambda_1})
\end{aligned}
$$

(4.159)

Finally, for $s \leq x < 0$, the solution of our equation (together with the boundary condition $d\phi(s)/dx = -C$) is

$$
\begin{aligned}
\phi(x) &= \frac{p}{r}(\frac{D}{r} - x) + \frac{1}{\lambda_1}(c - \frac{p}{r})e^{-\lambda_1(x-s)} \\
&\quad + \frac{(p + q)}{r(\lambda_1 - \lambda_2)} e^{-\lambda_2 s}[e^{-\lambda_1(x-s)} - \frac{\lambda_1}{\lambda_2}e^{-\lambda_2(x-s)}]
\end{aligned}
$$

(4.160)

Since x is unbounded from above, the term in $e^{-\lambda_2 x}$ vanishes in order to satisfy (4.156). As a result, we obtain that the (s, S) inventory policy is a solution of a simple sytem of two equations, or (Sulem [61])

$$S = \frac{(-p + cr)s + \frac{p+q}{\lambda_2}(1 - e^{-\lambda_2 s} - kr)}{q + rc}$$

$$e^{\lambda_1 S} = \frac{(-p + cr)e^{\lambda_1 S} + \frac{p+q}{\lambda_1 - \lambda_2}[\lambda_1 e^{(\lambda_1 - \lambda_2)s} - \lambda_2]}{q + rc}$$

(4.161)

The existence and uniqueness of a solution is guaranteed for such equations if $-p + rc < 0$. Now assume that instead, we consider an average cost objective

$$\bar{\phi} = \lim_{T \to \infty} \frac{1}{T}\int_0^T f(x)dt + \sum_i (k + cu_i)$$

(4.162)

Then, by Section 4.3, (ii) we have

$$\bar{\phi} = \lim_{r \to 0} r\phi$$

(4.163)

Thus, the optimum (s, S) inventory policy is

$$S = \frac{ps}{q} - \frac{(p+q)}{2Dq}\sigma^2[1 - \exp(-2Ds/\sigma^2)]$$

(4.164)

and

$$\frac{e^{-\lambda_2 s}}{\lambda_2}[\frac{p}{\lambda_2} - (p+q)s - \frac{(p+q)}{2\lambda_2} exp(\lambda_2 s)]$$

$$-\frac{1}{2}s^2 + \frac{p}{\lambda_2}s - \frac{q}{\lambda^2} + \frac{kDq}{k+q} = 0$$

(4.165)

where $\lambda_2 = -2D/\sigma^2$. Finally, when demand is deterministic, $\sigma \to 0$, and it can be verified that,

$$S = \frac{2pDK}{q(p+q)}; \quad s = -\sqrt{\frac{2qDK}{p(p+q)}}$$

(4.166)

while the inventory average cost is

$$CD + \sqrt{\frac{2qDK}{p(p+q)}}$$

(4.167)

To conclude, if we were to consider of Poisson demands with mean ρ and let these demand have the probability distribution $p(z)$, and use an (s, S) policy, we will then obtain in a stationary environment

$$-\rho \int_0^\infty [\phi(x + z) - \phi(x)]p(z)dz + r\phi(x) = f(x)$$

$$\phi(s) = \phi(S) + k + c(S - s)$$

$$\phi'(s) = -c, \phi'(S) = -c, S > s$$

(4.168)

Convergence of ϕ as $x \to \infty$

A complete treatment of these equations will lead to a solution of our problem. Evidently, such a solution will be analytical if explicit solutions for ϕ can be found, otherwise some numerical scheme will be necessary.

(iv) Optimal Production Sequence

Vickson [64], following a paper by New [47] suggested and solved a dynamic approach to "sequential production drifting off schedule because of random variations in job processing times." The purpose of vickson's paper (and this example) are twofold; first to solve continuous approximation operational job processing problems and second to consider a dynamic problem defined with respect to other variables than time. For example, a process can be defined in terms of production levels, experience and so on. Time, as a dimension along which a process is defined becomes then implicit, rather than explicit as we have assumed it throughout the book.

To make these points clear, say that $\bar{t} > 0$ is an expected processing time per job on a machine, when no attemp is made to supervise and control the production process, and let σ^2 be its processing time variance. The completion of the n first jobs would require (without controls and assuming that jobs processing times are independent) an amount of time given by a random variable z, where $E(z) = \bar{t}n$ and $var(z) = n\sigma^2$. If we define the Wiener process with $w(0) = 0, E(x(n)) = 0$ and $var(x(n)) = n$, then the completion time of the n first jobs, or $T(n)$ is written as follows

$$T(n) = \bar{t}n - \sigma w(n) \tag{4.169}$$

In differential form, we can write instead

$$dT(n) = \bar{t}dn - \sigma dw(n); x(0) = 0 \tag{4.170}$$

The controller can expedite production using faster machine speeds, overtime labor or simpler means. Thus, a job can have its expected processing time reduced from $\bar{t}$ to $\bar{t} - u$ where $u \in [0, r], (r < \bar{t})$ is a control variable. For a discrete job model the total reduction in expected processing time for the first n jobs due to accelerated production would be $U(n) = \sum_{k=1}^{n} u_k$ where u_k is the processing time reduction for the kth job. In continuous approximation this is given as follows:

$$U(n) = \int_0^n u(\tau)d\tau; u \in [0, r] \tag{4.171}$$

where $U(n)$ expresses the total overtime and $u(n)$ is the overtime rate of n. Now if we set

$$x(n) = T(n) - n\bar{t} \tag{4.172}$$

the deviation from expected processing time, we have (with overtime) the following equation

$$x(n) = x + \int_0^n u(\tau)d\tau + \int_0^n \sigma dw(\tau) \tag{4.173}$$

or, in differential form,

$$dx(n) = u(n)dn + \sigma dw(n); x(0) = x \tag{4.174}$$

Finally, if the down-time of the machine is given by $Z(n)$, then

$$dx(n) = u(n)dn - dZ(n) + \sigma dw(n) \tag{4.175}$$

Although Vickson analyses the problem with the downtime of the machine, we shall in our example avoid it. The costs to be considered consist for simplicity of the following: a linear cost $cu(c > 0)$, and an operating cost incurred when production takes place off-schedule. This has the form $K(x)$:

$$K(x) = \begin{cases} -kx, x < 0 \\ px, x \geq 0 \end{cases} \tag{4.176}$$

with $k \geq p > 0$. Explicitly, if we consider an average cost policy, given by solution of

$$\phi = \min \lim_{N \to \infty} \frac{1}{N} \int_0^N [cu + K(x)]dn \tag{4.177}$$

Following Section (vii) compute an optimal policy by finding a g and a $\phi(.)$ such that:

$$\frac{\sigma^2}{2} \frac{d^2\phi}{dx^2} + K(x) - g + \min_{u \in [0,r]} u(c + \frac{d\phi}{dx}) = 0 \tag{4.178}$$

where g is the average cost value and $\phi(x)$ is the relative value function in the sense that $\phi(x) - \phi(0)$ is the infinite horizon total cost difference between optimally controlled processes starting in states x and 0. Minimizing with respect to u we have

$$u = \begin{cases} r \text{ if } c + \dfrac{d\phi}{dx} < 0 \\[3mm] 0 \text{ if } c + \dfrac{d\phi}{dx} > 0 \end{cases} \tag{4.179}$$

which leads to an equation we can write in the following form:

$$\frac{\sigma^2}{2} \frac{d^2\phi}{dx^2} + K(x) - g = 0 \text{ if } c + \frac{d\phi}{dx} > 0$$

$$\tag{4.180}$$

$$\frac{\sigma^2}{2} \frac{d^2\phi}{dx^2} + r\frac{d\phi}{dx} + (rc + K(x) - g) = 0 \text{ if } c + \frac{d\phi}{dx} < 0$$

These equations, once integrated, involve 4 constants, 2 of which can be found as stated earlier while the remaining two are found by continuity of the objective function when we switch from no control to control. At this point $x = x^*$

$$\phi(x^{*-}) = \phi(x^{*+})$$
$$\frac{d\phi}{dx}(x^{*-}) = \frac{d\phi}{dx}(x^{*+}) \tag{4.181}$$
$$\frac{d\phi}{dx}(x^{*+}) = -c$$

which provides, 3 more equations, the added one being for a solution of x^*. As a result, a solution of u can be written as follows,

$$u(n) = \begin{cases} r \text{ if } x > x^* \\ 0 \text{ if } x \le x^* \end{cases} \tag{4.182}$$

Solution of our problem requires analytical integration of the dynamic programming equation above. This is an easy task, if we write (on the basis of the physical characteristics of the problem):

$$\begin{cases} \dfrac{\sigma^2}{2}\dfrac{d^2\phi}{dx^2} + K(x) - g = 0 \text{ if } x < x^* \\[4mm] \dfrac{\sigma^2}{2}\dfrac{d^2\phi}{dx^2} + \dfrac{d\phi}{dx} + rc + K(x) - g = 0 \text{ if } x.x^* \end{cases} \tag{4.183}$$

and the continuity requirement equations at $x = x^*$.

4.5.2   Queueing Optimization

Here We shall consider a special queueing stochastic control problem. Assume that n, the number of persons in a queueing system is regulated by a birth-death process so that in a small time interval Δt

$$\Delta n = \begin{cases} +1 & \text{w.p. } \lambda(n,u)\Delta t \\ -1 & \text{w.p. } \xi(n,v)\Delta t \\ 0 & \text{w.p. } [1 - \lambda\Delta t - \xi\Delta t] \end{cases} \tag{4.184}$$

with u and v, two control variables, which can be used to regulate the inflow rate λ and the service rate ξ respectively. We shall define three types of costs $c_0(n)$ = the cost of having n persons, $c_1(u)$ = cost of influencing inflow and $c_2(v)$ = cost of control in service. Over a finite period of time $(0, T)$ and discount rate r, the objective is to minimize

$$J = E\int_0^T e^{-rt}[c_0(n) + c_1(v)]dt \tag{4.185}$$

Define the optimum cost as follows

$$W = \inf_{u,v} J \tag{4.186}$$

then the Dynamic Programming equation is given by (see Section 4.3, (ii))

$$
\begin{aligned}
\frac{\partial W}{\partial t} + \min_{u,v}\{ & W(n+1,t)\lambda(n,u) + W(n-1,t)\xi(n,v) \\
& -W(n,t)(\lambda(n,u) + \xi(n,v)) + c_0(n) + c_1(u) + c_2(v))\} - rW = 0 \\
& W(n,T) = 0
\end{aligned}
\tag{4.187}
$$

which we can rewrite as follows:

$$
\begin{aligned}
\frac{\partial W}{\partial t} + \min_{u,v}\{ & [\lambda(n,u)\Delta W(n,t) - \xi(n,v)\Delta W(n-1,t)] \\
& c_0(n) + c_1(u) + c_2(v)\} - rW = 0 \\
& W(n,T) = 0
\end{aligned}
\tag{4.188}
$$

Special cases, assuming λ and ξ have known functional forms, c_0, c_1, c_2 known and specified domains of n ($n \geq 0$, or $0 \leq n \geq N$) may be considered as well. Consider the simplest possible case: $\lambda(n,u) = \alpha u$ and $\xi(n,v) = \beta v$, and $c_0(n) = n, c_1(u) = u^2, c_2(v) = v^2$, then if $T \to \infty$, we have

$$\min[\alpha u \Delta W(n) - \beta v \Delta W(n-1) + n + u^2 + v^2] - rW = 0 \tag{4.189}$$

Take derivatives with respect to u and v and obtain

$$u^* = -\frac{\alpha}{2}\Delta W(n,t); \quad v^* = +\frac{\beta}{2}\Delta W(n-1,t) \tag{4.190}$$

Inserting into our equation above we have

$$-\frac{\alpha^2}{4}\Delta W^2(n) - \frac{\beta^2}{4}\Delta W^2(n-1) + n - rW(n) = 0 \tag{4.191}$$

which is a non-linear difference equation which could be solved.

Assume further that $n \geq 0$, so that we obviously have a reflection at $n = 0$. In this case;

$$\frac{\partial W}{\partial t} + \min_{u}\{\lambda(0,u)\Delta W(0,t) + c_0(0) + c_1(u)\} = 0 \tag{4.192}$$

In stationary states $\partial W/\partial t = 0$ and therefore, we have (for continuous λ and c in u):

$$\frac{\partial \lambda(0,u)}{\partial c_1(u)} = \Delta W(0,t) \text{ at } n = 0 \tag{4.193}$$

In other words, whenever we reach the lower boundary $n = 0$, we stop the "service process" and activate the "arrival process". Similary, when u is constrained from above by a capacity M, then

$$n \leq M \tag{4.194}$$

and we obtain a reflection at $n = M$. In this case,

$$O = \frac{\partial W}{\partial t} + \min_v \{-\xi(M,v)\Delta W((M-1),t) + c_0(M) + c_2(v) - rW\} \tag{4.195}$$

which in stationary state is reduced to (for continuous ξ and c_2 in v):

$$+ \frac{\partial \xi / \partial v}{\partial c_2 / \partial v} = \Delta W(M-1) \tag{4.196}$$

In the special linear-quadratic cost case we pointed out earlier, we have

$$u = -\alpha/2\Delta W(n) \text{ at } n = 0$$
$$\tag{4.197}$$
$$v = \beta/2\Delta W(n-1) \text{ at } n = M-1$$

Or at $n = 0$

$$\frac{\alpha^2}{2} + \frac{\alpha^2}{4} / [\Delta W(0)]^2 = rW(0) \tag{4.198}$$

and at $n = M$

$$-\frac{\beta^2}{2} + \frac{\beta^2}{4} / [\Delta W(M-1)]^2 = rW(M) \tag{4.199}$$

Combining these equations together with the stationary Bellman equation, we obtain a system of difference equations we can resolve numerically.

Both for a computational and analytical treatment of queueing problems, approximations as pointed out in Chapter 3, are made. Consider as a special case the machine interference problem, consisting of N machines, each breaking down at a known rate λ. Thus if x denotes the number of failed machines, we have a (birth) breakdown rate $\lambda(N - x)dt$. Let the machines (death) repair rate be

$$\xi = \frac{(\alpha x + \beta N)}{\gamma x + N} N \tag{4.200}$$

and $x = 0, 1, 2, \ldots, N$. This rate includes various well known problems as special cases. For example, for $\beta = 0, \gamma = 0$, we obtain $\xi = \alpha x$, an exponential repair rate when there are sufficient repairmen. For $x = 0, \lambda_0 = \lambda N$ and $\xi_0 = 0$. For large N, it is possible to replace the above stochastic process by a diffusion approximation (as was shown by Arnold [3]). To do so, the mean evolution of the stochastic dynamic process is defined first and the deviations from this mean are approximated by the diffusion. Such an approach was explicitly followed by Karmeshu and Jaiswal [35]. In our case, the superposition of the arrival and repair process is given by:

$$dx = \{\lambda(N - x) - \frac{N(\alpha x + \beta N)}{\gamma x + N}\}dt$$

$$+\sqrt{\lambda(N - x)}dw_1(t) - \sqrt{\frac{N(\alpha x + \beta N)}{\gamma x + N}}dw_2(t)$$

(4.201)

where $\{w_1, w_2, t \geq 0\}$ are two dimensional Wiener processes, mutually independent. Define now:

$$x(t) = N\phi(t) + \sqrt{N}y(t)$$

(4.202)

where $\phi(t)$ is a deterministic component, and $y(t)$ a stochastic one. Then instead of dx above, write

$$d\phi = [\lambda(1 - \phi) - \frac{(\beta + \alpha\phi)}{1 + \gamma\phi}]dt$$

$$dy = [\lambda + \frac{(\alpha - \beta\gamma)}{(1 + \gamma\phi)^2}]ydt + \sqrt{\lambda(1 - \phi)}dw_1 - \sqrt{\frac{\beta + \alpha\phi}{1 + \gamma\phi}}dw_2$$

(4.203)

where ϕ is the mean value of x and y is the random fluctuation around x. The Fokker-Planck equation of this process is clearly

$$\frac{\partial P}{\partial t} = -[\frac{d}{d\phi}A_1(\phi)]\frac{\partial}{\partial y}(yP) + \frac{1}{2}B_1(\phi)\frac{\partial^2 P}{\partial y^2}$$

where

$$A_1(\phi) = \{\lambda - \beta + (\lambda\gamma - \lambda - \alpha)\phi - \lambda\gamma\phi^2\}/(1 + \gamma\phi)$$

$$B_1(\phi) = \{\lambda + \beta + (\lambda\gamma - \lambda - \alpha)\phi - \lambda\gamma\phi^2\}/(1 + \gamma\phi)$$

(4.204)

When, at time zero, $P(y, 0) = \delta(y)$, a solution for P can be checked to be:

$$P(y, t) = \frac{1}{\sigma_y\sqrt{2\pi}} exp[-y^2/2\sigma_y^2];$$

$$\sigma_y^2(t) = A_1^2(\phi)\int_{\phi_0}^{\phi(t)}[B_1(\mu)/A_1^3(\mu)]d\mu$$

(4.205)

Since $x = N\phi + y\sqrt{N}$, we necessarily obtain

$$P(x,t) = \frac{1}{\sigma_y^2\sqrt{2\pi N}} \exp\{-\frac{(x - N\phi)^2}{2\sigma_x^2 N}\} \qquad (4.206)$$

Using this approximation, many special cases can be obtained. For example if $\gamma = 0, \lambda_x = \lambda(N - x)$ and $\xi_x = \alpha x + \beta N$. Then

$$N\phi = \frac{n(\lambda - \beta)}{\lambda + \alpha} + N exp((-\lambda + \alpha)t)[\phi_0 - (\lambda - \beta)/(\lambda + \alpha)] \qquad (4.207)$$

and

$$\begin{aligned} \sigma_x^2(t) &= N\sigma_y^2(t) \\ &= \frac{N\{\lambda^2 + \alpha\beta + (\alpha^2 - \beta^2)\phi - e^{-2(\lambda+\alpha)t}[\lambda^2 + \alpha\beta + (\alpha^2 - \beta^2)\phi_0\}}{(\lambda + \alpha)^2} \end{aligned}$$

$$(4.208)$$

Evidently, other cases can be obtained by changing the assumption regarding the transition probabilities λ_x and ξ_x. The advantage of this approximation is that it does not necessitate a reflection boundary (to correct the possibility of the Wiener process moving the queue process into a physically unrealizable situation). Of course, this would be the case, as long as the mean state of the queue is "far" from zero - the natural boundary. The design of machine interference problems requires both the definition of the parameters to be controlled as well as the design objective. These problems are left as exercises however.

Finally, it shall be pointed out that the queueing literature has had abundant continuous approximations used in computer network and jobs processing problems. Some notable references are [25, 36, 37, 51, 67]. The application of stochastic control techniques to design queues has lagged however. Notable exceptions are Bremaud [21, 22] as well as Robin [51,52]. To demonstrate an application of stochastic control to a queueing problem we consider next an M servers queue, approximated by a diffusion.

(i) *A Queue Approximation*
Consider a queue with M servers whose mean service time is μ and the variance is σ_s^2, and let the (persons, jobs, etc.) arrival rate have a mean of λ and variance σ_a^2. Let $\{x, t \geq 0\}$ be the queue's length, define a stochastic process. Halachmi and Franta have approximated this queueing problem by a diffusion approximation which we reproduce below:

$$dx = [\lambda - \mu\min(x, M)]dt + [\lambda^2\sigma_a^2 + \mu^3\sigma_s^2 \, min(x, M)]^{1/2}dw \qquad (4.209)$$

where $(w(0) = 0)dw$ is a standard Wiener process. Say that for such a queue with M servers, we associate a cost of $k + Q(M)$ (including the fixed cost k of service stations and the wages of servers $Q(M)$ for the period of interest). Further, let cx, be the waiting time cost per person expressing the weight of "quality of service". For a planning horizon $[0, T]$, the total expected cost is:

$$J = E\{\int_0^T cxdt + k + Q(M)\} \qquad (4.210)$$

and by dynamic programming, we have the following cost:

$$\frac{\partial J}{\partial t} = [\lambda - \min(x, M)\mu]\frac{\partial J}{\partial x} +$$
$$+ \frac{1}{2}[\lambda^3\sigma_a^3 + \mu^3\sigma_s^2 \min(x, M)]\frac{\partial^2 J}{\partial x^2} + Cx \qquad (4.211)$$
$$J(x, T) = k + Q(M)$$

This equation can be solved by separating the state space into two regions, $x < M$ and $x \geq M$ and by imposing continuity requirements for J at $x = M$. Thus, the expected cost is

$$-\frac{\partial J}{\partial t} = [\lambda - \mu x]\frac{\partial J}{\partial x} + \frac{1}{2}[\lambda^3\sigma_a^2 + x\mu^3\sigma_s^2]\frac{\partial^2 J}{\partial x^2} + cx; \ x \leq M$$
$$(4.212)$$
$$-\frac{\partial J}{\partial t} = (\lambda - M\mu)\frac{\partial J}{\partial x} + \frac{1}{2}[\lambda^3\sigma_a^2 + M\mu^3\sigma_s^2]\frac{\partial^2 J}{\partial x^2} + cx; x \geq M$$

The boundary conditions are
(1) At $t = T, J(x, T) = k + Q(M)$

(2) At $x = M$

$$\frac{\partial J(M^-, t)}{\partial x} = \frac{\partial J(M^+, t)}{\partial x}$$
$$(4.213)$$
$$J(M^-, t) = J(M^+, t)$$

A solution to these equations will provide therefore a means against which the cost of waiting (c) can be contrasted against the cost of service ($Q(M)$) in selecting the optimum number of servers.

If we impose, a reflection boundary at $x = 0$, then by Section 4.3.8, we have in addition the following constraint at $x = 0$;

$$\frac{\partial J(t, 0)}{\partial x} = 0 \qquad (4.214)$$

4.5.3 Vehicle Dispatching

We return to the impulsive vehicle dispatching problem considered in Section 3.6, and solve it under special assumptions regarding the arrival process. Recapitualting, the problem is

$$u(x) = \inf_{\{\tau^i, i \geq 1\}} E\{ \int_0^T \exp[-\alpha s] f(x(s)) ds + \sum \exp[-\alpha \tau^i c(x_{\tau^i})] \}$$

Subject to: (4.215)

$$dx = n dt + q\mu(dt) - \sum_{i \geq 1} \delta(t - \tau^i) x_{\tau^i}$$

where $c(t, x) \geq k > 0$, and the time index is dropped for simplicity. Further, the planning time T will be assumed subsequently to tend to infinity and the parameters assumed stationary.

At any one time, there are always two possibilities:

(i) do not send the vehicle and let persons wait, incur a cost J_1;

(ii) send the vehicle and incur the cost J_2. Under the first alternative, the cost J_1 is given by the dynamic programming recursive equation as follows:

$$J_1 = E \int_t^{t+\Delta t} f(s, x(s)) ds + u(t + \Delta t, x + \Delta x)$$ (4.216)

where Δt and Δx are the time increments. Under the second alternative, we incur the fixed cost $c(t, x)$ and reduce the number of waiting persons to $x = 0$. Let this cost be J_2 thus

$$J_2 = c(t, x) + u(t, 0)$$ (4.217)

The optimum cost $u(t, x)$ is the least of these two costs, or

$$u(t, x) = \min(J_1, J_2)$$ (4.218)

which can be written as follows:

$$u(t, x) \leq J_1$$
$$u(t, x) \leq J_2$$ (4.219)
$$(u(t, x) - J_1)(u(t, x) - J_2) = 0$$

To evaluate the term $Eu(t + \Delta t, x(t + \Delta t))$, we assume as in Section 4 a regularity of the function u and expand our equation. Namely,

$$Eu(t + \Delta t, x(t + \Delta t)) = u(t + \Delta t, x + n\Delta t + q)\Delta t + o(\Delta t) +$$
$$u(t + \Delta t, x + n\Delta t + q(1 - \Delta t) - q\Delta t)(1 - \Delta t) + o(\Delta t)$$ (4.220)

Dividing by $\Delta t \to 0$, one gets at the limit, the equation for $u(t,x)$ (when discounting is null):

$$(i) \quad \frac{\partial u}{\partial t} + (n-q)\frac{\partial u}{\partial x} + [u(t,x+q) - u(t,x)] + f \geq 0$$

$$(ii) \quad u(t,x) \leq c(t,x) + u(t,0)$$

$$(iii) \quad (i) * (ii) = 0$$

$$(iv) \quad u(T,x) = 0$$

(4.221)

The condition (iii) implies that equality holds either in (i) or (ii). When the equality holds in (i) the system evolves alone (without dispatching) until the first time t_1 where

$$u(t_1, x(t_1)) - u(t_1, 0) = c(t_1, x(t_1)) \tag{4.222}$$

At that time a vehicle is dispatched. Therefore if we know $u(t,x)$, the solution of the system of equations (4.221), then (ii) determines two regions (Figure 4.3)

$$C = \{(t,x); u(t,x) - u(t,0) < c(t,x)\} \tag{4.223}$$

and

$$S = (t,x), u(t,x) - u(t,0) = c(t,x) \tag{4.224}$$

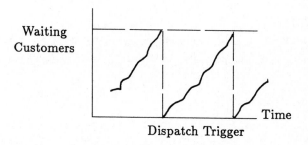

Figure 4.3: Optimum Non-Stationary Dispatching

When the state $(s, x(s))$ is in C no dispatching takes place but as soon as $(s, x(s))$ reaches the set S, a vehicle is dispatched.

Of course a general analytical solution for $u(x,t)$ is extremely difficult unless we make some simplifying assumptions. Alternatively, our conditions for optimality provide a set of equations agains which alternative dispatching rules can be tested for optimality. Below, we shall consider special cases which are often discussed in the dispatching literature which use long run average cost criteria. The first case we deal with consists of a stationary and discounted cost infinite horizon problem. The second case assumes a long run average cost where we show that the results obtained using the standard renewal-reward approach (Ross [55]), and our impulsive approach are similar. Later we resolve the Ross [55] problem completely using our method.

(i) *Discounted Cost, Infinite Horizon*

For an infinite planning horizon, stationary arrivals and discounted cost, define

$$u(x) = \inf_{v=\{\theta_i, i \geq 1\}} E\{\int_0^\infty e^{-\alpha s} f(x(s))ds + \sum_{i \geq 1} e^{-\alpha \theta_i} c(x_{\theta_i})\} \qquad (4.225)$$

where $\alpha > 0$ is the discount rate, f and c are independent of time and n and q are constants. Equations (4.225) becomes

$$(i) \quad (n-q)\frac{\partial u}{\partial x} + u(x+q) - u(x) + f - \alpha u(x) \geq 0$$

$$(ii) \quad u(x) - u(0) \leq c(x)$$

$$(iii) \quad \text{the product } (i) * (ii) = 0 \qquad (4.226)$$

$$(iv) \quad \text{the solution for } u(x) \text{ is bounded.}$$

Graphically, this means that dispatches are defined by the intersection of two curves: $c(x)$ and $[u(x) - u(0)]$ where $u(x)$ is defined by the solution of (4.226, (i)).

(ii) *Long Run Average Cost*

When we let α (the discount rate), tend to zero we must obtain the solution to the long run average cost. This cost can be written as $\bar{w}$;

$$\bar{w} = \lim_{T \to \infty} \frac{1}{T} E\{\int_0^T f(x(s))ds + \sum c(x_{\theta_i})\} \qquad (4.227)$$

where $\theta_i < T$. If τ is the cycle time of two successive dispatches we can show that the average cost is (starting from $x(0) = 0, \tau = \inf(s > 0, x(s) = 0)$),

$$\bar{w} = \frac{E\{\int_0^\tau f(x(s))ds + C(x_\tau | x_0 = 0)\}}{E(\tau | x_0 = 0)} \qquad (4.228)$$

and the optimum average cost $\bar{w}$ is given by minimizing (4.228) with respect to τ.

$$\bar{w} = \inf_{\tau} \frac{E \int_0^\tau f(x(s))ds + c(x^\tau | x_0 = 0)}{E(\tau | x_0 = 0)} \qquad (4.229)$$

The conditions corresponding to (4.226) starting from an $x_0 = x$, are then:

$(i) \quad (n - q)\dfrac{\partial w}{\partial x} + [w(x + q) - w(x)] - \bar{w} + f \geq 0$

$(ii) \quad w(x) - w(0) \leq c(x)$

$(iii) \quad$ the products$(i) * (ii) = 0$

$(iv) \quad w(x)$ bounded.

(4.230)

A solution yields the following result:

If $w(x)$ is regular and bounded and if $\bar{w}$ is constant satisfying equation (4.230), then $\bar{w}$ is the optimum long run average cost and the optimum cycle dispatching time is given by τ^*

$$\tau^* = \{\inf \; s \geq 0, \; w(x(s)) = c(x(s)) + w(0)\} \qquad (4.231)$$

From this result we deduce that the implicit optimum vehicle dispatching capacity x^* is given by the implicit solution of

$$w(x^*) = c(x^*) + w(0) \qquad (4.232)$$

We shall derive now explicit solutions to a given problem. For simplicity, assume that $n = 1, q = 1$ which leads to a Poisson arrival process, a waiting time cost $f(x) = ax$ and a fixed dispatching cost $c(x) = k$. Evidently:

$$\begin{aligned} x(t + \Delta t) - x(t) &= n\Delta t + \mu(\Delta t) \\ &= \Delta t + \mu(\Delta t) - \Delta t = \mu(\Delta t) \end{aligned} \qquad (4.233)$$

where $\mu(\Delta t)$, is a stationary Poisson arrival. For a long run average cost, x given and:

$$\tau = \inf(s \geq 0, x(s) = x); x \geq 1 \qquad (4.234)$$

we have from equation (4.232)

$$w(\tau) = [(a/2)x(x - 1) + k]/x \qquad (4.235)$$

A minimization of $w(\tau)$ the average cost, yields

$$\begin{aligned} x^* &= \sqrt{2k/a} \; \text{ if } \; \sqrt{2k/a} \geq 1 \\ \bar{u} &= w(\tau^*) \end{aligned} \qquad (4.236)$$

We now use our impulsive control approach and solve the quasi- variational inequality in (4.226) and obtain a similar result. Here w and $\bar{w}$ are a solution of

$$
\begin{array}{ll}
(i) & w(x+1) - w(x) - \bar{w} + ax \geq 0 \\
(ii) & w(x) \leq k + w(0) \\
(iii) & \text{The product } (i) * (ii) = 0
\end{array}
\qquad (4.237)
$$

Or, we seek a solution $x^*, w, \bar{w}, x \geq 1$ such that

$$
\begin{cases}
w(x+1) - w(x) - \bar{w} + ax = 0, \ \forall x \leq x^* \\
w(x^*) = w(0) + k; w(x) = w(x^*), \ \forall x \geq x^*
\end{cases}
\qquad (4.238)
$$

$$
\begin{cases}
w(x+1) - w(x) - \bar{w} + ax \geq 0 \ \forall x \\
w(x) \leq w(0) + k, \ \forall x
\end{cases}
$$

and

$$
w(x) = w(0) + x\bar{w} - (a/2)(x-1)x, \ x \leq x^*
\qquad (4.239)
$$

$$
w(x^*) = w(0) + k
$$

That is:

$$
k = x^*\bar{w} - (a/2)(x^* - 1)x^*
\qquad (4.240)
$$

Say that $w(0) = 0$ (which is possible since u is defined up to a proportionality constant, (4.239)-(4.240) therefore implies:

$$
\begin{aligned}
&x\bar{w} - (a/2)(x-1)x \leq k, \forall x \leq x^*, \\
&\bar{w} \leq ax \ \forall x > x^*
\end{aligned}
\qquad (4.241)
$$

Equations (4.237) and (4.238) are rewritten as:

$$
\begin{aligned}
&\bar{w} \leq (a/2)(x-1) + k/x, \ \forall x \leq x^* \\
&\bar{w} = (a/2)(x^* - 1) + k/x^* \\
&\bar{w} \leq ax, \ \forall x \geq x^*
\end{aligned}
\qquad (4.242)
$$

Since the function $(a/2)(x-1) + k/x$ obtains a unique minimum at $\bar{x} = \sqrt{2k/a}$, the conditions for optimality imply:

$$
\bar{w} = \inf_x[(a/2)(x-1) + k/x]
\qquad (4.243)
$$

If $\bar{w} \leq ax$ is satisfied, then (4.243) is equivalent to $x^* = \sqrt{2k/a} \geq 1$. Such a solution is expected, otherwise we would have to dispatch a continuous stream of vehicles on the route leading to an infinite cost.

The dispatching problem considered above belongs as well to a class of stochastic processes called by Stidham [60, 61], stochastic clearing systems. These are particularly applicable in public service problems and can be defined, as simple impulsive control problems with the stopping time equal to the clearing time.

Approximations as well as extensions of the dispatching problem considered here are of course possible. For example, we could consider the arrival process as a more general point process (see Section 2.5 of Chapter 2), or/and use diffusion approximations to obtain more tractable results.

Further Reading

The literature and applications of stochastic dynamic programming and control techniques is fare more extensive than indicated here. Books such as Howard [34], White [69], Dynkin [27], Bertsekas [18], Bersekas ans Shreve [14], Aoki [2], Astrom [4], Kushner [39, 40], in addition to those referred to in the text provide a glimpse of this extensive literature. Of course, these emphasize the "stochastic dynamic programming approach" as we have proceeded in this chapter. Attempts have been made, however, to generalize the Maximum Principle of deterministic control to stochastic systems. For example, Bismut [20], Haussman [31, 32, 33] (with solved problems) as well as Brock and Magill [23] have for example established a framework which provides an interpretation of the Lagrange multipliers in such stochastic optimization problems. Bismut, in particular has established appropriate optimality conditions for partially observed systems. The books by Fleming and Rishel [30] together with Fleming's papers [28, 29], are early treatment of such problems which are now extended throughout the literature. Problems with jumps, increasingly important in applications as we shall subsequently see (chapter 6 and 7), has received a thorough treatment by Bensoussan [11], and Lions [14, 15] but papers such as Pliska [49] provide also useful results and applications in management. In stopping problems, books by Shiryaev [59], Chow, Robbins and Siegmund [24] provide an important background to this field from the point of view of probability theory. In applications to inventory and production, Bensoussan [12], Bensoussan, Crouhi and Proth [13] provide an up-to-date account of stochastic control for production systems. Nevertheless, the early paper of Bather [5] and some recent work by Vickson [64, 65] are interesting formulations not treated by Bensoussan et al. [13]. Among the many additional applications, Vickson [66], Doshi [26], Puterman [50], Taksar [63], Pliska [49], Anderson and Friedman [1] are listed in our references.

Bibliography

[1] Anderson, R.F. and A. Friedman, 1977, "Optimal Inspections in a Stochastic Control Problem with Costly Information," *Mathematics of Operations Research*, 2, 155-190.

[2] Aoki, M., 1967, *Optimization of Stochastic Systems*, Academic Press, New York.

[3] Arnold, L., 1974, *Stochastic Differential Equations*, Wiley, New York.

[4] Astrom, K.J., 1970, *Introduction to Stochastic Control Theory*, Academic Press, New York.

[5] Bather, J.A., 1966, "A Continuous Time Inventory Model," *Journal of Applied Probability*, 3, 538-549.

[6] Bellman, R.E., 1957, *Dynamic Programming*, Princeton University Press, Princeton, N.J.

[7] Bellman, R.E.,1952, *Journal of Math. Mech.*, 6, 679-684.

[8] Bellman R.E. and S. Dreyfus, 1962, *Applied Dynamic Programming*, Princeton University Press, Princeton, N.J.

[9] Benes, V.E., 1971, "Existence of Optimal Stochastic Control Laws," *SIAM Journal of Control*, 9, 446-472.

[10] Benes, V.E., L.A. Shepp and H.S. Witsenhausen, "Some Solvable Stochastic Control Problems," *Stochastics*, 4, 39-83.

[11] Bensoussan, A., 1982, *Stochastic Control by Functional Analysis Methods*, North-Holland, Amsterdam.

[12] Bensoussan, A., 1982, "Stochastic Control in Discrete Time and Applications to the Theory of Production," *Mathematical Programming Study*, 18, 43-60.

[13] Bensoussan, A., M. Crouhi and J.M. Proth, 1983, *Mathematical Theory of Production Planning*, North-Holland, Amsterdam.

[14] Bensoussan, A. and J.L. Lions, 1975, "Nouvelles Methodes en Controle Impulsionnel," *Applied Mathematics and Optimization.* 1, 289- 312.

[15] Bensoussan, A. and J.L. Lions, 1978, *Applications des Inequations Variationnelles en Controle Stochastique*, Dunod, Paris.

[16] Bensoussan, A. and J.L. Lions, 1979, *Controle Impulsionnel et Inequations Quasi-Varionnelles*, Dunod, Paris.

[17] Bensoussan, A. and C.S. Tapiero, 1982, "Impulsive Control in Management: Prospects and Applications, *Journal of Optimization Theory and Applications*, 37, 419-442.

[18] Bertsekas, D.P., 1976, *Dynamic Programming and Stochastic Control*, Academic Press, New York.

[19] Bertsekas, D.P. and S.E. Shreve, 1978, *Stochastic Optimal Control*, Academic Press, New York.

[20] Bismut, J.M., 1976, "Theorie Probabiliste du Controle des Diffusions, *Memoirs of the American Mathematical Society*, 4, no. 167.

[21] Bremaud, P, 1976, "Bang Bang Control of Point Processes, *Advances in Applied Probability*, 8.

[22] Bremaud, P., 1976, "Sur l'Information Contenue dans les Processus Ponctuels," *These*, University de Paris IX, Paris.

[23] Brock, W.A. and M.J.P. Magill, 1979, "Dynamics Under Uncertainty," *Econometrica*. 47, 843-868.

[24] Chow, Y.S., H. Robbins and D. Siegmund, 1971, *Great Expectations: The Theory of Optimal Stopping*, Hougton Mifflin Co., Boston.

[25] Disney, R.L., 1975, "Random Flow in Queueing Networks: A Review and Critique," *AIIE Transactions*, 7, 268-288.

[26] Doshi, B., 1978, "Two-mode Control of a Brownian Motion with Quadratic Loss and Switching Costs," *Stochastic Process and Applications*, 6, 277-289.

[27] Dynkin, E.P., 1979, *Controlled Markov Processes*, Springer-Verlag, Berlin.

[28] Fleming, W.H., 1968, "Some Problems of Optimal Stochastic Control," in H.F. Karreman (ed.), *Stochastic Optimization and Control*, Wiley, New York, 59-64.

[29] Fleming, W.H., 1969, "Optimal Continuous Parameter Stochastic Control, *SIAM Review*, 11, 470-509.

[30] Fleming, W.H. and R.W. Rishel, 1975, *Deterministic and Stochastic Control*, Springer-Verlag, New York.

[31] Harrison J.M. and S.R. Pliska, 1981, "Martingales and stochastic Integrals in the theory of Continuous Trading", *Stochastic Processes and Applications*, 11.

[32] Haussman, V.G., 1978, "On the Stochastic Maximum Principle," *SIAM Journal of Control*, 16, 236-251.

[33] Haussman, V.G., 1981, "Some Examples of Optimal Stochastic Controls," *SIAM Review*, 23.

[34] Howard, R.A., 1960, *Dynamic Programming and Markov Processes*, Wiley, New York.

[35] Karmeshu, and N.K. Jaiswal, 1981, "A Nonlinear Stochastic Model for the Machine Interference Problem, *International Journal of Systems Science*, 12, 293-303.

[36] Kelly, F.P., 1979, *Reversibility and Stochastic Networks*, Wiley, New York.

[37] Kobayashi, H., 1972, "Some Recent Progress in Analytic Studies of System Performance, First USA-Japan Computer Conference," *Proceedings*, Session 5-1-1, 130-138.

[38] Krylov, N.V., 1980, *Controlled Diffusion Process*, Springer Verlag, Berlin.

[39] Kushner, H.J., 1967, *Stochastic Stability and Control*, Academic Press, New York.

[40] Kushner, H.J., 1971, *Introduction to Stochastic Control*, Holt, Rinehart and Winston, New York.

[41] Ladyzenskaya, D.A., V.A. Solonnikov and N.N. Vral'ceva, 1968, *Linear and Quasi-Linear Equations of Parabolic Type*, American Mathematical Society, Providence.

[42] Lanery, E., 1966, "Etude Asymptotique des Systemes Markoviens a Commandes, *Revue Informatique et Recherche Operationelle*, 5, 3-56.

[43] Lasry, J.M., 1974, *Controle Stochastique Ergodique*, Thesis, University of Paris IV, Paris.

[44] Lasry, J.M., 1975, "Controle Stationnaire Asymptotique," in A. Bensoussan and J.L. Lions (eds.), *Control Theory, Numerical Methods and Computer Systems Modelling*, Lecture Notes 107, Springer Verlag, Berlin.

[45] Mandl, P., 1968, *Analytical Treatment of One Dimensional Markov Processes*, Springer Verlag, Berlin.

[46] McCall, J., 1965, "The Economics of Information and Optimal Stopping Rules," *Journal of Business*, 35, 300-317.

[47] New, C.C., 1970, "A Common Error in Production Scheduling," *Opernl. Res. Quarterly*, 25, 283-292.

[48] Pliska, S.R., 1972, "Single Person Controlled Diffusion with Discounted Costs," *Journal of Optimization Theory and Applications*, 12, 248-255.

[49] Pliska, S.R., 1975, "Controlled Jump Processes," *Stoch. Proc. and Applications*, 3, 259-282.

[50] Puterman, M., 1975, "A Diffusion Process Model for a Storage System," *Logistics*, M. Geisler (ed.), *TIMS Studies in Management Science*, North Holland, Amsterdam, 1, 143-159.

[51] Robin, M., 1977, "Controle Impulsionnel des Processes de Markov," *These d'Etat*, INRIA, Le Chesnay, France.

[52] Robin, M., 1981, "On Some Impulse Control Problems with Long Run Average Costs," *SIAM Journal of Control*, May.

[53] Robin, M., 1983, "Long Term Average Cost Control Problems for Continuous Time Markov Processes: A Survey," *Acta Applicandae Mathematicae*, 1, 281-299.

[54] Robin, M. and C.S. Tapiero, 1982, "A Simple Verhicle Dispatching Policy with New Stationary Stochastic Arrival Rates," *Transportation Research*, 16B, 449-457.

[55] Ross, S.M., 1970, *Applied Probability Models with Optimization Applications*, Holden-Day, San Fransisco.

[56] Ross, S.M., 1982, *Stochastic Processes*, Wiley, New York.

[57] Ross, S.M., 1983, *Introduction to Stochastic Dynamic Programming*, Academic Press, New York.

[58] Sethi, S.P. and G.L. Thompson, 1981, "Simple Models in Stochastic Production Planning," in A. Bensoussan, P. Kleindofer and C.S. Tapiero (eds.), *Applied Stochastic Control in Econometrics and Management Science*, North Holland, Amsterdam, 295-304.

[59] Shiryaev, A.N., 1976, *Statistical Sequential Analysis*, Nauka, Moscow, (in Russian).

[60] Stidham, S. Jr., 1974, "Stochastic Clearing Systems," *Stochastic Processes and Applications*, 2, 85-113.

[61] Sulem A., 1986, "A Solvable One-Dimensional Model of a Diffusion Inventory System," *Math. of Operations Research*, 11, 125-133.

[62] Sulem, A., 1985, "Resolution Explicite de L'Inequation Quasi Variationelle Bidimensionelle Associee ā la Gestion d'Un Stock de Deux Produits," INRIA Report, Rocquencourt, France.

[63] Taksar, M.I., 1984, "Average Optimal Singular Control and a Related Stopping Problem," *Math. of Operations Research*, 9.

[64] Vickson, R.G., 1981, "Capacity Expansion Under Stochastic Demand and Costly Importation", University of Waterloo, Canada.

[65] Vickson, R.G., 1982, "Schedule Control for Randomly Drifting Production Sequences," *Infor*, 19, 330-346.

[66] Vickson, R.G., "Optimal Control of Production Sequences: A Continuous Parameter Analysis," *Operations Research.* 30, 659-697.

[67] Wald, A., 1947, *Sequential Analysis*, Dover Publications, New York.

[68] White, D.J., 1969, *Dynamic Programming*, Holden-Day, San Francisco.

[69] Wilde, L.L., 1980, "The Economics of Consumer Information" *Journal of Business*, 53, 143-157.

Chapter 5

APPLIED MODELING AND MARKETING UNDER UNCERTAINTY

5.1 *Introduction*

The brief outline of marketing and uncertainty of Chapter 1, Section 1.5, will be persued in this chapter in more specific terms. In particular, selected problems in marketing such as advertising, repeat purchasing, pricing, new products growth, etc. will be outlined. Our emphasis is on stochastic dynamic models and their use in reaching marketing decisions. Although such models are not commonly used by the marketing profession, there is an increasing awareness that they can be useful to obtain better decisions for products and markets management.

Stochastic effects in marketing may arise for example due to competitive forces in the market place, buyer (and seller) heterogeneity as well as memory lingering effects (or the carry-over effects in time) of a marketing mix history or consumers' recall of past states. In addition, the asymmetric distribution of information regarding product characteristics (such as reliability, quality, etc.) and consumers' responses to a marketing mix, render uncertainty in marketing, a pervasive effect to be reckoned with. These effects are too numerous to handle exhaustively but several problems will be dealt with in the context of particular applications. The implications to marketing strategies will be addressed as well.

5.2 *Advertising*

Advertising seeks to influence consumers' purchase decisions and to further the aims of marketing with respect to sales, product and firm positioning. To do so, it may act explicitly by being suggestive and convincing, but more often it may be used in influencing processes that are related to the marketing process. Such processes are usually extremely complex reflecting the dynamic and probabilistic considerations consumers may have and uncertain market forces. As a result, it is natural to describe models of sales response to advertising as stochastic and computing optimal advertising budgets by dynamic programming and control techniques.

To begin, we shall consider a sales response function to advertising which exhibits the uncertain effects advertising has on sales growth. Namely, hypothesize that

Increment in sales in a given interval of time	=	Deterministic growth, a function of current sales and current advertising effort a	+	Stochastic growth, a function of current sales and current advertising effort a

$$\Delta x = f(x,a)\Delta t + \sigma(x,a)\Delta w \qquad (5.1)$$

where Δt is a time increment, Δw is a Weiner process defined in Chapter 2.

Here the deterministic growth component, denoted by f is a "mean" response function and the stochastic component denoted by σ expresses the uncertainty regarding sales growth.

The firm defines a planning horizon over which it maximizes its utility of profits, a function of sales and advertising. As a result, the advertising-sales management process becomes a stochastic process and an advertising policy can be selected by the techniques of Chapter 4.

Specifically, consider the following problem:

$$\text{Max } J = E \int_0^T U(x,a)dt$$

$$a \in A; x(0) = s, \text{ subject to } (5.1)$$

(5.2)

with A closed and convex. Then, the dynamic programming equation of Chapter 4, yields

$$-\begin{array}{c} \text{The change of the firm's} \\ \text{objective in a small time} \\ \text{interval } (\Delta J/\Delta t) \end{array} = \begin{array}{c} \text{The current utility} \\ U \end{array}$$

$$+\begin{array}{c} \text{Mean, increment sales increase} \\ f \end{array} * \begin{array}{c} \text{Shadow price of additional} \\ \text{sales } (\Delta J/\Delta x) + \end{array} \quad (5.3)$$

$$+\begin{array}{c} \text{Variance, increment sales} \\ \text{increase } (1/2)\sigma^2 \end{array} * \begin{array}{c} \text{A "price" associated with an} \\ \text{increment in sales variance} \\ (\Delta^2 J/\Delta x^2) \end{array}$$

Note here that $\Delta J/\Delta t$ is the rate of change over time of the objective, or the evaluation of the firm's utility due to sales and advertising in the remaining period of time (t,T). Further, $\Delta J/\Delta x$ is the change in the objective due to a unit change in sales. In other words, $p = \Delta J/\Delta x$ is a shadow price associated with sales growth. Similarly, $\Delta^2 J/\Delta x^2$ is also a "shadow price" associated with change in the firm's objective due to a "marginal" change in sales (due to the advertising-sales uncertainty process only). This price is given by $\Delta p/\Delta x$ and will be discussed subsequently. It is important to understand the meaning of these terms so that they may be used in discussing optimization problems.

Say $f > 0$, i.e. we can induce higher sales by advertising. This means that advertising is sufficient to compensate both the natural "loss" of sales (due to attrition) and the increase of current and future sales (by the carry-over effect of advertising). This occurs when $p = \Delta J/\Delta x > 0$, i.e. there is a positive "shadow" price (income per unit sales increase) implying that we will go on increasing sales until the "price" p reaches the zero level. Then it may no longer be necessary to advertise, except to compensate sales losses due to various depreciating effects. At this stage, we are in a mean sense at the optimum sales level.

A second advertising effect occurs due to the carry-over effects as expressed in changes in p. This provides a mechanism to alter the shadow price of mean sales dynamics. How do we note this effect? Remember that $p = \Delta J/\Delta x$, thus, given $J(x)$, we can apply calculus rules to obtain an equation in $\Delta J/\Delta x$. To do so, let

$$- \Delta J/\Delta t = H \tag{5.4}$$

where H will be called a Hamiltonian, given through the previous equation by $H = U + pf + (1/2)\sigma^2(\Delta p/\Delta x)$, and expressing the net objective flow (over time). Thus, the "Hamiltonian" provides a time decomposition of the optimal objective since, obviously, J is always (by dynamic programming) the value of the optimal objective. This mechanism then provides a transformation of our multi-period advertising problem into a single period one by maximizing the flow. This can be done *provided* that we can compute the shadow price (benefit) of an additional sales, and the cost to be incurred due to sales uncertainty (i.e. p and $\Delta p/\Delta x$). This is represented simply in Figure 5.1 where we note that management must, (in order to determine a current advertising policy) forecast both the future sales realizations and their return-risk implications following some numeraire given by p and $\Delta p/\Delta x$. Unfortunately, these numeraires are not easily computable. It can be shown, however, that they can be computed implicitly. Namely, once the advertising policy has been established as a function of current information and current sales, then the rate of change in this numeraire per unit time (or $\Delta p/\Delta t$) is equal to the flow of the decomposed instantaneous objective of the firm (i.e. its Hamiltonian) per unit sales, (or $-\Delta H/\Delta x$), plus a random term proportional to the sales growth variance (σ), valued at the "shadow price of sales uncertainty" (or $\Delta p/\Delta x$). Recapitulating, since H is the net flow in the firm objective (for a given advertising policy) then p is the *value* of this flow due to a change in sales. This value is a function of both the change in the Hamiltonian and the *value* of the sales uncertainty it reduces. Next we obtain specific results by considering particular cases.

A Quantitative Approach

We follow a quantitative approach and formulate advertising models

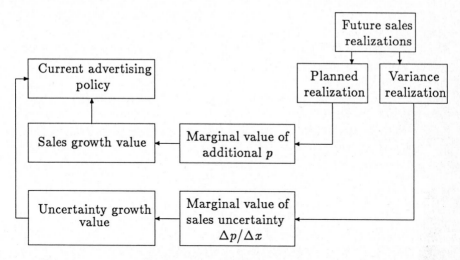

Figure 5.1: The Effects of
Uncertainty and Advertising

with carry over effects which assume that sales reflect past advertising efforts as well as the "forgetting" of these efforts over time. Notable examples are models suggested by Nerlove and Arrow [37], Stigler [49], Vidale-Wolfe [57] and others (see Gould [19] and Sethi [46] for a survey of these models). One basic assumption of these models is that sales response to advertising is deterministic. That is, given an advertising rate, given the effects of an advertising effort on sales, and given the parameters describing "forgetting" of past advertising by consumers, a resultant sales level can be uniquely determined by solving one or a system of differential equations. Each of these differential equations, implicitly and sometimes explicitly, makes specific assumptions concerning the market or the consumer memory mechanisms and advertising effectiveness functions. The choice of an advertising model, therefore, presupposes implicitly market behaviors that ought to be tested.

The random walk models of advertising we construct in this example demonstrate one approach to stochastic model building which renders explicit the assumptions made about the model (and thus about a market's behavior). Specifically, we assume that advertising expenditures affect the probability of sales at the margin and that in a small time interval Δt, the probability that sales will increase by one unit is a function of this advertising rate. Similarly, in a time interval Δt, the probability that sales will decrease by one unit is a function of the forgetting rate. In this manner we construct a random walk model as is given in Figure 5.2 We note here that sales are integer valued on the line and that our position on this line is influenced by forgetting (at a rate $m(x)$) and by advertising (at a rate $q(M, x, a(t))$. The movements (sales) over time on this line define a random function $\{x(t), t \geq 0\}$ which is a stochastic process of sales taking integer values between the two boundaries $x = 0, x = M$ or $x \in [0, M]$. Denote by $P(x, t)$ the probability of sales at time t. At time $t + \Delta t$, transitions to a sales state x can occur in three ways summarized in Figure 5.3. This figure although similar in concept to Figure 5.2 provides a switching probability approach to constructing random walk stochastic models. The switching probabilities are represented in Table 5.1.

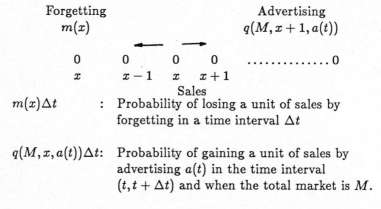

Figure 5.2: A Random Walk Model of Advertising

Table 5.1: Transition Probabilities

t	$P(x-1, t)$	$P(x, t)$	$P(x+1, t)$	Effect
$t + \Delta t$	$x - 1$	x	$x + 1$	
$P(x, t + \Delta t)$	$q(M, x-1, a(t))\Delta t$	$1 - m(x)\Delta t$	$m(x+1)\Delta t$	Forgetting
		$1 - q(M, x, a(t))\Delta t$		Advertising

From this Table, we can easily obtain an expression for the probability of selling x at time $t + \Delta t$ given the sales probability at time t. This is given by:

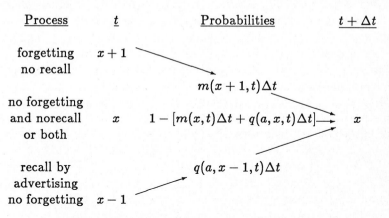

Figure 5.3: Probabilistic Model of Advertising

$$
\begin{aligned}
P(x, t+\Delta t) =\ & P(x-1,t)q(M,x-1,a(t))\Delta t+ \\
& P(x,t)[1-m(x)\Delta t][1-q(M,x,a(t))\Delta t]+ \\
& P(x+1,t)m(x+1)\Delta t
\end{aligned}
$$

When Δt is very small, $P(x,t)$ is reduced to a system of differential-difference equations:

$$
\begin{aligned}
dP(x,t)/dt =\ & m(x+1)P(x+1,t)-[m(x)+q(M,x,a(t))]P(x,t)+ \\
& q(M,x-1,a(t))P(x-1,t)
\end{aligned}
$$

$$(5.5)$$

with the boundary conditions

$$
\begin{aligned}
dP(0,t)/dt &= m(1)P(1,t)-q(M,0,a(t))P(0,t) \\
dP(M,t)/dt &= -[m(M)+q(M,M,a(t))]P(M,t)t+ \\
& \quad q(M,M-1,a(t))P(M-1,t)
\end{aligned}
$$

These equations determine the Kolmogorov equations for the process at hand and their solutions will yield the probability $P(x,t)$ of selling x at time t. Such equations are in general very difficult to solve and require that specific assumptions be made concerning the functional forms m and q. *These assumptions can in fact be construed as explicit hypotheses concerning a market's (or consumers) forgetting mechanism and advertising sales response functions.* Therefore, specification of the transition probabilities m and q provide a model of market behavior. We shall consider two hypotheses and then solve for $P(x,t)$. Proofs for these results can be found in

Chapter 2. The main point to note is that by changing the hypotheses we shall not only change the quantities of the stochastic process (i.e. the mean, variance evolutions, etc.) but the probability structure of the ensuing sales processes.

For the first hypothesis, which we call the Nerlove-Arrow hypothesis, $x(t)$ is interpreted in units of goodwill. It assumes that the probability of losing a unit by forgetting is proportional to the goodwill level $x(t)$ at time t. The advertising function is *not* a function of the market size which is assumed to be potentially infinite. The mean evolution is similar to the Nerlove-Arrow [37] model however. The second hypothesis is called the diffusion hypothesis. It assumes a finite market M and an advertising effectiveness function proportional to the remaining market potential $M-x$. This model has a mean evolution which is similar to that of Vidale-Wolfe [57] and Stigler [49]. Of course, by changing the hypotheses about the switching probabilities we will obtain again a different advertising model. In this manner we render explicit the hypotheses concerning consumer behavior.

Given these hypotheses, we substitute them whenever appropriate in the system of Kolmogorov differential-difference equations (5.5). Although an explicit solution of $P(x,t)$ is difficult to obtain, we can usually obtain the moment evolution by the probability generating function (pgf) of the (x,t) process. Specifically, define by $F(z,t)$ the pgf of $P(x,t)$; or

$$F(z,t) = \sum_{x=0}^{M} z^x P(x,t) \tag{5.6}$$

Using either the Nerlove-Arrow or the Vidale-Wolfe type of hypotheses, we obtain the moments evolutions given in Table 5.2, (Tapiero [50]). To obtain explicit solutions for $P(x,t)$ would require first solution of the partial differential equations given in Table 5.2. Such solutions are given in Table 5.3 where we clearly point out the limit distributions in case of a stationary advertising policy.

We turn now to the formulation of some advertising stochastic control problems of the Nerlove-Arrow and Vidale-Wolfe Type. First we consider the Nerlove-Arrow hypotheses and consider a feedback advertising policy of the form $a(x,t) = a_1(t)x + a_2(t)$ and q, a proportionality constant. The probability generating function of the advertsing stochastic process is given by

$$\partial F/\partial t = (qa_1(t)z - m)(z-1)\partial F/\partial z + qa_2(t)(z-1)F; \atop F(z,0) = z_G \tag{5.7}$$

where G is the initial goodwill. A general solution for (5.7) is known and given by [52]:

Table 5.2: The Evolution of Two
Advertising Models

	Nerlove-Arrow Model I	Vidale-Wolfe Model II
Hypotheses	mx $q(a)$	mx $q(a)(M - x)$
Probability Generating Function	$\partial F/\partial t =$ $(z - 1)(q(a)F - m\partial F/\partial z)$ $F(z, 0) = z^{q_0}$	$\partial F/\partial t = q(a)M(z - 1)F$ $\quad\quad + (m + q(a)(1 - z)\partial F/\partial z)$ $F(z, 0) = z^{q_0}$
Mean Evolution	$dy/dt = -my + q(a)$ $y(0) = q_0$	$ds/dt = -ms + q(a)(M - s)$ $s(0) = s_0$
Variance Evolution	$dv/dt = my + q(a) - 2v$ $v(0) = 0$	$dv/dt = q(a)M + (m - q(a))s-$ $\quad\quad 2v(m + q(a))$ $v(0) = 0$

$$F(z,t) = H^G(z,t,0)exp\{\int_0^t qa_2(\tau)(H(z,t,\tau) - 1)d\tau\}$$

$$H(z,t,\tau) = 1 + [exp(\rho')/(z - 1) - \int_t^\tau qa_1(y)exp(\rho')dy]^{-1} \left.\right\} \quad (5.8)$$

and also

$$\rho' = \int_\tau^t (m - a_1(\tau))d\tau$$

For an open-loop advertising strategy, $q(a(x,t)) = qa(t)$, (5.8) reduces to:

$$F(z,t) = \{1 + (z - 1)e^{-mt}\}^G \exp\{(z - 1)\int_0^t qa(\tau)e^{-m(t-\tau)}d\tau\} \quad (5.9)$$

which is the generating function of a sum of two random variables x_1 and x_2, where x_1 has a binomial distribution, and x_2 has a Poisson distribution. That is:

Table 5.3: The Probability Distributions
of Two Advertising Models

	Nerlove-Arrow	Vidale-Wolfe
Hypotheses	mx $q(a,t)$ $x = 0, 1, 2, ...$	mx $q(a,t)(M-x)$ $x = 0, 1, 2, ...M$
$P(x,t)$	$\frac{\Lambda(t)e^{-\Lambda(t)}}{x!}$ $\frac{d\Lambda}{dt} = -m\Lambda + q(a,t)$	
$P(x,t)$ $a = \bar{a}$	$\frac{\Lambda e^{-\Lambda}}{x!}$ $\Lambda = q\bar{a}/m$	$\Phi \sum_{j=0}^{s_0} \binom{M-s_0}{x-j}\binom{s_0}{j}\left(\frac{\beta\gamma}{\alpha\delta}\right)^j$ $\Phi = \alpha^x \beta^{M-s_0-x}$ $\alpha = qa(1 - e^{-\varepsilon t})/\varepsilon$ $\beta = (m + qae^{-\varepsilon t})/\varepsilon$ $\gamma = (qa + me^{-\varepsilon t})/\varepsilon$ $\delta = m(1 - e^{-\varepsilon t})/\varepsilon$ $\varepsilon = qa + m$

$$P(x_1,t) = \binom{G}{x_1}e^{-mx_1t}(1 - e^{-mt})^{G-x_1}$$

$$P(x_2,t) = exp[-\Lambda(t)]\Lambda(t)x_2/x_2; \qquad\qquad (5.10)$$

$$\Lambda(t) = \int_0^t qa(\tau)e^{-m(t-\tau)}d\tau$$

with mean goodwill and variance of given in Table 5.2.

If a firm establishes advertising budgets strictly in time varying proportions $a_1(t)$ to sales, then $a_2(t) = 0$ and the probability generating function (5.7) is reduced to

$$F(z,t) = H^G(z,t,0)$$

$$F(z,t) = \{1 + \alpha(t)/(z-1) + \int_0^t qa_1(\tau)\alpha(\tau)d\tau\}^{-1}G \quad \Bigg\} \quad (5.11)$$

$$\alpha(t) = \exp[mt - \int_0^t a_1(\tau)d\tau]$$

By taking successive derivatives of $F(z,t)$, the individual probability of sales can be found. For the linear feedback advertising policy, we find a mean-variance evolution given by:

$$\frac{ds(t)}{dt} = [qa_1(t) - m]s(t) + qa_2(t); \quad s(0) = 0$$

$$(5.12)$$

$$\frac{dv(t)}{dt} = [qa_1(t) + m]s(t) + 2[qa_1(t) - m]v(t) + qa_2(t); \quad v(0) = 0$$

which is a system of bilinear differential equations. By taking successive derivatives of $F(z,t)$ higher order moments may also be found.

Now consider a general advertising policy $a(x,t)$. A solution of (5.7) for its generating function becomes extremely difficult. Correspondingly, the evolution of the probability moments of $P(x,t)$ cannot be determined. Approximations can be established however, by taking a Taylor series approximation to $q(a(x,t))$. Specifically, a linearization of $a(x,t)$ about $s(t)$, the mean goodwill, yields: $a(x,t) \approx a(s,t) + (x-s)\partial a/\partial s$, which leads to a probability generating function found for the advertising linear feedback rule and hence moments are defined as above in (5.12) where a_1 and a_2 are replaced by: $a_1 = \partial a/\partial s$ and $a_2 = (a-s)\partial a/\partial s$. Such an approximation can of course, result from an assumption about the advertising decision process. Higher order approximations require solution of more complex stochastic processes. The meaning of this approximation is that feedback advertising strategies are expressed as a function of expected goodwill rather than as a function of the actual level of goodwill. Such an assumption corresponds to managerial behavior as goodwill states are not in general directly observable.

An alternative procedure to constructing a stochastic model of advertising and goodwill consists in randomizing the deterministic process given by the mean evolutions. Specifically ignoring for large G the boundary $x \geq 0$, (or assuming some reflection boundary at $x = 0$) we can transform it into a stochastic differential equation:

$$dx = [-mx + q(a(x,t))]dt + \sigma(x,a,t)dv; \quad x(0) = G \quad (5.13)$$

where dv is a standard Wiener process. That is dv is a stochastic process with independently distributed normal random variables with mean zero and variance one, uncorrelated in time. The mean evolution of x where $a(x,t)$ is open-loop or linear in x, clearly corresponds to $s(t)$ in Tables 5.2 and 5.3 respectively. Specification of the source of uncertainty requires however, that the function $\sigma^2(x,a,t)$ expressing the instantaneous variance of the x process be clearly defined. When $a(x,t)$ is of the open-loop type, a model for $\sigma^2(x,a,t)$ given by $(mx+qa)$, can be found by a diffusion approximation. Insertion of σ into (5.13) will demonstrate that at least the evolution of the first two probability moments in (5.13) and Table 5.2 are equal. If $a(x,t)$ is of the linear feedback type, then letting $\sigma^2(x,a,t) = [qa_2 + x(qa_1 + m)]$ we obtain again equal mean and variance evolutions to x and Table 5.2. In general, for linearized feedback advertising strategies, we obtain approximately

$$\sigma(x,a,t) = [mx + q(a(x,t))]^{1/2} \qquad (5.14)$$

This yields a non-linear stochastic differential equation for advertising which describes a continuous state stochastic model of goodwill as a function of advertising.

Similarly, for the diffusion (Vidale-Wolfe-Stigler) model, we may show that a mean variance approximation leads to:

$$\sigma^2(x,a,t) = mx + qa(M - x) \qquad (5.15)$$

and

$$dx = [-mx + qa(M - x)]dt + [mx + qa(M - x)]^{1/2}dw$$

McNeil and Schah [32] have considered an approximation to this model by an Ornstein-Uhlenbeck process (see also Feigin [16]). This approximation is reached as follows, we define

$$Z_M(T) = \frac{x(t) - (qa/qa + m)M}{\sqrt{M}} \qquad (5.16)$$

Then, as M - the market potential becomes very large ($M \to \infty$), $Z_M(t)$ converges in a weak Markov sense to the following Ito stochastic differential equation

$$dz = -(qa + m)zdt + [2qa/(qa + m)]dw$$
$$\text{with} \qquad\qquad\qquad\qquad\qquad\qquad\qquad (5.17)$$
$$x = (\sqrt{M})z + [qa/(qa + m)]M$$

or $\sqrt{M}z$ is the random deviation from long run equilibrium sales $Mqa/(qa+m)$. Denoting a new variable

$$u(t) = qa/(qa + m) \qquad (5.18)$$

we note that $qa = mu/(1-u)$ and therefore the corresponding sales stochastic differential equation with sales x is;

$$dz = [-mz/(1 - u)]dt + 2udw$$

with sales x $\qquad (5.19)$

$$x = (\sqrt{M})z + uM$$

To optimize these models it will be necessary to establish objective functions and proceed to an application of dynamic programming techniques, as we have shown previously.

Other stochastic models of advertising resolved are, for example, Dehez and Jacquemin [11] who have considered an uncertainty advertising problem by adding an error term to a firm's demand function as well as Pekelman and Tse [39] who have devised a discrete model of advertising and applied to it dual control techniques (see Chapter 7).

The choice of objectives is not without substantive problems however. Following Nerlove and Arrow [37], consider a monopolist facing the problem of choosing a time path for advertising $a(t)$ so as to maximize the present expected discounted value of profits J:

$$J = E\{\int_0^\infty Q(t)e^{-rt}\}dt \qquad (5.20)$$

where r is the discount rate of the firm. Assume that sales are a nonlinear function of goodwill, twice differentiable and that the profit function optimized by the firm is:

$$Q(t) = \pi(x) - w(a)$$

$$\qquad (5.21)$$

$$\partial\pi/\partial x > 0, \ \partial^2\pi/\partial x^2 < 0, \ \partial w/\partial a > 0, \ \partial^2 w/\partial a^2 \geq 0$$

That is, at the optimum price level sales relate to goodwill by the strictly concave function $\pi(x)$. Also, $w(a)$ is a non-linear increasing function of advertising. The optimum advertising control is thus reduced to maximization of (5.20) subject to an appropriate stochastic model of goodwill and advertising.

Consider a special problem, where advertising is a feedback function of sales. This means that the structure of the advertising policy is a function of the information pattern available at a given time. If the firm has full information on the goodwill state (and the ensuing distribution), its feedback policy will be of the general form $a(x,t)$. If the firm has only information on the moments of its goodwill, then the advertising policy will be given by a $(\Lambda, V, ..., t)$ where Λ is the mean goodwill, V the variance etc. If only moments of goodwill are known, we can show that the optimum advertising policy is given by the solution of a deterministic equivalent. For simplicity, state that advertising at time t is a function of the mean goodwill at that time. That is

$$a(x,t) = a(\Lambda, t) \qquad (5.22)$$

Inserting (5.22) into (5.10) we obtain a Poisson advertising process with parameter given by:

$$d\Lambda_2/dt = -m\Lambda_2 + qa(\Lambda_2, t); \quad \Lambda_2(0) = G \qquad (5.23)$$

which is a deterministic rather than a stochastic model.

Now let the optimum advertising control problem be based on some of the diffusion approximations established earlier. Namely, the problem faced by the firm is now

$$
\begin{aligned}
&\text{Maximize } J^0 = E\{\textstyle\int_0^\infty e^{-rt}(\pi(x) - w(a))dt\} \\
&a \in A \\
&\text{subject to} \\
&dx = (-mx + qa)dt + \sigma(x,a)dv; \quad x \geq 0
\end{aligned}
\qquad (5.24)
$$

In this problem, advertising is used to control not only the mean goodwill but also its random variations. Further, let $\sigma(x,a)$ be of any continuous form and differentiable such that advertising can increase or decrease sales uncertainty (expressed through $\sigma(x,a)$). Although in such a case analytical results can be difficult to obtain, we can proceed as we have done it earlier and obtain some insights about the optimum advertising policy, or obtain numerical results as indicated in Chapter 8. In this case, the dynamic programming equation is given by:

$$\text{Max}\{-rV + \frac{\partial V}{\partial x}f(x,a) + \frac{1}{2}\sigma^2(x,a)\frac{\partial^2 V}{\partial x^2} + \pi(x) - w(a)\} = 0 \qquad (5.25)$$

where V is the optimum value J^0, and $f(x,a) = -mx+a$, is the mean sales rate response to advertising and to sales losses (such as through forgetting). Also, by Ito differential rule for $p(x) = \partial V/\partial x$,

$$dp = \{\frac{\partial p}{\partial x}f + \frac{1}{2}\frac{\partial^2 p}{\partial x^2}\sigma^2\}dt + \frac{\partial p}{\partial x}\sigma dw \qquad (5.26)$$

Combining with equation (5.22) (with $p = \partial V/\partial x, f = [-mx+a], \partial f/\partial x = -m$, and if $\sigma^2 = [mx + a]^2, \partial\sigma^2/\partial x = 2m[mx + a]$,

$$dp = \{-\frac{\partial \pi}{\partial x} + p(r + m) + m[mx + a]\frac{\partial p}{\partial x}\}dt + \frac{\partial p}{\partial x}\sigma dw \qquad (5.27)$$

Further, from Bellman's Principle,

$$\frac{\partial w}{\partial a} = -[p + \frac{1}{2}\frac{\partial\sigma^2}{\partial a}\frac{\partial p}{\partial x}] > 0 \qquad (5.28)$$

and for $\partial^2\sigma^2/\partial a^2 > 0$,

$$\frac{\partial^2 w}{\partial a^2} = \frac{1}{2} - \frac{\partial^2\sigma}{\partial a^2}\frac{\partial p}{\partial x} > 0 \qquad (5.29)$$

In our special case, $\partial w/\partial a = -[p+(mx+a)\partial p/\partial x]$ and $\partial^2 w/\partial a^2 = -\partial p/\partial x$ since $\partial^2\sigma^2/\partial a^2 = 2$, and therefore $\partial p/\partial x < 0$. Of course, if $\partial^2\sigma^2/\partial a^2 < 0$, then $\partial p/\partial x > 0$ and the signs p and $\partial p/\partial x$ can be established, leading to insights regarding the "shadow prices of sales".

To compute p, $\partial p/\partial x$ and V - the optimum objective, Bellman's equation must be resolved. In equilibrium, when $dp = 0$, then in the mean, $E(dp) = 0$ and $p(x,t) = p(x)$, $\partial p/\partial x = dp/dx$. From equation (5.27), we thus obtain an ordinary differential equation

$$d\pi/dx = p(r + m) + m[mx + a](dp/dx) \qquad (5.30)$$

where a is defined by (5.28). If $\sigma^2 = [mx + a]^2$, and $w(a) = (1/2)a^2$, a solution for the optimum advertising program is $a = -[p + mxdp/dx]/[1 + dp/dx]$ which is inserted into (5.30) to yield a quadratic differential equation in dp/dx which can be resolved iteratively.

An Analytical Example

In [46], Sethi has solved a stochastic advertising control problem which is defined as follows:

$$\text{Max } V(x_0) = E \int_0^\infty [\pi x - a^2(x)]e^{-rt}dt$$
$$a(x) \geq 0$$
$$\text{Subject to} \qquad (5.31)$$
$$dx = [-kx + qa(x)\sqrt{1 - x}]dt + \sigma(x)dw$$
$$x(0) = x_0 \in (0,1)$$

where advertising dollars a are a function of the market share x, k is the market share depreciating effect and advertising effectiveness is proportional to $\sqrt{1-x}$. Also the following assumptions are made,

$$a(x) \geq 0, x \in (0,1), a(0) > 0$$

$$\sigma(x) > 0, x \in (0,1) \text{ and } \sigma(0) = \sigma(1) = 0$$

(5.32)

From Chapter 4, Section 4.3, the dynamic programming equation is

$$rV = (\pi x - a^2) + [qa\sqrt{1-x} - kx]\frac{\partial V}{\partial x} + \frac{1}{2}\sigma^2\frac{\partial^2 V}{\partial x^2} \qquad (5.33)$$

with an optimal feedback advertising control

$$a(x) = q\frac{(\partial V/\partial x)\sqrt{1-x}}{2} \qquad (5.34)$$

which leads (upon its insertions in the above equation) to:

$$rV = \pi x + [\frac{dV}{dx}]^2 q^2 \frac{(1-x)}{4} - \frac{\partial V}{\partial x}kx + \frac{1}{2}\sigma^2\frac{\partial^2 V}{\partial x^2} \qquad (5.35)$$

Because of the stationarity of the objective function V (remember that we have an infinite discounted horizon problem), the partial derivative $\partial V/\partial x$ is in fact a total derivative dV/dx (as well as $\partial^2 V/\partial x^2 \rightarrow d^2 V/dx^2$), we have therefore,

$$rV = \pi x + (\frac{dV}{dx})^2 q^2 \frac{(1-x)}{4} - kx\frac{dV}{dx} + \frac{1}{2}\sigma^2\frac{d^2 V}{dx^2} \qquad (5.36)$$

It can be verified that a solution for V is

$$V(x) = -\bar{\lambda}x + \bar{\lambda}^2 q^2/4r$$
$$\text{where } \bar{\lambda} = \frac{\sqrt{(r+k)^2 + q^2\pi} - (r+k)}{q^2/2} \qquad (5.37)$$

with $\bar{\lambda}$ denoting the marginal (shadow) price of market share x since $dV/dx = \bar{\lambda}$. Since V is linear in x it implies that $d^2V/dx^2 = 0$. The optimal (unconstrained) advertising policy would then be:

$$a(x) = (q\bar{\lambda}\sqrt{1-x})/2 \qquad (5.38)$$

as pointed out earlier.

5.3   Selected Applications and Problems

In this section, other quantitative problems are formulated and used to demonstrate the potential usefulness and applicability of stochastic dynamic systems in marketing. Essentially, we shall deal with problems of pricing, warranties, new products, repeat purchasing, etc.

5.3.1   Pricing

Pricing is an essential component of the marketing mix. It is also a complex decision which involves many considerations such as the quantitites produced and sold, product quality and differentiation, competition, market structure and so on. In the practice of marketing, pricing is an art. This is not a justification, however, for basing pricing decisions purely on the hunch of a talented manager. No less important are the principles of economics, marketing and model building to the successful study and practice of the art or pricing (Nagle [34]). There are many ways to reach a price (Monroe [31], Monroe & Britta [32]) depending on the available information regarding the company, competitiors and consumers sensitivity and responses to various schemes. The classical approach relating price p to quantity sold s uses relationships such as $s = s(p)$ in a static (or equilibrium) setting, or $s = s(p, dp/dt)$ in a dynamic setting (see the early papers by Evans [15],[16], Roos [43]). If $C(s)$ is the cost of production and the marketer is a monopolist with instantaneous profit, $\pi = ps - C(s)$, it is possible to resolve such a problem by the calculus of variations, control theory or deterministic dynamic programming as stated in Section 4.1. Stochastic models of pricing in this particular context can be constructed by letting sales be random (as in Dehez and Jacquemin [11] and discussed in the previous section).

The source of uncertainty in our model would then be due to a distributed price expectation which will affect the quantity sold by a manufacturer. Alternatively, we may conceive a model where quantitites sold are affected by relative prices. For example, let p^* be an "equilibrium" (or competition's price), then the difference $(p - p^*)$ can be used to construct a sales response model to pricing p. For example, we can "hypothesize" that the change is some function $f(.)$ of the price difference $p^* - p$, and describe the sales process by a Wiener process such as

$$ds = f(p - p^*)dt + bdw; \quad s(0) = x, \tag{5.39}$$

where b may be either a parameter or some function that can be estimated empirically or assumed. A "simple" pricing problem may then be formulated as a discounted profit and terminal market share objective given by

$$\text{Max } V(x) = E\{\int_0^T [ps - C(s)]e^{-rt}dt + e^{-rt}G(s,T)\}$$
$$p \in P$$

(5.40)

subject to (5.39)

where P is a convex constraint set on prices p and $G(s,T)$ expresses the desirability of a market share objective at time T, the final time. The "solution" of this problem, as shown in Chapter 4, is given by finding a pricing function $p^0(x)$ such that

$$-\frac{\partial V}{\partial t} = -rV + \frac{b^2}{2}\frac{\partial^2 V}{\partial x^2} - C(x) + \frac{\text{Max}}{p \in P}\{[f(p^* - p)\frac{\partial V}{\partial x} + px]\}$$

(5.41)

$$V(x,T) = G(x,T)$$

Assuming that an interior solution to p exists, the optimal pricing rule is given by

$$\partial f/\partial p = g(p) = x[\partial V/\partial x] \text{ and}$$

(5.42)

$$p^0 = g^{-1}(x[\partial V/\partial x])$$

Equation (5.42) can be used next to resolve $V(x)$, $\partial V/\partial x$ from (5.41) and subsequently compute the optimal price policy p^0 from (5.42). A second derivative of (5.41) with respect to p and x yields:

$$\Phi(x) = \frac{\partial^2 f}{\partial p \partial x}\frac{\partial V}{\partial x} + \frac{\partial f}{\partial p}\frac{\partial^2 V}{\partial x^2} + 1$$

(5.43)

By using the monotonicity property (or the modularity of the dynamic progamming equation) we have

$$\frac{\partial p^0}{\partial x} = \begin{cases} > 0 & \text{if } \Phi(x) > 0 \\ < 0 & \text{if } \Phi(x) < 0 \end{cases}$$

(5.44)

which establishes a condition for a change in the pricing policy as a function of sales x. If there were many firms so that an individual firm's sales does not affect the "equilibrium" price p then $\partial^2 f/\partial p \partial x = 0$ and $\Phi(x) = 1+$

$(\partial f/\partial p)\partial^2 V/\partial x^2$. This latter equation allows us to infer simply the change in prices as a function of changes in sales. For example, if $f(u) = au^3$, then $\partial f/\partial p = 3a[p - p*]^2 > 0$ which means that

$$\frac{\partial p}{\partial x} = \begin{cases} < \ 0 & \text{if } \frac{\partial V^2}{\partial x^2} < -1/3a(p - p^*)^2 \\ \\ > \ 0 & \text{if } " \quad > \quad " \end{cases} \tag{5.45}$$

The actual sign of $\partial^2 V/\partial x^2$ is defined of course by a solution of (5.41) and determined by the production cost function $C(x)$ and the target objective $G(x, T)$ at T.

Although in (5.39) we have assumed that p^* is externally given, in most marketing situations p^* may express the competition's reaction function to "our firm" prices. Thus, in fact we have: $p^* = p^*(p)$. Furthermore, such a price p^* may be function of aggregate industry sales (which we shall define by y), the number of firms n, their size etc. Thus, the "solution" we have provided is very restrictive and of little "practical value". To circumvent such difficulties and render marketing models closer to reality, games have been constructed providing a more rational formulation of the pricing problem. Such problems are not treated here but are clearly an important aspect of the dynamic systems literature. Alternatively, p^* may be defined on the basis of theoretical and economic considerations. Namely, let p^* be the industry equilibrium price, i.e. the price at which the long run industry profits are equal to zero. If y are industry sales and there are n identical firms, then an industry profit function is given by $F(z)$:

$$F(z) = \int_0^\infty e^{-\gamma t}[p^*y - nC(y/n)]dt; \quad z = y(0) \tag{5.46}$$

where γ is the industry discount rate and $nC(y/n)$ is the cost of producing y by n firms. Say that for each firm we have the sales response function (5.39), then for an industry, we obviously have (with reflection at $y = 0$):

$$dy = nf(p - p^*)dt + nbdw; \quad y(0) = z$$

$$\text{Prob } [y \geq 0] = 1 \tag{5.47}$$

The industry profit is thus given by the following dynamic programming equation (with reflection at $z = 0$)

$$0 = -\gamma F + nf(p - p^*)\frac{dF}{dz} + \frac{1}{2}b^2n^2\frac{d^2F}{dz^2} + pz - nC(z/n) \tag{5.48}$$

$$\partial F/\partial z = 0 \text{ at } z = 0$$

Remember that for zero profits $F(z) = 0$, such that (5.48) is reduced to:

$$nf(p - p^*)g(z) + \frac{1}{2}b^2n^2\frac{dg}{dz} + p^*z - nC(z/n) = 0$$

$$(5.49)$$

$$g(z) = dF/dz, \quad g(0) = 0$$

which is an ordinary differential equation of the first order whose solution is

$$\begin{cases} g(z) = \int_0^z \exp[-a_1(z - u)]a_2(u)du \\ a_1 = f(p - p^*)/(bn/2) \\ a_2(u) = [p^*u - nC(u/n)]/(b^2n^2/2) \end{cases}$$

$$(5.50)$$

and finally, integrating $g(z)$, we have

$$F(y) = \int_0^y \int_0^z \exp[-a_1(z - u)a_2(u)]dudz$$

$$(5.51)$$

Since $F(y) = 0$, we solve for p^* in (5.51). Specifically, let $a_2(u) = (p^* - c)u$, then

$$F(y) = \frac{(p^* - c)}{a_1^2}[\frac{1}{a_1}(1 - e^{-a_1y}) + \frac{a_1y^2}{2} - y]$$

$$(5.52)$$

A solution for a_1 from (5.52) is relatively easy. Say that n is very large, then a_1 is small so that $\exp[-a_1y] \approx 1 - a_1y$, then $a_1 = 0$ or $0 = f(p - p^*)$ is a solution to our equation. If $f(0) = 0$, then clearly $p^* = p$ is the solution, *which is the purely competitive pricing policy*. When n is not large, $\exp(-a_1y)$ may not be too small and a solution for a_1, is found by (5.52). Of course, if production costs are non-linear in the quantity produced, we would obtain a solution different than the one above. If $a_2(u) = p^*u - cu^{\alpha+1}$, then

$$F(y) = \int_0^y e^{-a_1z} \int_0^z \exp[a_1z][p^*u - cu^{\alpha+1}]dudz$$

$$(5.53)$$

Here note that $F(y) = 0$, implies

$$\frac{p^*}{a_1^2}[\frac{1}{a_1}(1 - e^{-a_1y}) + \frac{a_1y^2}{2} - y] =$$

$$= c\int_0^y \int_0^z e^{-a_1z}[e^{a_1u}u^{\alpha+1}]dudz$$

From integral Tables (Gradshteyn and Ryzhik [20], p. 318, eq. 3.383) we have

$$\int_0^z e^{a_1 u} u^{\alpha+1} du = \frac{1}{\alpha+3} z^{\alpha+2} \,_1F_1(\alpha+2, \alpha+3, a_1 z)$$

but (eq. 9.210 in [20])

$$_1F_1(\alpha+2, \alpha+3, a_1 z) \sim 1 + \frac{\alpha+2}{\alpha+3} a_1 z + \frac{\alpha+2}{\alpha+4}(\frac{a_1 z}{2})^2 + \frac{\alpha+2}{\alpha+5}(\frac{a_1 z}{3})^3 + \ldots$$

which provides an estimate for the above integral which is integrated by using the incomplete gamma integral

$$\int_0^y e^{a_1 z} z^{\beta-1} dz = a_1^{-\beta} \gamma[\beta, a_1 y]$$

to yield

$$\int_0^y \int_0^z e^{-a_1 z} [e^{a_1 y} u^{\alpha+1}] du\, dz =$$

$$= \frac{a_1^{-(\alpha+3)}}{\alpha+3} [\gamma(\alpha+3, a_1 y) + (\alpha+2) \sum_{n=4} \frac{\gamma(\alpha+n; a_1 y)}{\alpha+n-1}]$$

This leads to an equation in p^* and p given by:

$$\frac{p^*}{a_1^2}[\frac{1}{a_1}(1 - e^{-a_1 y}) + \frac{a_1 y^2}{2} - y] = \qquad (5.54)$$

$$= c \frac{a_1^{-(\alpha+3)}}{\alpha+3}[\gamma(\alpha+3, a_1 y) + (\alpha+2) \sum_{n=4} \frac{\gamma(\alpha+n; a_1 y)}{\alpha+n-1}]$$

If a_1 is small when n is large for example, then $\exp[-a_1 y] \sim 1 - a_1 y + a_1 y^2/2$ and the term multiplied by p^* is equal to zero and finally we require $\gamma(\alpha + 3, a_1 y) + (\alpha+2)\Sigma_{n=4}\gamma(\alpha+n, a_1 y)/(\alpha+n-1) = 0$ whose solution is $(a_1 = 0)$ the pure competition case, since all terms must necessarily be positive. When $a_1 y$ is not too small then we have $p^* = p^*(p, y)$ implicitly from the above equation which is inserted into (5.39) to provide an appropriate equilibrium price function. When all firms are in collusion so that industry profits are maximized in the long run, then we maximize with respect to p^* in (5.40). Assuming that an interior solution exists, it is given by:

$$n\frac{\partial f}{\partial p^*}\frac{dF}{dz} + z = 0, \frac{\partial f}{\partial p^*} < 0$$

or

$$z/n = |\frac{\partial f}{\partial p^*}|\frac{dF}{dz}$$

This means, that the firm's market share equals the industry marginal value of having more sales time the marginal effect the "industry" price has in increasing sales by one unit. To obtain a function p^* in terms of p, both f and dF/dz must be known however.

The problem we have resolved is of course limited to extremely simple marketing situations, which are rarely found in practice. Rather, the elements and the situation outlined in Table 5.4, are far more descriptive of the uncertainties marketers face when seeking to construct a pricing policy. Evidently, by handling the issues implied in Table 5.4 many problems can be formulated and resolved, providing thereby a fertile ground for the stochastic dynamic approach to pricing.

5.3.2   New-Products Diffusion: Stochastic Models

Sales growth diffusion models have had a major impact on the literature and practice of marketing science. Following the pioneering work of Bass [3], the basic diffusion model has been extended to incorporate various effects such as changes in the market potential; complementarity, subsitutability, contingent and independent relations of the new product with other brands in the market place; varying word-of mouth effects; various marketing mix effects (including the effect of price on both innovation and imitation coefficients or advertising effect on the innovation coefficient) competitive effects, and others.

Yet, it is surprising that the diffusion research tradition has ignored stochastic modeling considerations (for exceptions refer to [14], [23]). The desirability of a stochastic perspective is especially vital given the (a) uncertainty inherent in all marketing operations as evident by rapidly changing consumer tastes, unpredictable competitive activities, technology and other environmental conditions, and (b) the heterogeneity of any target adopting population as evident in the growing literature on market segmentation.

Our objective in this section is to provide an approach for applying stochastic modeling to new products diffusion and for formulating decision problems which use these models. The classical new product diffusion model may be formulated as follows:

Given a market protential N and a cumulative number of adopters x at time t hypothesize that the growth rate of new adopters is proportional

Table 5.4: Some Marketing Models

Sources of Uncertainty	Information Sources	Pricing policies structures	Objectives
consumers sensitivity to prices	consumer behavioral models	open-loop	profit maximization
price awareness	competition intelligence and information gathering	sales sensitive (feedback)	market share
competition's response and behavior	study of price effects on marketing mix and markets behavior	adaptive (with learning and adaption to new information)	skimming and peneration goals
inflation and environmental factors	sales force, reaction to prices and to price changes	timing problems in pricing policies	product line optimization
credit condition and "cost of money"	past performance and price experimentation, segmentation	pricing modes and price markets, image building, price discounting and price schedules (namely, non-linear pricing schemes)	promotional goals through pricing

to innovation and imitation effects. This can be stated as follows:

$$\Delta x = (N - x)(a + b)\Delta t; x(0) = 0, x = 0, 1, 2, ..., N$$

where a and b denote the innovation and imitation effects, and $\Delta x = x(t + \Delta t) - x(t)$ is a growth rate of adopters.

Alternatively, define by $P(t)$, a product adoption potential at a given time t, and let $y(t)\Delta t$ be the probability of new adoptions in Δt. In an expected sense, new adoptions are given by $P(t)y(t)\Delta t$. More generally, we cans state that new adoptions are uncertain, given by a process reflecting both the potential P and the probability of adoption $y\Delta t$, where the time subscript has been dropped for convenience. Or $\Delta x = F(P, y\Delta t)$, where F is a known function. In the special case $P = N - x, y = (a + bx)$, and F a product form function we obtain the Bass model.

If for simplicity, we assume that the potential is fixed and the adoption probability is identical for all (homogeneous) potential adopters, then the probability of adoption growth in Δt is simply given by a binomial distribution, or

$$\text{Prob}[\Delta x; P, t] = \binom{P}{\Delta x}(y\Delta t)^{\Delta x}[1 - y\Delta t]^{p - \Delta x}$$

$$(5.55)$$

$$\Delta x = 0, 1, 2, ...P$$

where Δt is very small, P and y fixed, it is easily checked that this is a Poisson process which we rewrite conveniently by;

$$\Delta x = \begin{cases} +1 & \text{w.p } Py\Delta t \\ 0 & \text{w.p } 1 - Py\Delta t \end{cases} \qquad (5.56)$$

$$x = 0, 1, 2, ...N$$

Since P and y are a function of both time and x, the process $\{x, t > 0\}$ can be interpreted as a general pure birth stochastic process with birth growth parameter $\lambda(x, t)$. In case of the "Bass" hypotheses, we have

$$\lambda(x, t) = (N - x)(a + bx) \qquad (5.57)$$

Combining this "growth hypotheses" together with the appropriate Kolmogorov equations we can find the probability of selling x units by time t. If there are no imitations but only innovations ($b = 0$) we have then the stochastic Vidade-Wolfe model outlined in the previous sections. These equations can be used also as a departure point for discrete state and continuous approximations to the new product sales growth process. Further, if we let the parameter N, a, b be a function of some marketing variable (such as price p, advertising A, etc.) we can derive generalized new sales growth processes.

The profit of the marketer in a small time interval dt is now πdt, where

$$\pi dt = (p - c)dx - Adt \tag{5.58}$$

where c is the unit production cost and dx are the sales in "dt" given by (5.56) when $\Delta t \to 0$. In expectation, we have

$$E(\pi dt) = (p - c)(N - x)(a + bx)dt - Adt \tag{5.59}$$

Now, let r be the marketer's discount rate and say that at $x = N$, we reach an absorbing state since no more units can be sold. In these circumstances the marketer's decision problem can be formulated as follows:

$$\text{Max } V(x_0) = E\{\int_0^\tau e^{-rt}\pi dt\}$$
$$p \in P; \ A \in \alpha$$
$$\text{subject to (5.56)-(5.59)}, \ x(0) = x_0 \text{ and} \tag{5.60}$$
$$\tau = \text{Inf}\{t \geq 0, x \geq N\}$$

and where P and α are convex constraint sets on prices and advertising. Application of the results in Chapter 4 yield instead of (5.60) and if $V(x_0)$ is regular and well defined:

$$-rV(x) + \underset{p \in P; A \in \alpha}{\text{Max}} \ \{(N - x)(a + bx)[V(x + 1) - V(x)] +$$
$$+(p - c)(N - x)(a + bx) - A\} = 0 \tag{5.61}$$
$$V(N) = 0$$

Say that $b = \log A$ and fix the price p to $\bar{p}$, then if an interior and feasible solution for A exists, it is found by solving

$$x(N - x)\{[V(x + 1) - V(x)] + (p - c)\} = A^0 \geq 0 \tag{5.62}$$

where A^0 denotes the optimal advertising budget. A solution of (5.61) and (5.62) by numerical means will provide a solution to our problem with advertising only. Such a solution is straightforward since at

$$x = N; \ V(N) = 0$$

and by recursion at

$$x = N - 1; \; V(N - 1) = (p - c) - \frac{e^{-(a+r)/N-1}}{N - 1}$$

and generally for all $x's$, the optimal value function may be found by simple iterations as will be shown in Chapter 8. It is easy to verify that the optimal advertising procedure is a declining function of the remaining sales potential (as expected).

Similarly, if we assume as Robinson and Lakhani [42] that price has a multiplicative effect on the adoption probability such that it is given by

$$y\Delta t = exp[-\varepsilon p][a + bx]\Delta t \tag{5.63}$$

and if $A = 0$ (no advertising), then optimization with respect to the price p can be shown to lead to

$$V(x) - \frac{exp[-\varepsilon p^0(x)](N - x)(a + bx)}{r} = 0 \tag{5.64}$$

where $p^0(x)$ is the optimal price function. To obtain a numerical characterization of this function, we resolve by recursive means and simultaneously solve equations (5.64) and (5.61) (with $A = 0$). If $\varepsilon p^0(x)$ is very small, a linear approximation to the exponentiald term in (5.64) yields

$$p^0(x) = \{1 - \frac{V(x)r}{(N - x)(a + bx)}\}\frac{1}{\varepsilon} \tag{5.65}$$

Extensions of this approach using the models outlined in Chapter 2 are of course possible. For example, we can assume that the potential or the adoption probability $y\Delta t$ in (5.55) are stochastic and derive the appropriate mixture models. Further, both P and $y\Delta t$ could be assumed to be given by empirical models (such as logistic regression models) which involve many factors, leading thereby to alternative versions of the Bass diffusion model. Finally, the Poisson model in (5.56) can also be generalized to jump processes of the type outlined in Section 2.6, and accounting for the probability that adoption occurs in groups rather than by individual consumers only (as implied through the Poisson process). These problems are left, however, as exercises as they are straightforward applications of the stochastic models of Chapter 2.

5.3.3   Repeat Purchasing

The marketing literature distinguishes between the purchase and repeat purchase processes. The latter process being a function of consumers satisfaction, the product life (or consumption time) etc. In this section, we shall

construct a stochastic dynamic process of repeat purchasing and show that
the empirically tested model of Ehrenberg [13] who found evidence for the
Negative binomial distribution is obtained here in the limit $(t \to \infty)$ of a
particular model. Of course, given such a process it is then possible to construct decision problems which can help us construct marketing programs
maximizing the value of repeat purchasing.

As in section 5.2 let $\{x, t > 0\}$ be a sales stochastic process and assume
that all sales can come from repeat purchasing with probability $a_2 \Delta t$ and
from new trial sales with probability $a_1 \Delta t$. Thus, if at time t, we have sold
x, the probability of increasing sales by one unit is given by $a_1 \Delta t + a_2 \Delta t$.
Similarly, assume that the probability of a purchaser being dissatisfied is
$m\Delta t$. Or, for x consumers, this probability is equal to $mx\Delta t$. As in section
5.2 we obtain a stochastic process given by

$$\Delta x = \begin{cases} +1 & \text{w.p } (a_1 + a_2 x)\Delta t[1 - mx\Delta t] \\ -1 & \text{w.p } mx\Delta t \\ 0 & \text{w.p } [1 - (a_1 + a_2 x)\Delta t][1 - mx\Delta t] \end{cases} \tag{5.66}$$
$$x = 0, 1, 2, \ldots$$

This leads to a probability process whose probability generating function is
given by:

$$\frac{\partial F}{\partial t} = [a_2 z - m](z - 1)\frac{\partial F}{\partial z} + a_1(z - 1)F; F(z, 0) = z^{x_0} \tag{5.67}$$

where x_0 are initial sales at time $t = 0$. Let $K = \log F$ then $\partial K/\partial z$
at $z = 1$ equals $\hat{x} = E(x)$, while $[\partial^2 K/\partial z^2 + E(x)]$ at $z = 1$ equals
$\text{var}(x) = v$ such that we can obtain by differentiation:

$$d\hat{x}/dt = (a_2 - m)\hat{x} + a_1; x(0) = x_0 \text{ given}$$
$$\tag{5.68}$$
$$dv/dt = [a_2 + m]\hat{x} + 2(a_2 - m)v, v(0) = 0$$

At the limit $t \to \infty, \hat{x} = \bar{x}, v = \bar{v}$

$$\bar{x} = a_1/(m^2 - a_2), m > a_2$$
$$\tag{5.69}$$
$$\bar{v} = a_1 m/[m^2 - a_2]^2,$$

and further

$$\frac{1}{F}\frac{dF}{dz} = \frac{a_1}{m - za_2} \tag{5.70}$$

A solution yields

$$F(z) = [m - za_2]^{-a_1/a_2} \tag{5.71}$$

which is the probability generating function of the negative binomial distribution used by Ehrenberg [13] to assess repeat buying. The mean and variance are given by equation (5.68) while the distribution is,

$$p(x = k) = \left| \begin{matrix} \frac{a_1}{a_2} + k - 1 \\ \frac{a_1}{a_2} - 1 \end{matrix} \right| (\frac{a_2}{m})^k (1 - \frac{a_2}{m})^{a_1/a_2} \tag{5.72}$$

Given the mean evolution however, we can follow the approximation approach of Chapter 2, and define the diffusion process. Finally, it is evident that problems regarding the choice of repeat buying parameters and marketing policies may be designed as optimization problems. For example, if a_1 is the advertising budget and a_2 expresses a quality of product (or service), a possible objective function to optimize would be,

$$E \int_0^\infty e^{-rt}\{[p - c(a_2)]x - a_1\}dt \tag{5.73}$$

where p is the price, $c(a_2)$ a per unit production cost function of a_2 (the repeat buying rate), x the sales level and a_1 is the advertising budget. The optimization problem thus defined can be resolved by application of the techniques of Chapter 4.

5.3.4   Need and Choice

The stochastic models considered in this chapter can be extended by considering multiple firms competing for buyers, by introducing multiple product lines, media and markets and by considering the simultaneous impact of the marketing mix on a firm marketing states. Concepts drawn from finance such as portfolio theory, options and risk management in general can be brought to bear on some of these problems providing thereby a decision framework which is sensitive to market's risk and utility preferences in attaining certain market states (such as market share, profits, penetration, limiting entries to competition etc.). Under uncertainty, these are mostly open problems for research.

    To terminate this chapter we shall consider an application to a class of marketing problems which are defined in terms of two behavioral decisions; "need" and "choice". In particular, we shall decompose a consumer-buyer decision into two probability events which occur sequentially but can be affected simultaneously by several firms and by various marketing instruments. These problems can be modelled suitably by using jump stochastic processes as defined and treated in Chapters 2 - 4.

Distinguish between the marketing "process of need arousal" and the "process of a consumer's choice". Needs may be aroused by aggregate industry advertising, product innovations, the need to repurchase, arousals by certain medias (as in television), new regulations regarding certain durable goods (such as cars), etc. In particular, when needs are aroused, they raise the potential for a marketing firm whose realization is reached (or not) only after the buyer has made a choice. This choice is then reached on the basis of product availability, display on shelve space in store, price, reputed quality, brand loyalty, sales effort etc. While, marketer may affect consumers' choices, their real purpose is to induce sales, increase the market share and reach desirable marketing states.

For demonstration purposes, let $A(t)$ be an industry advertising at time t which induces at that time a Poisson probability distribution of sales with parameter $\Lambda(t)$ (see section 5.2),

$$d\Lambda/dt = -m\Lambda(t) + A(t), \Lambda(0) = \Lambda_0 \qquad (5.74)$$

In other words, $\Lambda(t)dt$ is the probability that a need will be aroused. Alternatively, $\Lambda(t)$ can be interpreted as the rate at which new buyers enter the market. Once they have entered, however, they may choose a product (or not), from one of the competing firms. This choice will of course be exercised as a function marketers actions.

For simplicity, say that the probability of a buyer choosing a firm's i product, is given by f_i and is a function of the "marketing mix". For example, a logistic model such as:

$$\frac{f_i dt}{1 - f_i dt} = \beta(M_i, \bar{M}) \qquad (5.75)$$

where M_i denotes the ith firm's marketing mix effort and $\bar{M}$ the competitions effort can be used to estimate the choice probability. In this case, if x_i are the ith firm sale, the profit is π_i,

$$\pi_i = p_i x_i - c_i x_i - M_i(x_i) \qquad (5.76)$$

with M_i (potentially) a function of x_i, then the profit

$$V(x_i) = E \int_0^T e^{-rt} \pi_i dt + e^{-rT} G(x_i, T) \qquad (5.77)$$

(with r a discount rate) is given by

$$-\frac{\partial V}{\partial t} = -rV(x_i) + \Lambda\{[V(x_i+1) - V(x_i)]f_i\} + \pi \qquad (5.78)$$
$$V(x_1, T) = G(x_1, T)$$

where Λ, f_i and π_i are given by the equations above.

On the basis of these equations we can compute (at least numerically), the optimal policies to follow.

Further Reading

Marketing is an area where prolific and useful research has been conducted. Stochastic considerations regarding consumers' behavior combined with the carry over effects in time of marketing instruments and competitive advantage lead naturally to widespread applications of stochastic dynamic optimization. Although there are many books and research papers, the reader might benefit from some examples which include, Albrights and Winston [1], Sengupta [44], Schmalensee [45] and Wind [58].

Bibliography

[1] Albright, S.C. and W. Winston, 1979, "A Birth-Death Model of Advertising and Pricing," *Adv. in Appl. Prob.* 11, 134-152.

[2] Basar, T. and G.J. Olsder, 1982, *Dynamic Non-Cooperative Games*, Academic Press, New York.

[3] Bass, F.M., 1969, "A New Product Growth Model for Consumer Durables," *Management Science* 15, 215-227.

[4] Bettman, J.R., 1979, *An Information Processing Theory of Consumer Choice*, Addison-Wesley, Reading, Mass.

[5] Bismut, J., 1975, "Growth and Optimal Intertemporal Allocation of Risks," *Journal of Economic Theory* 10, 239-257.

[6] Blischke, W.R. and E.M. Scheuer, 1975, "Calculation of the Cost of Warranty Policies as a Function of Estimated Life Distributions," *Naval Research Logistics Quarterly* 22, 681-696.

[7] Bourguignon F. and S.P. Sethi, 1981, "Dynamic Optimal Pricing and (Possibly) Advertising in the Face of Various Kinds of Potential Entrants," *Journal of Economic Dynamics and Control* 3, 119-140.

[8] Brems, H., 1948, "The Interdependence of Quality Variations, Selling Efforts and Price, *QJE*, 62, 418-440.

[9] Brems, H., 1966, "Price Quality and Rival Response," in K. Hansen (ed.) *Readings in Danish Theory of Marketing*, North Holland, Amsterdam, 159.

[10] Case, J.H., 1979, *Economics and the Competitive Process*, New York University Press, New York.

[11] Dehez, P. and A. Jacquemin, 1975, "A Note on Advertising Policy Under Uncertainty and Dynamic Conditions," *The Journal of Industrial Economics* 24, 73-78.

[12] Dorfman, R. and P. Steiner, 1954, "Optimal Advertising and Optimal Quality," *American Economic Review* 44.

[13] Ehrenberg, A.S.C., 1972, *Repeat Buying*, North Holland, Amsterdam.

[14] Eliashberg, J, C.S. Tapiero and J. Wind, 1986, "Diffusion of New Products in Heterogeneous Populations Incorporating Stochastic Coefficients", University of Pennsylvania, *Working Paper*.

[15] Evans G.C., 1924, "The Dynamics of Monopoly," *American Math. Monthly* 31, 77-83.

[16] Evans, G.C., 1932, *Stabilite et Dynamique de la Production dans L'Economie Politique*, Memorial des Sciences Mathematique, Fasicule LVI, Paris, Gauthier-Villars.

[17] Feigin, P.D., 1976, "Maximum Likelihood Estimiations for Continuous Time Stochastic Processes, *Adv. in App. Prob.* 8, 712-736.

[18] Glickman, T. and P. Berger, 1976, "Optimal Price and Protection Period Discussion for a Product Under Warranty," *Management Science* 22, 1381-1390.

[19] Gould, J.P., 1970, "Diffusion Processes and Optimal Advertising Policy," in E.S. Phelps et al (eds.), *Microeconomic Foundation of Employment and Inflation Theory*, Norton, New York, pp. 338-368.

[20] Gradsteyn, I.S. and I.M. Ryshik, 1965, *Tables of Integrals, Series and Products*, Academic Press, New York.

[21] Horsky, D. and L.S. Simon, 1983, "Advertising and the Diffusion of New Products," *Marketing Science* 2, 1-17.

[22] Howard, R.A., 1963, "Stochastic Process Models of Consumer Behavior," *J. Advertising Research* 3, 35-42.

[23] Jeuland, A.P. and R. J. Dolan, 1982, "An Aspect of New Product Planning: Dynamic Pricing," in A.A. Zoltners (ed.), *Marketing Planning Models*, North Holland, 1-21, Amsterdam.

[24] Kalish, S., 1983, "New Product Diffusion Model with Price Advertising and Uncertainty," *Marketing Science*

[25] Kuehn A.A. and R.L. Day, 1964, "Probabilistic Models of Consumer Buying Behavior," *Journal of Marketing* 28.

[26] Lambin, J.J., 1976, *Advertising, Competition and Market Conduct in Oligopoly Over Time*, North Holland/American Elsevier, Amsterdam.

[27] Mamer, J.W., 1982, "Cost Analysis of Pro Rata and Free Replacement Warranties," *Naval Research Logistics Quarterly* 29, 345-356.

[28] Massey, W.F., D.B. Montgomery and D.G. Morrison, 1970, *Stochastic Models of Buying Behavior*, MIT Press, Cambridge, Mass.

[29] McNeil, D.R. and S. Schach, 1973, "Central Limit Theorems for Markov Population Processes," *J. Royal Stat. Soc.* 35, 1-23.

[30] Meyer, R.A., 1976, "Risk Efficient Monopoly Pricing for the Multiproduct Firm," *Quarterly Journal of Economics* 40, 461-474.

[31] Monroe, K.B., 1979, *Pricing: Making Profitable Decisions*, McGraw Hill, New York.

[32] Monroe, K. and A. Della Brita, 1978, "Models for Pricing Decisions," *Journal of Marketing Research*, 479-494.

[33] Montgomery D.B. and A.J. Silk, 1972, "Estimating the Dynamic Effects of Market Communications Expenditures," *Management Science* 18, 485-501.

[34] Nagle, T., 1983, "Economic Foundations for Pricing," *Marketing Science*.

[35] Nelson, P., 1970, "Information and Consumer Behavior," *Journal of Political Economy* 78, 311-329.

[36] Nelson, P., 1974, "Advertising as Information," *JPE* 82, 729-756.

[37] Nerlove, M. and K. Arrow, 1962, "Optimal Advertising Policy Under Dynamic Conditions," *Economica* 42, 129-142.

[38] Nicosia, F.M., 1966, *Consumer Decision Processes: Marketing and Advertising Implications*, Prentice Hall, Englewood Cliffs, NJ.

[39] Pekelman, D. and E. Tse, 1980, "Experimentation and Budgeting in Advertising: An Adaptive Control Approach," *Operations Research* 28, 321-347.

[40] Porter, M.E., 1980, *Competitive Strategy: Techniques for Analyzing Industries and Competitors*, The Free Press, New York.

[41] Rao, A.G., 1970, *Quantitative Theories in Advertising*, Wiley, New York.

[42] Robinson, B. and C. Lakhani, 1975, "Dynamic Price Models for New Product Planning," *Management Science*, 1113-1122.

[43] Roos, E., 1927, "Dynamical Economics," *Proc. Nat. Acad. of Sciences* 13.

[44] Sengupta, S.S., 1967, *Operations Research in Sellers' Competition*, Wiley, New York.

[45] Schmalensee, R., 1972, *The Economics of Advertising*, North Holland, Amsterdam.

[46] Sethi, S.P., 1977, "Dynamic Optimal Control in Advertising: A Survey," *SIAM Review* 19, 685-725.

[47] Sethi, S.P., 1983, "Deterministic and Stochastic Optimization of a Dynamic Advertising Model," *Optimal Control Applications and Methods* 4, 179-184.

[48] Spence, A.M., 1977, "Consumer Misperceptions, Product Failure and Producer Liability," *Review of Economic Studies* 44, 561-572.

[49] Stigler, G., 1961, "The Economics of Information," *Journal of Political Economy* 69, 213-225.

[50] Tapiero, C.S., 1975, "Random Walk Models of Advertising, Their Diffusion Approximation and Hypothesis Testing," *Annals of Economic and Social Measurement* 4, 293-309.

[51] Tapiero, C.S., 1975, "On Line and Adaptive Optimum Advertising Control by a Diffusion Approximation," *Operations Research* 23, 890-907.

[52] Tapiero, C.S., 1978, "Optimum Advertising and Growth Under Uncertainty," *Operations Research*, 26, 450-463.

[53] Tapiero, C.S., 1979, "A Generalization of the Nerlove-Arrow Model to Multi-Firms Advertising Under Uncertainty," *Management Science* 25, 907-915.

[54] Tapiero, C.S., 1982, "A Stochastic Model of Consumer Behavior and Optimal Advertising," *Management Science* 28, no. 3.

[55] Tapiero, C.S., 1982, "A Stochastic Diffusion Model with Advertising and Word of Mouth Effects," *Euro. J. of Operations Research* 12, 348-356.

[56] Taylor, J.W., 1974, "The Role of Risk in Consumer Behavior," *J. of Marketing* 38, 54-60.

[57] Vidale, M.L. and H.B. Wolfe, 1957, "An Operations Research Study of Sales Response to Avertising," *Operations Research* 5, 370-381.

[58] Wagner, H.M., 1969, *Principles of Operations Research*, Prentice Hall, Englewood Cliffs, NJ.

Chapter 6

RISK MANAGEMENT, INSURANCE AND FINANCE

In this chapter applications to finance and insurance are considered. The concept of utility and its use in optimization under uncertainty is outlined. Thereafter, portfolio problems, futures and options contracts are defined and discussed in the framework of stochastic decision models. In Section 6.4 problems of cash management are dealt with while in 6.5 a dynamic approach to the theory of the firm is presented by solution of a stochastic control problem resolved by Bensoussan and Lesourne [5]. Finally, in Section 6.6 three insurance problems are resolved. These are a stock, mutual and a re-insurance problem.

Our purpose in this chapter is to specify the usefulness and potential application of the dynamic approach to selected problems in finance and related fields. Current research in finance, insurance, international business and management abound with other problems and examples. To compensate for the partial treatment of the fields discussed, references will be given for further study.

6.1 *Utility and Risk Behavior*

Utility functions are functions that provide a consistent mean for comparing alternative rewards and which occur with some probabilities. Thus, utility functions express quantitatively decision makers' desires for higher rewards and their attitude towards the risk of such rewards. Of course, if instead of rewards, decision makers' objectives are expressed in costs, or penalties, then the utility function would become a disutility of such costs.

Say that $\{x, P(.)\}$ is a set of rewards x which are assumed to occur with probability $P(.)$ and define a function $u(.)$, the utility function. The basic utility theorem states that the expectation of the utility provides the objective index for comparing the desirability of rewards by a (risk sensitive) decision maker. In other words, the expected utility,

$$E(u(x) \mid P(.)) = \int u(x)P(x)dx; x \in X \tag{6.1}$$

can be used to select the reward which is best in the sense of a decision maker's valuation of alternative values of x, and their associated probabilities $P(x)$. Evidently, an expected utility can be interpreted either as the choice of a preferred probability distribution or as a regular expectation statement about $u(.)$. Typically, $P(.)$ would be a "subjective" estimate, or a belief, about the probabilities of rewards, or an "objective" estimate based on data and learning of the processes underlying the occurrence of the rewards and their probabilities (for further study, see Luce and Raiffa [30]). Thus, the objective index which is used to value the relative desirability of potential rewards is also a function of the model used in generating the probabilities $P(.)$.

This problem will be dealt with in Chapter 7 where notions of estimation (filtering, smoothing and forecasting) and dual control will be addressed. Given a probability $P(x)$ however, the basic assumptions regarding the utility functions are that alternative rewards

(1) can be compared

(2) can be ranked such that preferred alternatives have greater utility

(3) transitivity of preference

(4) indifference between alternative rewards implying an equal utility for such alternatives.

Other assumptions imposed on utility functions are continuity, increasing preference (i.e., the first derivative is positive) and the substitutability of alternative rewards. Of course, the expectation of utility in (6.1) need not equal the utility of the expectations. However, if $u(x)$ is a convex (concave) utility function with $\partial^2 u/\partial x^2 > 0 (\partial^2 u/\partial x^2 < 0)$, then these expectations are connected by Jensen's inequality, or

$$Eu(x \mid P(.)) \geq (\leq)u(E(x \mid P(.)))$$
(6.2)

and vice versa when the utility function is concave. This inequality is particularly useful when interpreting and comparing the results for decision making problems under certainty and uncertainty.

A definition of utility functions can then be used to describe functionally the decision maker's attitude toward risk. Three cases can be defined, (1) risk aversion, (2) risk seeking and (3) risk neutrality. Risk aversion expresses a behavior avoiding uncertainty and the preference of gambles that are more certain. For example, a risk averse decision maker will prefer a smaller reward if it can be obtained with more certainty, rather than the opposite. A risk seeker or risk loving decision maker has an opposite attitude to that of the risk averse. Although both prefer higher rewards, the "valuation" of such rewards are different. Finally, risk neutrality implies that rewards are valued at their objective measurement. Since for a risk averse decision maker the desire for more rewards with smaller probabilities will decrease (due to the increased risk associated with it), we note that this corresponds to a negative second derivative of the utility function (or to an assumption of concavity) and vice versa for a risk seeking decision maker as shown in Table 6.1.

To characterize quantitatively a risk attitude, we may define indices of risk behavior (see Arrow [1], Pratt [40] as well as McCall [35]) for further

Table 6.1: Utility Functions
and Risk Attitudes

	Assumptions
Utility Function	$u(.), \partial u/\partial x > 0,$ continuity
Risk Aversion	$\partial^2 u/\partial x^2 < 0,$ concavity in x
Risk Seeking	$\partial^2 u/\partial x^2 > 0,$ convexity in x
Risk Neutrality	$\partial^2 u/\partial x^2 = 0$

study). In particular, Pratt [40] defines an index of *absolute risk aversion* defined as follows:

$$\rho(x) = \frac{-\partial^2 u/\partial x^2}{\partial u/\partial x} = -\frac{\partial}{\partial x}\log(\frac{\partial u}{\partial x}) \qquad (6.3)$$

This basically expresses the amount by which a "fair bet" must be altered in order for a risk averse decision maker to be indifferent between accepting or rejecting the bet. In this sense, this is a cost associated with the increased risk of the marginal increase in reward.

The definition of utility functions appropriate for decision making purposes in managerial problems is difficult. For this reason, other means are often used to express the desirability of certain outcomes. For example, in a managerial problem, targets expressing desired operational outcomes can be sought, deviations from which induce a disutility. Similarly, constraints (as in regulation and reflection boundaries on processes) as well as probabilistic constraints (i.e. chance constraints equations) can also be used to express a behavioral attitude towards outcomes and risks. Such assumptions regarding decision makers preferences have been used earlier and will be used in this chapter.

Finally, utility functions can also be used to reflect the desirability of certain rewards at different times. These issues, discussed in Chapter 1 will be dealt with here by using the discounting mechanism. Namely, if $v(x,t)$ is the utility of a reward at time t, then a *separability* of the valuation with respect to x and t, is given by

$$v(x,t) = \alpha(t)u(x); 0 \leq \alpha(t) \leq 1$$

where $\alpha(t)$ is the weighting mechanism defined in $(0,1)$ and a function of time t, which reflects discounting with respect to time of the utility $v(x,t)$.

6.2 *Portfolio Problems*

Portfolio problems consist in selecting an allocation strategy among n competing alternatives, each yielding an uncertain payoff. For example, an investor having a budget of \$$W$ may invest them in any of the stocks available for purchase on the stock market. Each stock purchase is an alternative which can lead to a (speculative) profit or loss with various probabilities. When selecting several stocks to invest in, balancing the potentialities of gains with the risks of losing parts or the whole investment, the investor in effect constructs a portfolio. As a result, a porfolio is used to distribute the risk to be borne by the investor such that his expected utility, expressing the ordering of uncertain income and the risks of losses, are optimized in some way. In a similar vein, a marketer may wish to advertise in more than one medium (thereby constructing a portfolio of media advertising), produce a product line so that if one product fails, another may gain (see Wind et al. [53]). In R & D, we typically invest in several (often competing) projects, "hoping" that one project will succeed and bring large returns. A summary of such problems is given in Table 6.2 and is evident. This concern for risk management by construction of portfolios is even observed by large firms who diversify by buying other firms involved in completely unrelated business activities.

In this section, we shall first ouline the portfolio problem as a one period allocation problem under uncertainty. Thereafter, we extend it to a multi-period problem and, in particular, consider a stocks portfolio problem considered by Merton [36] - [38].

Denote by \$$W$ a budget to be allocated, and let $X_i, i = 1, ...n$ be the dollars allocated to each of the n available alternatives. Given this allocation to i, an uncertain payoff of size $\tilde{r}_i(X_i)$ ensues.

Define the sum or rewards by $\bar{R}$, a random variable. Thus, the allocation problem can be resolved by solving the following mathematical problem.

$$\text{Max } E\{U(\bar{R})\}$$
$$X_1, X_2, ...X_n \tag{6.4}$$
$$\text{subject to:}$$
$$\bar{R} = \sum_{i=1}^{n} \tilde{r}_i(X_i); \sum_{i=1}^{n} X_i \leq W, X_i \geq 0, i = 1, ..., n$$

Table 6.2: Portfolio Problems

Problem	Alternative	Allocation Decision	Criterion
Stocks Portfolio	Stocks with various returns and risks	Number of shares of each stock to buy	Maximize expected utility of speculative profits (dividends)
Salesmen allocation to territories	Territories with sales potentials	Number of salesmen to territories	Maximize profits (income from sales less selling effort)
R & D Project Allocation	R & D Projects with unknown returns possibilities	Dollars allocated for R & D	Maximize the expected utility of profits
Multi-media Advertising	Media involving uncertain sales as a function of advertising	Advertising dollars to media	Maximize sales and goodwill by allocating a fixed advertising budget
Multi-currencies portfolio	Foreign currencies with correlated price movement	Savings and income allocation to acquiring currencies	Maximize value of portfolio and satisfy currencies requirement
International production	Countries with production varying costs	Investments in new plants and facilities	Minimize expected production and shipment costs

where $U(.)$ is a utility function providing a return-risk ordering over all possible allocations. This problem has been resolved in many ways (for a study of the methods used, see [29]). Further, an important segment of finance theory deals with this problem even though it is quite general in nature, as we pointed out earlier. An early treatment of this problem was given by Markowitz in 1952 [34]. Specifically, let the return function be linear, such that $\tilde{r}_i(X_i) = \tilde{r}_i X_i$ with $(\tilde{r}_1...\tilde{r}_n)$ now a vector, normally distributed with means $\hat{r}_i$ and variance-covariance $\sigma_{ij}, i = 1,...n, j = 1,...n$. Mean returns are thus

$$\bar{R} = \sum_{i=1}^{n} \hat{r}_i X_i \tag{6.5}$$

while the returns variance σ_R is

$$\sigma_R = \sum_{i=1}^{n}\sum_{j=1}^{n} \sigma_{ij} X_i X_j \tag{6.6}$$

Markowitz then solved the following problem for all fixed return- variance $\sigma_R = \lambda$. Or

$$\text{Max } \bar{R}(X_1...X_n) \text{ s.t. } \lambda = \sigma_R \text{ and}$$
$$X_1...X_n \tag{6.7}$$
$$\sum_{i=1}^{n} X_i \leq W_i, X_i \geq 0$$

For a risk averse decision maker, an allocation $X_1...X_n$ will be chosen such that $\bar{R}$ will be largest, given that the variance is fixed. And inversely, for a given expected return, ρ, the variance has to be minimized. The locus of all such allocations, for fixed σ_R is called the efficient EV portfolio allocation while the locus of all EV efficient portfolios is called the EV-efficient frontier.

An alternative formulation of the problem is to add a Lagrange multiplier to σ_R in (6.7) and solve:

$$\text{Max } \bar{R} = \sum_{i=1}^{n} \hat{r}_i X_i + \theta[\sum_{i=1}^{n}\sum_{j=1}^{n} \sigma_{ij} X_i X_j - \sigma_R] \tag{6.8}$$

subject to:
$$\sum X_i \leq W, \; X_i \leq 0$$

Of course $\partial \bar{R}/\partial \sigma_R = -\lambda$ and therefore θ is interpreted as the price of "risk". Given such a function expessing the price of risk (found by empirical research on markets and investor's behavior), the porfolio allocation problem might be written as follow:

$$\text{Max } \bar{\theta} = \bar{R} - \theta u \tag{6.9}$$
subject to: Constraints on the $X's$

The portfolio procedure we have followed can be extended next to a multi-period setting.

Assume that an allocation at a given time t induces an income at the next time $t + \Delta t$ and that during the time interval Δt, a quantity of available resources (such as money) is consumed. This is shown graphically in Figure 6.1.

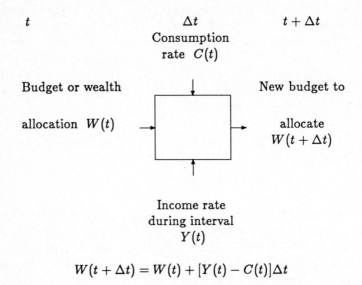

$$W(t + \Delta t) = W(t) + [Y(t) - C(t)]\Delta t$$

Figure 6.1: Budget Allocation Over Time

Income is generated by investments which in our problem is given as a function of our wealth or $Y(t) = Y(W,t)$. In our case, assume that all our wealth is invested in securities. Specifically, let $N_i(t)$ be the number of shares held at time t of security i whose price is $P_i(t)$. In a time interval Δt, the income obtained is derived from the change in prices $P_i(t + \Delta t) - P_i(t) = \Delta P_i(t)$, or

$$Y(t) = \sum_{i=1}^{n} N_i(t)\Delta P_i(t) \tag{6.10}$$

As a result, the change in wealth equations in figure 6.1 is given by

$$\Delta W(t + \Delta t) = \sum_{i=1}^{n} N_i(t)\Delta P_i(t) - C_i(t)\Delta t \tag{6.11}$$

which is a difference equation when $\Delta t = 1$. The stochasticity of this equation comes from the assumtion made regarding the price change. If prices vary randomly by some process, then $\Delta \tilde{P_i} = \tilde{P_i}(t + \Delta t) - P_i(t)$ is a random variable (assuming that we are at t and that prices P_i are observed perfectly at that time). In continuous time when $\Delta t \to 0$, we clearly have:

$$dW(t) = \sum_{i=1}^{n} N_i(t)dP_i(t) - C dt \qquad (6.12)$$

which is a stochastic differential equation if dP_i is a stochastic process (such as a diffusion, a jump process, etc.). In this case, assuming that the purpose of the decision maker is to maximize a discounted utility of consumption up to some planning time T, plus some functions over the terminal wealth at time T, we define stochastic control problems as shown in Table 6.3 for discrete and continuous time problems. For convenience, say that we invest a proportion θ_i of our wealth at t in security i, then essentially,

$$N_i P_i \;=\; \theta_i W, \text{ or } N_i = \frac{\theta_i W}{P_i} \qquad (6.13)$$

$$\sum_{i=1}^{n} \theta_i \;=\; 1$$

Insert these equalities into the general process of Table 6.3 and obtain the ammended process in the third row. The above formulation is often used in the portfolio finance literature. The problems, thus formulated can be solved by the techniques of Chapter 4, once the characteristics of the stochastic processes dP_i of price changes are given.

A problem of special interest consists in assuming that P_i are lognormal processes, in which case dP_i/P_i has a normal distribution with mean $\alpha_i dt$ and variance $\beta_i^2 dt$. Writing this as a diffusion process (see Chapter 2, Section 2.3),

$$dP_i/P_i = \alpha_i dt + \beta_i dw_i; \; P_0(0) = P_0 > 0 \qquad (6.14)$$

where w_i are standard Wiener processes.

Inserting into our wealth dynamic process, we obtain, for both discrete and continuous time,

$$W_{t+1} = W_t + \sum_{i=1}^{n} \theta_i W_t[\alpha_i + \beta_i \xi_i] - C_t; \; \xi_t \sim N(0,1), W_0 > 0 \qquad (6.15)$$

$$dW(t) = \sum_{i=1}^{n} [\theta_i \alpha_i W dt + \theta_i \beta_i W dw_i] - C dt$$

If the sum of $\theta_i \beta_i W dw_i$ (as well as $\theta_i W_t \beta_i \xi_i$) is a sum of uncorrelated random variables $dW_1...dW_n$ (or $\xi_1...\xi_n$), then the above equations can be written simply as follows:

$$W_{t+1} = W_t + \sum_{i=1}^{n} \alpha_i \theta_i W_t + W_t [\sum_{i=1}^{n} \theta_i^2 \beta_i^2]^{\frac{1}{2}} \xi - C_t \tag{6.16}$$

$$dW = [\sum_{i=1}^{n} \theta_i \alpha_i W - C]dt + w[\sum_{i=1}^{n} \theta_i^2 \beta_i^2]^{1/2} dw; \quad \sum_{i=1}^{n} \theta_i = 1$$

We can now turn to the solution of specific problems, in both discrete and continuous time.

Consider the problem stated in Table 6.3, in continuous time:

$$\text{Max } V(T) = E \int_0^T e^{-rt} U(C,t)dt + B(W(T))$$

$$C \in \Psi$$

subject to $\tag{6.17}$

$$dW = \sum_{i=1}^{n} \theta_i dP_i / P_i - Cdt; \quad \sum_{i=1}^{n} \theta_i = 1$$

where in addition we have n equations on $P_1...P_n$ describing the evolution of prices. As a result, we have by the dynamic programming procedure:

$$V(W_1, P_1, P_2, ..., P_n, t) = U(C,t)dt \tag{6.18}$$
$$+e^{-rt}[V(W + dW_1, P_1 + dP_1, ..., P_n + dP_n, t + dt)]$$

Say that prices evolve deterministically, then

$$V(W + dW_1, P_1 + dP_1, ..., P_n + dP_n, dt) = \tag{6.19}$$
$$= V + \frac{\partial V}{\partial t}dt + \sum_{i=1}^{n} \frac{\partial V}{\partial P_i}dP_i + \frac{\partial V}{\partial W}dW$$

Replacing $e^{-rdt} \approx 1 - rdt$, we obtain the following equation:

$$\frac{\partial V}{\partial t} + \sum_{i=1}^{n} \frac{\partial V}{\partial P_i}\frac{dP_i}{dt} + \frac{\partial V}{\partial W}(\sum_{i=1}^{n} \theta_i P_i \frac{dP_i}{dt} - C) + U(C,t) - rV = 0$$
$$V(W, P_1, ...P_n, T) = B(W(T)) \tag{6.20}$$

Now assume that prices evolve as a lognormal diffusion process (as in equation (6.14), then we use the continuous equation in (6.2) and obtain the following equation for V:

$$\frac{\partial V}{\partial t} + \sum_{i=1}^{n} \frac{\partial V}{\partial P_i}\alpha_i P_i + \frac{\partial V}{\partial W}\sum_{i=1}^{n}(\theta_i \alpha_i W - C) + \tag{6.21}$$
$$+ \sum_{i=1}^{n} \frac{\partial^2 V}{\partial P_i^2}\frac{\beta_i^2}{2}P_i^2 + \frac{\partial^2 V}{\partial W^2}(\sum_{i=1}^{n} \theta_i^2 \beta_i^2)\frac{W^2}{2}$$
$$+ U(C) - rV = 0$$
$$V(W_1, P_1...P_n, T) = B(W(T))$$

Table 6.3: Dynamic Portfolio

	Discrete Time ($\Delta t = 1$)	Continuous Time
Objective	Max $V(T) = E \sum_{t=0}^{T-1} (1+r)^{-t} U(C,t)$ $+B(W_T)$	Max $V(T) = E \int_0^T e^{-rt} U(C,t) dt$ $+B(W(T))$
	$U(.)$ a concave utility function	$U(.)$ a concave utility function
	$B(.)$ a concave terminal wealth function	$B(.)$ a concave terminal wealth function
	r = discount rate	r = discount rate
Process-General	$W_{t+1} = W_t + \sum_{i=1}^{n} N_{i,t}[P_{i,t+1} - P_{i,t}] - C_t$ $W_0 > 0$	$dW = \sum_{i=1}^{n} N_i dP_i - C dt$ $W(0) > 0$
Process-Amended	$W_{t+1} = W_t + \sum_{i=1}^{n} \theta_i W_t [\frac{P_{i,t+1} - P_{i,t}}{P_{i,t}}] - C_t$ $\sum_{i=1}^{n} \theta_i = 1$	$dW = \sum_{i=1}^{n} \theta_i (dP_i/P_i) - C dt$ $\sum_{i=1}^{n} \theta_i = 1$

The optimum consumption C and optimum θ_i are then found by solving for Optimum C:

$$-\frac{\partial V}{\partial W} + \frac{\partial U}{\partial C} = 0 \qquad (6.22)$$

Optimum θ's

$$\text{Max } \{W \frac{\partial V}{\partial W} \sum_{i=1}^{n} \theta_i \alpha_i + \frac{W^2}{2} \frac{\partial^2 V}{\partial W^2} \sum_{i=1}^{n} \theta_i^2 \beta_i^2\} \qquad (6.23)$$

subject to:

$$\sum_{i=1}^{n} \theta_i = 1, \theta_i \geq 0$$

It is simple to verify that a solution for θ_i is given by

$$\theta_i = -(\alpha_i/\beta_i^2) \frac{\partial V/\partial W}{\partial^2 V/\partial W^2} \qquad (6.24)$$

For two securities, $n = 2$ and $\theta_1 = \theta, \theta_2 = 1 - \theta$, we obtain:

$$\frac{\partial}{\partial W}\{[\theta\alpha_1 W + (1 - \theta)\alpha_2 W - C]V\} + \tag{6.25}$$

$$\frac{1}{2}\frac{\partial^2}{\partial W^2}\{[W^2\theta^2\sigma_1^2 + W(1 - \theta)^2\sigma_2^2]V\} - rV + U(C) = 0$$

For optimum C:

$$\frac{\partial V}{\partial W} = \frac{\partial U}{\partial C} \tag{6.26}$$

For optimum θ, we now have:

$$\frac{\partial}{\partial W}[(\alpha_1 - \alpha_2)WV] - \frac{\partial^2}{\partial W^2}[W^2(\theta\sigma_1^2 + \theta\sigma_2^2) - \sigma_2^2 W^2]V = 0 \tag{6.27}$$

If $U(C)$ is a (hyperbolic absolute risk aversion) utility function given by:

$$U(C) = \frac{(1 - \gamma)}{\gamma}((\frac{C}{1 - \gamma}) + \eta)^\gamma \tag{6.28}$$

and if we let $\sigma_2^2 = 0$, i.e., the second asset is not a risky one. Then a solution for W and C was shown by Merton [39, p. 390] to be proportional to W. For the case ($T = \infty$), a solution can be found by letting T tend to infinity in Merton's result

$$V(t) = \delta\beta^{-\gamma}e^{-\rho t}[\delta/(\rho - \gamma\nu)]^\delta[\frac{X}{\delta} + \frac{\eta}{\beta\gamma}]^\gamma \tag{6.29}$$

where $\delta = 1 - \gamma$ and $\nu = \alpha_2 + (\alpha_1 - \alpha_2)^2/2\delta\sigma^2$. At the initial time $t = 0$, we obtain:

$$V(W) = \delta\beta^{-\gamma}[\delta/(\rho - \gamma\nu)]^\delta[W/\delta + \eta/\beta r]^\gamma \tag{6.30}$$

Using (6.26), we find C^*, the optimum consumption rate,

$$C^* = \frac{(\rho - \gamma\nu)[W + \delta\eta/\beta r]}{\delta} - \frac{\delta\eta}{\beta} \tag{6.31}$$

while θ^* given by:

$$\theta^*W = \frac{(\alpha_1 - \alpha_2)W}{\delta\sigma_1^2} + \frac{\eta(\alpha_1 - \alpha_2)}{\beta\alpha_2\sigma_1^2} \tag{6.32}$$

When prices are correlated, we may replace the variance terms $\sum\beta^2\theta_i^2$ in (6.23) by

$$\sum_{i=1}^{n}\sum_{j=1}^{n}\theta_i\theta_j\beta_{ij} \tag{6.33}$$

where $\beta_{ii} = \beta_i^2$. Also, β_{ij} is the covariance between prices P_i and P_j. Other cases can be solved by specifiying various forms of the utility function as has been shown in [37] - [38], [31] and [23], for example.

Finally, by changing the interpretation of the variables used in constructing the above portfolio problems, other problems in marketing multi-products management, R & D projects allocation, etc., where portfolios have beneficial effects, can be constructed.

6.3 *Contracts Options and Futures*

Contracts are an agreement between two or more parties which involve some sort of an exchange. There are many types of contracts; a function of the purpose of contracting, the contractees and of course the environment and the information available to each of the parties. Contract examples in business, and generally in society, abound. Mostly, they establish the terms of exchange between parties for the purpose of managing the risk of the contractors. As instances of contracts consider the following cases:

An airline company contracts the acquisition (or the option to acquire) a new (technology) plane at some future time. The contract may involve a stream or a lump sum payment by the contractee to the contractor in exchange for the delivery of the plane at a specified time. Since the payments are often made prior to the delivery of the plane, a number of clauses are added in the contract to manage the risks for each of the parties of anyone deviating from the stated terms.

An investor may contract the acquisition (or the selling) of a stock, a given currency (denominated in certain quantitites), or a commodity at some future date. Such contracts involve a price and a delivery time (the exercise price). If the contractee has the right to exercise the contract at any time prior to the exercise date, then this will be called an option contract. If the exercise date is also the only exercise time, then the contract is called a forward contract. These and other contracts are particularly important in finance and will be presented subsequently.

In finance certain assets derive their value form the value (rights, claims, price) on other assets. Such assets are called contingent claim assets and include many financial instruments as special cases. For example, warrants, convertible bonds, convertible preferred stocks, options and forward contracts, etc. are some well known cases (see Elton and Gruber [20]). The intrinsic value of these assets is of course a function of the buyer and seller's objective and needs as well as the right these assets confer to each of the parties. When the number of buyers and (or) sellers is very large, these contingent assets are defined in standard terms to allow their free tradings. The number of such trades, has led to the creation of special stock exchanges (such as the Chicago, London, and Philadelphia commodities and currency exchanges) that manage the transactions of such assets.

A manufacturer can enter into binding bi-lateral agreements with a supplier, by which agreed (contracted) exchange terms are used as a substitute for the current market mechanisms of economic exchange. This can involve future contractual prices, delivery rates at specific times (to reduce inventory holding costs) and of course a set of clauses intended to protect each part against possible failures by the other party in fulfilling the terms of the contract.

Throughout the above cases the advantage resulting from negotiating a contract is to reduce, for one or both parties, the uncertainty concerning the future exchange conditions. In this manner, the manufacturer will be eager to secure long term sources of supplies, and their timely availability while, the investor, buyer of options, would seek to avoid too large a loss implied in the acquisition of a risky asset, currency or commodity, etc.

Since for each contract there, necessarily, need be a (or many) buyer and a (or many) seller, the "price" of the contract can be interpreted as the outcome of a "negotiation" process where both parties have an inducement to enter into a contractual agreement. For example, the buyer and the seller of an option can be conceived of as involved in a game, the benefits of which for each of the players are deduced from risk transference. In Figure 6.2, the main elements of a contractual situation are represented. Note that the utility of entering into a contractual agreement is always positive for all parties, otherwise there would not be any contractual agreement (unless such a contract would be imposed on one of the parties!). In this section we shall consider several examples of contracts while in Section 6.6 the use of contracts in insurance will be dealt with in detail.

Options

An option is a contract about an asset (securities, bonds, commodities, currencies, etc.) which confers the right to buy or sell the asset within a given time period subject to certain conditions. There are many types of options, as we shall briefly see. If the option is to buy, it is then called a *call option*, while if it is to sell, it is called a *put option*. Options may also be distinguished by the relationship between the exercise time (during which a decision to exercise or not the options can be taken) and the maturity date. If the exercise time is at the maturity date only, it is named a *European option* while if the maturity date is T, the option is bought at time t and if $[t, T]$ is the exercise time, it is then called an *American option*. To evaluate options we shall consider several examples.

Consider a metal trader who buys a *European (call) option* of a certain commodity, say copper, on the London stock exchange. Let $\{p, t \geq 0\}$

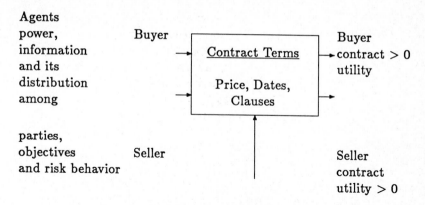

Figure 6.2: Valuing Contracts

denote the price of the commodity, defined by a stochastic process reflecting our belief about the future and its quantitiative characterization. Let $\pi(t)$ be defined as the contracted delivery price at maturity date T. This is also named the *strike price*. Finally, let Q be the contracted quantity (in some cases the strike price will be a function of Q), and let $f(p,t)$ be the probability distributions of the price at time t. For a risk neutral manufacturer, the value V of a unit of the options is at time T,

$$V = E \operatorname{Max} \{p(T) - \pi(T), 0\} \qquad (6.34)$$

where E is the expectations operator, or

$$V = \int_{\pi(T)}^{\infty} [p(T) - \pi(T)] f(p, T) dp \qquad (6.35)$$

Thus, if K is the premium paid to obtain the right of buying a unit of the commodity at time T, then clearly the solution of the resultant decision problem is:

$$\text{If } K < V; \text{ exercise the option} \qquad (6.36)$$
$$\text{If } K > V; \text{ do not exercise the option}$$

If there are n assets to buy, each at prices p_i, π_i and the premium per unit is K_i, then the optimal quantity to buy from each asset Q_i, can be otained by a solution of the following problem:

$$\text{Max } EU(\sum_{i=1}^{n} Q_i \text{ Max } [p_i - \pi_i, 0])$$

subject to   (6.37)

$$\sum_{i=1}^{n} K_i Q_i \leq B, \quad Q_i \geq 0$$

where $U(.)$ is the buyer's utility function and B is the total budget available that may be invested as premiums in some (or all) of the assets $i = 1, 2, ... n$. The problems defined above provide a "management science" approach to decision making with options. Next, we use another approach developed by Black-Scholes [8] and used in finance theory (see in particular references [4], [15], [16], [17] [37] for further study).

Assume a buyer of a call option and ignore all effects of taxes and transaction costs. In addition, say that markets trade continually (so we use a time-continuous model). An investor can borrow (or lend money) at the riskless rate r, i.e., (if he was to invest $1 without any risk, the rate of return would be for sure r). Assume as well a security (or a commodity) which is traded and define by $\{p, t \geq 0\}$ its price. Specifically, we shall assume a lognormal hypothesis for price variations. This means that dp/p has a normal distribution with mean μdt and variance $\sigma^2 dt$. In Ito's stochastic differential equation notation, we have

$$dp/p = \mu dt + \sigma dw \qquad (6.38)$$

where $w(.)$ is a standard Wiener process. Assume that options on the above (lognormal) assets are sold and let S be the exercise price of the option at time T, the maturity date. Our purpose is to characterize the value of such an option, or similarly its price, W, which is a function of p and t. Specifically, write

$$W = F(p, t), \qquad (6.39)$$

with $\partial F/\partial t$ continuous and F has existing two first derivatives with respect to p. If we invest P in the riskless asset, its value would be increasing at the following rate

$$dP = rP dt \qquad (6.40)$$

Instead of such an investment, say that we sell α units of the asset at its price p (at the cost αp) and buy an option whose value is W. Thus, the return on such a transaction would be $W - \alpha p$, or in differential terms; this equals $dW - \alpha dp$, which we equate to the riskless return dP (to obtain an equivalence between a riskless investment and an investment in the "risky" option). Combining these equations we have

$$dP = dW - \alpha dp \qquad (6.41)$$
$$= dW - \alpha[\mu p dt + \sigma p dw]$$

Since F is twice continuously differentiable, application of Ito's Lemma (see Chapter 2) to $W = F(p,t)$ yields,

$$dF = \frac{\partial F}{\partial t}dt + \frac{\partial F}{\partial p}dp + \frac{1}{2}\frac{\partial^2 F}{\partial p^2}(dp)^2 \qquad (6.42)$$

which can be written as follows:

$$dP = a dt + (\frac{\partial F}{\partial p} - \alpha)p\sigma dw \qquad (6.43)$$
$$a = [\mu p\frac{\partial F}{\partial p} - \alpha\mu p + \frac{\partial F}{\partial t} + \frac{1}{2}\sigma^2 p^2\frac{\partial^2 F}{\partial p^2}$$

Remembering that dP has a riskless return r, we can equate the above equation to $rPdt$.

To do so, an "Arbitrage Principle" is implied. This means that two investments with the same returns must have exactly the same price. Therefore, we necessarily have $adt = rPdt$ and $(\partial F/\partial p - \alpha)p\sigma = 0$.

This means that

$$\alpha = \partial F/\partial p \qquad (6.44)$$
$$rP = \mu p\frac{\partial F}{\partial p} - \alpha\mu p + \frac{\partial F}{\partial t} + \frac{1}{2}p^2\sigma^2\frac{\partial^2 F}{\partial p^2}$$

Inserting α we have

$$rP = \frac{\partial F}{\partial t} + \frac{1}{2}p^2\sigma^2\frac{\partial^2 F}{\partial p^2} \qquad (6.45)$$

Since, $P = F - \alpha p$, then inserting into the above equation we obtain the following second order differential equation in $F(p,t)$, the option's price, or

$$-\frac{\partial F}{\partial t} = rp\frac{\partial F}{\partial p} + \frac{\sigma^2}{2}p^2\frac{\partial^2 F}{\partial p^2} - rF \qquad (6.46)$$

To resolve this equation we require boundary conditions. Since this is a European option, which cannot be exercised before time T, its value in $[0,T]$ is zero, or

$$F(t,0) = 0, \ \forall t \in [0,T] \qquad (6.47)$$

At time T, the asset price is $p(T)$ and the strike price is S. If $p(T) > S$, the value of the option at this time $F(p,T)$ would then be $p(T) - S$. If

$p(T) \leq S$ then the option will not be exercised and its value would be zero. In other words,

$$F(p, T) = \text{Max} \,[0, p(T) - S] \qquad (6.48)$$

The differential equation above together with the boundary condition has been solved by Black-Scholes who have shown that

$$
\begin{aligned}
W &= F(p, t) = \bar{p}\Phi(d_1) - Se^{-rt}\Phi(d_2) \\
\Phi(y) &= (2\pi)^{-1/2} \int_{-\infty}^{y} exp(-u^2/2)du \qquad (6.49) \\
d_1 &= [log(\bar{p}/S) + \tau(r + \sigma^2/2)]/\sigma\sqrt{\tau} \\
d_2 &= d_1 - \sigma\sqrt{\tau}; \; \bar{p} = p(t)
\end{aligned}
$$

where $\tau = T - t$, is the remaining time until we can exercise the option. It can be shown that the option price (representing its value) W has the following properties

$$
\begin{aligned}
&\partial W/\partial p \geq 0, \; \partial W/\partial T > 0, \; \partial W/\partial S < 0, \\
&\partial W/\partial r > 0
\end{aligned}
\qquad (6.50)
$$

On the basis of such a price, a decision to buy or not buy the option can be taken. For example, if K is the premium to be paid for the option, then the following rule may be used

$$\text{If } K < F(p, T) \text{ buy the option} \qquad (6.51)$$
$$\text{If } K > F(p, T) \text{ do not buy the option}$$

In other word, the option valuation function $F(p, T)$ has provided an instrument for reaching decisions regarding the management of risk when acquiring options.

The Black-Scholes options' model considered has been extended in several directions. For example, price processes, other than the lognormal have been considered. Namely, normal and jump processes have been considered (see [31], [35] for further study). In addition, transaction costs together with discrete time models (and market incompleteness) for options trading have been studied. These problems are in general very difficult to resolve and provide fertile grounds for future research.

To conclude this section it is worth pointing out that there are many other prices used in stock exchange tradings and which have not been discussed here. Foremost are future prices which are an agreement to buy or sell a (say) commodity without any payment now (unlike options which required a premium payment) at a predetermined future date. In future contracts, the cost incurred by the buyer ususally includes a collateral to guarantee the ability to fulfill the terms of the contract. Each time that a commodity current (spot) price changes, the future's contract owner may be called upon to increase his payments to meet the collateral obligations.

6.4   *Cash Management*

Problems of cash management have attracted much attention in the short term finance literature. Foremost among the problems solved are Baumol's [2] 1952 paper and Miller and Orr [39] stochastic cash balance problem. Since then, a wide variety of cash managment problems have been suggested and resolved (e.g. see for example Sethi and Thompson [44], Constantinidis [13], Constantinidis and Richard [14], Eppen and Fama [21].

The Miller-Orr model as a case in point, considered a firm with two assets, cash and a portfolio of other liquid assets, yielding a given rate of return. The problem, as stated, consists in converting cash balances into other assets when a fixed transaction cost is incurred and when fluctuations in cash balances are governed by a random walk. Harrison and Taylor [24] pursued the problem as follows.

The firm has a reservoir of cash balances which is augmented by sales revenues and diminished by operating expenses. The level of these balances is generated by two random processes, one for addition to these balances, the other for deletions. The level of these balances can be controlled by transferring back and forth (as required and as prescribed by the cash management objective) funds between the liquid assets. Assuming that the return on cash is null while the return on the other assets is h per unit, per unit time, the cost of holding cash is the opportunity cost h. To make their model more specific, consider Figure 6.3, where all variables are clearly defined.

The cash management problem consists then in minimizing discounted costs subject to non-negativity constraints on the cash balances, or

$$W \geq 0 \tag{6.52}$$

The costs consist as pointed out earlier by the opportunity cost $hW(t)$, as well as the transfer costs in and out of the other assets, of $kdY(t)$ and $cdZ(t)$ respectively. The expected discounted cost to be minimized is then

$$\int_0^\infty E\{e^{-rt}(hW(t)dt + kdY(t) + cdZ(t))\} \tag{6.53}$$

Harrison and Taylor[24] show that a solution to this problem is given by a Barrier policy such that there is an S, with $0 \leq W(t) \leq S$, for all $t > 0$, where S is the unique solution of a transcendental equation. In other words, the "cash process" is a process with reflection at S and zero. At S we convert funds into the liquid asset and vice versa when cash balances reach the zero level.

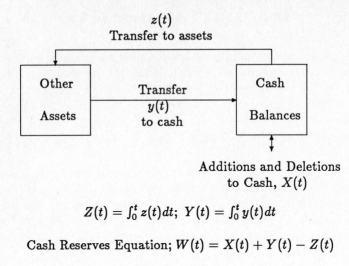

$$Z(t) = \int_0^t z(t)dt; \ Y(t) = \int_0^t y(t)dt$$

Cash Reserves Equation; $W(t) = X(t) + Y(t) - Z(t)$

Figure 6.3: A Cash Management Program

An alternative formulation of the Harrison and Taylor problem would be as follows (where time subscripts are dropped for convenience),

$$\text{Minimize } J = E \int_0^\infty e^{-rt}(hW + kw + cv)dt$$
$$u \in U, v \in V$$
Subject to:
$$dW = dx + udt - vdt, W(0) > 0 \text{ and } W \geq 0$$

(6.54)

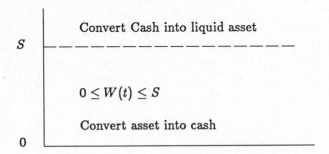

Figure 6.4: The Cash Barrier Policy

with $u = dY/dt$ and $v = dZ/dt$. If dx, the inflow-outflow of cash is given as in Harrison and Taylor by a diffusion model, with mean ξ and variance σ^2, the dynamic programming equation is,

$$-rJ + \mu dJ/dW + \frac{\sigma^2}{2}d^2J/dW^2 + (u - v)dJ/dW + (hW + ku + Cv) = 0$$
$$dJ(0)/dW = 0 \tag{6.55}$$

and $\lim J(W)$ converges as $W \to \infty$. The control u and v are found by minimizing,

$$\underset{u \in U, v \in V}{\text{Min }} u\{\frac{dJ}{dW} + h\} + v\{-\frac{dJ}{dW} + c\} \tag{6.56}$$

which means that

$$u = \begin{cases} \bar{u} \text{ if } h + dJ/dW < 0 \\ 0 \text{ otherwise} \end{cases}$$

$$\tag{6.57}$$

$$v = \begin{cases} \bar{v} \text{ if } c - dJ/dW < 0 \\ 0 \text{ otherwise} \end{cases}$$

where $\bar{u}$ and $\bar{v}$ are maximal convertible amounts. Evidently, because of $W \geq 0$, the quantitites v are prescribed by the amount of cash required to compensate negative cash balances. Further, since J is a function of W, then there is some W^* such that $dJ/dW = -h$, at this point, we convert funds into the asset. Since u can be as high as possible, realistically this can equal only the amounts which are above W^*. As a result, we obtain Harrison and Taylor's solution by putting $W^* = S$. Once having made this "observation", the remaining problem is to solve the differential equation (6.55) for $0 \leq W \leq S$ and finding the optimum S. Extensions, including fixed transaction costs, borrowings (such that levels $W < 0$ may be permissible) have been suggested and solved by Constantinidis [13] as well as Constantinidis and Richard [14]. The approach they used is based on the impulsive control approach (see Section 4.4).

Specifically, if we denote by x, the cash level at time t, the cost rate by $c(x) = \max (hx, -px)$, where

$$c(x) = \begin{cases} hx \text{ if } x > 0, \text{ opportunity cost} \\ px \text{ if } x < 0, \text{ shortage cost} \end{cases} \tag{6.58}$$

and if cash transfers at boundaries (x_1, x_0) involve fixed costs such that

$$B(x_1 - x_0) = \begin{cases} K^+ + k^+(x_1 - x_0) & \text{if} \quad x_1 > x_0 \\ 0 & \text{if} \quad x_1 = x_0 \\ K^- + k^-(x_0 - x_1) & \text{if} \quad x_1 < x_0 \end{cases} \qquad (6.59)$$

Then, Constantinidis [13] defines an impulsive stochastic control problem as follows:

$$\text{Minimize } J = \lim \frac{1}{T}\{E \int_0^T [C(x) + B^*(u)]dt + E \sum_{i=1} B(\xi_i)\}$$
$$T \to \infty \qquad (6.60)$$

subject to:
$$dx = udt - D(t, t + dt); \tau_i \leq t \leq \tau_{i+1}; \; x(\tau_{i+1}) = x(\tau_{i+1}^-) + \xi_i$$

where u are controlled cash additions, and $D(t, t + dt)$ are cash demands in the time interval $(t, t + dt)$, ξ_i is the quantity transferred incurring the cost (including a fixed cost) of $B(\xi_i)$. The solution to this problem is now straightforward by using section 4.4. If we let $dx = -\mu dt + \sigma dw$, and at τ_i, $x(\tau_i) = x(\tau_i^-) + \xi_i$ as well as a discounted and infinite horizon such that

$$J = E\{\int_0^\infty e^{-\beta t}C(x)dt\} + E\{\sum_i e^{-\beta t}B(\xi_i)\} \qquad (6.61)$$

then the optimality for J is found by,

$$(i) \quad -\beta J - \mu dJ/dx + \frac{1}{2}\sigma^2 d^2 J/dx^2 + C \geq 0$$

$$(ii) \quad J - \text{Inf}_\xi[B(\xi) + J(x + \xi)] \geq 0 \qquad (6.62)$$

$$(iii) \quad (i)^*(ii) = 0$$

and (Constantinidis and Richard [14]), if $h - \beta k^- > 0, p - \beta k^+ > 0$, then the optimum cash balance policy is of the following form

$$y(x) = \begin{cases} D & \text{if} \quad x \leq d \\ x & \text{if} \quad d \leq x < u \\ U & \text{if} \quad u \leq x \end{cases} \qquad (6.63)$$

which when reinserted in (6.62) above, provides an analytical solution to our problem.

Further extensions of the cash balance problem would consist in assuming that cash balances additions and deletions are governed by point processes and by considering in greater detail the relationship between investments, cash balances and borrowed funds.

6.5   *Dynamic Model of the Firm* [5, 6, 7]

The literature on corporate growth, or more generally on firm dynamics, has increased considerably. This has occurred hand in hand with the recognition that the firm is an anticipting, planning and adapting organism, plunged into a changing environment and having to face delays and uncertainties. The number of dynamic models of the firm we can address ourselves to is indeed very large, reflecting the specific issue at hand, the number of agents, the market structure, the firm's objective and even the managerial styles of the firm (see references [19], [52]). Here, we shall consider a model of optimal growth facing a risk of bankruptcy (Bensoussan and Lesourne [6]).

We assume that the firm model is given in terms of the following variables (Table 6.4) that are related as shown in Figure 6.5. Note that in Table 6.4, variables are explained and constraints stated. The objective of the firm is assumed to be dividend maximization, or

$$\Phi = \operatorname*{Max}_{D} E \int_0^\tau e^{-rt} D dt \qquad (6.64)$$

where r is the internal (shareholders) rate of discount and τ is the time of bankruptcy, at which the firm stops functioning, or

$$\tau = \{\operatorname{Inf} t \geq 0, m \leq 0\} \qquad (6.65)$$

Since Φ is the expected dividend payment over the lifetime of the firm, then by the dynamic programing formalism of Chapter 4, we have for $\Phi = \Phi(m, c, x)$:

$$r\Phi = \operatorname*{Max} \{D + u\frac{\partial\Phi}{\partial x} + v\frac{\partial\Phi}{\partial c} + (\lambda f(c) - v - D - ix + u)\frac{\partial\Phi}{\partial m}\} + \frac{\epsilon^2}{2}\frac{\partial^2\Phi}{\partial m^2}$$
$$|u| \leq a$$
$$v, D \geq 0 \qquad (6.66)$$
$$v + D \leq \lambda f(c) - ix + u^+$$
$$D \leq f(c) - ix$$

To this equation, we adjoin the boundary conditions at bankruptcy

$$\Phi(0, c, x) = 0 \qquad (6.67)$$

Table 6.4: Model and Variable Definitions

	Variable	Explanation	Constraints
Control Variable	$u(t)$	Borrowing rate	$\|u\| < a$
	$D(t)$	Dividends paid to shareholders	$D \geq 0$ $D < \lambda f(c) - ix$ $D \leq \lambda f(c) - ix$ $-v + u^+$
State Variables	$v(t)$	Investment in productive capital	$v \geq 0$
	$c(t)$	Productive capital	$c \geq 0$
	$x(t)$	Cumulative borrowed funds	$x \geq 0$
	$m(t)$	Cash on hand at time t, at $m = 0$, bankruptcy	$m \geq 0$
Parameters	i	Interest charge on borrowing	
	π	Profitability per unit time	
	$f(c)$	Production function	
	$\lambda f(c) dt$	Average profits in dt	
	ϵdw	Random profit in dt with mean zero and variance 1, dw, a standard Wiener process	

The Equations

$$dc = vdt; c(0) = c_0, \text{ initial capital}$$

$$dx = udt; x(0) = x_0, \text{ initial liabilities}$$

$$dm = [\lambda f(c) - v - D - ix + u]dt + \epsilon dw;$$

$$m(0) = m_0, \text{ initial cash holdings}$$

The Constraints

(i) $|u| < a$ - constraint on borrowing and debts return

(ii) $D \geq 0$ - dividends are always positive

(iii) $v \geq 0$ - investments are always positive

(iv) $m \geq 0$ - cash is positive, otherwise bankruptcy

(v) $0 \leq x/(c+m) \leq h, 0 \leq h \leq 1$ - limits on borrowing

(vi) $D \leq \lambda f(c) + u^+ - v - ix$ - dividends financed through excess earnings (and not borrowings)

(vii) $D \leq \lambda f(c) - ix$ - dividends smaller than average profits after interest charges

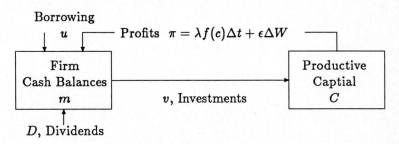

Figure 6.5: The Firm Model

The solution of (6.66) by analytical means is clearly difficult, but several insights can be obtained by an interpretation of the solution. We note that there are seven possible optimal policies corresponding to the maximization of u, v, D in (6.66). These are summarized in Table 6.6.

Further, we also note that with respect to i and r, the following situations occur: $i < r$: The firm borrows and invests without distributing until any dividends until it reaches an optimal equipment level. Then it stops investing and starts distributing. $i > r$: Two situations are possible, the firm never borrow but invests until it reaches an optimal equipment level. Then it stops investing and starts distributing (i very high); the firm borrows to accelerate growth, pays back its debt at a certain level of equipment, goes on investing until it reaches an optimal equipment level, then it stops investing and starts distributing (i moderately high).

For low borrowing interest rates, we find: When the firm has a good cash situation and a high level of equipment, it practices policy (I), i.e., does not invest, distributes and borrows, except if it is so close to the borrowing constraints that it is compelled to reimburse (policy IV), or if its cash situation is so favourable that it has to invest (policy VII). When the firm has a good cash situation with a low level of equipment, it practices policy (V), i.e., invests and borrows, except when it is so close to the borrowing constraints that it is compelled to reimburse (policy VI). When the firm has a low cash situation and a reasonable level of equipment, it gives priority to the improvement of its cash situation as soon as it is far enough from the borrowing constraints. Hence, it does not invest but distributes dividends (policy III). If it is too close to the borrowing constraints, it cannot avoid reimbrusements (policy IV). With a low cash situation and a low level of equipment (and hence a low level of average profits) the risk of bankruptcy is so high that the management saves the maximum for disaster and distributes (policy II) if it is far enough from the borrowing constraints. Otherwise, it cannot avoid reimbursing its debt (policy IV).

For high interest rates, the picture is slightly different. We shall only stress differences: A firm in a healthy situation (high level of equipment and high level of cash holdings) has no interest in being indebted since $i > r$. Hence, it distributes dividends and pays back its debt (policy II). During the course of its growth, such a firm may borrow to accelerate growth (policy V) and pay back its debt under defined circumstances (policy VI).

The analysis puts into evidence the three different roles of borrowing in the growth policy of a firm facing a risk of bankruptcy:

(a) Borrowing may be used to increase permantly the size of the firm's equipment when the borrowing interest rate is lower than the shareholders' interest rates. The firm will combine policies to remain as close as possible to $x = h(c + m)$.

(b) Borrowing may be used to accelerate growth of the firm either transitorily (during a part of the growth process) or permanently (during the whole growth process). (c) Borrowing may be used to avoid bankruptcy and improve the cash situation. This "emergency" borrowing occurs even for very high interest rates. It is generally coupled with a policy of no investment and no dividend distribution, but there exist cases in which this borrowing does not stop dividend distributions.

Since this model has a certain level of complexity, we shall illustrate the firm's strategy in the case of a self-financing firm ($x = 0$).

In this case, equation (6.66) may be written as,

$$r\Phi = \begin{array}{l} \text{Max } \{(1 - \frac{\partial \Phi}{\partial m})w + (\frac{\partial \Phi}{\partial c} - \frac{\partial \Phi}{\partial m})v + \frac{\partial \Phi}{\partial m}\lambda f(c)\} + \frac{\epsilon^2}{2}\frac{\partial^2 \phi}{\partial m^2} \\ v, D \geq 0 \\ v + D \leq \lambda f(c) \end{array} \qquad (6.68)$$

since u and x are equal to zero. Setting $z = \lambda f(c) - v - D$, the maximum in the right-hand side of (6.68) can be rewritten as:

$$\begin{array}{l} \text{Max } \{D + \dfrac{\partial \Phi}{\partial c}v + \dfrac{\partial \Phi}{\partial m}z\} \\ v, w, z \geq 0 \\ v + w + z \leq \lambda f(c) \end{array} \qquad (6.69)$$

which is equal to $\lambda f(c) \text{ Max } (\frac{\partial \Phi}{\partial m}, \frac{\partial \Phi}{\partial c}, 1)$. Hence, (6.68) becomes:

$$r\Phi = \lambda f(c)\text{Max}[\frac{\partial \Phi}{\partial m}, \frac{\partial \Phi}{\partial c}] + \frac{\epsilon^2}{2}\frac{\partial^2 \Phi}{\partial m^2} \qquad (6.70)$$

to which is adjoined the boundary condition:

$$\Phi(0, c) = 0 \qquad (6.71)$$

In that case, the optimal feedback strategy is extremely simple. The possible policies are reduced to three: A cash-policy (I) $v = D = 0$, $\dot{m} = \lambda f(c) + \epsilon\dot{w}$. The firm keeps its profit in order to improve its cash situation; An investment policy (II) $v = \lambda f(c), D = 0, \dot{m} = \epsilon\dot{w}$. The firm invests the whole of its average profit; A dividend policy (III) $D = \lambda f(c)$, $v = 0$, $\dot{m} = \epsilon\dot{w}$. The firm distributes its average profit.

Figure 6.6 shows the policies found in some numerical experiments for the three areas in R_+^2 in which a given policy is optimal, the cash position m corresponding to the first axis and the level of equipment c to the second. The evolution of the firm in time corresponds to a random walk in R_+^2. The firm switches to a different policy every time a border is crossed. These results are consistent with observed facts.

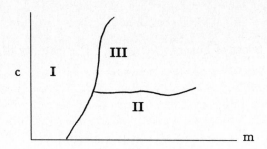

Figure 6.6: Optimal Policies

Finally, to develop a dynamic theory of the firm in an uncertain environment, it is important to deepen our knowledge of business reality and to improve our educational tools. Many managerial practices cannot be understood without reference to the occurrence of risks in the course of time. Whether these practices are consistent or not with some kind of optimal control of the stochastic evolution of the firm is an interesting theoretical issue. From that point of view, it is significant that the results of the model developed are roughly consistent with observed facts. But many other problems remain to be explored. Here are just a few examples:

- How to combine in a dynamic process investment projects by their expected profitability and by their level of risk?

- Is it possible to justify, theoretically, the banking rules imposing constraints on the structure of a firm's balance sheet? The idea underlying these rules is obviously that, if they are applied and if the firm is hit by an unexpected blow, the firm will have time enough to restore its profitability or to look for a solution avoiding a loss to the banks.

- What should be the loss announced to the shareholders at the beginning of the year by the manager of a firm in difficulty? The level should be such that the shareholders will not be unexpectedly confronted with a demand for cash and will have time to adapt to such a demand. Or, the contrary, is it unwise to darken too much the situation.

6.6   *Insurance*

In Chapter 1, we have described insurance as an instrument of risk management as well as the structure of insurance firms in a dynamic context. In this section, we shall develop the concepts outlined in Chapter 1 and construct two insurance models, one for a stock insurance firm and the

Table 6.5: The Optimal Policy

Policy	Action to Take
I	Borrow cash and distribute dividends. $u = a, v = 0, D = \lambda f(c) - ix, dm = adt + \epsilon dw$
II	Pay back debt out of cash and distribute dividends $u = a, v = 0, D = \lambda f(c) - ix, dm = -adt + \epsilon dw$
III	Borrow and give priority to cash holding $u = 0, v = 0, D = 0, m = [\lambda f(c) - ix + a]dt + \epsilon dw$
IV	Reimburse debt and give priority to cash $u = -a, v = 0, D = 0, dm = [\lambda f(c) - ix - a]dt + \epsilon dw$
V	Borrow and invest $u = a, v = \lambda f(c) - ix + a, D = 0, dm = \epsilon dw$
VI	Pay back debt and invest $u = a, v = \lambda f(c) - ix, D = 0, dm = -adt + \epsilon dw$
VII	Borrow, distribute dividends and invest $u = -a, v = a, D = \lambda f(c) - ix, dm = \epsilon dw$

other for a mutal insurance. In addition, the concept of re-insurance of great importance as a risk sharing scheme is considered in Section 6 (iii).

Basically, the insurance decision problem consists in transforming a stochastic process representing various risks (with varied severity) into a stream of "more" deterministic payments. Risk, in this case, is not reduced but is absorbed by the insurance firm which extracts for it a payment called the premium. There are many ways and techniques for computing these streams and has been an essential concern of actuarial science. For example, if x is a (risk) random variable, with density function $F(x)$, then actuaries are searching for some rule R such that a premium P can be paid by a policy holder for the "absorbtion" of x, or

$$P = R(F(x)) \tag{6.72}$$

Although there are alternative ways to compute this rule, the more prominent ones are based on the expected utility rule and the factor loading approach.

The expected utility rule states that there is a "fair" premium P such that

$$U(W) = EU(W + P - x) \tag{6.73}$$

where W is the initial wealth of the firm, P is the premium received for protection against risk x and E is the expectation operator.

The loading factor approach, however, seeks to determine a π such that $(1 + \pi)E(x)$ will equal the premium to be paid. This load is determined, as we shall see, by an optimization model where the insurance firm objective is well stated. Problems of risk sharing (as in mutual insurance), risk transfer (as in re-insurance), as well as insurance firm's investments, use both expected utility rules and loading factor policies when seeking economic arrangements for insurance protection. For references on these problems, [3, 9, 10, 12, 22, 42] may be helpful.

This section is organized as follows. In (i) a mutual insurance problem is considered, while in (ii) we consider a stock insurance firm model. In both models, a "normal" claim process is assumed while in (iii) applications of jump processes and re-insurance are considered.

(i) *Mutual Insurance*

Mutual insurance firms (unlike stock insurance firms), are firms whose stockholders are the bearers of insurance contracts. Insurance is then viewed as a collective process of N persons paying a fixed (or variable, contingent) amount monthly (the premiums) and seeking protection against claims that may occur to any one of them. For example, agricultural collectives may seek the participation of members of a collective in insuring each one of the members against possible damages or markets failures. Risk reduction for each is then exercised through a distribution of risk by aggregating individual risks and by accumulating cash (net of operating expense) to meet any possible contingent claims. Here, the problem is treated simply by assuming that the mutual insurance firm does not invest its moneys but reimburse insurees according to the cash position the firm may find itself in at any one moment. Alternatively, the firm can establish a contingent loading rate, meaning that insurees are required to make certain payments as a function of the cash level of the mutual insurance firm. In the first case, the firm loading factor is high, requiring that funds be returned. In the other, the loading factor is low, requiring that funds be sought from insurees. In both methods, the effects of uncertainty are different and the firm's optimal policy will depend on the objectives function. The cost function of the mutual insurer consits of two parts: a cost associated to maintaining cash reserves and administration costs. These costs will be deducted from the firm cash flow, and enter mutual insurees' objective through their imputation on the bankruptcy cost and through the payments required to maintain the mutual insurance firm functioning (i.e., not bankrupt and paying claims).

When firms cannot meet claims, the mutual partnership is dissolved and insurees have to self-insure or seek risk protection by alternative means. In this sense, the bankruptcy cost is the cost at which policyholders will refuse to increase premium payments and break apart their insurance mutuality.

Evidently, this is a function of policyholders' utilities in engaging in mutual protection compared to alternative risk sharing schemes (such as with stock insurance).

Granted that the policy holder finds it beneficial to participate in mutual insurance, we define an objective given by some function $L(p)$ of premiums p and K, the bankruptcy cost. Also, as pointed out earlier, our mutual insurance firm has no investments, since policyholders, being the stockholders as well, would prefer that excess funds be returned to them in the form of lower premium payments. Such payments, a sort of hidden "tax free" dividend is in some cases, favoring mutuals' competitive position.

For simplicity, we consider approximations and concentrate on simple results. A complete treatment can be found in [48].

State that the claims process is given by:

$$dz = \lambda(N)mdt + \sigma\sqrt{\lambda(N)}dw \tag{6.74}$$

The (deterministic) income rate is $(1+\pi)\lambda(N)mdt$, and the firm's carrying (policyholders' opportunity) cost hxdt and administrative expenses Cdt are deducted from cash flow so that the cash reserves held by the mutual firm to meet claims are given by:

$$dx = (\alpha_0\pi - hx - C)dt + \alpha_1 dw;$$
$$x(0) = W - \text{ the initial wealth} \tag{6.75}$$
$$\alpha_0 = \lambda(N)m \text{ and } \alpha_1 = -\alpha\sqrt{\lambda(N)}$$

The loading factor, expressing the rate (over mean claims) policy holders are required to pay in premiums is of course a decision variable which can be a function of time and a function of the mutual insurance cash position. When $\pi > 0$, this means that funds are accumulated at the mean rate $\pi\lambda mdt$, while for $\pi < 0$, this means that the firm reduces the required premiums to be paid by policyholders. For example, if a mutual insurance accumulates assets beyond "expectation", policyholders may note that members of the mutual firm can benefit through reduced premium rates.

Assume some function $L(\pi)$ that policyholders will minimize. Over time, letting $r > 0$ be the rate of discount of policyholders, and K the bankruptcy cost, and if τ denotes the bankruptcy time (i.e., granted no borrowing, this is the time at which the firm cash position reaches for the first time a negative level $x(t) \leq 0$), then the mutual insurance problem over a planning horizon $[0, \tau]$, is defined by the following:

$$\text{Minimize } J(W) = E_x\{\int_0^\tau e^{-rt}L(\pi)dt + Ke^{-rt}\}$$
$$\pi(t) \in \tilde{\pi} \tag{6.76}$$

subject to (6.75) and

$$\tau = \text{Inf}\{t > 0; x(t) \le 0\}$$

where $\tilde{\pi}$ is the set of feasible loading policies and $x_0 = W$ the firm's initial wealth.

We shall present intuitive optimization results and solve for an a priori constant loading factor policy. In [48], the linear minimum premiums objective with bankruptcy cost is considered in detail. Bellman's equation is

$$-rJ + (\alpha_0\pi - hx - C)\frac{dJ}{dx} + \frac{\alpha_1^2}{2}\frac{d^2J}{dx^2} + L(\pi) = 0; \qquad (6.77)$$
$$x \in [0, \infty), J(0) = K$$

For a given π (6.77) defines a second order differential equation which requires two boundaries for a solution. A first boundary is defined by the bankruptcy time τ, reached when $x = 0$ and when we incur the cost K. A second boundary is obtained by the covergence requirement for J as $x \to \infty$. Alternatively for some $x_1 > 0$, we define a stopping time such that

$$\tau = Inf\{t > 0, (x < 0) \cup (x > x_1)\} \qquad (6.78)$$

At the exit boundary $x = x_1, J(x_1) = \rho(x_1)$ and a constant is found by $\lim(\rho(x_1)) = \rho$, as $x_1 \to \infty$. Thus, K and ρ provide a complete solution to the cost estimate J. Since both the "mean" term $g(x, \pi) = \alpha_0\pi - hx - C$ and the "variance" α_1^2 are necessarily continuous, and bounded, the Ito stochastic differential equation (6.75) is well defined, and can be solved. Assuming that it has a unique solution and the objective exists and is the unique solution of (6.73), then an admissible control $\pi \in \Pi$ is also an optimal control if

$$- \alpha_0 dJ/dx = \partial L/\partial \pi \qquad (6.79)$$

These results derive directly from Bellman's principle and the continuity and differentiability of $L(.)$. For linear costs $L(\pi) = \psi\pi$ (to be dealt with next) note that the Bellman principle is expressed by minimizing over the admissible (loading factor) control policies:

$$\text{Min } \alpha_0\pi\frac{dJ}{dx} = \psi\pi \qquad (6.80)$$
$$\pi \in \Pi$$

The optimality principle expresses a "dynamic" marginal cost principle. If $L(\pi)$ is a disutility of policyholders in paying premiums at a loading factor π, then (at this factor, π) the marginal disutility per dollar mean claim $\alpha_0 = \lambda(N)m$, equals the negative marginal cost (and hence benefit) of increasing the mutual insurance wealth x. In other words, $-dJ/dx$ is a price policyholders are willing to pay per unit mean dollar claimed, for an optimum insurance protection.

Instead of optimizing the loading factor policy, say that we suppose that the premium policy is appropriately given by a per unit time payment $\alpha = \alpha_0(\pi_0 + 1)$, where α_0 is the mean claim rate, and π_0 the loading factor. Given that there is a fixed administration cost C per unit time, then the accumulation fund process is given by $dx = \beta dt + \alpha_1 dw$, with $\beta = \alpha - \alpha_0 - C = \alpha_0 \pi_0 - C > 0$. For such a process, assume that there is a terminal bankruptcy cost K and say that policyholders minimize both this cost and the cost of premiums $L(\alpha) = L[\alpha_0(\pi_0 + 1)]$. In this case, the expected cost $J(x)$, starting from initial wealth α, is given by the following equation:

$$\frac{\alpha_1^2}{2}\frac{d^2 J}{dx^2} + \beta\frac{dJ}{dx} - rJ + L(\alpha_0(\pi_0 + 1)) = 0 \qquad (6.81)$$
$$J(0) = K, \beta = \alpha_0\pi_0 - C > 0$$

In this case, a solution is straightforward,

$$J(x) = Ae^{\rho_1 x} + Be^{\rho_2 x} + L(\alpha_0(\pi_0 + 1))/r \qquad (6.82)$$

where ρ_1 and ρ_2 are the real two roots of the homogeneous equation in (6.82) given by

$$\rho_1 = -\frac{\beta}{\alpha_1^2} + \sqrt{(\frac{\beta}{\alpha_1^2})^2 + \frac{2r}{\alpha_1^2}} > 0$$

$$\qquad (6.83)$$

$$\rho_2 = -[\frac{\beta}{\alpha_1^2} + \sqrt{(\frac{\beta}{\alpha_1^2})^2 + \frac{2r}{\alpha_1^2}}] < 0$$

and A and B are two integration constants. Since at $x = 0, J(0) = K$ and for convergence of $J(x)$ to L/r as $x \to \infty$, we require $A = 0$ and $B = (K - L/r)$. Thus,

$$J(x) = Ke^{-px} + \frac{L}{r}(1 - e^{-px}) \qquad (6.84)$$

$$0 < p = \frac{\beta}{\alpha_1^2} + \sqrt{(\frac{\beta}{\alpha_1^2})^2 + \frac{2r}{\alpha_1^2}}$$

As a result, for initial wealth x, we distinguish between two costs, Ke^{-px} due to bankruptcy and the costs due to payments of premiums. Interpret

$exp(-px)$ as the probability of bankruptcy, then $J(x)$ is expressed in an actualized form as

(Cost of Future Bankruptcy) * (Probability of Bankruptcy)
+ (Cost of Future Premiums) * (Probability of no Bankruptcy).

which is equivalent in form to our equation (6.84). In our case, this probability is given specifically by:

$$y = exp\{-x[\frac{\alpha_0 \pi_0 - C}{\alpha_1^2} + \sqrt{\frac{(\alpha_0 \pi_0 - C)^2}{\alpha_1^2} + \frac{2r}{\alpha_1^2}}]\} \qquad (6.85)$$

Evidently, as x, the initial capital, increases, this probability of bankruptcy will be smaller. Thus, if we were to "regulate" the probability of bankruptcy, this could be done by an imposition on minimum reserves requirements $\bar{x}(x \geq \bar{x})$, so that the term in p in (6.84) could be compensated. Namely, say that α_1^2 is very large, then $p \to 0$ and reserves requirement will be very large. Inversely if α_1^2 is small, then smaller reserves requirements might be necessary. Other observations, such as high administration costs will reduce $p(\partial p/\partial C < 0)$ and therefore increase the pobability of bankruptcy, are evident from the above equation.

(ii) *A Stock Insurance Firm*

A stock insurance firm may be defined in terms of its assets K (or capital investments) yielding a rate of return, rK; a labor force L, consisting of agents paid proportionately to the income premiums they generate as well as a fixed wage. The firm collects premiums from insurees who have entered into (N) contractual agreements with the firm. The firm also pays claims, which occur following some random processes. This is presented graphically in Figure 6.7. A mathematical model is defined when we render precise the ways in which the above variables are interrelated. Evidently, there are many ways to do so, each way representing the structural properties of the firm investigated (see the previous section).

For simplicity, we shall define the following equations, given in Figure 6.7 with variables defined in Figure 6.8. The first equation (i) in Figure 6.8 describes the capital accumulation rate, which is a function of investmetns, desinvestments and the capital depreciation rate per unit time. The second equation expresses the labor dynamics where $H(t)$ is the hiring (or firing) rate and s the natural quit rate. To simplify the analysis, we shall assume that $H = sL$ and therefore the labor (agents) force is asumed to be stationary. Finally, the third equation measures cash balances. Cash income is given in terms of the premium income PN, income from desinvestments $(1-\gamma)g, 0 \leq \gamma < 1$ (where a portion γg is deducted from cash as a transaction cost of desinvestment), and the riskless asset rK (namely, returns from

investments in treasury bills, land, etc.). Cash outlays, however, are given
by the dividend payments D, investments $\beta I, \beta \geq 1$ (where $(\beta - 1)I$ is the
investment transaction cost, directly deducted from cash) and αPN is the
commission paid to agents which is a proportion α of the premium income.
In addition, claims by insurance contract holders, symbolically written by
$\varsigma(dt)$ are deducted from the cash balances. Since claims are usually random,
this is a stochastic differential equation.

Thus, given an insurance firm model we can assume that it's objective is
to maximize the discounted value of dividend distribution over the effective
life time of the insurance firm. This lifetime is defined as the planning
horizon over which the insurance firm does not default in payments to the
insureds. In other words, as long as the firm can meet instantaneously claims
by depleting its cash balances, or desinvesting, it will not default, but as
soon as it cannot meet a claim it will be bankrupt and dissolved. After such
a dissolution time, the insurance firm will no longer be capable of collecting
premiums, selling insurance and of course of distributing dividends.

The problem we formulated is thus a simplification of real situations
since no borrowing and no delays in payments and assets management are
possible. Let τ, the bankruptcy time, be the first instant reached when the
insurance firm cannot meet a claim, i.e.,

$$\tau = Inf\{t > 0; M(t) \leq 0\} \tag{6.86}$$

and the insurance firm discounted dividend maximization problem is

$$\text{Maximize } J(K_0, L_0, M_0) = E\{\int_0^\tau e^{-it} D(t) dt\}$$
$$I(t) \geq 0, g(t) \geq 0, D(t) \geq 0, H(t) \geq 0 \tag{6.87}$$
$$\text{Subject to equations (i)-(iii) in Figure 6.7}$$

where i is the internal rate of discount, and K_0, L_0, M_0 denote the known
current states at the optimization time. Furthermore, note that the premium rate P is given externally, imposed by competitive forces or through
regulation by national insurance authorities. Also, we may assume that
the number of contracts N is a function of premiums P and the agents
work-force L such that

$$N(t) = N_0 P^{-a} L^b, a > 0, b > 0, \partial N/\partial P < 0, \partial N/\partial L > 0 \tag{6.88}$$

In addition, physical constraints on the control variables require

$$0 \leq I(t)/M(t) \leq I_c, \ 0 \leq I_c \leq 1 \tag{6.89}$$
$$0 \leq g(t)/K(t) \leq g_c, \ 0 \leq g_c \leq 1 \tag{6.90}$$
$$0 \leq D(t) \leq D_{Max} \tag{6.91}$$

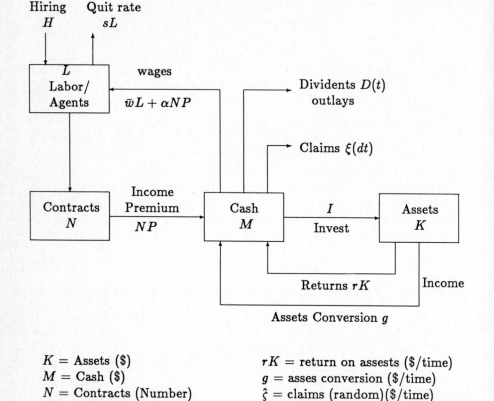

K = Assets (\$) rK = return on assests (\$/time)
M = Cash (\$) g = asses conversion (\$/time)
N = Contracts (Number) $\hat{\varsigma}$ = claims (random)(\$/time)
L = Labor (Agents) $\bar{w}$ = wage per agent (\$/agent/time)
P = Premium per contract α = Commissions rates
I = Investments (\$/time) s = natural quit rate (%)
D = Dividends (\$/time)
H = Hiring or firing (Agents/time)

Figure 6.7: The Insurance Firm (Model without Borrowing)

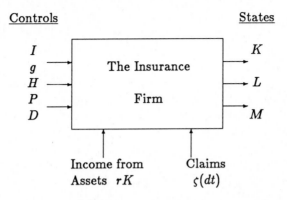

(i) $dK = (I - g - \delta K)dt; \; D_0 > 0$

(ii) $dL = (-sL + H)dt; \; L_0 > 0$

(iii) $dM = \{(1 - \alpha)PN(P, L) - \bar{w}L - \beta I + (1 - \gamma)g - D + rK\}dt - \varsigma(dt)$

$I(t) \geq 0, \; g(t) \geq 0, \; K(t) \geq 0, \; M(t) \geq 0, \; 0 \leq \alpha \leq 1, \; \beta \geq 1,$
$0 \leq \gamma < 1.$

Figure 6.8: The Insurance Firm Model, a state space Representation

where $I_c, g_c,$ and D_{Max} are known constants. Equation (6.89) states that no investment can be made by borrowing (Case $I_c = 1$) and more generally, at any one time, only a given proportion I_c of cash can be transformed into investments (thereby, expressing implicitly time delays required for converting cash into assets). Equation (6.90) points out the impossibility of selling all assets at the same time and that only a proportion g_c can be converted into cash. Finally D_{Max} in equation (6.91) provides an upper constraint on the quantity of dividends that might be distributed at any one time.

To resolve our problem we require still that the probability distribution of the claim process be defined, and an application of the techniques in Chapter 4. This is left as an exercise, although a solution yielding a barriers policy is provided in [49].

(iii) *Reinsurance*
The reinsurance contract between insurance firms is one of the essential

instruments firms have used to distribute and reduce risk. A great deal of attention has thus been devoted to perfecting these contracts both in theory and practice. A reinsurance contract is essentially an insurance policy issued by one company, the reinsurer, to another company usually called the ceding company or the direct underwriter. There are three forms of reinsurance arrangements: (a) proportional, (b) stop-loss and (c) excess loss (see [18], [47], [50] for references). Here we shall demonstrate how such contracts can be included as part of a dynamical model of an insurance firm. To keep ideas clear, the problem we deal with is simplified but could be applied to the models of (i) and (ii) without much difficulty.

Consider again an insurance firm collecting revenues at the rate of R at time t, and paying claims. Let these claims be defined by a Compound Poisson process. Specifically, claims occur according to a Poisson process with rate λ. Successive claims magnitudes $Y_1, Y_2, \ldots$ are assumed to be positive independent and identically distributed random variables having a known distribution function $F(.)$ (possessing first and finite second moments). Thus, the insurance cash position x is at any one time:

$$dx = Rdt - \varsigma(dt); \; x(0) = x_0 \tag{6.92}$$

where $\varsigma(dt)$ denotes the above claim process, explicitly written by:

$$dx = Rdt; \; x(0) = x_0;$$
$$x(\tau_i^+) = x(\tau_i^-) - Y_i, \; i = 1, 2, \ldots \tag{6.93}$$

where $\tau_1, \tau_2, , \ldots$ is a sequence of Poisson distributed random variables and $Y_1, Y_2 \ldots$ has density function $F(.)$. For simplicity (again), maximize the expected time to bankruptcy (assuming that it exists and is finite):

$$\text{Max } \bar{T} = E\{\int_0^T 1dt\}$$
$$T = Inf\{t \geq 0, x \leq 0\} \text{ and} \tag{6.94}$$
$$\text{subject to (6.93)}$$

Following the dynamic programming formalism of Chapter 4, the Bellman equation is then

$$1 + \frac{dT}{dx}R + \lambda \int_0^\infty [\bar{T}(x - y) - \bar{T}(x)]dF(y) = 0; \; \bar{T}(0) = 0 \tag{6.95}$$

The meaning of $\bar{T}(x)$ is that it is the expected time to bankruptcy when our cash position is x, and R, λ and $F(.)$ are stationary. A solution of this equation, an integro-differential equation, will provide the expected time to bankruptcy.

Now, assume that the insurance firm engages in excess loss reinsurance. In other words, the actual claim process associated with the ceding firm is now a Compound Poisson process with parameter λ and distribution function F_ρ^1

$$F_\rho^1(z) = \begin{cases} F(z) & \text{if } z < \rho \\ 1 & \text{if } z \geq \rho \end{cases} \qquad (6.96)$$

Similarly, the claim process associated with the reinsurer is also a Compound Poisson process having the Poisson parameter and distribution function:

$$F_\rho^2(z) = \begin{cases} 0 & \text{if } x < 0 \\ F(x+\rho) & \text{if } x \geq 0 \end{cases} \qquad (6.97)$$

Now let the ceding firm forego part of its income for reinsurance and let this be equal to c(ρ). As a result, the ceding and reinsurer cash position will be given by:

Ceding Firm(6.98)　　　　　　Reinsurer(6.99)

$$dx_1 = [R - c(\rho)]dt - \varsigma_1(dt) \quad dx_2 = c(\rho)dt - \varsigma_2(dt)$$

$$x_1(0) = x_{10} \qquad\qquad x_2(0) = x_{20}$$

where ς_1 and ς_2 are appropriately defined Compound Poisson processes (see equations (6.98) and (6.99)). Assuming each of these firms minimize the expected time to bankruptcy, we obtain instead of (6.95)

Ceding Firm

$$1 + [R - c(\rho)]\frac{d\hat{T}_1}{dx} + \lambda \int_0^\rho [\hat{T}_1(x-y) - \hat{T}_1(x)]dF(y) + \qquad (6.98)$$

$$+\lambda \int_\rho^\infty [\hat{T}_1(x-\rho) - \hat{T}_1(x)dF(y) = 0; \; \hat{T}_1(0) = 0$$

Reinsurer

$$1 + c(\rho)\frac{d\hat{T}_2}{dx} + \lambda \int_\rho^\infty [\hat{T}_2(x-\rho) - \hat{T}_2(x)]dF(y) = 0; \; \hat{T}_2(0) = 0 \qquad (6.99)$$

The solution of these equations, although more complex than that of (6.95), can still be otained by transforms techniques and by approximations. Of particular insterest in the study of such equations would be the effect of ρ on $\hat{T}_1$ and the economic implications regarding the willingness to pay ($c(\rho)$) and the expected time to bankruptcy. The actual solutions of such problems are, however, much more difficult, involving risk behavior by firms, market structure and gaming solutions.

Further Reading

The stochastic dynamic literature in finance, economics, insurance, cash management and the theory of the firm is far too great to be covered in one chapter. Further, there are many problems of interest which have not been treated. These include the problems of uncertainty and information in economics and finance (Hirschleiffer [25], Hirschleiffer and Riley [26]), bond problems [11], etc. Malliaris [31] provides a detailed outline of stochastic control in finance (see also [32] and [44]). In options pricing, the paper by Bensoussan [4] is particularly important. In insurance, the books we have referred to provide a useful point of departure for further study. In addition, the reader may consult the papers by Jewell [28] and Raviv [41] who deal with applications of Operations Research to insurance (Jewell) and with an interesting deterministic control formulation to special insurance problems (Raviv [41]). These are areas of burgeoning research however.

Bibliography

[1] Arrow, K.J., 1971, *Essays in the Theory of Risk Bearing*, Markham Publ. Co., Chicago, Ill.

[2] Baumol, W.J., 1952, "The Transaction Demand for Cash: An Inventory Theoretic Approach," *Quarterly Journal of Economics*, 66, 545-556.

[3] Beard, R.E., T. Pentikainen and E. Pesonen, 1979, *Risk Theory* (2nd ed.), Methuen and Co., London.

[4] Bensoussan, A., 1985, "On the Theory of Option Pricing," *ACTA Applicandae Mathematicae*.

[5] Bensoussan, A., and J. Lesourne, 1980, "Optimal Growth of a Self Financing Firm in an Uncertain Environment," in Bensoussan A. et al., *Applied Stochastic Control in Econometrics and Management Science*, North Holland, Amsterdam.

[6] Bensoussan, A., and J. Lesourne, 1981, "Growth of Firms: A Stochastic Control Theory Approach," in *Unternehmespplanung*, Springer Verlag, Berlin.

[7] Bensoussan, A., and J. Lesourne, 1981, "Optimal Growth of a Firm Facing a Risk of Bankruptcy," *Infor*, 19, 292-310.

[8] Black, F., and M. Scholes, 1973, "The Pricing of Options and Corporate Liabilities," *Journal of Political Economy*, 81, 637-659.

[9] Borch, K.H., 1968, *The Economics of Uncertainty*, Princeton University Press, Princeton, N.J.

[10] Borch, K., 1974, *The Mathematical Theory of Insurance*, Lexington Books, Lexington, Mass.

[11] Boyce, W.M., 1970, "Stopping Rules for Selling Bonds," *Bell Journal of Economics and Management Science*, 4, 27-53.

[12] Buhlmann, H., 1970, *Mathematical Methods in Risk Theory*, Springer Verlag, Berlin.

[13] Constantinidis, G.M., 1976, "Stochastic Cash Management with Fixed and Proportional Transaction Costs, *Management Science*, 22, 1320-1331.

[14] Constantinidis, G.M. and S.F. Richard, 1978, "Existence of Optimal Simple Policies for Discounted-Cost Inventory and Cash Management in Continuous Time," *Operations Research*, 26, 620-636.

[15] Cox, J.C. and S.A. Ross, 1976, "The Valuation of Options for Alternative Stochastic Processes," *Journal of Financial Economics*, 145-166.

[16] Cox, J.C. and S.A. Ross, 1978, "A Survey of Some New Results in Financial Option Pricing Theory," *Journal of Finance*, 31, 383-402.

[17] Cox, J.C., S.A. Ross and M. Rubenstein, 1979, "Option Pricing", Approach," *Journal of Financial Economics*, 7, 229-263.

[18] Dayananda, P.A.W., 1970, "Optimal Reinsurance," *Journal of App. Prob.*, 7, 134-156.

[19] Ekman, E., 1978, "Some Dynamic Models of the Firm," *The Economic Research Institute*, School of Economics, Stockholm.

[20] Elton, E.J. and M.J. Gruber, 1971, "Dynamic Programming Models in Finance," *Journal of Finance*, 26, 473-505.

[21] Eppen, G.D. and E.F. Fama, 1969, "Cash Balance and Simple Portfolio Problems with Proportional Costs," *International Economic Review*, 10, 119-123.

[22] Gerber, H.U., 1979, *An Introduction to Mathematical Risk Theory*, Monograph No. 8, S.S. Huebner Foundation, University of Penn., Philadelphia.

[23] Harrison, J.M. and S.R. Pliska, 1981, "Martingales and Stochastic Integrals with Theory of Continuous Trading," *Stoch. Proc. and Applications*, 11.

[24] Harrison, J.M. and A.J. Taylor, 1978, "Optimal Control of Brownian Storage Systems," *Stoch. Pro. and Appl.*, 6, 179-194.

[25] Hirschleifer, J., 1970, "Where are we in the Theory of Information," *American Economic Review*, 63, 31-39.

[26] Hirschleifer, J., and J.G. Riley, 1979, "The Analysis of Uncertainty and Information: An Expository Survey," *Journal of Economic Literature*, 17, 1375-1421.

[27] Iglehart, D.L., 1969, "Diffusion Approximations in Collective Risk Theory," *J. App. Prob.*, 6, 285-292.

[28] Jewell, W.S., 1974, "Operations Research in the Insurance Industry: A Survey of Applications," *Operations Research*, 22, 918-928.

[29] Levy, H. and M. Sarnat (eds.), 1977, *Financial Decision Making Under Uncertainty*, Academic Press, New York.

[30] Luce, R.D., and H. Raiffa, 1957, *Games and Decisions*, Wiley, New York.

[31] Malliaris, A.G., and W.A. Brock, 1982, *Stochastic methods in Economics and Finance*, North Holland, Amsterdam.

[32] Malliaris, A.G., 1981, "Martingale Methods in Financial Decision Making," *SIAM Review*.

[33] Markowitz, H.M., 1959, *Porfolio Selection*, Wiley, New York.

[34] Mason, S.P. and S. Bhattacharya, 1981, "Risky Debt, Jump Processes and Safety Covenants," *Journal of Financial Economics*, 9, 281-307.

[35] McCall, J.J., 1971, "Probabilistic Microeconomics," *Bell Journal of Economics*, 2, 403-433.

[36] Merton, R., 1969, "Lifetime Portfolio Selection Under Uncertainty: The Continuous Time Case, *Review of Economics and Statistics*, 50, 247-257.

[37] Merton, R.C., 1973, "Theory of Rational Option Pricing," *Journal of Economics and Management Science* 4, 141-183.

[38] Merton, R.C., 1977, "Optimum Consumption and Porfolio Rules in a Continuous Time Model," *Journal of Economic Theory* 3, 373-413.

[39] Miller, M.H. and D. Orr, 1966, "A Model of the Demand for Money by Firms,*Quarterly Journal of Economics*, 80, 413-435.

[40] Pratt, J.W., 1964, "Risk Aversion in the Small and in the Large," *Econometrica*, 32, 122-136.

[41] Raviv, A., 1979, "The Design of an Optimal Insurance Policy," *American Economic Review*, 69, 84-96.

[42] Seal, H.L., 1969, *Stochastic Theory of a Risk Business*, New York, Wiley.

[43] Sethi, S.P. and J.P. Lehoczky, 1984, "A Comparison of the Ito and Stranovich Formulations of Problems in Finance," *Journal of Economic Dynamic and Control*.

[44] Sethi, S.P. and G.L. Thompson, 1970, "Applications of Mathematical Control Theory to Finance: Modelling Simple Dynamic Cash Problems," *Journal of Quantitative and Financial Analysis*, 5, 381-394.

[45] Smith, C.W., 1976, "Option Pricing: A Review," *Journal of Financial Economics*, 3, 3-51.

[46] Sulem, A., 1984, "Resolution Explicite d'Inequations Quasi Variationelle en Dimension 1 Intervenant en Gestion de Stock," *Math. of Operations Research*.

[47] Tapiero, C.S., 1983, "The Optimal Control of a Jump Mutual Insurance Process,*Astin Bulletin*, 13, 13-21.

[48] Tapiero, C.S., 1984, "A Mutual Insurance Diffusion Stochastic Control Problem," *Journal of Economic Dynamics and Control*, 7, 241- 260.

[49] Tapiero, C.S., 1985, "A Dynamic Stock Insurance Firm Model and Dividend Optimization," *Journal of Large Scale Systems*.

[50] Tapiero, C.S. and D. Zuckerman, 1982, "Optimum Excess-Loss Reinsurance: A Dynamic Framework," *Stochastic Processes and Applications*, 12, 85-96.

[51] Tapiero, C.S., D. Zuckerman, and Y. Kahane, 1983, "Optimal Investment-Dividend Policy of an Insurance Firm Under Regulation," *Scand. Act. J.*, 65-76.

[52] Van Loon, P., 1983, *A Dynamic Theory of the Firm: Production, Finance and Investment*, Lecture Notes in Economic and Mathamatical Systems, Springer Verlag, Berlin.

[53] Wind, Y., V. Mahajan and R. Cordozo (eds.), 1981, *New Product Forecasting: Models and Applications*, Lexington Books, Lexington, Mass.

[54] Ziemba, W.T. and R.G. Vickson, 1975, *Stochastic Optimization Models in Finance*, Academic Press, New York.

Chapter 7

POT-POURRI

In this chapter we consider a pot pourri of applications and problems of interest which either were not treated in the book or provide fertile grounds for applications. Important issues such as estimation, learning and control will be introduced to provide a sense of the complexities they introduce. Evidently, the treatment of subjects in this chapter is in some cases superficial, defining mostly problems and their solution approaches rather than their actual solution.

7.1 *Estimation and Identification*

The estimation problem is defined by Kalman and Bucy [15] as follows:

> Given the actually observed values of a random process over some interval of time $[t_0, T]$, find the conditional probabilities of all values at time t of another related measurement random process.

Once the conditional probabilities relating the "model process" and the "measurement process" are found, the estimation problem is resolved. For example, consider the two processes (x_t, y_t) given by:

$$\begin{aligned}\text{Model process:} \quad & x_{t+1} = f(x_t, w_t) \\ \text{Measurement process:} \quad & y_t = h(x_t) + v_t \end{aligned} \qquad (7.1)$$

where w_t and v_t are two error terms which are assumed to be zero mean normal uncorrelated random variables with known variances. The function f denotes the model while h denotes the measurement. Since both processes are subject to random disturbances (w_t, v_t), the evolutions $\{x_t, t \geq 0\}$ and $\{y_t, t \geq 0\}$ define two stochastic processes. Let Y^T be the set of all measurements up to and including time T:

$$Y^T = \{y_0, y_1, ..., y_T\} \qquad (7.2)$$

Y^T is, of course, derived from the measurement (stochastic) process and stands for the observed values in the time interval $[t_0, T]$. The conditional probabilities relating the "model" and the "measurement" processes are given by:

$$P(x_t | y_0, ..., y_T) = P(x_t | Y^T)$$

The conditional mean estimate of $\hat{x}_{t/T}$ (based upon the measurement Y^T) is given by

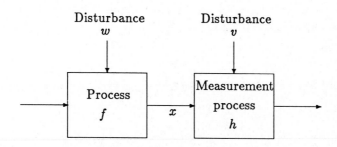

Figure 7.1: The Measurement Process

$$\hat{x}_{t|T} = E(x_t|Y^T) = \int_R x_t dP(x_t|Y^T)dx_t \qquad (7.3)$$

Define by $\varepsilon_{t|T}$ the error estimate. If $\varepsilon_{t|T}$ is an unbiased estimate of x_t with conditional error variance $V_{t|T}$, we write $E(\varepsilon_{t|T}) = 0$, $V_{t|T} = E(\varepsilon_{t|T}^2)$. We are concerned with the problem of selecting optimum estimates $(x_{t|T}, V_{t|T})$, (i.e. that all information contained in the observed data is taken into account).

If the measurement process Y^T leads (lags) the model process, i.e. $t > T(t < T)$, we obtain forecast (smoothing) estimates. When $t = T$, we obtain filter estimates. Thus, the time phasing of Y^T and x_t indicates the type of estimation problem we face.

Namely,

$$\begin{array}{ll}
\text{If } t = T \text{ filtering} \\
\text{If } t > T \text{ forecasting} \\
\text{If } t < T \text{ smoothing}
\end{array} \qquad (7.4)$$

The estimates $\hat{x}_{t|T}$ can be selected arbitrarily by intuition and judgement as is usually the case in management practice (when no "model process" is available). For complex problems, this is likely to lead to results which do not totally use the available information. Thus, it is necessary that a "model process" be constructed and that statistical techniques such as Bayesian estimation, least squares and maximum likelihood be used to use the available information for the estimation of the system's states.

We consider here the essential ideas of the Bayes and Least squares methods by solving a very simple one-dimensional filtering problem.

Consider the linear and discrete time stochastic difference equation

$$x_{t+1} = a_t x_t + w_t, \quad x_0 \sim N(\alpha, \sigma^2) \tag{7.5}$$

where a_t is a known time variable, x_t is the state variable, w_t is an error term with zero mean and known variance. The time record of x_t is given by a linear measurement model

$$y_t = h_t x_t + v_t \tag{7.6}$$

where h_t is given and v_t is a measurement error. We state,

$$\begin{aligned} E(v_t) &= E(w_t) = 0, \; E(v_t w_t) = 0 \\ E(v_t^2) &= q_t^2, \; E(w_t^2) = r_t^2 \end{aligned} \tag{7.7}$$

At each instant of time, a measurement y_t is drawn. At time $t = 0$, using Bayes theorem we have

$$p(x_0|y_0) = \frac{p(x_0)p(y_0|x_0)}{\int p(x_0)p(y_0|x_0)dx_0} = \text{const. exp.} \left[-\frac{(x_0 - x_{0|0})^2}{2V_{0|0}} \right]$$

where $p(x_0)$ is the prior probability distribution of x_0 which is known to be normal with mean α and variance σ^2. $p(y_0|x_0)$ is the likelihood which has normal distribution with mean $h_0 x_0$ and variance $h_0^2 \sigma^2 + q_0^2$. Since all these distributions are normal, they have a reproducing property. Thus, $p(x_0|y_0)$ also has a normal probability distribution where

$$\hat{x}_{0|0} = \frac{\alpha/\sigma^2 + h_0 v_0/q_0^2}{1/\sigma^2 + h_0^2/q_0^2}; \; 1/V_{0|0} = 1/\sigma^2 + h_0^2/q_0^2 \tag{7.8}$$

At time $t = 1$, we similarly obtain:

$$p(x_1|y_0, y_1) = \frac{\int p(x_0|y_0)p(x_1|x_0)p(y_1|x_1)dx_0}{p(y_1|y_0)}$$

All these distributions are also normal with

$$p(y_1|x_1) \sim N(h_1 x_1, q_1^2); \quad p(x_1|x_0) \sim N(a_0 x_0, r_0^2)$$

and after some manipulations:

$$\hat{x}_{1|1} = a_0 \hat{x}_{0|0} + K_1(y_1 - h_1 a_0 \hat{x}_{0|0})$$

$$1/V_{1|1} = h_1^2/q_1^2 + 1/(r_0^2 + a_0^2 V_{0|0}) \tag{7.9}$$

$$K_1 = h_1(r_0^2 + a_0^2 V_{0|0})/[h_1^2(r_0^2 + a_0^2 V_{0|0}) + q_1^2]$$

K_1 is called the Kalman gain at time $t = 1$ and expresses the weight attached to correcting the mean $\hat{x}_{1|1}$ when a time record y_1 is obtained at time $t = 1$. The term $(y_1 - h_1 a_0 \hat{x}_{0|0})$ is also called "the innovation". Assume that there is no error in measurement, then $q_1^2 = 0$, and therefore,

$$K_1' = 1/h_1$$

Since

$$K_1' > K_1$$

we note that the gain is at most equal to $1/h_1$. As the measurement error becomes larger, then the smaller the gain will be in adjusting K_1. When $h_1 = 1$, then $K_1' = 1$ and

$$\hat{x}_{1|1} = a_0 \hat{x}_{0|0} + y_1 - a_0 \hat{x}_{1|1} = y_1$$

which means that the mean is always taken as the record of the time series. The corresponding variance will naturally turn out to be zero since

$$1/V_{1|1}^2 = \frac{1}{0} + \frac{1}{r_0^2 + a_0^2} V_{0|0}^2 = \infty \text{ and } V_{1|1} = 0$$

In general, when Y^t is available, Bayes formula is

$$p(x_{t+1}|Y^t) = \frac{\int p(x_t|Y^t) p(x_{t+1}|x_t) p(y_{t+1}|x_{t+1}) dx_t}{p(y_{t+1}|Y^t)} \tag{7.10}$$

where

$$p(y_t|x_t) \sim N(h_t \hat{x}_{t|t}, q_t^2)$$
$$p(x_{t+1}|x_t) \sim N(a_t \hat{x}_{t|t}, r_t^2) \tag{7.11}$$

with $N(\alpha, \beta)$ denoting a normal probability distribution with mean α and variance β. Using the reproducing property of the normal distribution, we obtain the parameters of the conditional probability $p(x_{t+1}|Y^t)$ in recursive term form. Namely;

$$\hat{x}_{t+1|t+1} = a_t \hat{x}_{t|t} + K_{t+1}(y_{t+1} - h_{t+1} a_t \hat{x}_{t|t}) \tag{7.12}$$

$$\frac{1}{V_{t+1|t+1}} = \frac{h_{t+1}^2}{q_{t+1}^2} + \frac{1}{r_t^2 + a_t^2 V_{t|t}} \tag{7.13}$$

$$\tag{7.14}$$

$$K_{t+1} = \frac{h_{t+1}(r_t^2 + a_t^2 V_{t|t})}{h_{t+1}^2(r_t^2 + a_t^2 V_{t|t}) + q_{t+1}^2}$$

An extrapolation to the next period, without measurement (i.e. next period predictions) yields estimates which we denote by $(\hat{x}_{t+1|t}, V_{t+1|t})$. Obviously,

$$\hat{x}_{t+1|t} = a_t \hat{x}_{t|t}$$

$$1/V_{t+1|t} = 1/(r_t^2 + a_t^2 V_{t|t})$$

(7.15)

Thus the filter equations can be rewritten as:

$$\hat{x}_{t+1|t+1} = \hat{x}_{t+1|t} + K_{t+1}(y_{t+1} - \hat{x}_{t+1|t})$$

$$\frac{1}{V_{t+1|t+1}} = \frac{h_{t+1}^2}{q_{t+1}^2} + \frac{1}{V_{t+1|t}}$$

(7.16)

which describes the adjustment in estimates as a function of the past period's forecasts and the Kalman gain K_{t+1}. An extension to multivariate linear systems is straightforward (see [3, 4, 24]).

In a similar vein we may consider continuous time filtering problems. We use the least-squares approach for demonstration purposes. This will allow formulation of the filtering problem as a dynamic optimization problem. The model is given by

$$\frac{dx}{dt} = ax + w$$

(7.17)

with the continuous time record

$$y = hx + v$$

(7.18)

where x, a, w, y, h and v are function of time (with the time index t dropped for convenience) which were defined in the discrete time problem. Let x be the filter estimate

$$\hat{x} = \hat{x}(t|t) = E\{x(t)|Y^t\}$$

(7.19)

where Y^t is now a time continuous measurement:

$$Y^t = \{y(\tau), \tau \leq t\}$$

(7.20)

The error estimate is given by $\tilde{x} = x - \hat{x}$, with initial conditions $E[\tilde{x}(0)] = 0$ and $var[\tilde{x}(0)] = V(0)$. Assume that $\hat{w}$ is a control used to update the estimate $\hat{x}$ at time t,

$$d\hat{x}/dt = a\hat{x} + \hat{w}, \hat{x}(0) = x_0$$

(7.21)

and consider the least-square-fit criterion J in a time interval $[t_0, t]$

$$J = \frac{1}{2}\frac{\hat{x}^2(t_0)}{V(0)} + \frac{1}{2}\int_{t_0}^t [(y - h\hat{x})^2/q^2 + r^2 + \frac{\hat{w}^2}{r^2}]dt \qquad (7.22)$$

Minimization of J by a choice of $\hat{w}$ and subject to (7.19) is a standard quadratic (deterministic) cost problem whose solution is given by control or dynamic programming techniques. Let the Hamiltonian H be given by

$$H = \frac{1}{2}(y - h\hat{x})^2/q^2 + \frac{1}{2}\hat{w}^2/r^2 + V(a\hat{x} + \hat{w}) \qquad (7.23)$$

where $dV/dt = -\partial H/\partial \hat{x}; V(t_0) = V_0$ and $\partial H/\partial \hat{w} = 0$. A solution is then given by

$$d\hat{x}/dt = a\hat{x} + k[y - h\hat{x}]; x(0) = \hat{x}_0$$

$$\qquad (7.24)$$

$$dV/dt = 2aV - V^2 h^2/q^2 + r^2; V(0) = V_0$$

with the Kalman gain $k(t)$ given by;

$$k(t) = Vh/r^2 \qquad (7.25)$$

When the model and measurement processes are nonlinear or include parameter uncertainties, the results we obtain do not apply. We may then turn to approximate nonlinear filtering techniques and to adaptive filtering, as we shall briefly show next. Let the nonlinear model and measurement process be defined by:

$$x_{t+1} = f_t(x_t) + g_t(x_t)w_t$$

$$\qquad (7.26)$$

$$y_t = h_t(x_t) + v_t; \quad t = 1, 2, ...$$

where the statistics w_t and v_t are as defined in the linear case. Let Y^t be a set of measurements defined by (7.2). The conditional probability distribution of x_{t+1} is then given by:

$$p(x_{t+1}|Y^t) = \frac{p(y_{t+1}|x_{t+1})p(x_{t+1}|x_t)p(x_t|Y^t)dx_t}{\int\int p(y_{t+1}|x_{t+1})p(x_{t+1}|x_t)p(x_t|Y^t)dx_t dx_{t+1}} \qquad (7.27)$$

where $p(y_t|x_t)$ is a normal probability distribution given by

$$p(y_t|x_t) = \frac{1}{r(2\pi)^{1/2}}\exp[-\frac{1}{2}(y_t - h_t(x_t))^2/r_t^2] \qquad (7.28)$$

Predicition algorithms for $t > T$ are accomplished by solving:

$$p(x_{t+1}|Y^t) = \int p(x_{t+1}|x_t)p(x_t|Y^t)dx_t \qquad (7.29)$$

which is the continuous state, discrete time Chapman-Kalmogorov equation (see Chapter 2). If f_t and h_t are linear, then of course we obtain the filter equations (7.12) (or (7.14)). If f_t and g_t are nonlinear, all the moments (rather than just the first two used so far) of the probability distribution of conditional mean estimates are required. Equations (7.25) and (7.26) cannot therefore be resolved recursively. Approximations can be used however to allow computationally feasible solutions of (7.25). For a review of these approximations see Bucy and Joseph [3], Jazwinsky [14], and Sage and Melsa [24] for example. The procedures used to obtain approximate filters are numerous. The simplest consists in replacing the nonlinearities by their truncated Taylor series approximation around a nominal path (typically taken to be the conditional mean estimate). Alternatively, assumptions concerning the probability distribution of conditional estimates can be made which greatly reduce the problems of finding a solution of the nonlinear filter. For example, if the error term has a relatively small variance, a normal approximation is accurate and therefore the first two moments (i.e. two equations) can be used to represent the evolution of the conditional probability of x_t. When the error source is large, but the conditional distribution $P(x_t|Y^t)$ can be assumed to be symmetric (i.e. uneven moments except for the first one are equal to zero), all even moments can be expressed as a function of the first two moments. This property reduces the number of equations required to obtain filters. Other techniques can be found of course (see Mehra [19]).

For nonlinear continuous time systems, the problems outlined above remain the same. Specifically, consider the Ito stochastic differential equations

$$\begin{aligned} dx &= f(x,t)dt + g(x,t)dw \\[6pt] dy &= h(x,t)dt + rdv \end{aligned} \qquad (7.30)$$

with prior statistics given by:

$$\begin{aligned} E(dw) &= 0; \quad E(dw(t)dw(\tau)) = \delta(t-\tau)dt \\[6pt] E(dv) &= 0; \quad E(dv(t)dv(\tau)) = \delta(t-\tau)dt \end{aligned} \qquad (7.31)$$

To simplify the notations, define the Fokker-Plank diffusion operator (see also Chapter 2)

$$A = -\frac{\partial}{\partial x}f + \frac{1}{2}\frac{\partial}{\partial x^2}g^2 \qquad (7.32)$$

Then if $y = dz/dt$ and if Y^t is the time series generated by dz/dt, Kushner [17] has shown (using Ito's differential rule) that the conditional probability distribution $P(x|Y^t)$ is given by a solution of an extended Fokker-Plank diffusion equation:

$$dP = APdt + [h - E(h)](r^2)^{-1}(y - E(h)dt)P \qquad (7.33)$$

Since y is generated by the stochastic process $h(x,t) + rdv/dt$, equation (7.31) is a stochastic partial differential equation whose solution is unknown. It provides, however, a formal solution for the nonlinear filtering problem.

As a special case, we note that if the measurement variance is very large $((r^2)^{-1} \approx 0)$, then (7.31) is reduced to $dP = APdt$ which is the Fokker-Plank diffusion equation of the stochastic differential equation without measurement error.

7.2 Optimization and Learning, Dual Control[21]

Although we have not considered the effects of learning and information on decision processes, these are clearly important and crucial for any real application. Our purpose here is to compensate, albeit superficially, such simplifications by discussing a very simple model of the effects of learning and experimentation on the decision process (see Pekelman and Tse [21] and Pekelman and Rausser [20]). To illustrate the nature of the trade off between learning and control consider the two period problem with the following linear static system.

$$x_k = \alpha u_k + \varepsilon_k; \ k = 1, 2 \qquad (7.34)$$

where x_k is the observation, α is the unknown parameter which is normal with mean α_0 and variance σ_0, u_k is the control variable, and $\{\varepsilon_k\}$ is a sequence of equidistribution and independent normal variables with mean zero and variance q. The stochastic control problem is to find a control law

$$u_1 = u_1(q, \alpha_0, \sigma_0); \ u_2 = u_2(x_1, u_1, q, \alpha_0, \sigma_0) \qquad (7.35)$$

such that the cost

$$J = E\{x_1 + x_2 + \frac{1}{2}u_1^2 + \frac{1}{2}u_2^2\} \qquad (7.36)$$

is minimized. First, it should be noted that (7.32) is a static linear system since x_k is independent of x_{k-1} and therefore if α is known, the optimal closed loop law would be

$$u_1^* = u_2^* = -\alpha \tag{7.37}$$

and thus the optimal control law is open-loop in nature. For unknown α, a heuristic control law is to set

$$u_1^0 = -\alpha_0; \; u_2^0 = -\alpha_1 \tag{7.38}$$

where α_0 is the prior mean of α and α_1 is the updated mean of α after x_1 is observed and u_1^0 is determined. Since x_1 is a random variable (through ε before u_1^0 is applied), u_2^0 is also a random variable (before x_1 is observed). Such a control law is called *Certainty Equivalence* (CE).

Let u_1 be an arbitrary control law value applied to (7.32). After the observation of x_1, one can compute the aposteriori distribution for α which is normal with mean (see Section 7.1) and variance given by;

$$\alpha_1 = (\alpha_0 q + \sigma_0 u_1 x_1)/[u_1^2 \sigma_0 + q] \tag{7.39}$$

$$\sigma_1 = \sigma_0 q/[\sigma_0 u_1^2 + q] \tag{7.40}$$

From (7.38) it is noted that if $|u_1|$ is large, the updated variance for α will be small; in fact, if $|u_1| \to \infty, \sigma_1 \to 0$. This implies that a large control value at $k = 1$ helps one to learn the unknown parameter α. On the other hand, if $u_1 \approx 0, \alpha_1 \approx \alpha_0$ and $\sigma_1 \approx \sigma_0$; i.e., no additional knowledge on α will be obtained if a small control value is used at $k = 1$. In order to see what should be the proper, or optimum, value for u_1, one has to calculate the value, or the usefulness, of additional information on α, in the context of the given control problem, so that one can trade off present control (set $u_1 = -\alpha_0$) with additional learning for future control (set $|u_1|$ to be large). It should be noted that the CE control law ignores completely the benefit of future learning, as as a result, it may be far from optimal.

Let u_1 be the value of the control at $k = 1$, and x_1 be the resulting (random) observation. In minimizing the remaining cost

$$\begin{aligned} J_2 &= E\{x_2 + \tfrac{1}{2}u_2^2|x_1, u_1\} = E\{\alpha u_2|x_1 u_1\} + \tfrac{1}{2}u_2^2 \\ &= \alpha_1 u_2 + \tfrac{1}{2}u_2^2 \end{aligned} \tag{7.41}$$

where α_1 is given by (7.37). The optimum control law at $k = 2$ is

$$u_2 = -\alpha_1 = -(\alpha_0 q + \sigma_0 u_1 x_1)/(u_1^2 \sigma_0 + q) \tag{7.42}$$

Note that u_2 is random since x_1 is random. The minimum value function

$$J_2^*(x_1, u_1) = -\frac{1}{2}\alpha_1^2 = -\frac{1}{2}\left[\frac{(\alpha_0 q + \sigma_0 u_1 x_1)}{(u_1^2 \sigma_0 + q)}\right]^2 \qquad (7.43)$$

is a random variable through x_1. The cost of learning is negative and is represented by the expected minimum value function

$$E\{J_2^*(x_1, u_1)\} = -\frac{1}{2}\left[\frac{(\alpha_0 q + \sigma_0 u_1 x_1)}{(u_1^2 \sigma_0 + q)}\right]^2$$

$$= -\frac{1}{2}\left[\alpha_0^2 + \frac{\sigma_0^2 u_1^2}{(u_1^2 \sigma_0 + q)}\right] \qquad (7.44)$$

This indicates that learning is beneficial (negative cost) to future control. The overall cost of applying u_1 is:

$$J = E\{x_1 + \tfrac{1}{2}u_1^2\} + E\{J_2^*(x_1, u_1)\}$$

$$= \alpha_0 u_1 + \frac{1}{2}u_1^2 - \frac{1}{2}\{\alpha_0^2 + \frac{\sigma_0^2 u_1^2}{u_1^2 \sigma_0 + q}\} \qquad (7.45)$$

The optimum value for u_1 which will balance the present control (minimizing $\sigma_0 u_1 + (1/2)u_1^2$) and additional learning for future control (minimizing - $(1/2)\{\alpha_0^2 + (\sigma_0^2 u_1^2)/u_1^2 \sigma_0 + q\}$ is obtained by minimizing the "dual cost" given by (7.42). Unfortunately this minimization is not a simple analytical task. Therefore we can investigate a numerical solution by balancing the following to cost components

$$c_1(u_1) = \alpha_0 u_1 + (1/2)u_1^2$$

$$c_2(u_1) = -(1/2)\{\alpha_0^2 + \frac{\sigma_0^2 u_1^2}{u_1^2 \sigma_0 + q}\} \qquad (7.46)$$

A graphical plot of these costs for $\alpha_0 > 0$ will point out that;

(1) if q the variance of ε_k in (7.32) is small, $u_1^* \approx -\alpha_0$, since in this case, unplanned (or accidental) learning is sufficient to reduce the updated variance (7.39);

(2) if q is moderate, u_1^* is to the left of $-\alpha_0$, indicating that planned learning does pay off;

(3) if q is very large, $u_1^* \approx -\alpha_0$, since in the case of high noise intensity, planned learning does not pay off and thus the controller might consider his problem as a one-stage optimization problem. Similar conclusions can be drawn for different ranges for σ_0.

In this static example, the effect of the control value does not propagate in time through the system. Therefore the effects of learning and control can be distinguished easily. In a dynamic system, control applied at a certain time will influence the future state trajectory, and thus the dual effects of the control would be hard to separate. This example serves to point out one very important concept of dual control: namely that planned learning should be done only if

(1) accidental learning is not adequate, or

(2) learning does pay off (in terms of the objective function). This is the central theme of dual control theory.

As seen above, this two period static problem with a single parameter is difficult to solve analytically. Naturally, the general dynamic problem with multiple parameters and multiple periods poses a much higher level of difficulty and requires some form of approximation. For that purpose we can use the approach developed by Tse [28] (see also, Feldbaum [9], Florentin [10], Kendrick [16]).

We now turn to the application of this approach to the static example described above. The basis of the approach is the approximation of $J_2(x_1, u_1)$ by perturbation analysis around some nominal values $\{\alpha_2^0,\ u_2^0, x_2^0\}$ chosen as

$$\alpha_2^0 = \alpha_0, u_2^0 = -\alpha_2, x_2^0 = -\alpha_0^2 \tag{7.47}$$

i.e., the nominal values are the CE quantitites.

Let us expand now J_2 in (7.42) around x_2^0, α_2^0 and u_2^0 up to a second order. We then obtain

$$
\begin{aligned}
J_2 &= E\{x_2^0 + \delta x_2 + (1/2)(u_2^0)^2|x_1, u_1\} \\
&= x_2^0 + 1/2(u_2^0)^2 + E\{(\delta x_2)^2 + 1/2(\delta u_2)^2 + u_2^0 \delta u_2|x_1, u_1\} \quad (7.48) \\
&= -1/2\alpha_0^2 + E\{\delta x_2 + 1/2(\delta u_2)^2 - \alpha_0 \delta u_2|x_1, u_1\}
\end{aligned}
$$

An equation for δx_2 is given by

$$
\begin{aligned}
\delta x_2 &= x_2 - x_2^0 = (\delta\alpha + \alpha_0)(\delta u_2 + u_2^0) + \varepsilon_2 + \alpha_0^2 \quad (7.49) \\
&= \delta\alpha . \delta u_2 + \alpha_0 \delta u_2 - \alpha_0 \delta\alpha + \varepsilon_2
\end{aligned}
$$

Substituting (7.47) into (7.46) yields

$$J_2 = -1/2\alpha_0^2 + E\{\delta\alpha|x_1, u_1\}\delta u_2 + \frac{1}{2}(\delta u_2)^2 - \alpha_0 E\{\delta\alpha|x_1, u_1\} \tag{7.50}$$

Minimizing (7.48) with respect to δu_2 yields

$$\delta u_2 = -E\{\delta\alpha|x_1, u_1\} \tag{7.51}$$

and thus $J_2^*(x_1, u_1)$ can be approximated by

$$J_2^*(x_1, u_1) = (1/2)\alpha_0^2 - (1/2)E\{\delta\alpha|x_1, u_1\}^2 - \alpha_0 E\{\delta\alpha|x_1, u_1\} \tag{7.52}$$

and the dual cost

$$
\begin{aligned}
J &= E\{x_1 + (1/2)u_1^2 - \alpha_0^2 + (1/2)\alpha_0^2 - (1/2)E\{\delta\alpha|P_1\}^2 - \alpha_0 E\{\delta\alpha|P_1\} \\
&= E\{x_1 + (1/2)u_1^2 - (1/2)\alpha_0^2 - (1/2)E\{\delta\alpha|P_1\}^2\} \\
&= x_0 u_1 + (1/2)u_1^2 - (1/2)\alpha_0^2 - (1/2)\frac{\sigma_0^2 u_1^2}{\sigma_0 u_1^2 + q}
\end{aligned}
\tag{7.53}
$$

In this case, since J_2 is quadratic in δu_2, the perturbation analysis leads to the same solution as before, with no approximation. In general, since we expand the objective function only up to a second order, an approximation is introduced.

When we move from a two period problem with one parameter to the system of equations described before, many of the issues relating to the performance of the adaptive control scheme cannot be analyzed either analytically or graphically. We can construct however a simulation of the above system and investigate the impact of different policy rules on performance, in particular, the impact of our adaptive control scheme.

7.3 *Exhaustible Resources and Mining*

During the last two decades, attention has been increasingly devoted to the management of finite and depletable resources. These include, among others, quarry products, oil and gas and minerals (See Crabbe [5] for an extensive survey and references). These problems have been approached from both the (mining) firm and from governments' point of views in (economically) managing natural resources. To characterize mine problems, it is essential to distinguish between the basic features of depletable resources, the uncertainties and potential managerial actions that can be taken. Below, we shall outline a general framework highlighting several aspects of mining and the exhaustible resource management problem.

Basically, these problems consist of:

(1) A mine or a deposit from which we can extract a mineral of a given quality (i.e., composition). The costs of extraction are, typically, a function of the size of deposits, their location, composition-concentration, etc.

(2) Finite deposits at a given time that can be augmented by search and exploration. The effects of such activities on the stock of desposits is random, reflecting our lack of knowledge regarding the location of such deposits.

(3) Research and Development which can be applied to reduce extraction costs (i.e., augment accessibility), as well as seek alternative technologies and replacements to the depletable resources (such as finding more efficient ways to extract oil from tar sand and replace the need for gasoline by replacing it with alcohol).

(4) Other effects, such as regulation and market mechanisms dictating market prices, supplies and the proliferation of a wide variety of contracts. A Summary of these effects is given in Figure 7.2.

A stochastic control problem for managing such a mine can be constructed as follows. Let there be $i = 1, 2, ..., n$ quality grades of the resource, expressing the differing levels of quality. We define the following variables: $s_i(t) =$ the quantity of known deposits of grade i at time t, $s_i \geq 0$. $u_i(t) =$ the extraction rate of grade i deposits at time t, a decision variable $u_i \geq 0$. $p_i(t) =$ price of a unit of the resource of grade i at time t. $q(t) =$ exploration effort at time t, \$/time. $v_i(t) =$ investment in research and development for alternative resources - replacements \$/time, with $v_1 = dV_1/dt$ denoting cumulated investments. $v_2(t) =$ investment in research and development to augment the resource accessability and reduce extracting costs, \$/time, with V_2 denoting the cumulative investments. $\tau =$ the exhaustion time of the resources. $K =$ the "cost" of exhaustion of the resource. $\pi =$ profits at time t. $r =$ discount rate. $U(.) =$ a utility function of profits. The exhaustion time occurs when there are no resources left of any grade, such that:

$$\tau = \text{Inf}\{t \geq 0. \sum_{i=1}^{n} s_i(t) = 0\} \tag{7.54}$$

At this time a cost K is incurred, reflecting the replacement and transfer costs of dealing with other resources (such as switching from copper to aluminum, when there is no copper left!). This cost is conceptually similar to the bankruptcy cost considered in Chapter 6. In addition, however, past investment in research and development (V_1) seeking to find alternative resources and/or processes, can reduce the cost of replacement, such that:

$$K = K(V_1), \partial K/\partial V_1 < 0 \tag{7.55}$$

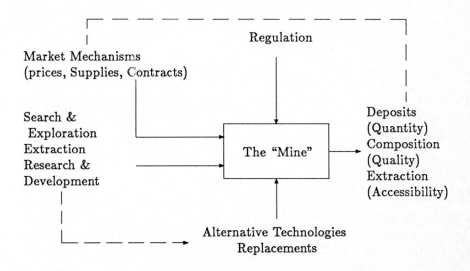

Figure 7.2: The "Mine" Extraction Problem

Given a profit measure π, the discount rate and a utility function of profits, the objective we can reasonably consider is:

$$\text{Maximize } J = E\{\int_0^\tau e^{-rt}V(\pi)dt + \exp[-r\tau]K(V_1)\} \qquad (7.56)$$

by a choice of policies, such as q — — the search and exploration effort, v_1 — — the investment in R & D to reduce extraction costs, and v_2 — — the investment in R & D for alternative resources. In addition, it is necessary to determine the profit function, as well as the dynamics of the stock equations, $s_i(t)$.

If $C_i(u_i, s_i, V_2)$ is the cost of extracting u_i when the stock is s_i and V_2 has been invested in R & D for cost reduction, then the profit at $t, \pi(t)$ is given by:

$$\pi(t) = \{\sum_{i=1}^n [p_i u_i - C_i(u_i, s_i, V_2)] - (v_1 + v_2 + q)\} \qquad (7.57)$$

Finally, the deposit stock equations will be given by:

$$ds_i(t) = -u_1 dt + \sum_{j=1} \delta(t - \theta_{ij})\varsigma; s_i(0) \geq 0, \varsigma \geq 0 \qquad (7.58)$$

where " $- u_i$ " is the depletion (extraction) rate and $\delta(t - \theta_{ij})\varsigma$ denotes the random discovery process, constructed as a point process. Specifically, we shall (for simplicity) assume that this is a Compound Poisson process with θ_{ij} the event (if $\theta_{ij} = t$ and $\delta(.) = 1$) of a discovery occurring and whose size has a random variable ς with known density function $F(.)$. Both processes (the discovery and its size) are assumed statistically independent. Let the discoveries be described by a Poisson process (See Chapter 2, Section 2.4) with parameter $\lambda, \lambda = \lambda(q), \partial\lambda/\partial q > 0$, a function of the exploration effort. Given such a discovery, the probability that it is of grade quality i is $x_i, i = 1, ..., n$. Thus, the discovery process has a Compound Poisson Process with mean rate of occurrence $\lambda(q)x_i$. Or $E(R_{ij}) = \lambda(q)x_i$, and $\varsigma \sim F(.), \theta_{ij}$ and ς independent.

The "mine" decision problem is, therefore, summarized by maximizing (7.54), subject ot (7.52) - (7.53), (7.55) - (7.56), and, of course, $dV_j/dt = v_j, V_j(0) = 0, j = 1, 2$. For other formulations of this problem and its solution, we refer to Desmukh and Pliska [7,8], Pyndick [22], Arrow and Chang [1], as well as Derzko and Sethi [6].

The solution of (7.54) is not without difficulties, however, since it is a stochastic control problem in $(n + 2)$ state variables and $n + 3$ control variables. For this reason, we shall consider below a simplified single grade problem for which only Bellman's equation is given.

(i) Single Grade Resource

The decision problem we consider is simplified by assuming no research and development and only a single grade. In this case, the problem is stated as follows:

$$\text{Maximize } J = E\{\int_0^\tau e^{-rt}U(\pi)dt + \exp[-r\tau]K\}$$
$$u \in U, q \in Q$$

$$\text{subject to} \qquad\qquad\qquad\qquad\qquad\qquad\qquad (7.59)$$
$$\tau = \text{Inf } \{t > 0, s(t) \le 0\}$$
$$\pi = pu - C(u, s) - q$$
$$dx = -udt + \sum \delta(t - \theta)\varsigma; \quad s(0) = s_0 > 0$$

In addition, $E(\theta) = \lambda(q)$ and $\varsigma \sim F(.)$. For this problem Bellman's equation is (see Chapter 4):

$$-rJ(s) - \frac{dJ}{ds}u + \lambda(q)\int [J(s+\varsigma) - J(s)]dF(\varsigma) + pu - C(u, s) - q = 0 \quad (7.60)$$

where at the boundary $s = 0$,

$$J(s = 0) = K \tag{7.61}$$

Also, for optimum extraction rate and constraint set $u \equiv (0, \bar{u})$

$$\text{Max } [pu - C(u, s) - \frac{u dJ}{ds}] \tag{7.62}$$
$$0 \leq u \leq \bar{u}$$

For optimum exploration effort and constraint set $Q \equiv (0, \bar{q})$:

$$\text{Max } [\lambda(q) \int [J(s + \varsigma) - J(x)][dF(\varsigma) - q] \tag{7.63}$$
$$0 \leq q \leq \bar{q}$$

Say that $C(u, s) = uc(s)$, and further that $\lambda(q) = \lambda_0 q$, then

$$u = \begin{cases} \bar{u} & \text{if } p - c(s) \geq dJ/ds \\ \\ 0 & \text{otherwise} \end{cases}$$

$$\tag{7.64}$$

$$e = \begin{cases} \bar{q} & \text{if } \lambda_0 \int [J(s + \varsigma) - J(s)] dF(\varsigma) > 1 \\ \\ 0 & \text{otherwise} \end{cases}$$

This property of the optimal solution can be used to "guess" that the solution is of the following form (which is true if J is strictly concave)

$$u = \begin{cases} \bar{u} \text{ for some } s > s_1 \\ \\ 0 \text{ otherwise} \end{cases}$$
$$q = \begin{cases} \bar{q} \text{ for some } s < s_2 \\ \\ 0 \text{ otherwise} \end{cases}$$

$$\tag{7.65}$$

As a result, a solution of equation (7.58) is given by:

$$\begin{cases} J(0) = K; s = 0 \\ \\ -rJ + \lambda_0 \bar{q} \int [] - \bar{q} = 0; \ 0 < s \leq s_1 \\ \\ -rJ - \dfrac{dJ}{ds} \bar{u} + \lambda_0 \bar{q} \int [] + p\bar{u} - \bar{u}c(s) - \bar{q} = 0, s_1 \leq s \leq s_2 \\ \\ -rJ - \dfrac{dJ}{ds} \bar{u} + p\bar{u} - \bar{u}c(s) = 0, \ s \geq s_2 \end{cases} \tag{7.66}$$

where $\int[]$ denotes the integral of $[J(s + \varsigma) - J(x)]f(\varsigma)$. In addition, the following boundary conditions are given by:

$$\begin{cases} \text{at } s = s_1 \\ J(s_1^+) = J(s_1^-) \\ p - c(s_1) = dJ/ds \text{ at } s = s_1 \end{cases} \qquad (7.67)$$

$$\begin{cases} \text{at } s = s_2 \\ J(s_2^+) = J(s_2^-) \text{ and} \\ \int[J(s + \varsigma) - J(x)]dF(\varsigma) = 1/\lambda_0 \end{cases} \qquad (7.68)$$

and, of course, the convergence requirement as $s \to \infty$. These constraints provide sufficient conditions for solving the three differential integral equations together with s_1 and s_2. For the solutions above to be optimal, however, note that (7.63) must be optimal. Since u and q are bang bang, then if $du/ds = -dc/ds - d^2J/ds^2 > 0$, meaning that if the extraction rate increases monotonically with the reserves, then there can be only one switch in the optimal u function. The condition on $du/ds > 0$ clearly implies $d^2J/ds^2 < -dc/ds$. By the same token $dq/ds < 0$ and there is one switch in the optimal q function if only $dJ(s+\varsigma)/ds < dJ(s)/ds$, which holds true if $d^2J/ds^2 < 0$ (i.e. J is concave in s). As a result, the proof of optimality of (u,q) in (7.63) is equivalent to a proof of concavity of $J(s)$. This can be shown to be the case by considering $J(s + \Delta s)$ in (7.57) and expanding in Taylor series to obtain finally a condition which states (for all points at which there is no switch),

$$\frac{u}{2}\frac{d^2J}{ds^2} < -r\frac{dJ}{ds} + \lambda_0 q \int [(\frac{dJ}{ds}(s + \varsigma) - \frac{dJ}{ds}(s))]dF(\varsigma) \qquad (7.69)$$

Say that $d^2J/ds^2 < 0$, then $dJ(s + \varsigma) < dJ(s)/ds$ and the above inequality always holds. Say that $d^2J/ds^2 > 0$, then when $q = 0$ and $u = 0$ (or positive), the equation above cannot hold. In this case, $d^2J/ds^2 < 0$ and J is concave proving thereby the optimality of (7.63).

7.4 *Quality Production and Maintenance*

The continuous quality production and maintenance problem defined in Chapter 3 can be solved analytically, leading thereby to some theoretical insights regarding maintenance procedures. We begin by assuming that maintenance is of the feedback type and that the machine quality production is observed continuously. The optimum feedback rule $u^0(y, n)$ stating "how much" to maintain a machine when its quality production is y and after having produced n units, is the solution of the production maintenance problem formulated in Chapter 3, Section 3.5 (ii). Application of dynamic programming for an autonomous system and with stopping level N leads to the following (Bellman) equation in J:

$$\frac{k^2 y^2}{2}\beta_0^2 \frac{d^2 J}{dy^2} - Py + \min_{0 \le u \le \alpha_0} \{-y[k(\alpha_0 - u) - \frac{k^2}{2}\beta_0^2]\frac{dJ}{dy} + Mu\} = 0 \qquad (7.70)$$

and the boundary conditions due to absorption at $y = \bar{y}$ and due to costless reflection at $y = 1$, $J(\bar{y}) = K$, $dJ(1)/dy = 0$. The optimum maintenance policy, found by minimization of (7.68) with respect to u yields;

$$u = \begin{cases} \alpha_0 \text{ if } M < -ky dJ/dy \\ \alpha_0 \text{ if } M > -ky dJ/dy \end{cases} \qquad (7.71)$$

Our next purpose is to characterize the form of the optimal policy.

Proposition Optimal control
The optimal maintenance policy is a barrier policy which is uniquely given by

$$u = \begin{cases} \alpha_0 \text{ for } y > y^* \\ \\ 0 \text{ for } y \le y* \end{cases} \qquad (7.72)$$

where $y^* = y_0, y^* = \bar{y}$ or y^* is the unique solution of the switching function $S(y^*) = 0$, with

$$S(y) = \frac{2ky}{k^2\beta^2}[\frac{M\alpha_0}{2}\frac{1}{y}(\frac{1}{y} - y) - P(1 - y)] + M \qquad (7.73)$$

Proof
Let $V(y) = dJ/dy$, then a solution for $V(y)$ in (7.68) with boundary condition $V(1) = 0$, yields

$$V(y) = \frac{2}{k^2\beta^2}\{\frac{P}{B(u)}[1 - y^{-B(u)}] - \frac{Mu}{[B(u) - 1]}[y^{-1} - y^{-B(u)}]\} \qquad (7.74)$$

where

$$B(u) = [2(\alpha_0 - u)/k\beta^2] - 1 \qquad (7.75)$$

The switching function $S(y) = M + kyV(y)$ given in (7.71) can then be computed explicitly by using (7.73). Say we begin by not maintaining (at which time $M + kyV(y) < 0$), then from (7.72) with $u = 0, V(y) < 0$ $(dV(y)/dy > 0)$ and therefore it is optimal to never maintain ($y^* =$

1). Alternatively, assume that we begin with maintenance (at which time $M + kyV(y) > 0$). Then from (7.72) with $u = \alpha_0$, we distinguish two cases:

$$V(y) = \begin{cases} > 0 \text{ if } P < \dfrac{M\alpha_0}{2}(\dfrac{1+y}{y}) \\[2mm] < 0 \text{ if } P > \dfrac{M\alpha_0}{2}(\dfrac{1+y}{y}) \end{cases} \tag{7.76}$$

Say that $(M\alpha_0/2)(1+1/y) > P$, then for all lower y's this inequality will be maintained, the switching function will be strictly increasing, as a result, it is optimal to always maintain, or $y^* = \bar{y} - -$ the overhaul absorption state. In the second case, $P > (M\alpha_0/2)(1+1/y)$, then $V(y) < 0$ and the switching function is strictly decreasing $(dV(y)/dy < 0)$ and a switch occurs at most when $S(y*) = 0$, $y^* > \bar{y}$ with $S(y) = M + kyV(y)$, with $B(u) = B(\alpha_0)$, or

$$S(y^*) = \frac{2ky}{\beta^2 k^2}[\frac{M\alpha_0}{2}(\frac{1}{y^*} - y^*) - P(1 - y^*)] + M = 0 \tag{7.77}$$

whose solution is

$$y^* = \frac{P}{2} \pm \sqrt{(\frac{P}{2})^2 - M(P - \frac{M\alpha_0}{2})(\frac{\alpha_0}{2} + \frac{k\beta^2}{2})} \tag{7.78}$$

Q.E.D.

A summary of the properties of $V(y)$ are given in Table 7.1. $J(y)$ can be obtained easily by integration of $V(y)$ in the ranges of (y_0, y^*) and $(y^*, \bar{y})$ and using the boundary condition $J(\bar{y}) = K$.

In practice, maintenance involves the shut-down of machines and numerous costs (such as opportunity costs) we might define as fixed costs. As a result, the maintenance policy is perhaps best characterized by an impulsive policy rather than a bang-bang one (see Chapter 4, 4.5). Specifically, maintenance costs would be $[c + m(u)]$, $c > 0$ and the effects of maintenance would be to alter discretely, at some (impulse) decision time the degradation dynamics. The solution of such a problem leads to quasi-variational inequalities which can be solved for some problems (as we have shown it when solving several problems in operations management in Chapter 4). Further areas of research would seek to bridge a gap between quality control and continuous production processes. In our formulation this means that states of machine quality are imperfectly observable and as a result, our dynamic programming approach incomplete. To amend such a situation, a measurement model sampling the quality of production at various levels of the continuous production process is required. In this case filtering equations providing quality estimates might be required to obtain the optimum maintenance program. This problem too is left as an area of further investigation.

Table 7.1: The Optimal Solution

	$u = 0$	$u = \alpha_0$
dV/dy	> 0	< 0
$V(y)$	$\dfrac{-2P}{k^2\beta^2}\dfrac{[1-y^\theta]}{\theta}$ $< 0 \;\; \forall y$ $\theta \; = \; 1 - 2\alpha_0/\beta^2 k^2$	$\dfrac{2}{k^2\beta^2}\{\dfrac{M\alpha_0}{2}(\dfrac{1}{y} - y) - P(1-y)\}$ < 0 if $P > \dfrac{M\alpha_0}{2} - (\dfrac{1+y}{y})$ > 0 if $p < \dfrac{M\alpha_0}{2} - (\dfrac{1+y}{y})$
$S(y)$	$> 0, \;\; \forall y$	< 0 if $P < \dfrac{M\alpha_0}{2} - (1 + \dfrac{y}{y})$ > 0 if $P < \dfrac{M\alpha_0}{2}(1 + \dfrac{y}{y})$

7.5 *Quality Control in a Dynamic Setting*

In this section we turn to the quality control problems defined in Chapter 3, Section 3, and resolve them. To do so, we shall consider only special cases and summarize essential results.

(i) Quality Control of a Discrete State Stochastic Quality Process.

As in Chapter 3, we consider the following stochastic quality control problem with curtailed and acceptance sampling. That is:

$$\text{Min } J = E\{\int_0^T c_0 N + c_1[ny + N(1-y)]dt + C_f(x(T))\}$$
$$(n, q), 0 \leq n \leq N, 0 \leq q \leq n$$

subject to

$$y = \sum_{j=0}^{q} \binom{n}{j} (1-\theta)^j (\theta)^{n-j}$$

$$dx = \begin{cases} +1 \text{ w.p. } (N-n)(1-\theta)ydt \\ 0 \text{ w.p. } 1-\theta \end{cases} \tag{7.79}$$

$$\partial C_f(x(T))/\partial x(T) > 0$$

The dynamic programming equation is:

$$-\frac{\partial J}{\partial t} = \underset{(n,q)}{\text{Min}} \quad \{c_0 N + c_1[ny + N(1-y)]+ \tag{7.80}$$

$$+(N-n)(1-\theta)y[J(x+1,t) - J(x,t)]\}$$

$$J(x,T) = C_f(x(T)); 0 \le n \le N, 0 \le q \le n$$

$$\frac{\partial C_f(x(t))}{\partial x} > 0$$

$$y = y(n,q) = \sum_{z=0}^{q} \binom{n}{z} (1-\theta)^z (\theta)^{n-z}$$

The solution is found by solving (7.78). Below we shall provide a solution for the curtailed sampling case where $q = 1$.

Proposition: Quality Control with Curtailed Sampling, $q = 1$
Define by $\Delta J = J(x+1,t) - J(x,t)$ then the optimal curtailed inspection plan n^* is either no inspection at all ($n^* = 0$) or is given by an interior solution.

$$n^* = \begin{cases} 0 \text{ if } c_1 + (1-\theta)\Delta J < 0 \\ \\ \text{interior solution if } " > 0 \end{cases} \tag{7.81}$$

where

$$n^* = \frac{c_1[1 - N\log\theta] - (1-\theta)\Delta J}{[\log\theta][c_1 - (1-\theta)\Delta J]} \tag{7.82}$$

Proof Derivation of (7.78) with respect to n, when $q = 1$ and $y = \theta^n$ yields

$$\alpha = \theta^n\{c_1[1 - (N-n)\log\theta] - (1-\theta)\Delta J[1 + n\log\theta] \tag{7.83}$$

When $\alpha = 0$, a solution to (7.81) yields the first order condition for an interior solution of the optimal inspection plan n^*. The solution to such an equation is given by (7.80). A second derivative of (7.79) with respect to

n or $\partial\alpha/\partial n$ provides a second order condition for n. If $\partial\alpha/\partial n > 0$, then (7.78) is convex in n and the solution is interior (since it is a minimization problem), and when $\partial\alpha/\partial n < 0$, then (7.78) is concave in n and the optimal solution is on either one of the boundaries N or zero. The condition for such convexity-concavity is given by $-c_1 + (1-\theta)\Delta J > 0$ (or < 0 respectively) as shown in equation (7.79). When the solution is on the boundary, we have

$$n^* = \begin{cases} N \text{ if } \alpha < 0 \\ 0 \text{ if } \alpha > 0 \end{cases} \qquad (7.84)$$

which leads after some manipulations to the following condition for $\alpha(n) < 0$ if $c_1 N |\log\theta| < [c_1 - (1-\theta)\Delta J][-1 + n|\log\theta|]$. In this case $n = N$ and therefore $\alpha(n) < 0$ implies, $N|log\theta|(1-\theta)\Delta J < (-1)[c_1 - (1-\theta)\Delta J]$. Since $\Delta J > 0$ and $c_1 > (1-\theta)\Delta J$ this is clearly a contradiction which means that $n^* = 0$ only.

Q.E.D

The interpretation of this solution is straightforward. Note that $J(x,t)$ is the "future" cost at time t when x units have already failed. Therefore, $\Delta J = J(x+1,t) - J(x,t) > 0$ is the cost increment at t due to having one additional unit failing. Since $(1-\theta)\Delta J$ is the expectation of such a unit cost increment, the switching function in (7.75) states that if the expected cost at t of an additional failed unit is greater than the unit inspection cost, it is then optimal to have no inspection at all. When the inspection cost is larger than the unit expected failure cost, then we obtain the sample size solution (7.80). Consider for discussion purposes the final instant of time T, then the switching function in (7.79) is:

$$(1-\theta)\Delta J - c_1 = (1-\theta)[C_f(x(T)+1) - C_f(x(T))] - c_1 \qquad (7.85)$$

Let $C_f(\bullet)$ be linear in $x(T)$ with proportionality parameter, c_f then if $c_1 > c_f(1-\theta)$ the optimal sample size is :

$$n^* = \frac{c_1[1 - N(T)\log\theta] - c_1(1-\theta)}{[c_1 + (1-\theta)c_f][\log\theta]} \in (0,N); \log\theta < 0 \qquad (7.86)$$

Clearly $\partial n^*/\partial N > 0$, such that the more we produce the larger the inspection sample size. Note however that n^*/N is not constant. When $c_1 < c_f(1-\theta)$, it is less expensive to deal with failed units after they have been sold such that it is optimal not to incur any inspection cost. The solution for q in (7.78) can be found by similar means. Minimization of (7.78) with respect to q and for fixed n yields

$$\text{Min } \{y(q)[-c_1 + (1-\theta)\Delta J]\} \atop 0 \le q \le n \tag{7.87}$$

Note that y is an increasing function of q and therefore the following proposition can be easily proved.

Proposition : Acceptance Sampling
The optimal acceptance number, for fixed sample size n is given by:

$$q^* = \begin{cases} n \text{ if } -c_1 + (1-\theta)\Delta J < 0 \\[2mm] 0 \text{ if } -c_1 + (1-\theta)\Delta J > 0 \end{cases} \tag{7.88}$$

This means that when inspection costs are larger than the expected cost of an additional unit that $q^* = 0$ and vice versa. Since the second case corresponds to $n = 0$ the jointly optimal solution (n*,q*) is given by (n*,0) with n* given by (7.80).

(ii) Quality Control and Post-Sales Failures
We return now to the problem defined in Chapter 3. application of the Bellman principle as in Chapter 4, is straightforward and yields for the finite time case.

$$V_t(x_t) = E(\pi_t)\beta EV_{t+1}(\alpha x_t + (1-\alpha)M_t(\phi)/N_t)$$

$$V_T(x_T) = Q(x_T); \; x \in [0,1] \tag{7.89}$$

For an infinite horizon problem and assuming stationary parameters and policies, equation (7.87) is reduced to

$$V(x) = E(\pi) + \beta EV(\alpha x + (1-\alpha)M(\Phi)/N); x \in [0,1] \tag{7.90}$$

The optimal quality control policy as well as the optimal manufacturing reliability are found by combining (7.88) with

$$V^*(x) = \text{Max } V(x : \Phi, \theta); \Phi \in \Gamma; \theta \in \nabla; x \in [0,1] \tag{7.91}$$

where Γ and ∇ are convex control sets for Φ and θ. Note that x_t takes naturally values in [0,1] thereby reducing the complexity of numerical computations by a discretization of the state space [0,1] into as many parts as are required for numerical precision, see Chapter 8.

An analytical solution to this problem can be obtained however, as shown in [27] (for a related problem see [25]).

7.6   *Renewable Resources (Pyndick [23])*

Renewable resources dynamic models have traditionally been used to describe "harvesting" policies given the natural growth of a "biological" resource stock function (e.g. see Clark [4]). For virtually, the natural rate of growth of the stock (or "Biomass") is in fact stochastic. For example, a fish or animal population reproduction process is basically stochastic. Similarly agricultural yields are a function of weather, etc., which renders the growth stock equations probabilistic at best.

The presence of "ecological" uncertainty raises important question about the behavior of renewable resource markets (see Gleit [11], Hutchinson & Fischer [13], Ludwig [18], and other references in these papers). These issues involve the effects of uncertainty on extraction of the resource, the life of species, the effects on rates of return dynamics of the *in situ* resource stock, regulation, etc.

Below, we shall consider a simple resource extraction, problem which was solved by Pyndick [23]. In addition to providing analytical solutions to an important economic problem, this application combines the dynamic programming approach with general optimality concepts regarding market behavior when there is a pure competition.

Assume that there are n firms (such as fishing firms) each harvesting under pure competition a natural resource. Let $\{x, t \geq 0\}$ be the stochastic processes of the natural resource stock, $f(x)$ is the mean natural growth rate whose growth dynamic is described by an Ito stochastic differential equation:

$$dx = f(x)dt + \sigma(x)dw; x(0) = x_0 > 0 \qquad (7.92)$$

with $\sigma(x)$ the growth rate diffusion coefficient $\sigma'(x) > 0, \sigma(0) = 0$ and $dw(.)$ is the standard Wiener process.

A firm harvest rate is q at time t. Thus, if all firms are identical, the aggregate harvest rate is $nq = Q$. Let p be the price at which each firm sales its harvest, and $p = p(Q), \partial p/\partial Q < 0$, reflecting the pure competition effects on the market prices and market demands. The harvesting cost is a function of the resource stock, such that q units costs $c(x)q$ to harvest and a firm profit $\pi = [p - c(x)]q$. The aggregate profit for all firms is of course $[p(Q) - c(x)]Q$. For a particular firm, whose discount rate is r, the problem it faces is defined by:

$$\text{Max } V_i(x, t) = E \int_t^\infty e^{-r(s-t)}[p - c(x)]q(s)ds \qquad (7.93)$$

$$0 \leq q(t) \leq \bar{q}$$

subject to:
$$dx = [f(x) - q]dt + \sigma(x)dw$$
$$x(0) = x_0 > 0, i = 1, ...n$$

Of course, since (7.91) is an infinite horizon problem and if $f(x)$ and $\sigma(x)$ are independant of time then $V_i(x)$ is stationary and Bellman's equation is:

$$rV_i = [f(x) - q]\frac{dV_i}{dx} + \frac{1}{2}\sigma^2(x)\frac{d^2V_i}{dx^2} + [p - c(x)]q \qquad (7.94)$$

The optimum extraction rate is in such a case given by:

$$q = \begin{cases} \bar{q} \text{ if } [p - c(x)] > dV_i/dx \\ 0 \text{ if } [p - c(x)] < dV_i/dx \end{cases} \qquad (7.95)$$

This means that a firm will harvest all it can if the return it can fetch for its harvest is greater than the marginal value of leaving the resource unharvested which is given by dV/dx. If all firms were to act in such a manner then $\bar{Q} = n\bar{q}$ will increase, reducing the price $p(Q)$. Therefore, under pure competition, there is a price p corresponding to a harvesting level Q such that:

$$p(Q) - c(x) = dV/dx \qquad (7.96)$$

This equation, of course, is a classical marginal revenue principle. Since dV_i/dx is the same for all firms and reflects the effect of aggregate harvesting on the value of keeping the resource unharvested. The optimality equation (7.94) is economically equivalent to a single aggregate firm, which extracts the optimal quantity $Q^* = Q^*(x)$ at the aggregated revenue:

$$\int_0^{Q^*} p(Q)dQ - c(x)Q^* \qquad (7.97)$$

where $c(x)Q^*$ is the aggregate harvesting cost while the integral of $p(Q)dQ$ is the surplus that all firms have and which maximizes the optimal harvest (or $q^* = Q^*/n$), then the dynamic programming program is resolved by:

$$rV = \int_0^{Q^*} p(Q)dQ - c(x)Q + [f(x) - Q^*]\frac{dV}{dx} + \frac{1}{2}\sigma^2(x)\frac{d^2V}{dx^2} \qquad (7.98)$$

$$p(Q) - c(x) = dV/dx$$

This equation has been solved for several growth functions by Pindyck, summarized in Table 7.2. By inserting these solutions into (7.96), these can be verified easily. An economic interpretation of $V(x), dV/dx$ and the optimal extraction rate as a function of the problem's parameters provide insights regarding the economic management of natural resources.

Table 7.2: Analytical Examples

$f(x)$	$\dfrac{dV}{dx}$	$Q*(x)$	$V(x)$
$\delta x(1 - x/K)$	$\dfrac{\phi_1}{x^2}$	$b(\phi_1 + c)^{-1/2}x$	$frac-\phi_1 x - \dfrac{\phi_1\delta}{rK}$
$\delta x \log \dfrac{K}{x}$	$\dfrac{b}{x(r+\delta)}$	$\dfrac{b(r+\delta)x}{b+(r+\delta)c}$	$\dfrac{b}{r+\delta}\log x + \phi_2$
$r\sqrt{x} - \dfrac{rx}{\sqrt{K}}$	$\phi_3\sqrt{x}$	$\dfrac{bx}{(\phi_3+c)^2}$	$2\phi_3\sqrt{x} + \dfrac{\delta\phi_3}{r}$

$$\phi_1 = 2b^2 + 2b[b^2 + c(r+\delta) - \sigma^2]^{1/2}/[r+\delta-\sigma^2]^2$$

$$\phi_2 = \frac{1}{r}\{b \ \log \ [\frac{b(r+\delta)}{1+(r+\delta)c}] - b + (\delta \log \ K - \sigma/2)/(r+\delta)\}$$

$$\phi_3 = -c/2 + \tfrac{1}{2}[c^2 + 4b/(2r + \delta/\sqrt{K} + \sigma^2/4)]^{1/2}$$

$$Q(p) = bp^{-n}$$

$$\sigma(x) = \sigma x$$

$$c(x) = cx^{-\gamma}$$

7.7 *International Insurance : Premium Valuation*

International insurance contracts, while diversifying insurance firms portfolio add on a currency exchange risk which compounds further the risk of claims. Further, the time varying character of exchange rates add on a perspective which requires a dynamic approach to the valuation of international contracts. Such an approach may provide a methodological foundation useful for the determination of "fair premia" in international insurance (see also [26]).

Our purpose here will be to devise a premium valuation formula specifically adapted to the stochastic and dynamic environment of exchange rates and their effects on international contracts valuation. In particular, we use an expected utility equivalence formula and reformulate it in a dynamic setting to account for the time variation and uncertainty of exchange rates.

Consider a domestic insurance firm whose wealth is initially known and given by W. Further, let this firm engage in international insurance contracting in a given country and let the portfolio of foreign insurance contracts have a known claim probability distribution. For simplicity, assume that such claims are given by a compound Poisson process (see Chapter 2), with mean claim rate q and known (and independent) claim density function $(dF(z), z \geq 0)$, denoted in the foreign currency. Although the insurance firm has both domestic and foreign portfolio insurance contracts, consider the foreign portfolio only.

Foreign exchange rates are assumed to be lognormally distributed over time and given by the following Ito stochastic differential equation;

$$dy/y = adt + bdw; y(0) = s \tag{7.99}$$

where a is the mean rate of growth of exchange rates and b is the instantaneous standard deviation growth rate. Finally $dw(.)$ is a standard Wiener process with $w(0) = 0$. The initial exchange rate is known and given by s. The insurance firm is assumed to collect over time premium payments in the foreign currency at the rate Pdt at time t (the mode of premium payments can be generalized to other forms as well, indexed to the firm's domestic curreny wholly or partially, or expressed as a function of exchange rates variations). Thus, the insurance firm's wealth increments, if no claim occurs and in a small time interval dt is given by Pdt. In a time interval $[h_i, h_{i+1}]$, no claims occur then wealth growth occurs at the rate dx and is given by:

$$dx = Pdt, t \in [h_i, h_{i+1}]j; \quad x(0) = w \tag{7.100}$$

Note that if premiums are paid in the domestic currency, we have $P = P(t)$ while, if premiums are paid in the foreign currency, we have instead, $P = P(t)y$ where $P(t)y$ is equal to the foreign premium payment valued in the domestic currency at the time premium payments are made.

When a claim occurs at the (Poisson) random times $h_j; j = 1, 2, 3, ...$ the firm's wealth is depleted by converting local funds into foreign ones. Thus, if $\{z, z \geq 0\}$, is a random claim with known density function $dF(*)$, occurring at the random times h_i, then the cost of such a claim in local currency terms is $zy(h_i) = z_i$. At this time, we have $x(h_i) = (x(h_{-i}) - z_i; z_i = zy(h_i))$.

Let $U(*)$ be the insurance firm utility function and r be its discount rate. Further, let k be the first instant of time at which claims exceed wealth (including the initial wealth) and at which time bankruptcy occurs. That is:

$$k = \text{Inf } \{t > 0, x \leq 0\}. \tag{7.101}$$

The insurance firm's current, expected and discounted utility is thus, given by $J(x, y)$ with:

$$J(x, y) = E\{\int_0^k U(x)\exp(-rt)dt + U(0)\exp(-rk)\} \tag{7.102}$$

where $(x, y) = (s, u)$ are the informational states of wealth and current exchange rates at the initial time $t = 0$ and r is the discount rate. Finally, $U(0)$ is the terminal utility of no wealth and facing the demise of the insurance contract (i.e., the firm no longer participates in insurance since it has no wealth to cover claims). Note that for a stationary premium payment as well as stationary parameters a and b in (7.97), that $J(x, y)$ is only a function of the information available regarding wealth x and the exchange rate y. Further, using the dynamic programming arguments of Chapter 4 it can be easily shown that $J(x, y)$ satisfies the following functional equation:

Proposition: For a lognormal exchange rate process as in (7.97) with stationary parameters a and b and a Compound Poisson Claim Process $\{q, F(.)\}$ the actualized utility of the international insurer is given by:

$$-rJ(x, y) + P(.)\partial J(x, y)/\partial x + ay\partial J(x, y)/\partial y +$$

$$b^2 y^2 \partial^2 J(x, y)/2\partial y^2 + qE_z\{J(x - zy, y)\} + U(X) = 0 \tag{7.103}$$

$$J(0, y) = U(0)$$

In the above equation, q is the Poisson rate at which claims z with density function $F(*)$ occur. Further, $P(.)$ is defined as a function of the mode of premiums payments. If premiums are paid in the domestic currency, then $P(.) = Py$ while if the premiums are paid in a lump sum P at the beginning of the insurance contractual time, then $P(.) = 0$, but the initial wealth is $W + P$.

The actual fair premium in the expected utility sense is of course given by noting that for $x = W$ the current weath and $y = s$ the current exchange rate, that the current utility equals the actualized utility of foreign insurance countracts. Specifically,

Proposition The actual fair premium rate P^*, is given by a solution for P in:

$$J(W, s) = U(W) \tag{7.104}$$

The proof of (7.102) is a direct outcome of expected utility equivalence in premium valuation (see Chapter 6). Note that in such a case that the actual fair premium is a function of $r - -$ the rate of discount reflecting an attitude towards time, exchange rates evolution (a) and uncertainty (b), claims z and of course the utility effects of bankruptcy (at $x = 0, U(0)$). A generalization of the above propositions to international insurance in N countries is straightforward and left as a simple exercise. A generalization to an excess of loss reinsurance scheme with

$$z = \begin{cases} x \text{ if } z \geq V \\ \\ V \text{ if } z > V \end{cases} \tag{7.105}$$

amends equation (7.102) to:

$$-rJ + P(.)\partial J/\partial x + ay\partial J/\partial y + (1/2)b^2 y^2 \partial^2 J/\partial y^2 +$$

$$q \int_0^v [J(x - zy, y) - J(x, y)]dF(z) + \tag{7.106}$$

$$q[J(x - Vy, y) - J(x, y)]\text{Prob}[z \geq V] + U(x) = 0$$

with $J(0, y) = U(0)$

Although these equations are extremely difficult to solve analytically, they provide a formulation for the expected utility equivalence principle for premium calculations in international insurance which can be handled easily by numerical means.

Bibliography

[1] Arrow, K.J. and Chang ,1980,"Optimal Pricing, Use and Exploration of Uncertain Natural Resources Stock," in P.T. Liu (ed.) *Dynamic Optimization and Mathematical Economics*,Plenum Press, New York.

[2] Beddington, J.R. and M. May, 1977, "Harvesting Natural Populations in a Randomly Fluctuating Environment, *Science* 197, 463- 465.

[3] Bucy R.S. and P.D.Joseph, 1970,*Filtering for Stochastic Processes with Application to guidance*, Wiley, New York.

[4] Clark, C.W., 1978, *Mathematical Bio-economics: The Optimal Management of Renewable Resources*, Wiley, New York.

[5] Crabbe, P.J., 1982, "Sources and Types of Uncertainty Information and Control in Stochastic Economic Models of Non-Renewable resources," in G.Feichtinger (ed.), *Optimal Control Theory and economic Analysis*, North-Holland, Amsterdam.

[6] Derzko N.A. and S.P. Sethi, "optimal Exploration and Consumption of a Natural Resource – Stochastic Case," *International Journal of Policy Analysis and Information Systems* 5, 185-200.

[7] Desmukh, S.D. and S.R. Pliska, 1980, "Optimal Consumption and Exploration of Nonrenewable Resourcs under Uncertainty," *Econometrica* 48, 177-200.

[8] Desmukh, S.D. and S.R. Pliska, 1983, "Optimal Consumption of a Nonrewnewable Resource with Stochastic Discoveries and a Random Environment," *Review of Economic Studies* L, 543-554.

[9] Feldbaum, A., "Theory of Dual Control", *Automation and Remote Control* 1960-61, (21-9, 21-11, 22-1, 22-3).

[10] Florentin, J.J., 1962, "Optimal Probing, Adaptive Control of a Simple Bayesian System", *Journal of Electronics and Control*, Series 1, 13, 165-177.

[11] Gleit, A., 1978, "Optimal Harvesting in Continuous Time with Stochastic Growth", *Math. Biosciences* 41, 111-123.

[12] Goel, S., and N. Richter, 1974, *Stochastic Models in Biology*, Academic Press, New York.

[13] Hutchinson, C.E. and T.R. Fischer, 1979, "Stochastic Control Theory Applied to Fishery Management", *IEEE Trans. on Systems, Man, Cybernetics* SMC-9, 5, 252-259.

[14] Jazwinsky, A.H., 1970, *Stochastic Processes and Filtering Theory*, Academic Press, New York.

[15] Kalman, R.E. and R.S. Bucy, 1961, "New Results in Linear Filtering and Prediction Theory," *Journal Basic Engineering*, 83D, 95- 108.

[16] Kendrick, D.A., 1981, *Stochastic Control for Economic Models*, McGraw Hill Book Co., New York.

[17] Kushner, H., 1971, *Introduction to Stochastic Control*, Holt, Rinehart and Winston, New York.

[18] Ludwig, D., 1979, "Optimal Harvesting of a Randomly Fluctuating Resource," *SIAM Journal of Applied Mathematics*, 37, 1, 166-205.

[19] Mehra, R.K., 1972, "Approaches to Adaptive Filtering," *IEEE Trans. on Automatic Control*, 17, 693-698.

[20] Pekelman, D. and G. Rausser 1978, "Adaptive Control Survey: Methods and Applications," in A Bensousan, P. Kleindorfer and C.S. Tapiero (eds), *Applied Optimal Control*, TIMS Studies in Management Sciences, Vol. 9, North-Holland, New York.

[21] Pekelman, D. and E. Tse, 1976, "Experimentation and Control in Advertising, An Adaptive Control Approach," *Working Paper 76-04-01 Wharton School*, University of Pennsylvania, Philadelphia.

[22] Pyndick, R.S., "Uncertainty and Exhaustible Resources Markets," *Journal of Political Economy*, 88, 1203-1225.

[23] Pyndick, R.S., "Uncertainty in the Theory of Renewable Resource Markets", *Rev. of Econ. Stud.* 1984, 289-303.

[24] Sage, A.P. and J.L. Melsa, 1971, *Estimations Theory with Applications to Communications and Control*, McGraw Hill, New York.

[25] Tapiero, C.S., 1986, "Quality Control by the Control of a Discrete State Stochastic Process," *International Journal of Production Research*, 24, 927-937.

[26] Tapiero, C.S. and L. Jacque, 1987, "Premium Valuation in international Insurance," *Scandinavian Actuarial Journal*.

[27] Tapiero, C.S., A. Reisman and P. Ritchken, 1987, "Product Failures, Manufacturing Reliability and Quality Control: A Dynamic Framework," *INFOR*.

[28] Tse, E., 1976, "Sequential Decision and Stochastic Control," *Math. Progr. Studies* 5, 227-243.

Chapter 8

THE COMPUTER AND NUMERICAL APPROACH

8.1 *Introduction to Computational Techniques*

The numerical solution of a stochastic control problems is, as we pointed out repeatedly in the text, a necessity for applications in management science. Although, in some cases analytical solutions were obtained, these are exceptions rather than the rule. But they are, of course, useful for both pedagogical purposes and to yield analytical insights. For most problems, we have no choice but to turn to numerical solutions, or to simulation in the attempt to define an optimal (or close to optimal) policy.

The numerical techniques we can use are varied and usually involve a great deal of computation time. For example, references such as Polak [25], Kushner [23], Kushner and Clarck [24], Goursat and Quadrat [16], Quadrat [26] are but a few of the available literature which has dealt directly with the numerical solution of stochastic control problems (see also [2], [4], [20], [28], [30]).

We can distinguish among three groups of techniques for solving stochastic control problems. These are based on:

(i) classical numerical analysis of the Bellman equation, or the dynamic programming approach,

(ii) discretization of the stochastic control problem and its solution as a Markov Decision Process, or the probability approach; and

(iii) special purpose numerical algorithms and approximation techniques.

We shall briefly discuss each of these approaches, and will concentrate our treatment on stochastic control problems with Wiener processes.

8.1.1 Classical Analysis of Bellman's Equation

Bellman's equation (in case of Wiener processes) is given by a differential equation whose solution yields the objective. In general, this is a nonlinear partial (or ordinary) differential equation, requiring a large memory for its solution, and degenerating into a curse of dimensionality as soon as more than two (or more) state variables are considered. Once Bellman's equation "is written" there are several alternative ways to handle the equation. Popular approaches include the finite element method [6] and discretization. The computer programs we shall use are based on discretization and for this reason, we shall consider this technique in greater detail.

(i) Discretization of Ordinary Differential Equations

For simplicity, assume an ordinary differential equation such as:

$$\frac{dy}{dt} = f(y,t); \ y(0) = Y_0 \tag{8.1}$$

defined over an interval $[0,T]$. Discretization consists in subdividing the interval into N parts of length $\varepsilon = T/N$ and seek approximate values of

$y(t)$, at each of the points $t_n = n\varepsilon, n = 0, 1, 2, ..., N$. The discretization techniques differ one from the other on how estimates for $y(t_n)$ are obtained. The simplest approach is to state,

$$Y_{n+1} = Y_n + \varepsilon(\frac{dy_n}{dt}) \tag{8.2}$$

where for convenience we have written $Y_n = Y(t_n)$ and $dy_n/dt = dy(t_n)/dt$, and

$$Y_{n+1} = Y_n + \varepsilon f(t_n, Y_n). \tag{8.3}$$

Alternatively, we can integrate first dY_n/dt in the interval (t_n, t_{n+1}) with initial condition $Y_n = Y(t_n)$ and then obtain a difference equation of the form (8.3). Specifically, consider the time interval (t_n, t_{n+1}), then for $t \in (t_n, t_{n+1})$, by Taylor approximation,

$$\frac{dy(t)}{dt} = \frac{dy_n}{dt} + \frac{1}{\varepsilon}(t - t_n)\Delta\frac{dy_n}{dt} + \frac{1}{2!\varepsilon^2}(t - t_n)(t - t_{n-1})\Delta^2\frac{dy_n}{dt} + ... \tag{8.4}$$

where the operator Δ is;

$$\Delta(.) = (..)_n - (..)_{n-1}. \tag{8.5}$$

Intergrating the above Taylor approximation in (t_n, t_{n+1}) we obtain

$$Y_{n+1} = Y_n + \varepsilon(\frac{dy_n}{dt} + \frac{1}{2}\Delta\frac{dy_n}{dt} + \frac{5}{12}\Delta^2\frac{dy_n}{dt} + \frac{3}{8}\Delta^3\frac{dy_n}{dt} + ...) \tag{8.6}$$

which is a discretization of $y(t)$ which uses more points. This is called the Adams-Bashforth formula. Other formula vary by the choice of intervals over which they are integrated (see for example, Fox [12]).

General difference approaches can be summarized by recursive equations of the k-order difference form;

$$\sum_{i=0}^{k} \alpha_i Y_{n+i} = \varepsilon \sum_{i=0}^{k} \beta_i f(t_{n+1}, Y_{n+1}) \tag{8.7}$$
$$n = 0, 1, ..., N - k, \alpha_k \neq 0$$

and initial conditions

$$Y_r = Y_{0,r}, \quad r = 0, 1, ..., k - 1. \tag{8.8}$$

The choice of the method is usually cumbersome involving a comparison of methods in so far as speed of computation, precision and stability (convergence) are concerned in solving the differential equation. Popular formulas for solving differential equations are given in Table 8.1 (Babuska, Prager and Vitazek [1]). The first three difference equations in Table 8.1 are based on Adams-Bashforth type formulas (based on integration of the derivation at t_n over an interval $t_n - t_{n-1}$). For practical purposes, these formulas are simple to apply and have also good stability properties.

Table 8.1: Difference Formulas for the Ordinary Differential Equation

$\dfrac{dy}{dt} = f(t, y)$	
Formulas	Order k
$Y_{n+1} = Y_n + \varepsilon \dot{Y}_n$	1
$Y_{n+2} = Y_{n+1} + \frac{1}{2}\varepsilon(3\dot{Y}_{n+1} - \dot{Y}_n)$	2
$Y_{n+3} = Y_{n+2} + \frac{1}{12}\varepsilon(23\dot{Y}_{n+2} + 16\dot{Y}_{n+1} + 5\dot{Y}_n)$	3
$Y_{n+1} = Y_n + \varepsilon \dot{Y}_{n+1}$	1
$Y_{n+1} = Y_n + \frac{1}{2}\varepsilon(\dot{Y}_{n+1} - \dot{Y}_n)$	1
$Y_{n+2} = Y_{n+1} + \frac{1}{12}\varepsilon(5\dot{Y}_{n+2} + 8\dot{Y}_{n+1} - \dot{Y}_n)$	2

In these difference formulas we clearly see the importance of initial conditions since a recurrence relationship is (except in the simple cases) carried over to two and more intervals. To resolve this difficulty, techniques based on one-step ahead formulas have been developed. These are of the following form:

$$Y_{n+1} = Y_n + \varepsilon \phi_f(t_n, Y_n, \varepsilon) \qquad (8.9)$$

where ϕ might be nonlinear and is determined in terms of the function f of equation (8.1). Foremost among these techniques are the Runge-Kutta methods (see Henrici [18]). These equations assume however that starting from some initial value, a recursive calculation of Y_n provides a solution of (8.1), When there may be more than one boundary conditions, (such as the two- points boundary value problems recurring in deterministic control), a solution to our equation is more complex, requiring some scheme to translate the multiple boundary value problem to an initial value problem.

The difference methods used for solving first order differential equations can be extended without much difficulty to the solution of higher order equations. In particular, note that Bellman's equation for a large number of (Wiener noise) problems, was written in the following form (for stationary problems):

$$
\begin{cases}
\underset{u}{\text{Min}} \; \{LJ - rJ + c\} = 0 \\
\\
LJ = f(x,u)\dfrac{dJ}{dx} + \dfrac{1}{2}\sigma^2(x,u)\dfrac{d^2J}{dx^2}
\end{cases}
\tag{8.10}
$$

where boundary conditions are imposed according to the problems definition. "Solution" of this equation (8.10), equivalent to the problem's solution has meant

(i) providing an optimum control $u^0(x)$, which for every state x provides the rule u^0, the feedback rule, which minimizes (8.10); and

(ii) computing the optimum cost $J^0(x)$, which uses the optimal feedback rule $u^0(x)$ when the state is x.

To clarify the discretization procedure in solving the above problem, assume that the state space x is confined between "0" and "1", or $0 \le x \le 1$. Instead of segmenting t, as we have done it in (8.1), segment x into say N parts such that each part has length $1/N$ (see Figure 8.1).

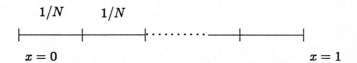

Figure 8.1: Segmenting a State Space

thus

$$
x = \{0, \frac{1}{N}, \frac{2}{N}, \frac{3}{N}, ..., \frac{(N-1)}{N}, 1\}
$$

At a point "0", $x = 0$, at point "1", $x = 1/N$, etc. at the Nth point, $x = 1$. Consider point 1 (off the boundary), then, Bellman's equation is

$$
f(\frac{1}{N}, u_1)\dot{J}_1 + \frac{1}{2}\sigma^2(\frac{1}{N}, u_1)\ddot{J}_1 - rJ_1 + c(\frac{1}{N}, u_1) = 0
$$

where $\dot{J} = dJ/dx$ and $\ddot{J} = d^2J/dx^2$. This is an equation in $u_1, J_1, \dot{J}_1$ and $\ddot{J}_1$. Optimization with respect to u_1 either by analytical or numerical means, provides of course a solution $u_1^0 = u_1^0(1/N, \dot{J}_1, \ddot{J}_1)$, which when reinserted into the above equation provides an equation of the following form,

$$F_1\left(\frac{1}{N}, J_1, \dot{J}_1, \ddot{J}_1\right) = 0$$

Our problem is to replace $\dot{J}_1$ and $\ddot{J}_1$ by appropriate discretized formulas. If we use the (simplest) formulas in Table 8.1, we then have (for the first formula)

$$J_2 = J_1 + (1/N)\dot{J}_1$$

or also (if we use the fourth formula),

$$J_1 = J_0 + (1/N)\dot{J}_1$$

Of course a solution for say $\dot{J}_1$ requires a boundary condition. Namely, say that the problem is defined such that we have absorption at $x = 0$ and the cost is k, thus, at $x = 0, J(0) = J_0 = k$, and by the second formula above

$$\dot{J}_1 = (J_1 - J_0)N = N(J_1 - k)$$

which is an equation in the known parameters N and k. Now consider the second derivative, $\ddot{J}_1$, and by similarity with the first derivative, write

$$\dot{J}_1 = \dot{J}_0 + (1/N)\ddot{J}_1$$

and

$$(\dot{J}_1 - \dot{J}_0)N = \ddot{J}_1$$

or

$$(N(J_1 - k) - \dot{J}_0)N = \ddot{J}_1$$

Since J_0 is independent of $x = 0$ (since it equals k), then $\dot{J}_0 = 0$ and

$$\ddot{J}_1 = N^2(J_1 - k)$$

Insert both $\ddot{J}_1$ and $\dot{J}_1$ into $F_1(1/N, J_1, \dot{J}_1, \ddot{J}_1)$ and obtain one equation in J_1 which can be solved implicitly. As a result, we have $\dot{J}_1, \ddot{J}_1$ which is used together with J_1 in solving the recursive equations, when we move from $x = 1/N$ to $x = 2/N$, to $x = 3/N$ and until $N/N = 1$.

Of course, the problems we deal with are varied requiring (in some cases) numerical techniques to find optimal controls, such that within an optimization routine, there may be one or more other optimization routines. Further, in some cases, the control rule u might not be computed explicitly, as we have assumed it, but rather implicitly. In such a case we would face two equations - the Bellman equation and the implicit control rule equation. While computationally this may be cumbersome, requiring other numerical techniques (such as solving one or a system of equations, which may be subject to constraints), conceptually the problem's solution procedure remains the same. In the applications we shall consider, these procedures will be made far more explicit. But at this stage, the formidable problems of solving Bellman's equation should become apparent. The procedure we have followed has sought to provide a "feel" of how a solution might be obtained. Of course, if we had in our problem two reflection boundaries at $x = 0$ and $x = 1$, then this would mean that

$$\frac{dJ}{dx} = 0 \text{ at } x = 0, 1$$

which is a 2 points boundary value problem! for the differential equation (8.10). Also, when the state space x is unrestricted ($x \in (-\infty, +\infty)$), the segmentation of space may be meaningless, requiring a "special" treatment. This problem in particular, will be treated in our applications by seeking the transformations of the state space, such that it is confined to the bounded $(0, 1)$ space. These and other problems we shall refer to, have implications on the stability of computations, accuracy, convergence, etc., of the numerical procedure. Although in applications we often use computer prgrams and techniques, we do not understand fully, it is essential to gain some basic comprehension of the factors involved in finding numerical solutions of stochastic control problems

(ii) Discretization of Partial Differential Equations

When Bellman's equation is given by a partial differential equation (such as a Parabolic one), discretization procedures can also be applied (for references see [16], [24]). For example, consider the following equation,

$$\frac{\partial J}{\partial t} + \underset{u}{\text{Min}} \left[f(x, u)\frac{\partial J}{\partial x} + \frac{1}{2}\sigma^2(x, u)\frac{\partial^2 J}{\partial x^2} - rJ + c(u, x) \right] = 0$$

$$(8.11)$$

$J(x, T)$ given, $x \in [0, 1]$

where x, the state space has, again, been restricted to a closed $[0, 1]$ space. Next we replace the partials by difference approximations and obtain a set of simultaneous equations in $J(t,x)$, where $x = \{0, \varepsilon, 2\varepsilon, \ldots, 1\}$, and ε is the size of steps in the state space. Thus for $\partial J/\partial t$;

$$\frac{\partial J}{\partial t}(t,x) = \frac{J(t+h,x) - J(t,x)}{h} \qquad (8.12)$$

with $h =$ the time step. For $\partial J/\partial x$, the choice of discretization is selected on the basis of properties of f and σ (see Quadrat [26], a comparison of discretization procedures) such that

$$\frac{\partial J}{\partial x}(t,x) = \begin{cases} \dfrac{J(t,x+\varepsilon) - J(t,x-\varepsilon)}{2\varepsilon}, & \text{if } \sigma^2/f \text{ is large and } f > 0 \\[2ex] \dfrac{J(t,x+\varepsilon) - J(t,x)}{\varepsilon}, & \text{if } \sigma^2 \text{ is small and } f > 0 \\[2ex] \dfrac{J(t,x) - J(t,x-\varepsilon)}{\varepsilon}, & \text{if } f < 0 \end{cases} \qquad (8.13)$$

The discretization above can be taken at t+h rather than at t, reflecting the lead-lag character of the approximation of $\partial J/\partial t$. When it is taken at $t + h$, the resultant recurrence equations (in the Backward solution of (8.11)) are explicit and are therefore simple to resolve, while when taken at t, the recurrence equations are implicit and therefore more complex to compute. Finally, for the second order partial $\partial^2 J/\partial x^2$ we have,

$$\frac{\partial^2 J}{\partial x^2} = \frac{J(t,x+\varepsilon) - 2J(t,x) + J(t,x-\varepsilon)}{\varepsilon^2} \qquad (8.14)$$

which provides the last equation necessary to discretize the Bellman equation (8.11). Of course, alternative discretization procedures will lead to alternative definitions on which numerical computation for $J(t,x)$ are made.

For demonstration purposes, say that in our problem, $J(T,x) = 0$, i.e., regardless of where we are at the "end" of the problem, the value J equals zero. Then "pick" a state in $(0,1)$, say x and move backwards to all possible states, which are (because of the Markov process), $x + \varepsilon, x, x - \varepsilon$. In the discretized Bellman equation, we have

$$\frac{\partial J(T-h,x)}{\partial t} = \frac{J(T,x) - J(T-h,x)}{\varepsilon}$$

or

$$\frac{\partial J(T-h,x)}{\partial t} = -\frac{J(T-h,x)}{\varepsilon}$$

When we use the explicit formulation of $\partial J/\partial x$ (i.e., $t = t + h$) and with $f < 0$, for simplicity

$$\frac{\partial J(T-h,x)}{\partial x} = \frac{J(T,x) - J(T,x-\varepsilon)}{\varepsilon} = 0$$

and

$$\frac{\partial^2 J(T-h,x)}{\partial x^2} = \frac{J(T,x+\varepsilon) - 2J(T,x) + J(T,x-\varepsilon)}{\varepsilon^2} = 0$$

and therefore, (after insertions in (8.11)):

$$-J(T-h,x) + \varepsilon r J(T-h,x) + \varepsilon c(x,u) = 0$$

which provides a solution for $u, \partial c/\partial u = 0$ and as a result,

$$J(T-h,x) = \frac{\varepsilon c(x,u^0(x))}{1-\varepsilon r}$$

We repeat these computations for all $\{T-2h, T-3h, ..., 0\}$ and $\{0, ..., x - \varepsilon, x, x+\varepsilon, ..., 1\}$ and obtain a solution of the Bellman equation. The solution, as our procedure has indicated, strongly depends on the boundaries imposed on Bellman's equation. Generally, boundaries can be more complex, and located in different points. For example, if at $x = 0$, we have a reflection, then for all t,

$$\frac{\partial J}{\partial x}(t,x) = 0 \text{ at } x = 0$$

which provides a further set of equations we must reckon with when solving the discretized Bellman equation. Other cases can be solved, as the applications in Sections 8.3 will show. When the planning time T is not too large and time steps not too small, the discretization procedure can lead to quick solutions. Of course, by decreasing the time steps, the computation time may be excessive. A rule of thumb would be to take smaller time steps when the process variance is larger and vice versa, when the process variance is small.

Finally, when we consider problems in more than two state variables, the computations required for solving the Bellman equations become immense, which tends for this reason, to limit the usefulness of computational methods to a "reasonable number of state variables".

8.1.2   The Probability Approach

The probability approach consists in transforming the stochastic control problem into a Markov Decision Process (MDP). This is done in two steps; first discretize the problem and then apply one of the algorithms that solve MDP's. The underlying assumption of this approach, proved originally by Billingsley [5] is that the discretized Markov process converges (in a weak sense) to the continuous diffusion process (see also Strook and Varadhan [3], Quadrat [26]). It is Kushner [23] however, that has realized the potential of this approach for the solution of stochastic control problems. To transform a continuous process into a discrete state one, we proceed as follows.

As in the previous section, assume that the state space is defined exhaustively in $[0, 1]$, such that $0 \leq x \leq 1$, and that a partition of the interval in N segments yields N values $(x_0, ..., x_N)$, where $x_i = i/N$. Now define an event i as follows

$$\text{i if } x_{i-1} \leq x \leq x_i \; ; \; i = 1, 2, ..., N$$

In other words, at any time t, the value and the state $x(t)$ can take, are exhaustively defined by the events i. Specifically, consider two successive instants of time $(t, t + h)$;

$$x(t + h) = x(t) + f(x(t), u)h + \sigma(x(t), u)\Delta w$$

$$\Delta w = w(t + h) - w(t) \tag{8.15}$$

where

$$t \in [T, T - h, T - 2h, ...0]$$

$$x \in [0, \Delta x, ...N\Delta x], \; \Delta x = 1/N$$

where, Δw has a zero mean normal probability distribution with variance h. Say that at time $t, x(t) \in i$, meaning that $x_{i-1} \leq x(t), \leq x_i, i = 1, ...N$. At $t + h$, the new state $x(t + h)$ can obtain a value such that $x(t + h) \in j, x_{j-1} \leq x(t + h) \leq x_j, j = 1, ...N$ depending upon the transition probabilities. Namely, the random event Δw, the control selected and applied in $(t, t + h)$ as well as the system structure (expressed by the functional forms f and σ) determine the various (controlled) chances of switching from $x(t + h) \in i$ to $x(t + h) \in j$. For the Wiener process defined by (8.15), switches can occur to neighboring points only. In other words, if we replace the process (8.15) by its equivalent random walk (as shown in Chapter 2, section 2.2) then given that we are in state x, we look for the probability of moving upwards ($\Delta x = +1$), downwards ($\Delta x = -1$) or remaining ($\Delta x = 0$) in the same place. Let these probabilities be denoted by $P_{x,x+\Delta x}(t)$ and $P_{x,x}(t)$ where

$$\Delta x = \begin{cases} +\varepsilon & \text{with } P_{x,x+\Delta x}(t) \\ -\varepsilon & \text{with } P_{x,x-\Delta x}(t) \\ 0 & \text{with } P_{x,x}(t) \end{cases}$$

where ε is a small number denoting the size of the jump on the line. Clearly, since Δx has a known mean and a known variance, we have (dropping terms in h^2),

$$E(\Delta x) = f(x,u)h = (P_{x,x+\Delta x} - P_{x,x-\Delta x})\varepsilon$$
$$var(\Delta x) = \sigma^2(x,u)h = (P_{x,x+\Delta x} + P_{x,x-\Delta x})\varepsilon^2$$

Therefore, a solution for $P_{x,x+\Delta x}$ and $P_{x,x-\Delta x}$ yields

$$P_{x,x+\Delta x} = \sigma^2 h/2\varepsilon; \; P_{x,x-\Delta x} = \sigma^2 h/2\varepsilon - fh/2\varepsilon \qquad (8.16)$$

Now, if we denote by $f^+ = \max(f,0)$ and $f^- = \max(-f,0)$ and let $\varepsilon = \Delta x$ be the size of the jump, the equations for $P_{x,x\pm\Delta x}$ above can be written by

$$P_{x,x\pm\Delta x} = \sigma^2 h/2(\Delta x)^2 + hf^\pm/(\Delta x) \qquad (8.17)$$

At the boundaries $x = 1,0$, we also have $x = 1, f^+ = 0, \sigma = 0$ and $P_{1,1+\Delta x} = 0$, while at $x = 0, f^- = 0, \sigma = 0$ and $P_{0,0-\Delta x}$. In other words, the probability of being in state x at time $t + h$ is given by:

$$x(t+h) = (x+\Delta x)P_{x,x+\Delta x} + (x-\Delta x)P_{x,x-\Delta x} + (x)P_{x,x} \qquad (8.18)$$

where each of the probabilities are given explicitly in (8.16) and (8.17). Of course, the actual multiplication will bring us back to our equation (8.15).

To observe how such transformations (discretization) of the stochastic process affect our dynamic optimization problem, we consider the following problem:

$$V(t,x) = \begin{array}{c} \text{Min}\{L(t,x,u)h + EV(t+h,x+\Delta x)\} \\ u \in U \end{array} \qquad (8.19)$$

$$V(T,x) = Q(x); \; t = 0, h, 2h, 3h, ...T \qquad (8.20)$$

Then explicitly we have

$$V(t,x) = \begin{cases} \text{Min } \{L(t,x,u)h+ \\ u \in U \\ +V(t+h,x)P_{x,x}(t) \\ +V(t+h,x+\Delta x)P_{x,x+\Delta x}(t) \\ +V(t+h,x-\Delta x)P_{x,x-\Delta x}(t) \end{cases} \qquad (8.21)$$

when $\Delta x \to 0, h \to 0$, we obtain again the continuous time equation of problems (8.19). This equation together with the boundary equation (8.20), equation (8.16) and optimization for u at each time step, provides a numerical solution of our problem.

Next, denote by P_{ij} the chance (probability) of switching from i to j in $(t, t + h)$, (see Chapter 2), written explicitly as a function of time and the control u;

$$P_{ij}(t) \equiv \text{Prob}\{x(t) \in i \to x(t + h) \in j\} \qquad (8.22)$$

Since P_{ij} are transition probabilities they define a Markov Chain $P(t, u)$ at a given time t, with

$$P = \begin{vmatrix} P_{11} & \cdots & P_{1N} \\ & & \\ & & \\ P_{N1} & \cdots & P_{NN} \end{vmatrix} ; \sum_{j=1}^{N} P_{ij} = 1, P_{ij} \geq 0 \qquad (8.23)$$

The process defined above is thus reduced to a set of simultaneous (and linear) equations,

$$x_j^{t+h} = \sum_{j=1}^{N} P_{ij}^t(u) x_i^t, \; j = 1, ..., N \qquad (8.24)$$

where x_j^{t+h} states that we are at time $t + h$ in state x_j and P_{ij} denotes the probability of switching to state j from state i, when a control u is exerted. In matrix notation, we have

$$x(t + h) = Px(t); \; x(0) = \text{ given initial condition} \qquad (8.25)$$

Next discretize the loss function ℓ entertained when choosing an optimum control u. For simplicity, say that $h = 1$, such that if $t_0 = 0$, then $t_1 = t_0 + h = 1, t_2 = 2, ...$ until $T = M(= T/h)$, the final planning time. Thus,

$$c_{ij}(t, u) = \ell(j; i, u)h$$

i.e., $c_{ij}(t, u)$ is the cost of being in state j at $t + 1$ conditioned by the event being in i at time t. In other words, given that at time s we are in state (event) x_i, the cost-to-go till the final time T (corresponding to the Mth discretization step) is given by:

$$I(i, s) = \sum_{t=s}^{M} \sum_{j=1}^{N} P_{ij}(t, u) c_{ij}(t, u) \qquad (8.26)$$

and so, the dynamic (backward) recurrence equation is

$$I(i, s) = \sum_{j=1}^{N} P_{ij}(s, u)\{c_{ij}(s, u) + I(j, s+1)\} \tag{8.27}$$

If the final cost, at $s = M$ equals zero, we have the boundary equation

$$I(j, M) = 0, \; j = 1, 2, ... N \tag{8.28}$$

The above two equations are of course solvable, by applying recursive techniques. For example, at $M, J(j, M) = 0$ for $j = 1, ..., N$. At $s = M - 1$, however,

$$I(i, M-1) = \underset{u}{\text{Min}} \; \sum_{j=1}^{N} P_{ij}(M-1, u)c_{ij}(M-1, u) \tag{8.29}$$

which is one equation in one unknown u, which we can solve analytically or numerically. Say that the optimal u is u^0, then clearly the computed controls u^0 consist of N values $u^0(i)$ or, at $s = N - 1$,

$$\{u^0(M-1), i\} = \{u^0(M-1, 1), u^0(M-1, 2), ..., u^0(M-1, N)\} \tag{8.30}$$

stating what action to take at time $M - 1$, conditioned by the state i we might be in at that time. At time $M - 2$, we have

$$I(i, M-2) = \sum_{j=1}^{N} P_{ij}(M-2, u)\{c_{ij}(M-2, u) + I^0(j, M-1)\} \tag{8.31}$$

where $I^0(j, M-1)$ is calculated by substitution of u^0 in $I(j, M-1)$ or

$$I^0(j, M-1) = \sum_{j=1}^{N} P_{ij}(M-1, u^0(M-1, i))c_{ij}(M-1, u_0(M-1, i)) \tag{8.32}$$

Again, $I(i, M-2)$ is a function in u we optimize. We repeat the above procedure for $s = M - 3, M - 4, ...$ till the initial time. At this time we obtain the decision Table $u^0(s, i)$, which prescribes what to do at time s if we are in state i. At the initial time, the optimum cost of a solved problem is then summarized by;

$$I^0(i, 0) = \sum_{t=0}^{M} \sum_{j=1}^{N} P_{ij}(t, u^0(t, i))c_{ij}(t, u^0(t, i))$$

or

$$I^0(i, 0) = \sum_{j=1}^{N} P_{ij}(0, u^0(0, i))\{c_{ij}(0, u^0(0, i)) + I^0(j, 1)\} \tag{8.33}$$

representing equivalent ways to write the optimum cost.

Although we have "computed" earlier $u^0(t, i)$ by backward recursion, this may not be always feasible, nor simple. Thus, if T is large and discretization steps h small, M may become far too large, requiring considerable computation time. Also, there may be more direct ways to solve the Markov decision problem, prospecting the special structure of Markov processes. Two approaches used in the literature for solving these equations are the *Value* and the *Policy Iteration Techniques*. These techniques, have led in some special cases to simple and efficient algorithms. Each of these approaches is outlined next by considering an infinite horizon (stage) problem.

(i) The Policy Iteration Technique

Consider an infinite horizon decision problem with constant parameters. In this case, if we use a discount rate r, the backward recurrence (dynamic programming) equation (8.33) is time independent (see Chapter 4), and is reduced to;

$$J(i) = \sum_{j=1}^{N} P_{ij}(u)[c_{ij}(u) + J(j)r] \qquad (8.34)$$

and a convergence requirement on J. It is convenient to write this equation in matrix notation; with $\bar{J}(u) = J(i; u)$, $i = 1, ..., N$, $C(u) = \|c_{ij}(u)\|$, $P(u) = \|p_{ij}(u)\|$, then

$$\bar{J}(u) = P(u)[C(u) + r\bar{J}(u)]$$
$$\text{or} \qquad\qquad\qquad\qquad\qquad\qquad\qquad\qquad (8.35)$$
$$\bar{J}(u) - rP(u)\bar{J}(u) = P(u)C(u)$$

which means that u is a solution of:

$$\bar{J}(u) = [I - rP(u)]^{-1}P(u)C(u) \qquad (8.36)$$

where I is now the identity matrix. Of course for $\bar{J}$ to exist (the convergence requirement in (8.34)), it is necessary that $[I - rP(u)]$ be of full rank and that $r < 1$,

$$\text{rank}[I - rP(u)] = N; r < 1 \qquad (8.37)$$

Technically, however, the solution of the Markov decision process is reduced to the solution of a system of simultaneous equations. Howard [20] in particular, has suggested an iterative algorithm based on an iteration of the policy u which (it can be shown) converges to the optimal control. The proof follows the procedure we shall outline in case of value iteration in the next section. The algorithm followed by Howard for policy iteration is

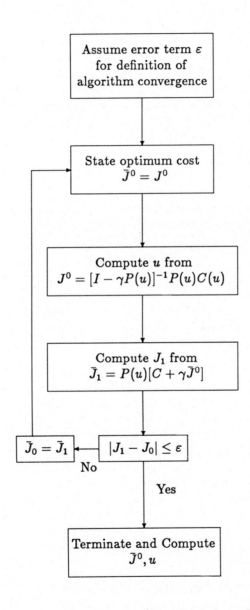

Figure 8.2: Value Iteration (The Stationary Case)

summarized in Figure 8.2. The advantage of this algorithm is of course its simplicity.

(ii) Value Iteration Technique

The value iteration technique is based on an iterative (and converging) computation of the optimum cost, rather than computation of the optimum policy. To present this approach, we shall consider again an infinite stage problem and subsequently, show application of the technique on an infinite horizon stochastic control problem with diffusion processes. When the decision process is a discounted cost problem, the discretized dynamic programming recurrence equation (8.32) is

$$J(i,s) = \sum_{j=1}^{N} P_{ij}\{c_{ij} + \gamma J(j, s+1)\}; \ \gamma = (1+r)^{-1} \qquad (8.38)$$

where r is the discount rate and p_{ij} and c_{ij} are function of the control, u only. In vector notation, this is written as follows;

$$\bar{J}(s) = P(u)C(u) + \gamma \bar{J}(s+1). \qquad (8.39)$$

For an infinite horizon problem, $\bar{J}(s) = \bar{J}(s+1)$ such that (as noted earlier)

$$\bar{J}(s) = [I - \gamma P(u)]^{-1}P(u)C(u). \qquad (8.40)$$

The last two equations above define the value iteration algorithm. Say that $\bar{J}^0$ is the optimum cost, then substituting in (8.30), we obtain a set of equations in u. Given u, we insert in (8.40) and solve for $\bar{J}^1$ by letting $\bar{J}^1 = \bar{J}(s)$ and keeping $\bar{J}(s+1) = \bar{J}^0$. Repeating this procedure, a sequence of costs is obtained which it can be shown (Quadrat [26]) converges to the optimum cost. This procedure is summarized in Figure 8.3, and an intuitive proof is given for the continuous case we consider next.

Consider now the dynamic programming equation of an infinite horizon problem with a diffusion process (see Chapter 4, Section 4). The cost function is in this case given by

$$-rJ(x) + \underset{u}{\text{Min}} \ \{L(u)J(x) + C(x,u)\} = 0 \qquad (8.41)$$

where $L(u)$ is the diffusion operator,

$$L(u) = f(x,u)\frac{\partial}{\partial x} + \frac{1}{2}\sigma^2(x,u)\frac{\partial^2}{\partial x^2}$$

r is the discount rate and C the instantaneous cost. Evidently, the cost $J(x)$ is stationary and a function of the initial condition of the state equation. Over a finite time T, the dynamic programming equation was shown to be;

$$\frac{\partial J}{\partial t} + \underset{u}{\text{Min}} \{L(u)J + C(x,u)\} - rJ = 0 \qquad (8.42)$$

with appropriate boundary at $t = T$. As in the previous section. discretize $\partial J/\partial t$,

$$\frac{\partial J}{\partial t} \approx \frac{J(t+h,x) - J(t,x)}{h}$$

thus the dynamic programming equation above, in its discretized form is

$$0 = \frac{J(t+h,x) - J(t,x)}{h} + \text{Min}\{L(u)J(t+h,x) + C(u,x)\} - rJ(t+h,x)$$

Rearranging the terms in $J(t+h,x)$, we have

$$J(t,x) = \underset{u}{\text{Min}}\{[I - rh + hL(u)]J(t+h,u) + C(x,u)\} \qquad (8.43)$$

If we denote $t = mh$, and replace $J(t,x)$ by $J(m)$, then

$$\begin{cases} J(m+1) = \underset{u}{\text{Min}}\{M_r(u)J(m) + C(x,u)\} \\ M_r(u) = [I - rh + hL(u)]. \end{cases} \qquad (8.44)$$

For J to be stationary however (and optimal), it has to be a solution of (8.43), or at a given stage,

$$\underset{u}{\text{Min}}\{L^m(u)J(m) + C(x,u)] - rJ(m)\} = 0. \qquad (8.45)$$

Combining with the previous equations, the value iteration algorithm becomes;

a) assume a term ε for the policy improvement algorithm;

b) assume an initial value J^0;

c) solve for u from (8.36) by letting $J(m) = J^0$;

d) compute $J(m+1)$ from (8.35);

e) if $|J(m+1) - J(m)| \leq \varepsilon$, stop and end computations, if not write $J^0 = J(m)$ and go to C.

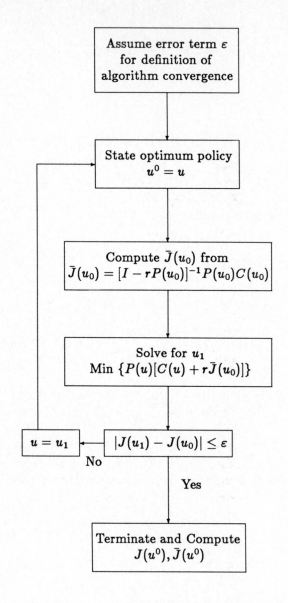

Figure 8.3: Policy Iteration (The Stationary Case)

To prove that with this procedure we reach the optimum stationary cost J^0, we proceed as follows. Note that for h small $M_r(u)$ has the following properties;

$$M_r(u)|_{ij} \geq 0, \ \forall ij \text{ and } \forall u$$

$$\sum_{i=1}^{N} M_r(u)|_{ij} = 1 - rh$$

By definition

$$J(m+1) - J(m) = \underset{u}{\text{Min}}\{M_r(u).J(m) + C(x,u)\} -$$
$$- \underset{u}{\text{Min}}\{M_r(u)J(m-1) + C(x,u)\}.$$

Let u^m be the mth stage optimal control. Thus,

$$J(m+1) - J(m) = M_r(u^m)J(m) + C(x,u^m)$$
$$-M_r(u^{m-1})J(m-1) + C(x,u^{m-1})$$
$$\leq M_r(u^{m-1})J(m) + C(x,u^{m-1})$$
$$-M_r(u^{m-1})J(m-1) + C(x,u^{m-1}).$$

The last inequality is obtained by the definition of the optimum u. Thus,

$$|J(m+1) - J(m)| \leq |M_r(u^{m-1})(J(m) - J(m-1))|$$
$$\leq (1 - \lambda h)|J(m) - J(m-1)|$$

which clearly proves the contraction property of the value iteration algorithm i.e., that each iteration improves the estimate of the stationary optimum cost J^0, since

$$\lim_{m \to \infty} |J(m+1) - J(m)| \to 0.$$

8.1.3 Special Procedures

Under this heading various approaches are included, consisting mostly in the transformation of the stochastic control problem into a problem which is numerically tractable, or approximating the control problem if it belongs to a special class. For example, chance-constraint programming, stochastic programming (and more generally nonlinear programming) can be used for solving special control problems. This will involve mainly open- loop controls, loosing the important feedback feature of dynamic programming solutions (for references see Sengupta [29], Gonedes and Lieber [14], Kleindorfer [22] and Ziemba [32]). Other approaches have sought some procedures transforming the original stochastic control problem to equivalent open-loop stochastic control problems.

For example, the dynamic programming equation has been solved iteratively by *perturbing* the optimal control around some nominal trajectory and improve successively our guess of this trajectory. This approach, called differential dynamic programming, has been applied successfully by Jacobson and Mayne [21] to specific problems (including bang bang controls) and was shown in some cases to converge quickly to the optimum solution. Its essential advantage is in the relatively small amount of memory required to implement the technique, while its disadvantage, is that it produces open loop controls. Further, inequality constraints on say, state variables are easily handled.

Alternatively, for problems involving many states, which are practically impossible to solve, Quadrat [26] has suggested and applied to problems of dam and energy management (see [9], [7]), an approximation method based on a class of local feedbacks. This approach presumes however a special structure of the systems equations which allow decomposition (Quadrat and Viot [27]).

Finally, it is worth pointing out that techniques based on Monte Carlo simulation of the stochastic control problem [7,9] as well as deterministic approximation when the noise is small are also used (e.g., Holland [19], Fleming [10]). In this latter case, the numerical solution of the stochastic control problem is found by applying optimal (deterministic) control techniques, such as Pontryagin's Maximum Principle.

In actual applications, the choice of the method to use depends on several factors, including familiarity of the researcher with the numerical technique, convergence and computer efficiency which may vary for a particular problem from method to method. With the increasing use of stochastic control, and the required need to solve problems of several state variables with small discretization steps (for precision), the choice of the method will become acute. Throughout this chapter, we shall use however a discretization approach of the Bellman equation. The Kushner-Howard approach, based on solution of Markov problems has been practiced for awhile and computer routines are currently available. (The algorithms outlined earlier are conceptually simple to apply). Next, we shall turn our attention to specific applications and specific computer programs.

8.2 *The Computer's Approach*

The numerical techniques outlined in the previous section set the ground for their integration and application in the solution of specific management science problems. These techniques, taken together, form a whole, which provides alternative ways of handling a problem, and lead to solution characterisitics which can differ from problem to problem. As we have pointed out earlier, these characterisitics (such as accuracy, speed, convergence, etc. of the iterative-algorithm technique used) are both problem and algorithm specific. It is therefore desirable that in our attempt to solve stochastic control problems, that the computer programs used, be problem specific, reflecting the special features desired in the solution of the problem. The basic purpose of an expert program in Stochastic Control would be to integrate in a computer, (i) segments representing the various numerical techniques we can potentially use, (ii) artificial intelligence languages, and (iii) a set of rules that can manipulate these segments in developing programming a special procedure to solve a special problem. This is a formidable task, whose realization provides an opportunity for applying routinely complex optimization procedures to dynamic and stochastic management problems. It cannot, however, be used to solve unsolvable or ill-formulated problems. Here too, the well known adage GIGO (Gargage in, Garbage out) applies. Since, unless a stochastic control problem is well formulated, satisfying existence conditions, possibly uniqueness, well isolated poles (i.e., points of divergence to infinity) or none at all, the computer program generated will not provide a solution.

A decision support system for stochastic control problems which facilitates the use of dynamic systems for management planning and decision making under an uncertain environment, has been developed by Gomez Quadrat [13]. It provides FORTRAN generated programs that solve the Bellman equation and its optimal control, and is based on an internal choice of methods. The outcome of a query is expressed in a SUBROUTINE which is then integrated into a MASTER PROGRAM provided by the user. These subroutines require for their functioning;

(i) parameters (constants) of the problem denoted by $zzi, i = 1, 2, ...$;

(ii) discretization for time;

(iii) the number of segments, or discretization of the state space;

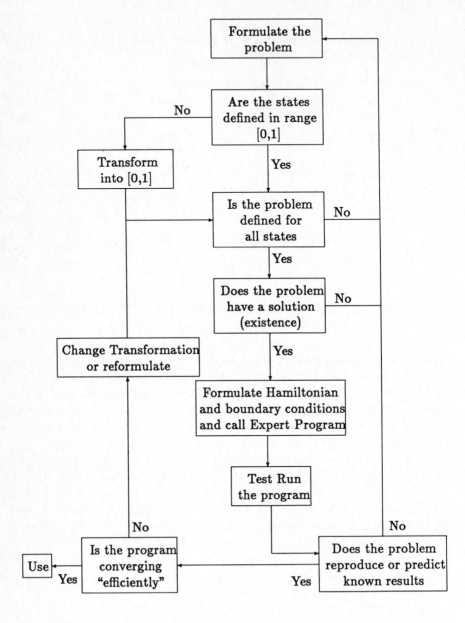

Figure 8.4: Application Procedure for Automatic Program Generation

(iv) the maximum number of iterations to be applied in solving Bellman's equation;

(v) specification of the error which defines the "convergence" of the iterative algorithm.

The optimization subroutine, however, is generated by specifying;

(i) the number of state variables used in the dynamic program;

(ii) the Hamiltonian, representing the problem's definition

(iii) the behavior at the boundaries and the costs;

(iv) the choice of implicit, or explicit techniques for dicretization;

(v) the numerical solution applied to obtain the optimal control (such as, Newton's algorithm or some other technique).

Finally, as in Section 8.1, the program accepts program formulations whose states are defined in [0,1]. We shall show in our applications that this is not an important limitation, since a problem can be transformed in the state to satisfy the above requirement.

The procedure we follow in applications is summarized in Figure 8.4, where we compare the numerical results obtained by the solution of a stochastic control problem with predictable results or insights on properties of the solution that can be reached theoretically by the solution of the small problem. This is essential, as an ultimate test of confidence in the (numerical) program generated. In this vein, the applications to be considered in the next section, invariably present;

(i) a summary mathematical formulation;
(ii) a transformation of the problem;
(iii) analytical treatment of the problem – if possible;
(iv) a computer generated FORTRAN program;
(v) numerical results obtained by the program.

Subsequently, the results are interpreted as solutions to management science problems.

8.3   *Applications*

8.3.1   A Production Program

We return to the production problem (see Chapter 4 as well as Chapter 3, Section 3.2) and assume in addition that both production programs and inventory holding capacity are constrained, with

$$0 \leq u \leq u; \ \bar{u} > 0; \ -m \leq x \leq M; \ m \geq 0, \ M > 0$$

This means that the inventory equation has reflecting boundaries at $x = -m$ and $x = M$, which have to be considered in the program optimization. Also, we let the demand be lognormal (although this need not be the case) and define the following (general) production control problem;

$$\mathrm{Min} J = E\{\int_0^T [c(u) + h(x)]e^{-rt}dt + g(x(T))e^{-rT}\}$$
$$0 \leq u \leq \bar{u}$$

subject to :

$$dx = (u - D)dt + \sqrt{\theta}Ddw \qquad (8.46)$$

$$x(0) = x_0 \in [-m, M]; \ \mathrm{Prob}[-m \leq x \leq M] = 1$$

where $c(u)$ is the production cost, $h(x)$ is the inventory cost, $g(x)$ is the terminal inventory cost and r the discount rate. First, note that x does not have a $[0, 1]$ bounded interval, but can be obtained by a simple variable transformation,

$$y = \frac{x + m}{m + M}$$
$$y = 1 \leftrightarrow x = M \qquad (8.47)$$
$$y = 0 \leftrightarrow x = -m$$

Applications of Ito's differential rule, to obtain a dynamic equation is straightforward, since $\partial y/\partial x = (1/M + m), \partial^2 y/\partial x^2 = 0$, and finally the transformed problem is;

$$\text{Minimize } J = E\{\int_0^T e^{-rt}\{c(u) + H(y)\}e^{-rt}dt + C(y)e^{-rT}\}$$

$$0 \leq u \leq \bar{u}$$

subject to

(8.48)

$$dy = \frac{(u - D)}{M + m} dt + \frac{\sqrt{\theta} D}{M + m} dw; \quad y(0) = \frac{x_0 + m}{M + m}$$

Prob$[0 \leq y \leq 1] = 1$, or reflection at $x = 0, 1$

and where H and G are appropriately adjusted functions of y. Without reflection, Bellman's equation is

$$-rJ + \frac{u - D}{M + m} \frac{\partial J}{\partial y} + \frac{1}{2} \frac{\theta D^2}{(M + m)^2} \frac{\partial^2 J}{\partial y^2} + c(u) + H(y) = -\frac{\partial J}{\partial t} \qquad (8.49)$$

and at the final time (boundary) T

$$J(y, T) = G(y) \qquad (8.50)$$

Two other boundaries are imposed due to reflection at $y = 0, 1$. At $y = 1$, reflection is costless, since we can always stop production, in which case,

$$\frac{\partial J(1, t)}{\partial y} = 0 \qquad (8.51)$$

At $y = 0$, (or $x = -m$) we suppose that a cost of α is incurred per unit of rejected sale, then

$$\frac{\partial J(0, t)}{\partial y} = \alpha D(t) \qquad (8.52)$$

Finally, the optimum production program is given by solving for each (y, t)

$$\begin{aligned} &\text{Min } u \frac{\partial J}{\partial y} + C(u)(M + m) \\ &\text{subject to} \\ &0 \leq u \leq \bar{u} \end{aligned} \qquad (8.53)$$

Equations (8.49) - (8.53) provide a statement of optimum production which clearly is difficult to solve (although special cases have been solved analytically, e.g., Bensoussan, Crouhy and Proth [3]). Say that $C(u)$ is a continuous and differentiable function in u, then if $u^0 \in [0, \bar{u}]$, we have

$$\frac{\partial J}{\partial y} + \frac{\partial c}{\partial u}(M + m) = 0$$

which leads to an analytical form

$$u^0 = u^0\left(\frac{\partial J}{\partial y}, y\right)$$

and

$$u^0 = \begin{cases} \bar{U} \text{ if } u^0 \geq \bar{u} \\ u^0\left(y, \frac{\partial J}{\partial y}\right) \text{ if } u^0 \in [0, \bar{u}] \\ 0 \text{ if } u^0 \leq 0 \end{cases}$$

which means that the optimal control is calculated explicitly rather than implicitly as a function of the discretized state y and $\partial J/\partial y$. We simplify, by considering the special objective function

$$C(u) \quad = \quad c_1 u + c_2(u - u^*)^2 + h_1 x + h_0(x - x^*)^2 \text{ if } x \geq 0$$

$$H(x) \quad = \quad -h_2 x + h_0(x - x^*)^2 \text{ if } x < 0$$

$$G(x) \quad = \quad \gamma(x - x^*)^2 \text{ at } t = T$$

and generate program PROD1 as given in the appendix. This program has 11 parameters $ZZ_1 - ZZ_{11}$, the time t is replaced by x_1 while the state space is denoted by x_1, v denotes the optimum cost, $p_1 = \partial v/\partial x, q = \partial v/\partial x^2$, etc. (see comments within the SUBROUTINE PROD1). Parameters' notation is given in Table 8.2, while the mean demand $D(t)$ is an arbitrary function of time, given functionally in the program by $ZFD(x_0)$, and for example,

$$D(t) = 5 + 2\sin X_0 + (0.1)X_0.$$

Evidently, by changing the function $ZFD(x_0)$ we can obtain another type of demand. Also, a SUBROUTINE ZS is defined to express more particularly how the inventory costs are generated. Finally, using the the program both the optimal production levels and the optimum cost as a function of time are computed. Such analyses are the solution of the discretized Bellman equation and can be used for several purpose as in Chapter 5 when dealing with an advertising problem. Graphically, we see that production declines (expectedly) with inventory, and that over time, production is more responsive to instantaneous demands (rather than future ones). To assess the effects of inventory storage limitations and their costs, we can take at some time t, the optimum costs $J(x, t; M)$ and $J(x, t : M')$ and check whether we ought to invest and increase (or reduce M) to more appropriate levels, by comparing these costs.

An extension of our production problem to a two (or more) joint products problem is not straightforward. Difficulties arise essentially due to the

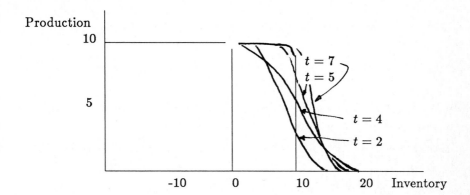

Figure 8.5: The Optimal (Feedback) Production

cost reduction (or increase) effects of dealing with more than one product at a time, demand dependence as well as joint constraints on inventory storage capacity which does not simplify the definitions of $[0,1]$ state-space for each of the products.

8.3.2 An Advertising Program

We consider an advertising model of the Vidale-Wolfe type (see Chapter 5, section 5.2) approximated by a diffusion with reflection at both extreme points of the state space. Let x be the sales and M be the total potential. Thus, $y = x/M$ is the firm's market share and $y \in [0,1]$ with reflection at $y = 0$ and at $y = 1$. The advertising problem we deal with is a profit maximization problem with a target market share objective y^* at time T, which we summarize as follows:

Maximize $J(y_0) = E\{\int_0^T e^{-rT}(pMy - a)dt + e^{-rT}(y(T) - y^*)^2\}$
$a \in A$
Subject to :

$$dy = [-my + qa(1 - y)]dt + \sigma(y, a)dw$$

$$y(0) = y_0, \ \sigma^2(y, a) = my + qa(1 - y), \ \text{Prob}[0 \le y \le 1] = 1$$

The program defined in this manner has 8 parameters summarized in Table

8.3, while the computer program based on a discretization of the Bellman equation associated to the problem is given in the appendix. For a given set of parameters, summarized in Table 8.3, we obtain the optimal advertising policy given in Tables 8.4 and 8.5. These Tables state how much to advertise when the market share is observed and given by a specific number such that the objective is maximized. The behavior of the optimal advertising policy is, as expected, similar to the kind of results described in Chapter 5 when studying the problem from a qualitative- analytical point of view. Of course, the usefulness of this computer based "numerical instrument" depends on the validity of the model in representing truly sales response to advertising effort. For practical purposes, much more elaborate models will be required, involving competitive actions and the simultaneity of other factors which affect sales, advertising budgets and their effectiveness.

8.3.3   Quality Production and Maintenance

Earlier (Chapter 3) we formulated and resolved under alternative cost assumptions and models, a continuous quality production and maintenance problem. This was achieved by considering a quality-degradation state function, and transforming it into a linear control problem for which an analytical solution was obtained. For more complex cases we can deal with the problem by solving the Bellman equation numerically. This is achieved next by a computer program characterizing numerically the maintenance policy. The computer program (see the appendix) solves the following stochastic control problem for a given definition of functions $F(y), G(y)$ and $P(y)$;

$$\text{Min } J = E\{\textstyle\int_0^N [Mu - P(y)]dn + K\}$$
$$0 \leq u \leq \bar{u}$$

$$N = \text{Inf}\{n \geq 0, y = \bar{y}\}$$

$$dy = [F(y) + kuy]dn + \sqrt{2G(y)}\,dw$$

with a reflection boundary at $y = 1$.

The program uses a state discretization, which allows the transformation of the continuous production problem into a discrete one (albeit with as many steps as necessary for program precision). Further, noting, on theoretical grounds, that the optimum maintenance policy is of the Bang- Bang type, simplifications can be used. Let $y \in [\bar{y}, 1]; 0 \leq y \leq 1$, be the quality domain of definition, and then define a new variable between zero and one such that

Table 8.2:

Parameters of the Advertising Program

Model Notation	Computer Notation	Run 1 Parameters	Run 2 Parameters
M	zz1	10.000	10.000
m	zz2	.1	.1
q	zz3	.05	.03
γ	zz4	0	1000
p	zz5	1.0	1.0
y^*	zz7	—	.6
A	zz8	50	50

Numerical Solution Parameters		
Discretization of State	η_1	23
Discretization of Time	η_0	201
Time Step	h_0	.005

Table 8.3: Run 1

$$q = 0.05, \ \gamma = 0$$

Market	Time									
Share	0	0.2	0.4	0.6	0.8	1	1.2	1.4	1.6	1.8
.1	2488	2330	2222	2135	2058	1990	1928	1870	1817	1767
	10.29	5.81	4.6	4	3.6	3.3	308	2.9	2.76	2.6
.2	1593	1479	1392	1312	1260	1207	1160	1117	1078	1043
	8.91	7.75	6.70	6.01	5.5	5.2	4.91	4.68	4.5	4.33
.3	897	845	799	760	726	697	670	646	625	605
	7.16	7.3	6.92	6.55	6.24	5.98	5.77	5.59	5.43	5.3
.4	3.99	391	381	371	362	353	345	337	330	324
	4.87	5.24	5.50	5.61	5.6	5.62	5.6	5.55	5.51	5.47
.5	100	109	118	124	130	134	138	141	143	146
	1.75	2.1	2.6	3.	3.4	3.6	3.9	4.15	4.34	4.5
.6	.18	4.07	8.4	13.	18.5	23.9	29.4	35.	40.	45.8
	0	0	0	0	0	0	0	0	0	0
.7	99.5	91	83.2	76.3	70.3	65.2	60	57.2	54.3	52
	0	0	0	0	0	0	0	0	0	0
.8	398	373	350	327	307	287	268	250	234	219
	0	0	0	0	0	0	0	0	0	0
.9	897	852	811	720	730	691	654	618	584	551
	0	0	0	0	0	0	0	0	0	0

Table 8.4: Run 2

$$q = 0.03, \ \gamma = 1000$$

Market					Time					
Share	0	0.2	.4	.6	.8	1	1.2	1.4	1.6	1.8
.1	-2844	-2320	-2198	-2096	-2904	-192	-104	-1765	-1643	-1623
	17	9.36	7.82	6.81	6.17	5.7	5.36	5.08	4.8	4.68
.2	-1593	-1457	-1347	-1251	-1164	-108	-100	-935	-865	-798
	14.8	13.0	11.3	10.3	9.65	9.14	3.75	8.45	8.2	8.01
.3	-395	-313	-734	-661	-591	-52.5	-46	-398	-336	-276
	11.9	12.3	11.9	11.4	11.1	10.8	10.6	10.4	10.3	10.3
.4	-397	-348	-296	-245	-191	-73.8	-8.4	-29.8	-246	-79.3
	8.07	8.96	9.7	11.01	10.4	10.7	7.9	11.6	11.6	11.4
.5	-98	-57	-15.4	28.4	74	121	17	220	271	323
	2.8	3.9	5.01	6.09	7.1	8	9	9.67	10.63	10.9
.6	28.2	58.6	113	167	219	272	300	376	429	483
	0	0	0	0	0	0	0	0	0	0
.7	-96	-17.8	58.8	134	207	280	350	419	487	554
	0	0	0	0	0	0	0	0	0	0
.8	-394	-290	-187	87.5	10.6	10.6	201	293	384	473
	0	0	0	0	0	0	0	0	0	0
.9	-393	-758	-628	-499	-373	-248	-12.5	-56.2	11.2	22.7

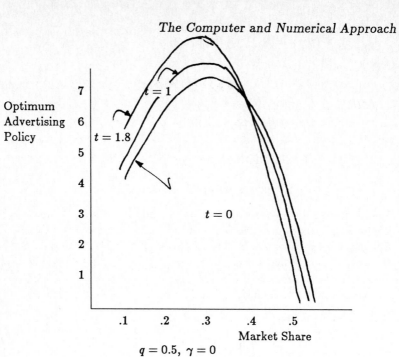

Optimum
Advertising
Policy

$q = 0.5$, $\gamma = 0$

Figure 8.6: Run 1

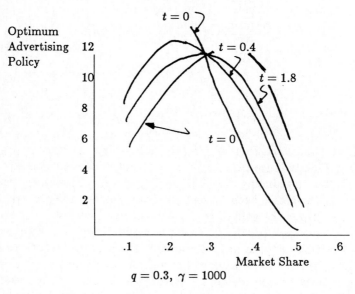

Optimum
Advertising
Policy

$q = 0.3$, $\gamma = 1000$

Figure 8.7: Run 2

$$x_1 = (y - \bar{y})/(1 - \bar{y}), \bar{y} < 1$$

The Bellman equation would of course be amended correspondingly (as well as its boundary conditions). Let the price $p(y)$ be an arbitrarily defined function, rather than a linear one. Namely, we let in our problem,

$$yf(y) = \text{FUNCTION } F(Y); \quad yg(y) = \text{FUNCTION } G(Y); \quad \text{and}$$

$$p(y) = \text{FUNCTION } P(Y).$$

The program which resolves the corresponding Bellman equation is given, in the appendix where the functions F, G and P have been defined explicitly. For the parameters below we obtained an optimal maintenance policy which is naturally bang-bang and where $y = y^*$ is the quality level at which maintenance is started until overhaul. Results for $M = 40$, the cost of maintenance and $k = .8, 1. -$ the quality parameters, are given by $y^* = .21$ and .15

(i)   Function $F(Y) : -y(k\alpha - k^2/\beta^2/2)$
(ii) Function $G(Y) = (ky\beta)^2/2$
(iii) Function $P(Y) = py$

Parameters

Model Notation	Computer Notation	Numerical Values
M	zzM	40
K	zzT	20
k	zzK	.8 and .1
$\bar{y}$	zzY	.6
$\bar{u}$	zzu	.05

Here we see that as the maintenance cost increases, we (expectedly) maintain less the machine. Further, when k (the quality-degradation parameter) decreases, maintenance expenditures increases since maintenance becomes more effective in reducing the machine degradation. Finally, for alternative degradation functions, such as the log-normal process, the program remains valid if we change the definition of the functions F and G. Then we could write, $F = \alpha y \log y + (y\beta^2)(\log y)^2$ and $G = \beta^2 y^2 (\log y)^2/2$. When the price-quality function $P(y)$ is not a linear one, the definition of the function P in our program has to be amended as well. In particular step price-quality functions could be considered as alternatives to our simple linear model. While the above assumptions complicate the analytical treatment of our problem, they do not do so when the problem is treated numerically.

8.4 *Simulation*

When stochastic control problems are too difficult to resolve, either due to the dimensionality of the problem or due to numerical considerations, it is possible to use simulation techniques. Basically, simulation allows us to conduct experiments on the dynamic model by using the computer. These experiments can provide a means to investigate the model's response to changes in policy, changes in parameters etc. and on that basis reach decisions. In Figure 8.8, we describe a typical simulation cycle which uses the generation of random numbers together with a model's structure and parameters to obtain at least an outcome. Multiple repetitions of this cycle lead to a set of outcomes which can be interpreted as sample paths, characterizing the probabilistic response of the dynamic model to a pre-selected set of parameters and possibly, decision strategies.

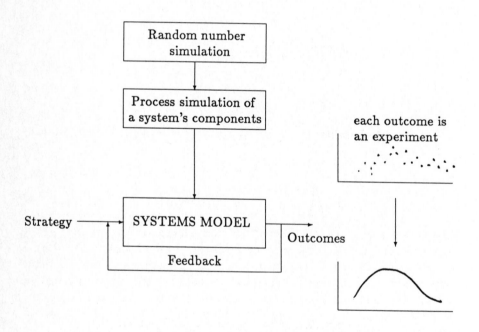

Figure 8.8: A Simulation Cycle

Through the simulation of a dynamical model, we can obtain a sample of a "future reality". This future reality is not what will occur, but a set of such future realities generated by computer simulation, provides an

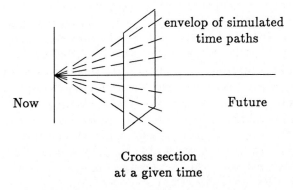

Figure 8.9: Probabilistic Evolution

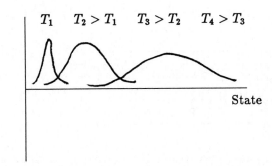

Figure 8.10: A Cross Section at a Given Time

empirical mechanism for characterizing the probability of future outcomes. As we simulate further into the future, the outcomes are less and less certain as is shown in Figure 8.9. If we choose a cross section of the expanding cone at a specific instant of time, we obtain a probability distribution of the set of possible outcomes at that given time. If we compare such cross sections at different instants of time, we obtain distributions that are schematically described in Figure 8.10. Simulation, therefore, does not consist only in extrapolating a particular process in time, but in constructing the relative chances of future realities to occur.

A simulation model for a dynamic process can be constructed by simply programming the process at hand and testing its behavior. Alternatively, there are many simulation languages which have been designed to facilitate the simulation of dynamic and stochastic systems. Popular languages include DYNAMO, CSMP, GPSS, SLAM, SIMAN and many others (see references [8], [11], [15], [17], [24]). These languages are usually adapted to deal with special types of problems and each may have features which can be deemed useful in the context of specific problems. For example, while DYNAMO and CSMP (and to a lesser extent SIMAN) can be interpreted as languages for integrating systems of dynamic (differential or integral) equations, languages such as GPSS, SLAM, SIMAN are particularly suited for discrete state stochastic processes such as queueing problems. Application of these languages to management problems abound and can be found throughout the management professional literature and reviews. The combination of simulation techniques together with optimality seeking methods provides a very powerful instrument, translating theoretical and quantitative constructs into an effective way to resolve real management problems.

Bibliography

[1] Babuska, I.M. Prager and E. Vitazek, 1966, *Numerical Processes in Differential Equations*, Wiley Interscience, New York.

[2] Bensoussan, A., 1982, *Stochastic control by a functional analysis methods*, North Holland, Amsterdam.

[3] Bensoussan, A. M. Crouhi and J.M. Proth, 1983, *Mathematical Theory of Production Planning*, North-Holland, Amsterdam.

[4] Bertsekas, D.P., 1976, *Dynamic Programming and Stochastic Control*, Academic Press, New York.

[5] Billingsley, P., 1968, *Convergence of Probability Measures*, Wiley, New York.

[6] Ciarlet, P.F., 1978, *The Finite Element method for Elliptic Problems*, North Holland, Amsterdam.

[7] Colleter, P.F., Delebecque, F. Falgarone and J.P. Quadrat, 1980 "Application of Stochastic Control Methods to the Management of Energy Production in New Caledonia", in A. Bensoussan, P. Kleindorfer and C.S. Tapiero (Eds.) *Applied Stochastic Control in Econometrics and Management Science*, North-Holland, Amsterdam, pp. 203-232.

[8] CSMP/IBM, 1974, "Continuous System Modeling Program", User's Manual, Program No. 5734, X59, White Plains, New York.

[9] Dodu, J.C., M. Goursat, A. Hertz, J.P. Quadrat and M. Viot, 1981, "Methode de Quadient Stochastique pour l'Optimization des Investissements dans un Reseau Electrique", *EDF Bulletin*, Serie C, No. 2.

[10] Fleming, H., 1971, "Control for small noise intensitites", *SIAM J. Control*, 9, No. 3.

[11] Forrester, J.W., 1968, *Principles of Systems*, Cambridge, Wright-Allen Press, Boston.

[12] Fox, L., 1962, *Numerical Soultions of Ordinary and Partial Differential Equations*, Pergamon Press, Oxford.

[13] Gomez, C., J.P. Quadrat and A. Sulem, 1982, "Towards an expert system in stochastic control: the Hamilton-Jacobi Part", INRIA Report.

[14] Gonedes, N.J. and Z. Lieber, 1974, "Production Planning for a stochastic demand process", *Operations Research*, 22.

[15] Gordon, G., 1969, *Systems Simulation*, Prentice-Hall, Englewood Cliffs, N.J.

[16] Goursat, M. and J.P. Quadrat, 1983, "Numerical Methods in Optimal Stochastic Control", INRIA paper, France.

[17] Harris, C.J., 1977, "Modeling, Simulation and Control of Stochastic Systems with Applications in Wastewater Treatment", *Intl. J. on Systems Science*, 8, 393-411.

[18] Henrici, P., 1962, *Discrete Variable Methods in Ordinary Differential Equations*, Wiley, New York.

[19] Holland, C.J., 1974, "Small noise open loop control", *SIAM J. Control*, 12, 380-388.

[20] Howard, R., 1960, *Dynamic Programming and Markov Processes*, MIT Press, Cambridge, Mass.

[21] Jacobson, D.H. and D.Q. Mayne, 1970, *Differential Dynamic Programming*, Elsevier, New York.

[22] Kleindorfer, P.R., 1978, "Stochastic control models in management science: theory and computation", in *Applied Optimal Control*, TIMS Studies in Management Science, North-Holland, Amsterdam, 9, 69-88.

[23] Kushner, H.J., 1977, *Probability Methods for approximation in stochastic control and for elliptic equations*, Academic Press, New York.

[24] Kushner, H.J. and D.S. Clarck, 1976, *Stochastic Approximation Methods for Constrained and Unconstrained Systems*, Springer-Verlag, Berlin.

[25] Mihram, G.A., 1972, *Simulation*, Academic Press, New York.

[26] Polak, E., 1973, "A Historical Survey of Computational Methods in Optimal Control", *SIAM Review*, 15, 553-584.

[27] Quadrat, J.P., 1980, "Existence de Solution et Algorithme de resolution numerique de problems stochastique degenerees ou non", *SIAM Journal on Control*, March.

[28] Quadrat, J.P. and M. Viot, 1980, "Product form and optimal local feedback for multi-index Markov chains", Allerton Conference (INRIA Report).

[29] Ross, S.M., 1983, *Introduction to Stochastic Dynamic Programming*, Academic Press, New York.

[30] Smith, G.D., 1969, *Numerical Solution of Partial Differential Equations*, Oxford U. Press, London.

[31] Stroock, F., and S.R.S. Varadhan, 1979, *Multidimensional Diffusion Processes*, Springer-Verlag, Berlin.

[32] Ziemba, W.T., 1971, "Transforming Stochastic Dynamic Problems into Nonlinear Programs", *Management Science*, 17, 450-462.

APPENDICES

Computer Programs

A.1 Production Program

```
      REAL U(1,23,101),V(23,101)
      WRITE(*,10)
10    FORMAT (2X,' PRODUCTION PROBLEM WITH CONSTRAINTS')
      WRITE(*,11)
11    FORMAT(2X,'INPUT THE PARAMETERS OF THE PROBLEM BELOW')
      WRITE(*,12)
12    FORMAT(2X,'PARAMETERS FOR THE DEMAND FUNCTION')
      WRITE(*,13)
13    FORMAT(1X,'CONSTANT=,F10.3,LINEAR TREND=,FO.3,QUADRATIC TREND=,
     1F10.3,CYCLICAL SINE AMPLITUDE=,F10.3,MAGNITUDE OF TIME ANGLE=,
     2F10.3')
      READ(*,201)A1,A2,A3,A4,A5
201   FORMAT(4(F10.3/),F10.3)
      WRITE(*,14)
14    FORMAT(1X,'PARAMETERS FOR RUNNING THE PROGRAM')
      WRITE(*,15)
15    FORMAT (1X,'NUMBER OF POINTS FOR STATE DISCRETISATION(I3), NUMBER
     1OF TIME PERIODS(I3),WITH TIME STEP,F5.3, THE CONVERGENCE PARAMETE
     2R,F5.3,MAX NO. OF ITER. (I3)')
      READ(*,202)N1,NO,HO,EPS,NMAX
202   FORMAT(1X,I3/I3/F5.3/F5.3/I3)
      WRITE(*,16)
16    FORMAT (1X,'THE PROBLEM SYSTEM AND COST PARAMETERS ')
      WRITE (*,17)
17    FORMAT(1X,'LINEAR COST PER UNI FOR PRODUCTION ?,F10.4')
      READ(*,203)ZZ1
203   FORMAT(F10.4)
      WRITE (*,55)
55    FORMAT(1X,'COST OF DEVIATING FROM PROD. DESIRED LEVEL ?,F10.4')
      READ(*,203)ZZ2
      WRITE(*,56)
56    FORMAT(1X,'PROPORTIONAL QUADRATIC COST OF INVENTORY ?,F10.4')
      READ(*,203)ZZ3
      WRITE (*,57)
57    FORMAT(1X,'HOLDING COST PER UNIT/PER UNI TIME ?,F10.4')
      READ(*,203)ZZ4
      WRITE(*,58)
58    FORMAT(1X,'SHORTAGE COST PER UNIT/PER UNIT TIME ?,F10.4')
      READ(*,203)ZZ5
      WRITE(*,59)
59    FORMAT(1X,'UPPER INVENTORY HOLDING QUANTITY ?,F10.4')
      READ(*,203)ZZ6
```

```
       WRITE(*,60)
    60 FORMAT(1X,'LOWEST INVENTORY SHORTAGE ?,F10.4')
       READ(*,203)ZZ7
       WRITE(*,61)
    61 FORMAT(1X,'TERMINAL COST,DEVIATION FROM DESIRED LEVEL ?,F10.4')
       READ(*,203)ZZ8
       WRITE(*,62)
    62 FORMAT(1X,'DESIRED INVENTORY LEVEL ?,F10.4')
       READ(*,203)ZZ9
       WRITE(*,63)
    63 FORMAT(1X,'VARIANCE TO MEAN RATIO FOR DEMAND ,F10.4')
       READ(*,203)ZZ10
       WRITE (*,64)
    64 FORMAT(1X,'DESIRED PRODUCTION LEVEL ?,F10.4')
       READ(*,203)ZZ11
       WRITE(*,65)
    65 FORMAT(1X,'COST OF FALLING BELOW LOWEST SHORTAGE, ?,F10.4')
       READ(*,203)BB
       CALL PROD1(N1,NO,HO,V,U,EPS,NMAX,ZZ1,ZZ2,ZZ3,ZZ4,ZZ5,ZZ6,ZZ7
      1,ZZ8,ZZ9,ZZ10,ZZ11,A1,A2,A3,A4,A5,BB)
       STOP
       END
C
       SUBROUTINE PROD1(N1,NO,HO,V,U,EPS,NMAX,ZZ1,ZZ2,ZZ3,ZZ4,ZZ5,ZZ6,
      1ZZ7,ZZ8,ZZ9,ZZ10,ZZ11,A1,A2,A3,A4,A5,BB)
       REAL V(N1,NO),U(1,N1,NO),U1,Q1,P1,WW,WO
C      THIS PROBLEMS SOLVES A STOCHASTIC CONTROL PROBLEM IN CONTINUOUS
C      TIME, WHOSE BELLMAN EQUATION IS GIVEN BY;
C      THE PARAMETERS ZZ1,ZZ2,ZZ3,ZZ4,ZZ5,ZZ6,ZZ7,ZZ8,ZZ9,ZZ10,ZZ11
C      THE STATE VARIABLE IS DENOTED BY X1 WHILE XO IS TIME
C      IF V DENOTES THE COST FUNCTION AND ITS PARTIAL DERIVATIVES ARE
C      P1 (FIRST DERIVATIVE) AND Q1 (SECOND DERIVATIVE), BOTH TAKEN
C      WITH RESPECT TO X1 (THE STATE), THEN THE OPERATOR IS:
C
C      PLUS[Q1*ZFD*ZZ10] MINUS[P1(U1-ZFDO)+(U1-ZZ11)**2*ZZ2+U1*ZZ1+ZS(X1)
C           --------------      ----------
C           ZZ7+ZZ6            ZZ7+ZZ6
C
C      THE PROBLEM IS OF THE PARABOLIC TYPE
C      THE TIME DOMAIN IS DEFINED BY 0, TO (NO-1)*HO
C      THE FINAL TIME COST IS ZZ8*(X1-ZZ9)**2
C      THE CONDITIONS AT THE BOUNDARIES ARE:
C         X1 = 0    -P1=-BB*ZFD
C         X1 = 1     P1=0
C      THE DISCRETISATION POINTS ARE NO AND N1 WITH NO--TIME, N1--STATES
C      WITH  X1 VARIES FROM X1=0 (EQUIVALENT TO I1=2)
C                       TO   X1=1 (EQUIVALENT TO N1-1)
C      DISCRETISATION IN TIME IS EXPLICIT
C      THE HESSIAN MATRIX IS CONDUCTED FORMALLY
C      THE METHOD USED IS TO USE NEWTON ITERATIVE TECHNIQUES
C      IN MINIMIZING THE HAMILTONIAN
```

```
C       NMAX IS THE MAXIMAL NUMBER OF ITERATION BY THE METHOD OF NEWTON
C       EPS DENOTES THE CONVERGENCE ERROR USED IN THE NEWTON ITERATION
        H1=FLOAT(1)/(N1-3)
        U1=U(1,1,1)
        HIH1=H1**2
        H21=2*H1
        NMO=NO-1
        NM1=N1-1
        DO 113 I1=1,N1,1
        X1=H1*(I1-2)
        V(I1,NO)=ZZ8*(X1*(ZZ6+ZZ7)-ZZ7-ZZ9)**2
  113   CONTINUE
        DO 100 IIO=1,NMO,1
        IO=NO-IIO
        XO=HO*(IO-1)
        V(N1,IO+1)=V(N1-2,IO+1)
        V(1,IO+1)=H1*ZFD(XO)+V(3,IO+1)
  110   CONTINUE
        DO 109 I1=2,NM1,1
        X1=H1*(I1-2)
        Q1=(V(I1+1,IO+1)-2*V(I1,IO+1)+V(I1-1,IO+1))/HIH1
        P1=(V(I1+1,IO+1)-V(I1-1,IO+1))/H21
        NITER=0
        WO=-1.0E+20
  101   CONTINUE
        NITER=NITER+1
        IF(NITER-NMAX) 102,102,103
  103   CONTINUE
        WRITE(*,901) I1,IO
  901   FORMAT(' THE NEWTON ITERATIVE SCHEMA HAS NOT CONVERGED ',2I3)
        GOTO 104
  102   CONTINUE
        U1=((2*ZZ11*ZZ2-ZZ1)*ZZ7+(2*ZZ1*ZZ2-ZZ1)*ZZ6-P1)/(2*ZZ2*ZZ7
       1+2*ZZ2*ZZ6)
        IF(U1.LE.0.0) U1=0.0
        IF (U1.GE.ZZ11) U1=ZZ11
        WW=P1*(U1-ZFD(XO,A1,A2,A3,A4,A5))/(ZZ77+ZZ6)+(U1-ZZ11)**2*ZZ2
       1+U1*ZZ1+ZS(X1,ZZ3,ZZ4,ZZ5,ZZ6,ZZ7,ZZ9)
        ER=ABS(WW-WO)
        IF (ER-EPS) 104,104,105
  105   CONTINUE
        WO=WW
        GOTO 101
  104   CONTINUE
        U(1,I1,IO)=U1
        WO=WW
        W1=Q1*ZFD(XO,A1,A2,A3,A4,A5)*ZZ10/(ZZ7+ZZ6)
        WO= W1+WO
        VNEW=HO*WO+V(I1,IO+1)
        V(I1,IO)=VNEW
  109   CONTINUE
```

```
      XT=(IO-1)*HO
      WRITE (*,950)
  950 FORMAT(2X,'TIME,INVENTORY STATES,COST AND PRODUCTION CONTROLS')
      DO 111 I1=1,N1,1
      XI=-ZZ7+H1*(I1+1)*(ZZ6+ZZ7)
      WRITE(*,900) IO,XT,I1,XI,V(I1,IO+1),U(1,I1,IO)
  900 FORMAT(1X,I3,1X,F6.2,1X,I3,1X,F6.2,1X,E14.5,1X,E14.5)
  111 CONTINUE
  100 CONTINUE
      RETURN
      END
C
      FUNCTION ZS(X1,ZZ3,ZZ4,ZZ5,ZZ6,ZZ7,ZZ9)
C     FUNCTION FOR CALCULATING THE INVENTORY COST
      B=(ZZ6+ZZ7)*X1-ZZ7
      C=ZZ7/(ZZ6+ZZ7)
      IF(X1.GE.C) A=ZZ4*B
      IF(X1.LT.C) A=-ZZ5*B
      ZS=ZZ3*(C-ZZ9)**2+A
      RETURN
      END
C
      FUNCTION ZFD(XO,A1,A2,A3,A4,A5)
C     THE PRODUCT MEAN DEMAND GENERATOR
      A=A1+A2*XO+A3*XO**2+A4*XO**3+A5

      ZFD=A
      RETURN
      END
```

A.2 Advertising Program

```
C
C     PROGRAM FOR THE OPTIMIZATION OF A STOCHASTIC
C     PUBLICITY PROGRAM OF THE VIDALE WOLFE TYPE
C     WITH REFLECTION BOUNDARIES AT BOTH STATE ENDS.
      COMMON V(23,51),U(1,23,51)
      OPEN(5,FILE='B:PUB.DAT')
      OPEN(6,FILE='B:PUB.OUT')
C     READING PROGRAM COMPUTATIONAL DATA
      READ(5,7)N1,NO,NMAX,HO,EPS
    7 FORMAT(3I5,2F5.3)
C     READING PROBLEMS' PARAMETERS
      READ(5,8)ZZ1,ZZ2,ZZ3,ZZ4,ZZ5,ZZ6,ZZ7,zz8
    8 FORMAT(8F10.4)
C     PRINTING OF PARAMETERS
      WRITE(6,9) N1,NO,NMAX,HO,EPS
    9 FORMAT(2X,'COMPUTATIONAL PARAMETERS'/
     12X,'NUMBER OF DISCRETE STATES N1= ',I5/
     22X,'NUMBER OF TIME STEPS      NO= ',I5/
```

```
       32X,'MAX NO. OF ITERATIONS    NMAX= ',I5/
       42X,'TIME STEP (UNIT OF TIME)  HO= ',F5.4/
       52X,'CONVERGENCE ERROR TEST    EPS= ',F5.3/)
        WRITE(6,10) ZZ1,ZZ2,ZZ3,ZZ4,ZZ5,ZZ6,ZZ7,ZZ8
    10 FORMAT(/2X,'PROBLEM PARAMETERS'/
       12X,'FINAL PROPOR COST       ZZ1= ',F10.2/
       22X,'FORGETTING RATE         ZZ2= ',F5.4/
       32X,'ADVERT EFFECT.PARAM     ZZ3= ',F5.4/
       42X,'TOTAL INDUSTRY SALES    ZZ4= ',F10.3/
       52X,'PRICE OF GOODS SOLD     ZZ5= ',F5.3/
       62X,'DESIRED TERMINAL M.SHARE ZZ6= ',F5.3/
       72X,'TOTAL MARKET POT. (1)    ZZ7= ',F10.3/
       82X,'UPPER BOUND ON ADV. EXP. ZZ8= ',F5.2)
        CALL PUB1(N1,NO,HO,EPS,NMAX,ZZ1,ZZ2,ZZ3,ZZ4,ZZ5,ZZ6,
       1ZZ7,ZZ8)
        STOP
        END
C
C

        SUBROUTINE PUB1(N1,NO,HO,EPS,NMAX,ZZ1,ZZ2,ZZ3,ZZ4,ZZ5,ZZ6,
       1ZZ7,ZZ8)
        COMMON V(23,51),U(1,23,51)
C       INTIALIZATION OF MATRICES
        DO 12 I=1,N1
        DO 12 J=1,NO
        U(1,I,J)=0.0
    12 V(I,J)=0.0
        AN1=N1
        H1=1./(AN1-3.0)
        U1=U(1,1,1)
        HIH1=H1**2
        H21=2.*H1
        NMO=NO-1
        NM1=N1-1
        XOO1=HO*(NO-1)
C       TERMINAL COST COMPUTATIONS
        WRITE(6,1000)
  1000 FORMAT(2X,'TERMINAL COSTS'/)
        DO 113 I1=1,N1,1
        X1=H1*(I1-2)
        V(I1,NO)=ZZ1*(X1-ZZ6)**2
        WRITE(6,900)I1,X1,NO,XOO1,V(I1,NO)
   113 CONTINUE
C
        DO 100 IIO=1,NMO
        IO=NO-IIO
        XO=HO*(IO-1)
        V(N1,IO+1)=V(N1-2,IO+1)
        V(1,IO+1)=V(3,IO+1)
   110 CONTINUE
        DO 109 I1=2,NM1,1
```

```
      X1=H1*(I1-2)
C     COMPUTAION OF THE FIRST (P1) AND SECOND PARTIALS (Q1)
      Q1=(V(I1+1,I0+1)-2*V(I1,I0+1)+V(I1-1,I0+1))/HIH1
      P1=(V(I1+1,I0+1)-V(I1-1,I0+1))/H21
C
      NITER=0
      WO=-1.0E+20
  101 CONTINUE
      NITER=NITER+1
      IF(NITER-NMAX) 102,102,103
  103 CONTINUE
      WRITE(6,901)I1,I0
  901 FORMAT(1X,'THE NEWTON TECHNIQUE HAS NOT CONVERGED', 2I3)
      GOTO 104
  102 CONTINUE
C     COMPUTATION OF THE OPTIMAL CONTROL
      DIVISOR=ZZ3**2*(ZZ7-X1)**2
      A10=-(X1*ZZ7-X1**2)*ZZ2*ZZ3
      A11=P1*ZZ3*(X1-ZZ7)-1
      UINF=A10/DIVISOR
      IF (Q1-1.0E+6) 572,572,573
  573 U1=UINF
      GO TO 569
  572 AQ1=ABS(Q1)
      IF (AQ1- 1.0E-6)567,567,568
  567 IF (A11.GT.0.0) U1=ZZ8
      IF (A11.LE.0.0) U1=0.0
      GO TO 569
  568 IF(P1-10.0E+10) 571,571,570
  570 U1=0.0
      GO TO 569
  571 A21=P1/Q1
      A20=-A21*(ZZ7-X1)-1/Q1
      U1=(A20+A10)/DIVISOR
      IF(U1.LT.0.0) U1=0.0
      IF(U1.GT.ZZ8) U1=ZZ8
  569 CONTINUE
C
C     BELLMAN'S EQUATION WITH COST= PROBCOST
      PROBCOST=U1-X1*ZZ4*ZZ5
      WW=Q1*(U1*ZZ3*(ZZ7-X1)+X1*ZZ2)**2/2.0+P1*(U1*ZZ3*(ZZ7-X1)-X1*ZZ2
     1)-PROBCOST
C
      ER=ABS(WW-WO)
      IF(ER-EPS)104,104,105
  105 CONTINUE
      WO=WW
      GOTO 101
  104 CONTINUE
      U(1,I1,I0)=U1
      WO=WW
```

```
      VNEW=HO*WO+V(I1,IO+1)
      V(I1,IO)=VNEW
  109 CONTINUE
  100 CONTINUE
      WRITE (6,89)
   89 FORMAT(2X,'PRINTING OF OPTIMAL COMPUTATIONAL RESULTS'/)
      WRITE(6,90)
   90 FORMAT(6X,'STATE',7X,'TIME',6X,'OBJECTIVE',3X,'ADVERTISING')
      DO 111 IO=1,NO,1
      IE=NO-IO+1
      XO=HO*(IO-1.)
      DO 111 I1=1,N1,1
      X1=H1*(I1-2)
      WRITE(6,900)I1,X1,IE,XO,V(I1,IE),U(1,I1,IE)
  900 FORMAT(1X,I3,F7.3,1X,I3,F7.3,2(1X,E14.4))
  111 CONTINUE
      RETURN
      END
```

A.3 Maintenance Program

```
      COMPUTER PROGRAM FOR QUALITY AND MAINTENANCE

      COMMON/PARAM/YB,ALPHA,BETA,P,ZZZ
      DIMENSION V(22),IESP(1,22)
      WRITE(*,1000)
 1000 FORMAT(2X, 'QUALTITY  MAINTENANCE PROGRAM',1X/)
      WRITE (*,1001)
 1001 FORMAT (1X,'INPUT THE PARAMETERS AS SPECIFIED BELOW')
      WRITE(*,1002)
 1002 FORMAT (1X,'N1(I3)',1X,'EPSIMP(F4.0)',1X,'IMPMAX(I5)')
      READ(*,1005)N1,EPSIMP,IMPMAX
 1005 FORMAT(I3,F4.0,I5)
      WRITE(*,1005)N1,EPSIMP,IMPMAX
      WRITE(*,1003)
 1003 FORMAT(1X'RO(F5.2)',1X,'ZZM(F5.2)',1X,'ZZT(F5.2)',1X,
     1'ZZK(F5.2)',1X,'ZZY(F5.2)',1X,'ZZU(F5.2)')
      READ(*,1004)RO,ZZM,ZZT,ZZK,ZZY,ZZU
 1004 FORMAT(6F5.2)
      WRITE(*,1004)RO,ZZM,ZZT,ZZK,ZZY,ZZU
      WRITE(*,1006)
 1006 FORMAT(1X,'INPUT THE MODEL PARAMETERS; ALPHA, BETA, YB,P,ZZZ,IN
     1FORMATS OF F5.2')
      READ(*,1007)ALPHA, BETA,YB,P,ZZZ
 1007 FORMAT (5F5.2)
      WRITE (*,1007)ALPHA,BETA,YB,P,ZZZ
      CALL QUALM (N1,EPSIMP,IMPMAX,V,IESP,RO,ZZM,ZZT,ZZK,ZZY,ZZU)
      STOP
      END
```

```
C
      SUBROUTINE QUALM(N1,EPSIMP,IMPMAX,V,IESP,RO,ZZM,ZZT,ZZK,ZZY,ZZU)
      COMMON/PARAM/YB,ALPHA,BETA,P,ZZZ
      DIMENSION V(N1), IESP(1,N1)
C
C     THIS PROBLEM RESOLVES THE BELLMAN EQUATION IN THE CASE WHERE
C     THE PARAMETERS ARE ZZM,ZZT,ZZK,ZZY,ZZU
C     TIME IS DENOTED BY X1
C     THE DYNAMIC SYSTEM IS DESCRIBED BY THE FOLLOWING OPERATOR;
C       PLUS{Q1*ZZG(X1),MIN[P1*(ZZK*ZZU*X1+ZZF(X1)]+
C               ZZM*ZZU-ZZP(X1)  P1*ZZF(X1)-ZZP(X1)]}
C     WHERE V DENOTES THE OPTIMAL COST
C     P1 IS THE FIRST DERIVATIVE OF V WITH RESPECT TO X1
C     Q1 IS THE SECOND DERIVATIVE OF V WITH RESPECT TO X1
C     THE PROBLEM IS STATIONARY WITH THE FOLLOWING BOUNDARY CONDITIONS;
C     AT   X1=0, V=ZZT
C     AT   X1=1, P1=0
C     THE NUMBER OF DISCRETISATION POINTS ARE N1 WITH
C     X1=1 CORRESPONDING TO I1=N1-1
C     X1=0 CORRESPONDING TO I1=1
C     THE DISCOUNT RATE EQUALS ZERO
C     IMPMAX IS THE MAXIMUM NUMBER OF ITERATIONS OF THE IMPLICIT SYSTEM
C     ERIMP IS THE CONVERGENCE ERROR OF THE IMPLICIT SYSTEM
C
      H1=FLOAT(1)/(N1-2)
      HIH1=H1**2
      H21=2*H1
      NM1=N1-1
      DO 114 I1=1,N1,1
      V(I1)=0
  114 CONTINUE
      IMITER=1
  108 CONTINUE
      ERIMP=0
      V(N1)=V(N1-2)
      V(1)=ZZT
  106 CONTINUE
      DO 105 I1=2,NM1,1
      X1=H1*(I1-1)
      Q1=(V(I1+1)-2*V(I1)+V(I1-1))/HIH1
      P1=(V(I1+1)-V(I-1))/H21
      WO=P1*ZZF(X1)-ZZP(X1)
      W1=P1*(ZZK*ZZU*X1+ZZF(X1))+ZZU-ZZP(X1)
      WO=MIN(W1,WO)
      IESP(1,I1)=0
      IF(WO-W1) 102,101,102
  101 CONTINUE
      IESP(1,I1)=1
  102 CONTINUE
      W1=Q1*ZZG(X1)
      WO=W1+WO
```

```
       WO=WO
       VNEW=RO*WO+V(I1)
       V(I1)=VNEW
       ERIMP=ABS(WO)+ERIMP
 105   CONTINUE
       IMITER=IMITER+1
       IF (IMITER-IMPMAX)111,110,110
 111   CONTINUE
       IF (EPSIMP-ERIMP)108,107,107
 110   CONTINUE
       WRITE (*,907)
 907   FORMAT('THE IMPLICIT SCHEMA HAS NOT CONVERGED')
 107   CONTINUE
       WRITE(*,910)
 910   FORMAT(' THE STATE ',2X,'OPTIMAL MAINTEANCE ',2X,'OPTIMAL VALUE')
       DO 112 I1=1,N1,1
       WRITE(*,903) I1,IESP(1,I1),V(I1)
 903   FORMAT(I3,2X,I3,8X,E14.5)
 112   CONTINUE
       RETURN
       END
C
       FUNCTION ZZF(X1)
       COMMON/PARAM/YB,ALPHA,BETA,P,ZZZ
C      THE FUNCTION DENOTING  X1*F(X1) AND DEFINING THE MEAN PRODUCTION
C      DEGRADATION  WITHOUT MAINTENANCE
C      THE PARAMETERS ARE YB,ZZK,ALPHA AND BETA
       Y=YB+X1*(1-YB)
       ZZF=-Y*(ZZK*ALPHA-(ZZK*BETA)**2/2.)
       RETURN
       END
C
       FUNCTION ZZG(X1)
       COMMON/PARAM/YB,ALPHA,BETA,P,ZZZ
C      THE FUNCTION DENOTING X1*G(X1) DEFINING THE VARIANCE COMPONENT IN
C      PRODUCTION DEGRADATION.  THE PARAMETERS ARE YB, ZZK AND BETA
       Y=YB+X1*(1-YB)
       ZZG=(ZZK*Y*BETA)**2/2.
       RETURN
       END
C
       FUNCTION ZZP(X1)
       COMMON/PARAM/YB,ALPHA,BETA,P,ZZZ
C      THE PRICE FUNCTION GIVEN IN TERMS OF QUALITY X1.
C      THE PARAMETERS ARE YB AND P
       Y=YB+X1*(1-YB)
       ZZP=P*Y
       RETURN
       END
```

AUTHOR INDEX